SHEFFIELD CITY
POLYTECHNIC LIBRARY
POND STREET
SHEFFIELD S1 1WB

100213662 8

TELEPEN

10

28 MAR 2001

D1338127

ELD HALLAM UNIVERSITY
EARNING CENTRE
DRAWN FROM STOCK

HOUSING POLICY IN BRITAIN: A HISTORY

The government in Britain has a long tradition of involvement in housing. This book provides a comprehensive history of housing policy in Britain from the beginning of the twentieth century to the end of the 1970s. For every period the author gives a detailed account of the housing situation in which policies operated, the policies pursued, their rationale, owner-occupation, and privately owned rented housing are fully discussed. Particular emphasis is placed on the financial and economic aspects of housing policy, including the impact on it of the natural economic situation. The growth of the population and in the number of households is also discussed fully.

HOUSING POLICY IN BRITAIN

A HISTORY

A.E. Holmans

CROOM HELM
London • Sydney • Wolfeboro, New Hampshire

© 1987 A.E. Holmans
Croom Helm Ltd, Provident House, Burrell Row,
Beckenham, Kent, BR3 1AT
Croom Helm Australia, 44-50 Waterloo Road,
North Ryde, 2113, New South Wales

British Library Cataloguing in Publication Data

Holmans, A.E.
    Housing policy in Britain.
    1. Housing policy — Great Britain — History
    I. Title
    363.5′56′0941   HD7333.A3

    ISBN 0-7099-3789-X

Croom Helm, 27 South Main Street,
Wolfeboro, New Hampshire 03894-2069, USA

Library of Congress Cataloging-in-Publication Data

Holmans, A.E.
    Housing policy in Britain.
    Includes index.
    1. Housing policy — Great Britain — History. I. Title.
HD7333.A3H64 1987   363.5′8   86-19930
ISBN 0-7099-3789-X

Printed and bound in Great Britain by Mackays of Chatham Ltd, Kent

CONTENTS

PREFACE

When this book was being written, the author was a Senior Economic Adviser in the Department of the Environment. All the views expressed are of course the author's own and do not reflect any views of the Department. The views expressed and the conclusions reached are based on published information, and no reference has been made to unpublished records relating to the formation of policy. Likewise, for reasons of propriety, no comments are made about the policies of the present Government, and the policies of the previous Government are commented on sparingly. All the calculations and estimates, other than those drawn from official published sources, are the author's own and have no official status.

The author is indebted to David Donnison, Duncan Maclennan, and Mark Boleat who read all or part of the text and made helpful comments.

Tables V.16 and V.17 are reproduced from the General Householder Survey by kind permission of the Controller of H.M. Stationery Office.

A.E. Holmans
London, 1986

1

CHAPTER I

SCOPE AND COVERAGE OF A HISTORY OF PUBLIC POLICY AND HOUSING

The purpose of this book is to examine why, how, and with what results government became so deeply involved with housing; and especially why the degree of involvement increased so much in the three decades after 1945, notwithstanding the exceptionally rapid rise (by past British standards) in real income and owner-occupation taking place of renting as the majority tenure. The policies pursued in the three decades after 1945 followed directly from the policies of the inter-war years, so the inter-war experience must be recounted in some detail. The pre-1914 background to the policies of the inter-war years has necessarily to be discussed in somewhat less detail, but an outline of it is essential for an understanding of what happened after 1918. In discussing the nineteenth century origins of housing policy as a function of government in England, it is important to consider how far the conditions and problems to which the policies were addressed really were novel in any sense other than scale. Insanitary housing and overcrowding did not begin with the Industrial Revolution, even though the response was different in the nineteenth century from what had gone before.

Public policy can only be described and assessed in terms of the circumstances of the time and the underlying causes of the problems with which it sought to deal. Much of this history is therefore devoted to the way in which housing conditions responded to demographic change and to development and change in the British economy. The number of households to be housed, what they were able and willing to pay for housing and what housing cost to provide were all of the greatest

2

importance for public policy, and so must be described in enough detail both to explain the context
of policies and to provide the material required
for any conclusions about the appropriateness or
otherwise of the policies pursued.

The history of housing policy after 1918 in
England cannot be recounted except with a heavy
emphasis on housing tenure. For the period from
World War I to the 1970s there are, therefore,
separate chapters on owner-occupation, local authority housing, and renting from private landlords,
with overview chapters on the inter-war years and
the post-war decades to describe the economy, population and households, and housing conditions in
the aggregate. The pre-1914 background is discussed in a single chapter, to set the scene for
what came after. World War I, far more than World
War II, was the watershed for British housing.
Both the development of the housing system and the
evolution of policy in the sixty years that followed World War I contrasted very sharply with the
century that preceded it. The difference between
pre- and post-1914 were far greater than any differences between sub-periods within those eras.

Given the long period to be covered, the
present book must necessarily be written from
secondary sources, for instance reports of surveys
and censuses, reports and minutes of evidence of
Royal Commission and Departmental Committees, and
statistical publications. This secondary material
is voluminous but very scattered, and much of value
may be derived from bringing it together in a
coherent way. This is as true of the recent past
as of the more distant past, if anything more so
owing to the greater volume of material. There
are, indeed, risks and disadvantages to crossing
the boundary between history proper and current
affairs in the way that is inherent in writing in
the mid-1980s about the 1960s and the 1970s. Lack
of perspective long enough to see any but short
term consequences limits a history of housing
policy in these decades to being an orderly record
of what was happening and what was done, and the
immediate consequences. But such an orderly record
has considerable value, for the speed with which
events become overlaid with myth and legend is
great. What was said in the heat of the moment on
controversial issues may be remembered as if it
were the last word on the subject, and forebodings
of feared consequences very readily become mixed

3

with actual consequences. Moreover, the boundary
between history and current affairs is not the same
for everyone.   By the mid-1980s there was a whole
generation of younger householders, voters,
councillors, and MPs for whom the 1957 Rent Act was
not even a childhood memory.

Mention has next to be made of why the title
should refer to Britain, even though many of the
statistics that are cited refer to England and
Wales or to England, and many of the Acts of
Parliament commented on did not apply to Scotland.
Scotland retained her separate legal system under
the Act of Union, and Scottish local government
remained different from English.   There has as a
consequence been a separate body of Scottish law on
housing standards and housing finance, administered
separately from English, under the supervision of a
separate Government Department (The Scottish
Office) and Minister (the Secretary of State for
Scotland). As well as a separate legal and administrative identity, Scotland has had since 1861 a
separate statistical identity in most matters to do
with housing. With the beginning of civil registration of births, deaths, and marriages in Scotland in 1855, a Scottish General Register Office
was set up, and from 1861 onwards, this office
managed the census in Scotland.   From 1801 to 1851
the census was under a single control throughout
Great Britain, but from 1861 there were separate
censuses in Scotland and in England and Wales.
There have been differences of definition, classification, and presentation of the results, which
sometimes prevent consistently defined Great
Britain figures from being produced.   To combine
Scottish figures with those for England and Wales
or to 'stretch' figures for England and Wales to
cover Scotland as well would often require a substantial amount of estimation which could be described adequately only by taking up a disproportionate amount of space.   Surveys on housing subjects have generally covered either England and
Wales or Scotland, but not both.   Multi-purpose
surveys from which housing information has been
obtained that have covered Great Britain (the
General Household Survey) or the United Kingdom
(Family Expenditure Survey) are exceptions to the
rule.   With national income accounts statistics
(e.g. gross fixed investment in dwellings in comparison with gross domestic product) and most financial statistics (e.g. of mortgage lending and rates

4

of interest) the whole of the United Kingdom is covered. To try to exclude Northern Ireland (or the whole of Ireland before 1920) would likewise require a wholly disproportionate amount of space.

In general, however, housing conditions have changed in similar ways in Scotland and in England and Wales, and the substance and thrust of housing policy has been the same. On most aspects of the finance of local authorities' housing there has been separate Scottish legislation, but it has almost always passed through Parliament not long after the corresponding legislation for England and Wales, and has been designed to achieve the same result. One important body of legislation on housing, the Rent Acts (Rent Restrictions Acts in 1939 and earlier) has always applied throughout Great Britain. A history of housing policy in Britain can therefore be written without needing to refer often to specifically Scottish detail.

Economic Aspects of Housing

Introductory comment is also necessary here about some of the economic aspects of housing, as they have an important bearing on the history of public policy. Houses can be regarded both as investment goods (i.e. as the "plant" used in producing services that are or might be sold); and as consumers' durable goods of a special kind. The former is the way in which rented houses can appropriately be regarded. But how best to regard owner-occupied houses is more open to argument. In a society where owner-occupation is the majority tenure, to regard the owner-occupier as an investor who lets to himself (in effect his own landlord) would appear to most people as artificial. In such circumstances owner-occupied houses are probably best regarded as very costly and very long lasting consumers' durable goods. This is not just a point about classification or about how to treat housing in national income accounts that span a period long enough to begin when renting was by far the largest tenure and end when owner-occupation predominates. It has an important bearing on how the tax system should treat owner-occupied housing if the principles that apply in the system as a whole apply equally to housing as well. That houses can be both investment goods and consumers' durable goods means that there exist side by side markets in which the houses themselves are bought and sold and

other markets where only the use of house room is
bought and sold. Households can often move from
one of these housing markets to the other, and
houses likewise can be transferred between rental
and ownership markets. The result is complications
that have no parallels in other markets.

The housing market also differs from other
markets in that houses are fixed in location
(numerically unimportant exceptions apart) and take
up large amounts of land. Purchase or renting of
housing is therefore the purchase or renting not
just of accommodation, but of accessibility as
well.

Accessibility to employment opportunities has
generally been the most important aspect of it,
though for those in a position to choose other
aspects of accessibility - for instance to city
centre services, or to the countryside - are important as well. Accessibility to employment opportunities has attracted most attention, and there is
now a large literature on the subject, especially
the relationship of rents or house prices to
distance from the city centre, and the way households in different circumstances respond to this
relationship (1). To review that literature here
would be out of place; but the subject matter with
which it deals has been extremely important in the
development of urban and suburban housing. The way
in which limits to accessibility have forced households to trade quality of accommodation against
accessibility is a major part of the explanation of
bad housing conditions in towns. An important part
of an analysis of how and why housing conditions
have changed therefore lies in the way in which
some of those constraints on accessibility have
changed. They range from the purely geographical
such as sea coasts and lake shores, through those
constraints which are a mixture of policy and
geography, like the Green Belts that became so
important a part of the planning orthodoxy in post-
war Britain, to constraints caused by the technology of passenger transport and by real incomes.
The tighter the constraints on accessibility the
smaller the area in which large numbers of people
had to live, and hence came crowding, high rents,
and high land prices.

Through their effect on accessibility, changes
in transport had a very large effect on housing, in
particular between 1900 and 1939 the development of
the electric tram, the motor bus, and the electric

6

passenger train; and then in the 1950s and 1960s the spread of car ownership. Rising real incomes also worked to relax the constraints both through increasing ability to pay the out-of-pocket costs of longer journeys to and from work, and through shorter working hours leaving more room for time spent travelling.

The limitations on accessibility, and hence on the supply of land that was usable for housing, were without much doubt the main reason why rents and house prices rose relative to the general price level throughout the period studied, from the early nineteenth century to the later twentieth century, the inter-war years alone excepted. This rise in rents and house prices in real terms (over and above increases that were caused by houses being built to higher standards) is an important aspect of the history of housing, particularly in explaining why rising real incomes in the half century before 1914 did not do more to reduce the amount of bad housing. Rising rents and house prices will be met with in the history of nineteenth and early twentieth century housing, and again in the years after 1945. The inter-war years were the great exception, when innovations in public transport combined with the absence of any very effective regulation of land use produced a huge increase in the supply of land that was usable for housing. So although the demand for housing was extremely strong, the supply could increase sufficiently to meet it without price increases, in contrast with what happened both earlier and subsequently. The growth of the population in the nineteenth century, and the growing concentration of that growth in the larger towns increased the importance of accessibility in limiting the supply of land for housing. There is here the main part of the explanation of why land ownership and taxation of land values were such a contentious subject in the half century before 1914, and again in the 1960s and 1970s. High land prices aggravated many of the problems that faced housing policy.

Houses in Britain, as in the countries of western Europe and North America, are too expensive in relation to income for households to buy a house for ready money at the beginning of their housing career or accumulate the purchase money from prior savings. Most householders must therefore either hire a house, or buy one with borrowed money. Housing must therefore be <u>financed</u>, and the finance

has to be for a long term. For the purchaser with
borrowed money the loan must be for a long term of
years if the repayments of principal are to be
spread thinly enough to be met out of income year
by year. The investor in houses to let can usually
obtain from the rent in any one year enough to pay
off only a small part of the debt incurred to
finance the purchase of the house.

Much the same considerations apply to houses
built for letting by public authorities. The very
high capital cost of houses would make payment of
the full cost directly from taxation extremely
expensive, in most circumstances prohibitively so.
The principles of local authority finance that
applied in Britain since the mid-nineteenth century
always drew a distinction between expenditure
chargeable to revenue, for which borrowing was not
permissible, and capital expenditure which could be
financed from loans so long as the loans were
properly amortized. The type of expenditure that
can be classed as 'capital' has always included
expenditure incurred for buildings and works that
provide services over a long period of years.
Roads and bridges are one class of example, schools
were another when local authorities acquired responsibility for education, and housing fitted in
with these principles without any difficulty.
Nineteenth century principles about balancing the
budget applied to expenditure chargeable to
revenue, including of course the loan charges
(interest and amortization) on loans raised to meet
capital expenditure, but loan finance for capital
expenditure was regarded as entirely proper. The
distinction between capital expenditure and expenditure chargeable to revenue is bound to be somewhat arbitrary at the margin, a point taken by
those who advocated financing local authority
housing directly from taxation. Military expenditure was so financed, including costly and long
lasting items like capital ships, and as a consequence the defence budget was not burdened by
interest charges in the way that housing accounts
were. So why not houses? The size of the tax
burden that would be caused is part of the answer;
fairness between successive generations of taxpayers is another.

High capital costs and long term loan finance
cause interest payments to be a uniquely high proportion of current housing costs. This is true
whether the housing is rented or being bought on

mortgage. In the late 1960s and 1970s, some 55-60% of owner-occupiers' outgoings consisted of interest payments; for housing let by local authorities the proportion was over 60%, and in the inter-war years had been as high as 80%. There are no other public services where interest costs are anything like so high a proportion of total current costs as this; and no other goods or services purchased by consumers where interest predominates among costs in this way. Housing costs are therefore uniquely sensitive to interest rates, both in absolute (or "nominal") terms and relative to the rate of change of the general price level (i.e. in real terms). High and rising nominal interest rates consequently imposed stresses and strains on housing finance in the 1960s and 1970s that were both severe and novel, not just in Britain but in most Western countries. How these strains were coped with will be discussed at some length in later chapters. Dependence on long term loan finance necessarily makes privately owned housing, whether for owning or letting, very dependent on capital markets and financial institutions. Developments in capital markets are therefore important in any history of housing. Not only privately owned housing but housing provided by public authorities is affected by conditions in capital markets. There were several occasions during the period studied when the policies the monetary authorities wished to pursue in managing the National Debt worked against local authorities being able to borrow the amounts that appeared to be called for on grounds of housing policy. This first happened in 1920, within little more than a year of the Exchequer becoming involved in housing finance. Entanglement with management of the National Debt presupposes that government is involved in financing housing at all. How it came to be so will emerge from the history. But that part of the history can be the more readily recounted with the aid of a small amount of the economic theory of public finance.

Some Introductory Theory of Public Finance as Applied to Housing

The reasons for provision of services wholly or partly at the expense of public funds are usually grouped under four heads:

a)   Provision of 'public goods'; these are

9

services which cannot be charged for directly, either because there is no way at all of withholding the service (e.g. defence or law and order) from those who choose not to contribute towards the cost, or because to charge would be excessively costly (e.g. for using roads with many access points). They therefore have to be provided publicly and financed from taxation.

b) Externalities, i.e. costs falling on people other than those who produce - or occasionally consume - the goods or services in question; or benefits that accrue to people other than the direct consumer who pays.

c) Paternalism, i.e. action by government because individuals on their own may act in ways that are contrary to their own best interests or those of their families owing to ignorance or short-sightedness.

d) Income redistribution, either literally or by distributing the benefits from a service differently from the distribution of the burden of the taxation levied to finance it.

Putting the argument this way may convey the impression that the provision of services by private enterprise through markets is the norm from which exceptions have to be justified individually on specific facts. That may be criticized as evidence of bias in 'orthodox' economics towards laissez faire; but nonetheless, it accords with the history during the period studied of gradual and incremental increases in the range and scale of tax-financed services, and with the fact that because tax increases are unpopular, choices must be made about public expenditure and public opinion convinced of the need for new or expanded services.

The theory of 'public goods' has little relevance to housing. A system where the guiding principle was that 'you get only what you pay for, and pay only for what you get' would encounter no technical difficulty if the consequences were acceptable. That the consequences were not acceptable to substantial sections of opinion in a large part of the period studied was due to the poor standard of housing of many households when all that they got was what they could afford unaided.

Externalities, especially the effect of bad housing on health and hence the costs imposed not just on those who are ill but on the community as a

whole which has to support families whose earning
power is lost through illness or premature death of
the breadwinner, are met with from time to time as
an argument for supporting housing from public
funds, but have not, as a matter of history, been a
major influence on the development of policy in
Britain. There is a considerable body of modern
literature about whether poor housing does give
rise to social costs, especially through poor
health (reviewed in detail by Burns and Grebler
(2), but in essence, the argument about this class
of externalities is that put forward by Chadwick in
1842 (3). After pointing to the evidence he had
collected about the connection between insanitary
living conditions and disease and death, he wrote:

> "To whatever extent the probable duration of
> life of the working man is diminished by
> noxious agencies .... so much productive
> power is lost; and in the case of destitute
> widowhood and orphanage, burdens are created
> and cast either on the industrious survivors
> .... or on the contributors of the poor's
> rates ...."

Government action about housing in Britain, though,
was not based on a belief that there would be
financial savings of the kind Chadwick referred to,
and indeed such savings from better housing have
not been convincingly demonstrated in this country.
Much more important have been those externalities
to do with public health and fire risks. Neither
take government action very far. Public health, in
the sense of risks to the health of people other
than those that actually live in the house, may
provide good reason for requiring proper sanitation
but hardly more. Protection against the spread of
fire calls for rules about the materials to be used
in houses in built up areas, but has nothing to do
with convenience or comfort.
Far more important than externalities was a
combination of paternalism and (in a very special
sense) redistribution of income. Paternalism may
be seen in the growing body of legislation, and
more effective enforcement of it, to set minimum
standards for new houses built, and to close,
demolish, or compulsorily improve the very worst
housing. These were actions to try to drive the
very worst accommodation off the market, for the

protection of those who might otherwise have lived in it. There is an obvious analogy with preventing the sale of contaminated or adulterated food, as was noted by nineteenth century housing reformers. The difference from externalities is to be found in the action being for the protection of the house-holders who might otherwise have rented very defec-tive housing, not for the protection of third parties. To succeed in driving the poorest and hence cheapest accommodation off the market is to compel households to spend more on housing. If they cannot afford to do so, assistance is needed. Owing to the inter-connection between minimum stan-dards, costs, rents and subsidy, it is very hard to say where paternalism ends and redistribution of income begins.

What economists termed 'income redistribution' in this area was seldom regarded as such by the housing specialist, whether Member of Parliament, Councillor, administrator, or reformer. On the contrary, they have historically seen themselves as engaged in the provision of housing on terms that enable people with low incomes to get access to good housing, and assisting people for whom the obstacles to access to good housing are more complex than simply low income. For whom such access to good housing should be facilitated, on what scale, at what cost, and what should consti-tute 'adequate' housing made up much of the sub-stance of housing policy after 1918, and were coming towards the centre of debate well before then.

Redistribution of Income and Housing Policy

Because income redistribution figured so pro-minently in economists' discussions of housing policy for many years, even though practitioners of housing policy seldom saw income redistribution as what they were about, it is worth pausing briefly over the issues involved. There were two lines of economists' criticism of post-1919 housing policy that came from looking at it in terms of its object being to redistribute incomes. One was that subsi-dizing particular goods or services (in this instance housing) is less satisfactory as a means of redistributing income than cash payments. The second was that if the goods or services subsidized are consumed by all households and the subsidy is made available irrespective of means, then the

redistributive effect is small or non-existent.
Large sums are raised from all households as taxpayers, and repaid to all of them (or nearly so) as
consumers; considerable administrative costs are
incurred, work incentives are harmed and discontent
aroused by the tax burden, and no redistributive
effect achieved. The second of these lines of
criticism, the alleged lack of redistributive
effect when a high proportion of households benefit, did not really apply in England until the
1960s and later. But the first, the alleged
inferiority of housing subsidies to income supplements, applied much earlier. Housing subsidies
began in 1919; and it has been argued that the
legislation of the 1860s and 1870s to provide for
minimum housing standards was an attempt to do what
could have been done better by income supplements
to enable people to afford adequate housing (4).
    The basis of the contention about the inferi-
ority of housing subsidies to income supplements is
two-fold. On the standard assumptions of welfare
economics it is possible to show without difficulty
that consumers' well-being is increased less by a
subsidy tied to consumption of specific goods and
services than by a cash sum of equal amount (5),
provided that both are equally feasible and, not
quite the same thing, those who provide the funds
either have no preferences as to which method is
used, or their preferences are treated as irrelevant. Subsidized housing was also alleged to lead
to the growth of vested interests in the supply of
particular kinds of housing irrespective of what
households want, whereas income supplements can be
spent on the kind of housing that people prefer, if
indeed they prefer more housing rather than more of
something else. Economic arguments on these lines
made a powerful contribution to debates on policy
in the later 1950s, the 1960s and 1970s. But
nevertheless, policies up to then had taken a very
different course. So why did policies take the
course they did notwithstanding the economic arguments in favour of cash supplements to income
rather than subsidies?
    Mention has already been made of the fact that
housing reformers did not see themselves as advo-
cating income redistribution. The link between
this fact and the economic theory lies in the
proviso about the preferences of those who provide
the funds. On one level this is no more than a
minor theoretical refinement; but on another it is

13

a practical consideration of the greatest importance. Although many of the social ills that
stirred the passions of reformers can be seen to
have had their origins in low levels of income and
an unequal distribution of income and wealth,
reformers seldom looked to redistribution of income
as the remedy. They campaigned instead for specific remedies for specific ills: better education,
better health services, better housing. The same
was generally true of political parties when they
came to take an interest; promises of better services were much more common than proposals for
general redistribution of income. Bad housing,
poor educational opportunities, or lack of access
to adequate medical care aroused feelings of compassion and sympathy, and feelings that "something
must be done", among people who would have been
unmoved by a demonstration of the inequality in the
distribution of income. Specific consequences of
an unequal distribution of income and wealth were
what were adjudged socially undesirable, inequitable or (in extreme circumstances) inhumane. Bad
housing is highly visible, and its power to shock
correspondingly great. Lord Shaftesbury's reaction
to what he saw when walking through the slums in
London were: ".... by turns [I] was sad, by turns
wild. I felt and now feel indignant to fury" (6).
This is perhaps an extreme example, but it exempli-
fies the reactions of people who would be unmoved
by inequalities of income as such.

Such responses to bad housing were matched by
similar responses to preventable or curable ill
health, deficient or non-existent education, and
destitution. Such conditions offended against
widespread sentiments about fairness and human
dignity, even if the inequalities of income and
wealth from which they sprang were regarded as
being part of the natural order of things. In the
words of a housing reformer of the first quarter of
the twentieth century:

> "We have to face two facts in this world:
> one is that inequality is in the eternal
> order of things, and the other is that in
> the human heart there is forever a
> passionate determination to remove it." (7)

The impact that this passion to reduce
inequalities has had on politics and policy has
varied through time. As we shall see, it increased

14

greatly in the two World Wars of the twentieth century, especially the second.

The principle of action to reduce inequality in access to particular goods and services, notably health services, education, and housing has been termed "specific egalitarianism" (8). "Selective egalitarianism" would perhaps be a more apt term for the proposition that access to those goods and services should be distributed much less unequally than income and wealth in total. When and why housing came to be included in the "selective egalitarian" group of services, considerably later than education, for instance, in Britain is an aspect of the history of public policy and housing that will be discussed in some detail in subsequent chapters.

"Selective egalitarianism" is at least conceptually an alternative to egalitarian redistribution of income and wealth in total, if the consequences of the distribution that emerges from the combination of market forces and inheritance are adjudged unacceptable. General redistribution has had its supporters. The idea of getting the distribution of income "right" and then leaving everything else other than public goods (in the sense used earlier in this chapter) to competitive markets has had a considerable appeal to economists, not least socialist economists like Evan Durbin and Arthur Lewis as well as to economists of more conservative views.

General redistribution of income and wealth is however extremely difficult to achieve. The inequality of the primary distribution of income from employment and property is very deeply rooted. The spread of weekly earnings of manual workers in Britain was first measured in 1886, and when measured in 1968 was found to be virtually the same (in proportionate terms) as it had been over 80 years before (9). The position of workers in different industries, trades, and occupations in the distribution had altered, but the shape of the distribution had hardly changed. That the distribution had changed so little over a period that included two world wars and the Great Depression does not inspire confidence in the ability of government policies to influence it, for instance by policies intended to raise the pay of those at the lower end of the distribution. To make large changes in the secondary distribution of incomes (i.e. after tax and cash payments from public funds) is likewise very difficult to do owing to the weight of taxation required to do it, the effect on incentives, and the possibilities of evasion and capital flight. There is nothing in the least surprising in action to reduce or remove the most objectionable consequences of the unequal distribution of income and wealth being preferred to an attempt to reduce the inequality of money incomes.

"Selective egalitarian" policies could be criticized as being for the purpose of defending a very unequal distribution of income and wealth by mitigating those effects of inequality that caused the most grievance while leaving the basic inequalities unaltered. From the opposite political standpoint a critic might maintain that better education, better health services, and better housing for those with larger incomes are part of the reward for the effort by which such incomes are earned, so that if large incomes do not bring advantages in these as well as other ways, work incentives are harmed.

But although "selective egalitarianism" can explain why housing conditions became the subject of government action, it does not explain why provision of houses to let at subsidized rents was the form it took. The comparison was frequently made with food and clothing, both necessities of life like housing and also, again like housing but unlike education and health services, needed all the time. Adequate standards of food and clothing have been secured by cash payments (very rare exceptions apart), not direct provision by government; so there is something to be explained about adequate housing not being secured in the same way. That income supplements would be preferable has frequently been suggested, for instance, "A redistribution of income .... is best achieved by income subsidies .... the replacement of all housing subsidies by income subsidies should be the major component of social policy" (10).

An important part of the answer lies in the cash payments from public funds intended to ensure adequate food and clothing being made for the most part to people whose income from work is interrupted (by illness, injury, or unemployment) or ended (most commonly by retirement). Only Family Allowances (and Family Income Supplement) were exceptions to this generalization. Income supplements to ensure access to adequate housing would

16

have to be paid primarily to people in full-time employment. If paid to everyone regardless of income the cost would be very high. But supplements to earnings that vary according to how far earnings are below a standard level raise issues totally different from payments to unemployed, sick, or retired people. Nineteenth century opinion regarded payments from public funds to supplement wages as highly objectionable. The 1834 Royal Commission on the Poor Law's denunciation of them was regarded as authoritative, and became part of the received view of the 'political nation'. Trade unions were just as opposed to what they regarded as a threat to proper wages that would make their members dependent on the goodwill of government instead of on wages earned as of right. In the mid-twentieth century the "poverty trap" and the "poverty surtax" were the subject of concern.

As well as these reasons of principle why supplements to incomes were not seriously considered in the formative years of housing policy, there were cogent practical reasons. Means-testing millions of households and paying them money according to how far their actual income fell short of standard was beyond the administrative capacity of the nineteenth or early twentieth century state. The mechanism that could have been used to run a 'negative income tax' or 'reverse income tax' was ultimately provided not by social reform but by war finance. Wartime increases in the coverage of income tax and changes in the method of collecting it brought almost everyone in paid employment (other than domestic employment) within the scope of the tax system with tax collected and overpayments refunded weekly or monthly. Not until after 1945 therefore, did income supplements become a practical proposition as a way of dealing with substandard housing. But by that time local authority housing in Britain had become a very powerful going concern. Provision of houses to let at subsidized rents had for long been well within the capacity of local authorities, given the political will and the finance. By the late nineteenth century the larger urban local authorities had become powerful organizations providing a wide range of services.

Provision of houses to let at subsidized rents was for many years the main way in which an attempt was made to enable as many households as possible to obtain and keep satisfactory housing at a price within their means. Part of the history of housing policy is the emergence of the concept of a "need" for separate accommodation, and gradual broadening of accepted views about who "needs" a house or flat to themselves. That families with children should have a separate house or flat was at first an objective of housing reformers rather than a generally accepted view about social rights and obligations (11), but by 1945 had become widely enough accepted for a government statement on post-war housing policy to include as an objective "A separate home for every family that wishes to have one" (12). Subsequently the broadly held view about who "needs" a separate dwelling widened to include childless couples, and widowed survivors of families that wish to carry on living independently. By the later 1970s the argument had shifted to whether single people "needed" separate accommodation, and in what circumstances their "needs" were such as to give rise to a social and political obligation on the part of government (and hence on taxpayers and ratepayers) to enable them to get accommodation if they could not buy it or rent it in the market.

The concept of housing "need" was an integral part of selective egalitarianism as applied to housing and went with minimum standards. The concept of minimum standards of housing is best seen in two parts: the standard from which nobody should be debarred by inability to pay; and the compulsory minimum standard, which householders could be compelled to have regardless of whether they would prefer to make do with something less and spend more of their money in other ways. The former is "selective egalitarian" in its inspiration; the latter, embodied in the law on unfitness of human habitation and overcrowding, is paternalist in the most clear cut way. That the former is a relative standard that might be expected to rise with income was easy to accept; but that the compulsory minimum should rise in the same way beyond what is required for the protection of health and morals was far less obvious and much more open to debate. The distinction between the two separate types of minimum standard emerged only gradually. Selective egalitarianism as applied to housing, unlike health and education, never envisaged equal standards irrespective of income. With health services and (with more reservations) education, users accept the judgement of professionals about what service they need. Housing is very different in the enormous variation and variety that make it unsuitable for supply on the same lines as health services. Diversity goes with a market, and with a market go higher standards for those who can afford them and want them.

Notes and References

(1) See among others A.W. Evans,
    The Economics of Residential Location,
    Macmillan, London, 1973.
(2) L.S. Burns and L. Grebler,
    The Housing of Nations,
    Macmillan, London, 1977.
(3) E. Chadwick,
    Report on the Sanitary Conditions of the
    Labouring Population of Great Britain,
    ed. M.W. Flinn, Edinburgh University Press,
    Edinburgh, 1965.
(4) R. McKie,
    Housing and the Whitehall Bulldozer,
    Institute of Economic Affairs, London, 1971.
(5) See D.C. Stafford, The Economics of Housing,
    Croom Helm, London, 1978 pp.69-70 for an
    exposition of this proposition as applied to
    housing.
(6) G.B.A.M. Finlayson,
    The Seventh Earl of Shaftesbury
    Methuen, London, 1981, p.276.
(7) H. Barnes, Housing, Benn, London, 1923, p.231.
(8) A.B. Atkinson, The Economics of Inequality,
    Oxford University Press, Oxford, 1975, p.32,
    quoting J. Tobin.
(9) E.H. Phelps Brown, The Inequality of Pay,
    Oxford, 1977, p.319.
(10) D.C. Stafford, Economics of Housing, pp.13-14.
(11) See the dedication of Barnes, Housing,
    "To the homeless. One dwelling, one family.
    Every family a dwelling".
(12) Ministry of Reconstruction, Housing,
    (Cmd. 6609, 1945), paragraph 4.

CHAPTER II

THE PRE-1914 ANTECEDENTS OF HOUSING POLICY

The First World War was the watershed in the development of housing policy in Britain, but the conditions that constituted "the housing problem" as successive governments, councillors and households were to know it after 1918 had been laid down long before then. Policies after 1918 must be looked at in the context of what had gone before if any assessment is to be made of how great the impact of the war on the development of housing policy really was. How greatly altered was the development of housing policy by what in that context was a huge historical accident? Whether the course that policy took after 1918 was in any real sense the logical outcome of what had gone before has of late been disputed with some vigour, and earlier views that saw subsidized council housing as the inevitable answer to the pre-1914 "housing question" upbraided as being part of a 'Whig' approach to the history of housing (1). To see what is at issue in this controversy one must look in some detail at conditions in the pre-1914 decade, and more cursorily at the preceding three quarters of a century.

The origins of State action on housing are conventionally traced back to the reports of the 1840s (notably Chadwick's <u>Report on the Sanitary Condition of the Labouring Population of Great Britain</u> (2) and the reports of the Royal Commission on the State of Towns (3), and the legislation to which they led. There is much substance in such an account, but it is incomplete. For one must ask whether the conditions regarded as cause for concern and calling for action were novel; or whether recognition of the worst housing conditions as being a social evil was the consequence of

21

changes in attitudes towards conditions that had existed for decades or even centuries without arousing such a response. "The condition of England" and "the housing question" are nineteenth century expressions. In the nineteenth century housing conditions became the subject of public concern, which they certainly had not been in earlier centuries. Why this was so is obviously important in a history of housing. The most usual explanation is in terms of the Industrial Revolution having created masses of insanitary urban housing. Such an explanation is the more appealing if what is generally termed the 'pessimistic' view of the effect of the Industrial Revolution on living standards is accepted. There is, however, ample evidence of equally bad housing conditions in rural England; there is little reason to attribute bad housing to 'industry' and every reason to attribute it to poverty.

Chadwick's report and the report of the 1844-45 Royal Commission, and before them the reports by Drs Arnott, Kay, and Southwood Smith on disease and squalid housing in the East End of London described living conditions which, at their worst, make horrifying reading, which is what they were intended to do. Chadwick, Southwood Smith, and the Royal Commission were concerned to demonstrate to the 'political nation' that grossly insanitary living conditions made action necessary, and so concentrated on the worst conditions to demonstrate how prevalent they were. The inquiries into the health of towns have been criticized, like the inquiries into child labour in the factories and the mines, for concentrating on the worst and so not presenting a balanced picture or anything like it. Chadwick's 1842 report and the reports of the Royal Commission, though, were not nineteenth century precursors of the House Condition surveys of the 1960s and the 1970s, and should not be read as if they were. So long as the reader does not assume that the conditions described were universal, there is little risk of misunderstanding. To demonstrate that bad conditions are widely prevalent is quite sufficient to establish the case for action; it is not necessary to prove that they are universal and without exception.

Nevertheless, it is important to recall that the conditions described had existed in London in the eighteenth century and earlier without arousing public concern in the way that conditions that were no worse in the industrial towns (and in London as well) did in the nineteenth century. The growth of public concern about the health of towns and (more sporadically) rural housing must therefore be explained in terms of changed attitudes to long-existing conditions rather than to the conditions that aroused concern being novel. When one of the Assistant Commissioners of the Royal Commission on the Employment of Children, Young Persons, and Women in Agriculture wrote that rural cottages were "deficient in almost every requisite that should constitute a home for a Christian family in a civilized community" (4), he was speaking the language of the nineteenth century, not the eighteenth or earlier centuries. Such concerns about housing, health, and 'the conditions of the people' generally were among the outcomes of a much larger shift of sentiment and attitudes from the robust or coarse ways of the eighteenth century towards more sensitivity or humanity. The reform of the criminal law is one well known example; eighteenth century Parliaments added frequently to the list of capital offences, mostly offences against property; in the nineteenth century the offences punishable by death were continually reduced, eventually to murder and treason only. More positively, there was a growth of societies for missionary activity of all kinds, including moral wellbeing at home as well as abroad. This shift of sentiments and attitudes was not universal, of course, and there were exceptions in both directions. The reasons for it lie beyond the scope of a history of housing, particularly how far the explanations lie within the realm of religion. But that religious enthusiasm, of which Shaftesbury is the best known example, was important in early and mid-nineteenth century reform movements, is hardly open to dispute, any more than that some of the support that those movements received in Parliament came from Members attached to the landed interest who welcomed an opportunity to attack the manufacturing interest.

Indignation about bad conditions was one thing; what to do was another. There were strong objections to central control over local affairs, and the administrative and financial resources of civil government, both central and local, did not amount to much. The 'reform' tradition in British politics ever since the 1770s had been in favour of reductions in the civil as well as the military

23

establishments as a means to lower expenditure and lower taxation. More public expenditure and more public services as the 'reform' policy lay far in the future. Even the most radical political movement of the day, the Chartists who spoke of 'physical force' and drew their mass support from the victims of economic depression, had a programme of reforms solely of political institutions. There was thus a very long way to go before the rising concern about health (and housing) in the towns could be translated into effective action. Attempts to legislate began early on, though. The first was the Bills introduced by Lord Normanby (Home Secretary in Melbourne's government from 1839 to 1841) to impose what were for the time high minimum standards for new house building. His Bills came to grief in Committee, being strongly opposed on grounds of the effect they would have on house building costs (5). There were some advocates of reform who ignored the problem of costs altogether; others assumed, without (as far as is known) investigation, that it could be dealt with at the expense of the investors' returns from the cheaper kinds of rented housing. As an example of the former we may take the views of a Dr Davidson (senior physician at the Glasgow Royal Infirmary), included by Chadwick in his 1842 report.

"Why .... should we not have a legislative enactment that would level these hovels to the ground - that would regulate the width of every street - that would regulate the ventilation of every dwelling house .... for what right .... has any man to form streets, construct houses, and crowd them with human beings, so as to deteriorate health and shorten life, because he finds it profitable to do so? As well might the law tolerate the sale of unwholesome food because it might be profitable to the retailer of it" (6).

A somewhat similar view was expressed by Nassau Senior, Professor of Political Economy at Oxford University, a leading member of the Royal Commission on the Poor Laws, and a noted opponent generally of state intervention in economic matters, who opposed legislation to limit hours of work in factories on the ground that a reduction in hours would be ruinous to employers because the

24

profit was earned in the last hour of work. He wrote:

> "With all our reverence for the principle of non-interference, we cannot doubt that in this matter it has been pushed too far. We believe that both the ground landlord and the speculating builder ought to be compelled by law, though it should cost them a percentage on their rent and profit, to take measures which shall prevent the towns which they create from being the centre of disease" (7).

Nassau Senior evidently thought that owners of urban house property received a rate of return considerably greater than that which would have been sufficient to induce them to invest. If this were not so, then action which would cost them "a percentage of their rent and profit" would lead to a reduced supply of new houses being built to let and, if nothing else was done, to more sharing and crowding. Dr Davidson and others of like opinion ignored this problem altogether; and the 1840 Select Committee on the Health of Towns opined that the higher rents that town workers would have to pay for more sanitary housing would be good value for money because less working time (and hence pay) would be lost through illness, but did not consider whether those concerned could afford to pay such additional rent. Unless letting poor quality housing was so profitable that the cost could be forced up by statutory regulation and the yield forced down while still leaving sufficient inducement to invest, revulsion that led to enforcement of minimum standards but no more would be ineffective until rent-paying capacity increased. It is here that one sees an element of justification, in regard to housing, for Professor Gash's contention that ".... Peel's budgets .... did more for the working classes of Britain than all Shaftesbury's reforms put together" (8). Between 1842 and 1851 the import duty on timber was first reduced and then repealed, as were the taxes on glass and bricks, thereby reducing the cost of house building. They had been taxed not in order to place imposts on housing in particular, but as part of later eighteenth century war finance, to tax anything and everything within reach in the absence of an income tax. The reintroduction of the income tax in 1842 and the reduction in taxes on consumer goods shifted the tax burden in a way advantageous to poorer people, but could only make a small impact on the poverty that was the basic cause of bad housing.

Disease and death in the towns caused by lack of sanitation could be tackled, though, by means which were not nullified by inability to afford better housing. This is not the place for an extended discussion of public health in Victorian England, for which reference may be made to Wohl (9). The role of legislation and public administration in the provision of adequate systems of sewers, sewage disposal, and water supply can be studied there, and in the works of Finer (10), Lewis (11), and Lambert (12). Sanitation and water supply had of necessity to be provided publicly, so the question of interference with private enterprise or going beyond the proper functions of government did not really arise, once opinion was convinced that action was necessary. By the mid-nineteenth century what to do and how to do it had become clearly recognized and well understood: "What we want most now" wrote Florence Nightingale to Chadwick "is not to know but to do" (13). What was needed was the political will together with a sufficient amount of administrative ability. The reform of municipal corporations had helped local government to become a force to be reckoned with in the middle and later nineteenth century; superintendence by central government, carried out by enthusiasts of the calibre of Chadwick and Simon, applied further stimulus. The power to investigate and report was used to great effect where statutory powers of compulsion were lacking. The pace at which action was taken varied locally, with cost and economy important influences, but the eventual outcome was not in doubt.

Public health measures before long went beyond the provision of sewerage, water supply and street cleansing, and began to regulate the standards to which new houses were built. Proposals for legislation to do this went back to the 1840s. Powers to prevent the unhealthy use of existing houses and remedy conditions that were dangerous to health have a history almost as long. Rather later came powers to close and demolish insanitary houses, and then powers for area clearance. A brief outline of the legislation is useful here. The powers conferred on local authorities by the nineteenth

26

century legislation can be grouped into three
categories:

i) the Public Health Act powers over new building, and (less comprehensive and more difficult to exercise) to prevent the unhealthy
use of existing houses and to remedy conditions that were dangerous to health;
ii) powers to close or demolish individual houses
that were unfit for human habitation;
iii) powers to demolish and clear areas of insanitary housing.

The Public Health Act of 1875 is the best
known of the Acts that conferred powers on local
authorities to enforce minimum standards for new
houses. It owes much of its fame to its reputed
political context, being seen as part of Disraeli's
response to the interests of the urban workers
enfranchised by the 1867 Reform Act. Disraeli's
words 'sanitas sanitatum omnia sanitas' are well
known (14); but his reputation as head of a reforming administration has always contained a large
element of myth, and this is no exception. Public
health and housing were not issues that divided the
political parties; reforms were promoted (and
opposed) by members of both parties, and back-
benchers were often as prominent as ministers. The
previous administration (Gladstone's first
Ministry) had appointed the Royal Commission on the
Sanitary Laws in 1869, under the chairmanship of
C.B. Adderley, and many of its recommendations were
enacted into law under the same Ministry by the
Sanitary Act of 1872. The Public Health Act of
1875 was, in fact, largely a consolidating measure,
originating in the Local Government Board (15) and
piloted into law by Sclater-Booth, the President of
the Board, and Disraeli took little interest in it
(16). The Act did, however, equip local authorities with wide-ranging powers in a form probably
easier to use than in the earlier legislation that
it consolidated. There were powers to regulate new
house building, including both the houses themselves (e.g. connection to sewers, water supplies,
size of rooms, natural lighting and ventilation)
and their arrangement (e.g. width of streets,
prohibition of building of courts and alleys, and
of back-to-back houses). To assist local authorities to use those powers, the Local Government
Board in 1877 issued "model bye-laws" which local

authorities could adopt. Subsequent legislation, notably the Public Health Act of 1890, widened further the range of aspects of new house building that local authorities could regulate by bye-laws.

Many of these bye-law making powers were adoptive only, which meant that their effect on the minimum standards of houses built was gradual, though cumulative. In the bye-laws the phrase "to the satisfaction of the local authority" occurred frequently; and in determining what this meant in practice, the views and professional status of medical officers of health and their inspectors were important. The growing prestige and higher status of medical officers of health worked to raise the standards required, and towards stricter enforcement. This raising of minimum standards of new houses raised their cost as well; and by 1913 concern had begun to be expressed about whether the standards had been raised to levels that so raised costs as to worsen the problem of providing adequate housing for the lower paid (17). Powers to regulate the standards to which new houses were built were much easier to exercise than powers relating to existing houses. Such powers had first been provided by the Public Health Act of 1848, and extended by the Nuisances Removal Acts before being consolidated by the 1875 Public Health Act. These Acts provided powers to inspect insanitary houses, compel remedial work, and if necessary close them. These powers could be used, and stage by stage were used, to require the provision of proper sanitation to houses built without it, and could be used to demolish houses so as to open up badly ventilated 'courts'. Powers were provided (originally by the Nuisances Removal Act 1855) to require abatement of overcrowding where this was dangerous to the health of the inhabitants and the inhabitants were not all of one family. This was in principle a power to restrict the letting of single rooms to families and sub-letting where the result was overcrowding severe enough to be harmful to health; but, as was very soon realized by the medical officers of health that had to use these powers, they were of very little practical value when such accommodation was all that those who lived in it could afford. To try to enforce the law in such instances would not reduce overcrowding, only move it around (18).

There was a close affinity between the public health powers just described and the powers to demolish or close individual houses that were unfit

28

for human habitation. The body of law providing these powers was commonly known as the Torrens Acts (after William Torrens MP, sponsor of the Bills that became the first of this series of Acts), and comprised the Artisans and Labourers' Dwellings Act of 1868, amended in 1879 and again in 1882, and consolidated as Part II of the Housing of the Working Classes Act of 1890. The powers to secure the closing or demolition of individual houses that were unfit for human habitation were effective enough in themselves. The main obstacle to using them was the absence of any provision for rehousing the occupiers who were displaced. Torrens had included rehousing provisions in his original Bill, but was unable to carry them through Parliament (19).

Powers to demolish whole areas of insanitary housing (as distinct from individual houses) were provided by the so-called 'Cross Acts', the Artisans and Labourers' Dwellings Improvement Act 1875, amended in 1879 and 1882 and consolidated as Part I of the Housing of the Working Classes Act 1890. Whereas Torrens was a back-bench MP, Cross was Home Secretary (in Disraeli's Cabinet), and his Act was the first piece of specifically housing legislation to be sponsored by the government of the day. Cross was able to carry the rehousing clauses in his Bill, notwithstanding opposition on grounds of "municipal socialism". Sale of the cleared sites to charitable trusts and "model dwelling companies" was the preferred method of providing for rehousing, but local authorities were empowered to build for rehousing on the cleared sites (subject to central government approval) if model dwelling companies were not willing or able to do so. The preference for model dwelling companies was subsequently removed, so that local authorities could undertake the rehousing themselves if they wished (but wholly at their own expense); the London County Council (brought into being by the Local Government Act 1888) was particularly active in this respect.

There is not the information to make a precise estimate of the number of houses demolished and the number of new houses built under the Cross Acts. For London detailed figures of new houses built were collected, viz 9,700 by philanthropic organizations and individuals, 3,400 by London County Council, and 900 by the Metropolitan Boroughs (20), making 14,000 in all. The number of dwellings

29

demolished was greater than this, though just how much greater is not known. A history of slum clearance in the English provincial cities has still to be written; there was a considerable amount done in Birmingham, Liverpool and Sheffield, but all told, it is unlikely that the total number of new houses built exceeded 20,000 to 25,000. In physical terms, a somewhat larger number of insanitary houses were demolished; but in human terms the results were more equivocal. The view of the Royal Commission on the Housing of the Working Classes was:

> " .... although the health and appearance of London have been vastly improved in consequence .... and though [demolitions] have been a boon to the better class of the poor, yet they have been accompanied by the severest hardship to the very poor, increasing overcrowding and the difficulty of obtaining accommodation, and sending rents up accordingly" (21).

This was written in 1885, but it remained substantially true in later years even when local authorities were doing the rehousing. The most poorly paid occupations were very sparsely represented among the occupations of the London County Council tenants. The reason is not far to seek: although the sites were disposed of cheaply (often at a small fraction of what they might have fetched in other uses) and finance for new building could be had from the Public Works Loans Commissioners at interest rates not much above what Government paid, rents sufficient to meet those interest charges and cover running costs of dwellings built by local authorities were beyond what the very poor could afford. Poverty was the primary reason why they lived in slums; and slum clearance with unsubsidized new building could not make them better housed.

Provision of New Houses by Private Benevolent Initiative

The charitable housing trusts and "model dwelling companies" did not build for letting at subsidized rents, but rather at non-profit-making rents. They embodied the nineteenth century charitable and philanthropic endeavour as applied to housing.

Something of the flavour of these endeavours is
conveyed by the stated aims of the Society for
Improving the Condition of the Labouring Classes,
formed in 1844 following a meeting attended by
(among others) Lord Ashley (22) and Dr Southwood
Smith: "effecting great benefits for the working
classes .... by raising a planned dwelling or
cottages, for a certain number of families, so
contrived as to unite comfort with economy" (23).
Men of goodwill, they thought, could organize the
provision of housing on much more advantageous
terms than it was currently being provided.

An extended discussion of the philanthropic
housing movement would be out of place here; it has
been studied in some detail by Tarn (24), and Wohl
(25), though activity in the provinces has attracted much less attention than philanthropic housing
activity in London. In general what was attempted
was to provide accommodation to let on limited
profit terms. The expression "five percent philanthropy" (not a low return when Consols yielded
about 3 percent) has stuck, but such a yield was
not always achieved. The Medical Officer of Health
for Exeter, for example, told the Royal Commission
that the Industrial Dwelling House Company, which
had been "got up with philanthropic motives to
start proper housing for the poorer classes" had
never paid dividends of more than 2% or 2½%, and
that its shares were at a 50% discount (26). There
was "charity by accident" of this kind; there were
outright gifts (most notably by George Peabody,
used to found the housing trust that still bears
his name); there were companies that paid their 4%
or 5%, notably Sir Sidney Waterlow's Improved
Industrial Dwellings Company; and also (and in no
sense least) there was a considerable indirect
involvement of public funds.

Public funds came in by two routes. The
earlier of the two (and long continuing) was loans
from the Public Works Loans Commissioners who were
authorized by the Labouring Classes Dwelling Houses
Acts of 1866 and 1867 to lend at 4%, repayable over
40 years to "model dwelling companies" and trusts.
These were much more favourable terms than were
offered by any commercial lenders, and were in
effect making the State's credit available to the
philanthropic housing movement. Also important
were the sites obtained, for far less than would
have to have been paid on the open market, from
public authorities that had carried out clearance

31

schemes under the Cross Acts, as mentioned above. These Acts required the cleared sites to be used for housing (in the hope of rehousing as many as possible of the displaced inhabitants), and to that end allowed land to be sold at less than the cost of purchase and clearance, and regardless of the price the land might fetch in other uses. The Metropolitan Board of Works made extensive use of its slum clearance powers, and the Peabody Trust did most of the rebuilding work. Not all the sites built on by the model building companies were slum clearance sites; some were provided, for the good of the cause, by wealthy ground landlords like the Marquess of Westminster. But to overlook the importance of indirect public funding of the 'philanthropic' housing movement is easy; and if it is overlooked, too sharp a contrast may be drawn between nineteenth century private beneficence and twentieth century publicly financed provisions of housing.

Why was the Housing Question so Intractable Notwithstanding the Rise in Real Incomes?

Given the absence of any definite rise in real wages in the first half of the nineteenth century it is small wonder that there was no definite improvement in housing conditions. But the second half is another matter altogether, for real incomes in general and real wages rose substantially. Real wages on average doubled between the 1850s and the end of the century. Though as an annual rate this is not a spectacular increase, only about 1.4% a year, cumulatively such an increase sustained for half a century might reasonably be expected to have made considerable inroads into the problems caused by the gap between the cost of housing of a standard that was regarded as adequate and what large numbers of poorer households could afford to pay. Yet although there was a definite improvement in housing conditions on average, the worst was extremely bad and there was a lot of it. Contemporaries were in no doubt that "the housing question" was far from being solved. The reasons why rising real wages had done so little towards a solution to the problem warrant comment, as they are so highly relevant to the policies pursued and any others that might have been pursued.

In looking for explanations of why even in 1911 effective demand by well over a million households was too low in relation to costs for them to have a separate house, regard must be had both to the demand side of the market, particularly the relationship of the demand for housing to income; and to the supply side, particularly the cost of capital, building costs, and land. An explanation in terms of the short run, that 1911 is not a representative year to take, is unconvincing. By 1911 new house building had fallen away steeply from the boom years at the beginning of the decade. Although the land tax provisions of the 1909 Budget (which did not become law until 1910 owing to the rejection of the Finance Bill by the House of Lords) were widely alleged to have been harmful to new house building, their effects on the housing stock in 1911 can only have been minimal. New house building was falling fast well before the 1909 Budget. Interest rates rose in the pre-1914 decade, but there is little doubt that satiation of effective demand in the boom was the main reason why house building was falling. The balance of houses and households does not suggest that 1911 is an unrepresentative year for short-term reasons. Explanations must be sought in the longer term.

On the demand side, we may start with the amounts spent on housing in relation to income. The figures available are in general average or representative figures, and as such do not pick up the effects of dispersions around averages; nevertheless, they are important as a starting point. In 1906 average weekly earnings of men working full time in manual occupations varied from 27s to 34s a week according to industry (27), and in 1912 the average rent of four-roomed houses in towns outside London was 5s 3d a week including rates (28). As rates averaged about one-quarter of gross rents at the time (29), the implied net rent was about 4 shillings a week. This figure is confirmed by working back from the inter-war average net rent of 6 shillings a week for controlled lettings (30) to 4s 3d in 1914. The increase in wages between 1906 and 1912 was slow enough for 1906 earnings to be compared with 1912 rents without introducing serious error. The average rent, net of rates, of the typical house, was equal to about one-seventh of average wage earnings; if rates (almost invariably paid with the rent) are included, the proportion was between one-sixth and one-fifth. By the standards of subsequent periods, these were high ratios of rent to average earnings, even though, as we shall shortly see, such rents could not provide a commercial return on newly built houses of a standard that was adequate according to the opinion of the time. In his study of family budgets in York, Rowntree found a median ratio of rent to income of about 16%. Average rents in York were very similar to the average for provincial towns (31). That the ratio was as high as this tells against a general explanation of poor housing conditions in terms of mere unwillingness as distinct from inability to pay the rent that would secure a better house. Some contemporary comment did indeed attribute bad housing, along with many other ills, to unwise use of income and in particular excessive expenditure on alcoholic drink. In view of the very large amounts spent on alcoholic drink and the wealth of evidence about how poverty was aggravated by drink (32) there is no doubt that in some instances bad housing could be attributed to drink. But as a general explanation of bad housing, though, an explanation in terms of excess expenditure on alcoholic drink was no more than the direct ancestor of the explanation in the 1970s of rent subsidies in terms of local authority tenants spending their money on prestige cars and foreign holidays.

The rent of 4s a week excluding rates was an average for the whole stock of "working class" houses, and was considerably lower than the rents which would just cover the cost of providing new houses. The average cost of all new houses (excluding land) was estimated at £250 (33), so £200 including land is as low a figure as may reasonably be taken as the cost of "working class" housing that complied with legal standards but probably little more. A 5% net return, including amortization over 60 years, would be £10 12s; and expenditure on repairs, management, and rent collection about £2 10s (34), making £13 a year, 5 shillings a week. Rates would add about 1s 6d to this, making 6s 6d a week, not far short of a quarter of average weekly earnings of adult men in manual work. The implication was that rents of new houses were within the reach of only the better paid of workmen, earning well above average. An increase in the supply of housing for families with average earnings or less depended on "filtering", in the sense of tenants of new houses releasing the houses they previously occupied. With the number of households rising so fast, filtering could bring

34

about a marked improvement in conditions for those who could not afford the rent of new houses only if the number who could afford them was rising just as fast.

How fast would be the increase in the number of households able to afford better housing depended on the demand side on the income elasticity of demand (35). For the information from which to estimate it, recourse must be had to Rowntree's budget studies (36). Rowntree's data on rents and incomes are in grouped form and so can give only an approximate indication of the income elasticity of demand for housing. But given this limitation, they suggest an elasticity in the region of 0.4 to 0.5, which is close, perhaps surprisingly so, to the estimates of 0.6 to 0.7 found for owner-occupiers in the 1960s and 1970s (37), and closer still to the estimate of 0.4 for tenants in the 1960s. That rising real incomes did not do more to reduce sharing and overcrowding cannot, on the evidence that there is, be attributed to a low income elasticity of demand for housing in Victorian and Edwardian England.

Since an explanation is not to be found on the demand side of the market, one must turn to supply. Building costs are an obvious place to look for explanations of why the rise in real incomes did not bring about a greater improvement in housing conditions. The movement of building costs is shown in Table II.1. Rents are shown in the same Table.

The movement of the building cost index follows closely the swings in output of new building, so comparisons with the general price level has to be between years that were at fairly similar phases of the building cycle. 1874 and 1900 were both boom years; in 1896 and 1913 activity was at a lower level. Comparison of years at similar phases of the building cycle suggests that there was no long-term increase in building costs in real terms up to 1900. In the early years of the twentieth century there is more suggestion of increase, though there must be some doubt about it owing to variation according to the timing and severity of the building cycle.

With the possible exception of the decade or so before 1914, there is thus no evidence of a long run increase in building costs in real terms. Like building costs, the cost of capital was subject to medium term declines and increases, and one of the

Table II.1 - Index Numbers of House Rents and Building Costs

(1900 = 100)

	Rents (Weber)	Building Costs (Maywald)	Consumers Expenditure Deflator (Feinstein)	"Real" Rents	"Real" Building Costs
1874	82.6	107.3	108.8	75.9	98.6
1880	90.5	94.5	101.8	88.9	92.8
1890	92.7	89.0	95.5	97.1	93.2
1896	95.8	83.6	92.8	103.2	90.1
1900	100.0	100.0	100.0	100.0	100.0
1913	102.4	101.7	106.8	95.9	95.2

Note: 1874 is the starting point because that is the first year for which the assessed values of houses exempt from duty were published; 1896 is the year in which the general price level was at its lowest in this period.

Source: The rent index was constructed from House Duty valuations by B. Weber, and published posthumously in Appendix 13 of J. Parry Lewis Building Cycles and Britain's Economic Growth. Consumers expenditure deflator from C.H. Feinstein National Income, Employment and Output of the United Kingdom 1855-1965, Table 61; building costs from Table 63.

increases took place in the decade before 1914. It happened at a time when static or declining real wages restrained the ability of tenants to pay high rents and when increasing local rates restricted still further the rents that landlords could charge. It was this combination of circumstances that made rising capital costs appear significant as a cause of housing problems in the pre-1914 decade; but over the longer term there is little sign of any long-term increase in the cost of capital for housing (38). The rent series in Table II.1 (Weber's) was derived from the House Duty valuations, and so measures average rentals. It therefore includes the effects of rising quality of houses as well as the true rent increase. There is no wholly reliable way of separating the contributions made by increases in quality. But if the allowance for increases in quality assumed in the estimates of gross fixed investment are anywhere

near right, the increase in the average quality of
the stock can have been only about 0.3% a year
(38), so there appears to have been a rise of about
0.8% a year, on the average, in rents in real terms
in 1874-1900, after excluding the increase due to
improvements in the quality of the housing rented.
This was rather more than one-half of the rate of
rise in real earnings in the same period. Such an
increase in the price of housing in real terms
would seem to go far towards explaining the limited
effectiveness of rising real incomes in providing
answers to "the housing question". Over and above
the increase in rents there was an increase in
local rates in real terms. In the decade before
1914 the increase in rates averaged about 16% (39).
Rates were probably about one-quarter of gross rent
and hence about one-third of the net rent, so the
increases in rates added about 5% to gross rents
over the decade. With rates included, real rents
appear to have run steady over the period from the
turn of the century to 1913 when the trend of real
earnings was downwards. That British local government was financed from a tax on real property, and
especially house property, meant that controversies
over local government finance were closely bound up
with housing policy.
     If neither building costs in real terms nor
the cost of capital for financing house building
can go very far towards explaining why house rents
rose relative to prices generally, there remains an
explanation in terms of the supply of 'accessible'
building land being limited by concentration of
population growth in the towns and by the high cost
of travel. The extent to which the demand for
space for housing could be met by living further
away from workplaces was limited by the long
working day. Right down to 1914 the standard
working day remained at the ten hours, not counting
meal-breaks, that had been campaigned for in the
1840s and generally achieved in most factory
employments. The Board of Trade's inquiry in
1906/07 into earnings and hours, recorded average
hours in a full working week (excluding overtime)
in 54 industries and trades. In only two of them
was the average less than 50 hours, and the average
for all was 54.1 hours (40). A ten-hour working
day plus meal breaks does not leave much time for
travelling to or from work. For casual workers,
especially numerous in London, there were added
pressures to live near to the places where work

might be had. That pressures of demand on a limited supply of land had led to increased rents was the view of Marshall, the leading British economist of the day. In his Principles of Economics he wrote:

".... ground rents in towns have risen, both extensively and intensively. For an increasing proportion of the population is living in houses on which ground rents on an urban scale have to be paid, and that scale is rising. But house rent proper, that is what remains of the total rent after deducting the full rental value of the ground, is probably little, if at all, higher than at any previous time for similar accommodation" (41).

In Marshall's terms, the "extensive margin" of house building could not move out fast enough to obviate a rise in what he termed "ground rents on an urban scale". The reason why it could not can be summed up in the term 'accessibility', which is a function both of transport technology and incomes. With higher incomes, greater travel to work costs became acceptable.

Differences in average rents associated with the size of town provide a measure of support for Marshall's view. The 1912 information on rents gives the following averages.

Table II.2 - Index Numbers of Average Rents in 1912

London Inner Zone	116
London Middle Zone	100
London Outer Zone	87
Towns with populations over 250,000	62
Towns with populations between 100,000 and 250,000	63
Towns with populations between 50,000 and 100,000	55
Towns with populations under 50,000	51

Source: Cd. 6955, 1913, pp.4-5 (modified by excluding towns in Scotland and Ireland). The definition of the three London "zones" is at p.xv.

These effects on the pressure of demand for urban land help explain why rents, land values, land ownership, and land taxation generated so strong a head of political steam in the forty years before 1914, which issued forth in such ways as

Chamberlain's "unauthorized programme" in 1885, Lloyd George's land tax proposals in the 1909 budget (42), and the campaigns in favour of replacing local rates wholly or partly by taxation of site values. They also help explain why land reform and proposals to reform the basis of local taxation had their supporters as means of making progress with the "housing question".

Contemporary Answers to "The Housing Question" Before 1914

The emphasis placed on land values and local taxation in the previous section reflects their prominence in controversies about housing, particularly in the pre-1914 decade. As mentioned at the beginning of the chapter, there has been something of a reaction against the view that subsidized house building was the inevitable outcome of the gap between what adequate housing cost to provide and what large numbers of households could afford to pay, with the problem facing historians being how to explain why the inevitable took so long to happen (43). The 'revisionist' approach puts heavy emphasis on the pressures for land reform and reform of local taxation as ways of tackling "the housing question". To see how these came into the picture, and whether they could have achieved the results eventually achieved by subsidy, it is useful to catalogue the logically possible ways of working towards the reduction of bad housing. Four lines of approach may be distinguished:

i) stronger enforcement of public health legislation to drive the worst housing off the market, rather in the manner of contaminated food;

ii) redistribute income, for instance by minimum wage legislation, so that adequate housing could be afforded more readily;

iii) reduce the cost of supplying housing by lowering the price of land and transferring part of the weight of local taxation away from housing;

iv) build houses for letting at subsidized rents, with part of the cost met from central taxation or local rates, or both.

These four were not, of course, mutually exclusive. In particular, Liberal thinking often combined (ii) and (iii).

Building houses to let at subsidized rents was not just objected to on grounds of expense, but on principle as well. Here the nineteenth century humanitarian impulse, that 'something ought to be done' about squalid and crowded housing, came into conflict with the other strongly held ideas about the limited functions of government and the acceptable level of taxes and rates, and the moral virtues of 'self-help'. The tension was particularly great, with two sets of moral considerations pulling in opposite directions. Shaftesbury wrote:

> "If the state were required to provide houses for the working classes at nominal rents, it would while doing something for their physical condition utterly destroy their moral energies" (44).

Others saw houses let at subsidized rents as tantamount to public doles, in terms of if local authority provided subsidized houses then why not food, clothing, etc. Anything that appeared to savour of a grant in supplementation of wages was widely regarded as anathema. Octavia Hill told the Royal Commission on the Housing of the Working Classes:

> " .... If you assume that it is your duty to provide houses for the poor at a price that they assume they can pay, it will just be a rate in aid of wages like the old poor law system" (45).

A prominent example of the first method of dealing with poor housing, a policy of compulsion combined with putting as much as possible of the cost onto landlord and ground rents, may be found in the policies advocated in the 1880s by Joseph Chamberlain. An enthusiastic supporter of heavy taxation of landowners and ground rents, he was of the view that the responsibility of ensuring that the poor were properly housed should be borne by property owners, not by government (46). The way in which this was to be done was, as outlined to the Royal Commission: " .... making provision for the destruction of unhealthy and overcrowded dwellings" and "proper bye-laws to prevent a re-creation of the evil" (47). That such policies would force up rents he acknowledged: "I think the

very poor people spend too little in rent ....
They waste the money they save on rent on something
much less to their advantage. I would not object
to a system under which they would be compelled to
attribute a larger proportion of their income to
house rent than they do at the moment" (48). The
difficulties that would be encountered by such a
policy are evident from the relationship between
housing costs and income, and how ineffective in
practice the London medical officers of health
found their powers against overcrowding. A policy
of driving off the market poor but cheap accommodation that fell short of adequate standards was
beyond the powers of local government in pre-1914
England; and would have failed even with considerably stronger powers. With the level and distribution of income as they were, a policy that relied
solely on compelling people to spend more of their
income on housing could not succeed.

Equally beyond the power of the State in pre-
1914 was another line of action, redistributing
income, in particular raising wages, to enable most
households to afford adequate housing at a commercial rent. The group of supporters of the Liberal
Government (including Rowntree) who were Lloyd
George's Land Enquiry Committee expressed the
following view in 1914:

".... in the interest of housing alone ....
the time has come for the nation to
seriously consider the problem of low wages
and deal with it..... If the legal fixing
of minimum wages is materially to help in
the solution of the housing problem, the
statute should lay down the requirement that
the minimum fixed for men of normal ability
must be at least the sum necessary to maintain a family of moderate size in a state of
physical efficiency and to enable them to
pay an economic or commercial rent for a
sanitary dwelling" (49).

If this were done, the laws about overcrowding, sanitation and nuisance could be properly
enforced. The "residuum unable to pay an economic
rent" would be provided for by a combination of
filtering and municipalization; with their rent-
paying power reinforced, wage earners would
generate effective demand for new houses; what they
vacated could be bought by the local authority and

41

let to the very poor. Just how this would work, what it would cost, and how it would be financed was not discussed, but at least the idea had the merit of recognizing that rising real wages would not solve the housing problem for everybody. To lump together the very low paid, casual workers, the disabled, widows, and the elderly as the "residuum" may seem remarkably insensitive; but this was the first time this particular aspect of ability to pay for housing was given any attention at all.

What would have been the wider economic effects of such an attempt to shift the distribution of income in favour of wages is open to argument. For agricultural workers the redistribution was intended to be at the expense of land rent; but since only 11% of employment was in agriculture most of the redistribution would have to have been at the expense of profits. Whether such an attempt at redistribution would in anything but the short-term have done more harm to real wages (by slowing down capital accumulation and the rise in output per head) than good is very arguable. But in this context it is a purely hypothetical question, for the means to bring about such a redistribution of income did not then exist. There were the powers under the Trade Boards Act of 1909 to set minimum wages in the "sweated" trades, as a substitute for collective bargaining; and the minimum wages set for coal mining in 1911 as a means of imposing on the coal owners a settlement of the coal mining pay dispute of that year. But none of this could be developed into general minimum wages, still less the controls needed to ensure that compulsory increases in money wages were not passed on as higher prices. The comment of the majority report of the Royal Commission on Housing in Scotland that: "The Local Authority, as housing authority, cannot profitably interfere between employer and employed, nor can the housing needs of the working classes wait for a settlement of claims by labour for a larger share of the profits of production" (paragraph 2024) was a sagacious comment; and the second part would have been true even if central government had tried to "interfere between employer and employed".

What then of the third possibility, land reform and reform of local taxation? That radical reformers should be in favour of putting more of the burden of both national and local taxation on

urban landowners can be readily understood when in
the 1880s 65% of central government revenue came
from customs and excise duties and only 35% from
income tax and death duties. Even in 1907 the
proportions were still 53:47. The support for
taxing site values as a source of local government
revenue in place of rates charged on occupiers
according to rental values had similar origins
(50). Rates were regressive in their incidence and
a heavy charge on households. Just how heavy can
be judged from the estimate (51) of rates being on
average about a quarter of gross rents paid by
'working class' tenants and one-third of the net
rent. With gross rents equal on average to around
a sixth of earnings, the implication is that rates
were equivalent to about 4% of wage earners'
incomes. The demands and obligations on local
authorities, particularly for education, were
increasing: between 1885 and 1913 local authorities' expenditure out of revenue increased by some
185% in real terms (52). In the 1880s 85-90% of
local authorities' revenue came from rates and only
10-15% from central government grants; in 1907 70-
75% and 25-30%. Between 1872 and 1900 rates per
inhabited house rose by between 70% and 75% in real
terms; and between 1900 and 1913 by another 33%
(53). Small wonder that local government finance
became a highly charged and contentious subject,
and that few local authorities were willing to
build houses for letting when the cost fell
entirely on the rates.

Conservatives tended to argue that land and
housing together were being over-taxed, and that
more of the cost of provision of public services
should fall on commerce and finance, which in
practice meant national rather than local taxation.
The contrary view was that owners of land paid too
little, and that the burden could be shifted away
from house owners and their tenants onto ground
landlords. This is not the place to review these
controversies in any detail, for which reference
may be made to Offer (55). The point here is that
very considerable scepticism is in order about what
might have been achieved by site value taxation or
rating, and particularly whether a worthwhile
contribution could have been made to improving
housing conditions. The comprehensive review by
Professor A.R. Prest of British attempts to tax
increases in land values, from Lloyd George's land
taxes in the "people's Budget" of 1909 through the

"development charge" of the 1940s, the Betterment Levy of the 1960s to the Development Land Tax of the 1970s, shows how meagre were the results in comparison with expectations. That much contemporary opinion in the decade before 1914 looked to land reform and land taxation for answers to the 'housing question' does not imply that they could provide any. They were wholly unknown quantities in cash terms.

The other possibility, subsidized house building, had its contemporary supporters and was by no means an ex post rationalization. A very clear statement of the case was made by the Royal Commission on Housing in Scotland. It was set up in 1912, and although it did not report until 1917 it concerned itself with pre-war conditions. The detail reviewed was Scottish, but the reasoning would have applied with equal force as well to England, not least because in the two decades before 1914 industrial Scotland was one of the most prosperous parts of the United Kingdom. The Commissioners reported (55):

> "Private builders had for a long time prior to the war failed to provide in anything like adequate numbers the houses necessary for the working class population .... the fundamental [reason was] that an economic rent could not be got ...." (paragraph 1964).

They drew the conclusion:

> "The housing of that section of the community that cannot by reason of low wages or disability affecting their earning capacity pay an adequate rent is one of the most important questions with which we have to deal .... it is no concern of the private property owner to house these people .... who is to house them? It can only be the Local Authority" (paragraph 2022).

The Royal Commission's Minority Report advocated a subsidy, payable to men with three children or more, equal to the difference between the average rent of a two-roomed-dwelling and "the higher rent of which would be requisite for the proper housing of the family on the higher standard to be enforced in the near future". Such a subsidy "would have the advantage of being a direct and avowed subsidy for a clearly understood purpose, and could thus be effectively limited in scope" (56). This is the first instance in a British official report of advocacy of a subsidy to households rather than to "bricks and mortar". But it was an idea which was not to be taken up again for many years.

Supplementation of income to enable poorer people to pay the market price of 'adequate' accommodation was, with the single exception just referred to, not a contemporary concept in discussions of the housing problems before 1914, but a development of the 1950s and later. The question has been asked, retrospectively however, why this approach was not followed at a time when great store was set on keeping the activities of government as small as possible. McKie, for example, wrote:

> "The mid-Victorian reformers might have been expected to work through the market rather than against it; to have subsidized the labourer so that he could compete in the market ....
> .... why is it that the mid-Victorians never experimented with direct housing subsidies tied to family circumstances but tacitly rejected the orthodox market philosophy in relation to the housing of the labour poor?"

McKie's view is that the answer lay in the "moralistic approach of the Victorian philanthropists .... 'Labouring men' were not trusted to maximize their satisfactions in a sober and sanitary manner acceptable to the middle classes. Tory paternalism and nonconformist compassion could be alike the enemies of choice" (57).

Such a policy would however, have been anathema both to the 'political nation' and (in all probability) to the 'labouring men' who might be intended to benefit; and far beyond the resources of nineteenth and early twentieth century public administration to operate. Moreover, the attitudes surrounding the Poor Law ensured that the time was far distant before cash payments to men in employment would get anything other than a highly unsympathetic hearing; and that prospective recipients would keep well away from anything connected with or savouring of the Poor Law. Direct cash payments by the State to individuals, other than as outdoor relief under the Poor Law, did not appear in Britain until 1909, when the Old Age Pensions Act 1908 came into effect, after nearly twenty years of controversy and discussion including no less than three official enquiries (58). The pensions were financed and administered in a way that would keep them completely apart from the Poor Law: they were financed wholly from national taxation; the means testing was done by officers of Customs and Excise; and payment was made through the Post Office (also a branch of national government). That they were separate from the Poor Law added to their popularity. This was the sum total of cash payments to individuals from public funds, apart from sick benefit and (for a small range of trades only) unemployment pay under the National Insurance Act of 1911. In the later nineteenth and early twentieth centuries there was neither the will nor the machinery to make payments on the scale needed to tackle bad housing by housing allowances.

It is hard to avoid the conclusion, therefore, that the only feasible way in which housing that was adequate by the standards of the day could be brought within the financial reach of the very large number of households that could not afford it unaided was by building for letting at subsidized rents. That there were numerous and influential advocates of other approaches is certainly true; but there are no convincing reasons for thinking that those other methods could have worked, and many reasons for thinking that they would not have done so. Local authorities had been involved in a small way in house building since the 1880s, initially to replace slums demolished under the 'Cross' Acts when no other body could be found to take it on, but before long for broader purposes. The Housing of the Working Classes Act of 1885, which followed the report of the Royal Commission, redefined "lodging houses" (which local authorities were empowered to provide under an Act of 1851) to include separate dwellings and cottages for the working classes. By this curiously elliptical means the power to build was conferred, at the behest of Lord Salisbury (Primer Minister at the time) who defended the Bill with vigour against the charge that what was proposed was 'socialism'. The 1885 Act was consolidated as Part III of the Housing of the Working Classes Act of 1890. It was there, as in the 1885 Act, purely a permissive power that depended for its effect on local authorities choosing to adopt it. It was used most extensively by the London County Council; the LCC did not adopt Part III of the 1890 Act until 1899, but by 1914 it had completed over 3,700 houses. In 1900, in one of the sequence of amending Acts, the LCC gained the power to buy land and build outside its boundaries. The same Act gave the newly formed Metropolitan Boroughs power to build under Part III of the Act of 1890; by 1914 they had built 2,400 dwellings. The total number of houses built before 1914 under Part III of the Housing of the Working Classes Act of 1890 was about 20,000 (59).

In the decade before 1914 there was considerable debate over whether the power to build houses under Part III of the 1890 Act should remain purely permissive, or whether it should be made in some circumstances a duty. The Housing, Town Planning Act 1909 went a considerable distance towards making it a duty, by giving the Local Government Board the power to require local authorities to adopt Part III of the Act of 1890; and also provided that four householders could petition the Local Government Board to hold a public enquiry, and, if the facts as found on enquiry so justified, find a local authority in default. These powers were criticized as being dictatorial but in operation were much less impressive than they appeared on paper. The default powers when used proved to be extremely cumbersome, as was demonstrated by the example of Potterne in Wiltshire (60), where four years of activity, including three formal enquiries by the Local Government Board's inspectors, were needed to get provision made (in the form of tenders accepted) for six houses. Against local authorities' unwillingness to act, central government in the circumstances of the time could achieve little. The explanation for the widespread unwillingness of local authorities to take action lay in the financial pressures already discussed. When they were already hard pressed they were unwilling to take on a new and expensive obligation. Particularly was this so for the larger cities and towns, which as county boroughs were responsible for education. They were pressing the government hard for more Exchequer grants to help meet the cost of their existing statutory responsibilities, and could not take on a large new commitment wholly at their own expense. If they were to build houses for letting at subsidized rents, central government would have to bear a substantial

47

share of the cost. There were indeed proposals to
this end. Bills to provide for such subsidies were
introduced annually in 1910 to 1914. Their most
prominent supporter was Sir Arthur Griffith-
Boscawen, a back-bench Conservative MP, who had for
two years been Chairman of the LCC Housing
Committee, backed by Colonel W.K. Taylor, Chairman
of Liverpool City Council's Housing Committee (61).
Griffith-Boscawen proposed a fund of £1 million (in
total, not annually) for housing, contributed by
the Exchequer, on the ground that ".... if neither
private enterprise nor the landowner can afford [to
house the poor] and the local authority can only do
it at a huge cost to rates, then the State must
come in to meet the great national evil" (62). The
government of the day, first under Campbell
Bannerman and then Asquith, resisted, and the Bills
were not much more than gestures as the days had
long passed when members of the opposition back-
benches could carry major legislation through the
House of Commons.

The reasons why the Government did not move on
the question of an Exchequer subsidy for housing
owed something to the Liberal views about land
taxation and hence not burdening the Exchequer with
costs that should properly fall on property owners;
but more important, as will be seen in more detail
in Chapter VII, the combination of the heavy expenditure caused by the 'battleship race' with Germany
and the cost of the reforms already introduced by
the post-1906 Liberal administration, notably old
age pensions and national insurance, pressed very
hard on the existing sources of revenue. Lloyd
George's land taxes produced little revenue; so
higher public expenditure would require either a
substantially higher income tax, or tariffs on
imports. To Liberals at the time, tariffs were
anathema. Majority opinion among Conservatives (or
Unionists) supported 'tariff reform' that would
comprise a protective tariff on manufactured goods,
and a tariff on food from foreign countries (as
distinct from what was then the 'empire'). To some
sections of opinion, the revenue that a tariff
would bring was seen as providing the opportunity
for social reform that could not be financed from
existing sources. To others, using some of the
tariff revenue to finance social reform was seen as
a way of making more acceptable a fiscal reform
that would be regressive in its incidence, particularly the food tariff, which would raise the price

48

of imported wheat and hence bread prices. Income tax rates were already high by the standards of the day; resistance to any sizeable increase was strong, and could have been overcome only through a prolonged political struggle. What would have happened if war had not drastically altered political and public perceptions of what were tolerable tax rates, can be no more than a historical 'if'. By 1914 there was an impasse.

Notes and References

(1) See, for instance, the discussion at a conference in 1981 on housing market studies 1860-1930 reported in D. Reeder (ed.) <u>Urban History Year-book 1983</u> (Leicester University Press, Leicester, 1983), pp. 81-82. The term is pejorative and implies a parallel with an outmoded interpretation of English (and then British) constitutional history, in which the growth of liberty and Parliamentary government was traced, with moral approbation as progress, from Magna Carta through the Long Parliament and the Revolution of 1688 to the Reform Bill of 1832 and beyond.

(2) Edwin Chadwick, <u>Report on the Sanitary Condition of the Labouring Population of Great Britain 1842</u>, ed. M.W. Flinn, Edinburgh University Press, Edinburgh, 1965.

(3) Royal Commission for Enquiring into the State of Large Towns and Populous Districts, First Report, Parliamentary Papers 1844 Vol. VXII.

(4) Paragraph 14 of Report of Rev. J. Fraser, annexed to First Report of the Royal Commission on the Employment of Children, Young Persons and Women in Agriculture (Parliamentary Papers 1867/68, Vol. XVII).

(5) See I.C. Taylor, 'The Insanitary Housing Question and Tenement Dwellings in Nineteenth Century Liverpool in A. Sutcliffe (ed.), <u>Multi-Storey-Living</u>, Croom Helm, London, 1974.

(6) Chadwick, <u>Sanitary Conditions of the Labouring Population</u>, p.216.

(7) Report of Commissioners on the Condition of the Hand Loom Weavers, p.73, (Parliamentary Papers 1841, Vol. X).

(8) N. Gash, <u>Aristocracy and People</u>, Arnold, London 1979, p.4.

(9) A.S. Wohl, <u>Endangered Lives</u>, Dent, London, 1983.

(10) S.E. Finer, <u>The Life and Times of Sir Edwin Chadwick</u>, Methuen, London, 1952.

(11) R.A. Lewis, <u>Edwin Chadwick and the Public Health Movement</u>, Longmans, London, 1952.

(12) Royston Lambert, <u>Sir John Simon</u>, Macgibbon and Kee, London, 1963.

(13) Quoted in Lambert, <u>Sir John Simon</u>, pp.521-22.

(14) Speech by Disraeli at the Crystal Palace in
      1872 and quoted by among others, R.C.K.
      Ensor, England 1870-1914, Oxford University
      Press, Oxford, 1936, p.56. This phrase is a
      pun on 'vanitas vanitatum, omnia vanitas' -
      'Vanity of vanities, all is vanity', the
      opening words of the Book of Ecclesiastes.
(15) This department was formed in 1871 by amalga-
      mation of the Poor Law Board, the Medical
      Department of the Privy Council, and the
      Local Government Act Office. The 'Board' had
      only a nominal existence (like the Board of
      Trade and the Board of Education). The
      President of the Board was a Minister who was
      sometimes but not always a member of the
      Cabinet. The Local Government Board remained
      the Department responsible for public health,
      housing, and the Poor Law until the Ministry
      of Health was formed in 1919.
(16) R.N.W. Blake, Disraeli,
      Eyre and Spittiswoode, London, 1966.
(17) The Land, Vol. 2 Urban, pp. 85 and 131-44.
(18) See Wohl, The Eternal Slum, pp.116-119 for
      full discussion, with extensive quotations
      from medical officers of health.
(19) See Wohl, The Eternal Slum, pp.84-91 for the
      legislative history of Torren's Bills.
(20) Wohl, The Eternal Slum, quoting London
      Statistics, 1910/11 and 1914/15.
(21) Royal Commission on the Housing of the
      Working Classes, Report, p.17, 1885.
(22) Later the Earl of Shaftesbury, by which title
      he is better known.
(23) J.N. Tarn, Five Percent Philanthropy,
      Cambridge University Press, Cambridge, 1973,
      p.15.
(24) Tarn, Five Percent Philanthropy.
(25) Wohl, The Eternal Slum.
(26) Royal Commission on the Housing of the
      Working Classes 1884/85, Minutes of Evidence,
      Q.8450.
(27) British Labour Statistics Historical Abstract
      Table 37.
(28) Board of Trade, Report of the Enquiry into
      Working Class Rents and Retail Prices,
      (Cd.6955) 1913, p.xxv.
(29) Ministry of Labour, Departmental Evidence to
      the Inter-Departmental Committee on Rent
      Acts, 1931.

(30) Report on the Inter-Departmental Committee on the Rent Acts (Cmd. 5621, 1937) paragraph 42. The Rent Restrictions Act set controlled rents at (generally speaking) 40% above the rent paid in 1914.

(31) Board of Trade, Enquiry into Working Class Rents, pp.2-3. Rents in York were 55% of the average for "Middle" London, compared with an average of 57% for the English provincial towns.

(32) See, for instance, E.H. Hunt, British Labour History 1815-1914, Weidenfeld and Nicolson, London, 1981, pp.124-25.

(33) A.K. Cairncross, Home and Foreign Investment, Cambridge University Press, Cambridge, 1953, p.108.

(34) Departmental Committee on the Rent Restrictions Acts,. 1920, Minutes of Evidence, Q.251.

(35) The relationship between a specified increase in income and the consequent increase in demand for a good or service, in this instance housing.

(36) B. Seebohm Rowntree, Poverty, A Study in Town Life (1913 Edition), p.201.

(37) Cairncross, Home and Foreign Investment, Table 49.

(38) Derived from the assumptions by Cairncross and Feinstein about increases in the quality of new houses, and Miss Riley's estimates of the age of the housing stock. K.M. Riley, 'An Estimate of the Age Distribution of the Housing Stock of Great Britain', Urban Studies, Vol. 10 (1973) pp.373-79.

(39) The Land, Vol.2, p.85.

(40) British Labour Statistics Historical Abstract Table 36.

(41) Alfred Marshall, Principles of Economics (8th Edition) Macmillan, London, 1922, p.676.

(42) See A.R. Prest, The Taxation of Urban Land, Manchester University Press, Manchester, 1981.

(43) See for example, the Editor's introduction in M.J. Daunton (ed.) Councillors and Tenants, Leicester University Press, Leicester, 1984.

(44) Quoted in G.B.A.M. Finlayson, The Seventh Earl of Shaftesbury, Methuen, London, 1981, p.589.

(45) Royal Commission on the Housing of the Working Classes, Minutes of Evidence, Q.8870.

(46) Quoted by A.S. Wohl, The Eternal Slum, Arnold, London, 1977, p.230.
(47) Royal Commission on the Housing of the Working Classes, Minutes of Evidence, QQ.12356, 12400, 12403, 1885.
(48) Royal Commission on the Housing of the Working Classes, Minutes of Evidence, Q.12616, 1885.
(49) The Land, Vol.2, pp.161-62
(50) For a full discussion, See A. Offer, Property and Politics 1870-1914 Cambridge University Press, Cambridge, 1981.
(51) See reference (29).
(52) B.R. Mitchell and P. Deane, British Historical Statitistics, Chapter XIV, Table 10. Revalued to constant price by the consumers' expenditure deflator from C.H. Feinstein, National Income, Employment and Output, Table 61.
(53) Mitchell and Deane, British Historical Statistics, Chapter XIV, Table 9. Revaluation to constant prices as in reference (144). Inhabited houses from Table II.7 above.
(54) Offer, Property and Politics, has a full discussion.
(55) Royal Commission on the Housing of the Industrial Population of Scotland, Urban and Rural, Report (Cd. 8731, 1917).
(56) Minority Report, paragraph 258.
(57) R. McKie, Housing and the Whitehall Bulldozer, Institute of Economic Affairs, London, 1971, pp.24-25.
(58) The Royal Commission on the Aged Poor, Report (Parliamentary Papers 1895, Vol.XIV); Departmental Committee on Old Age Pensions, Report (Parliamentary Papers 1898, Vol. XLV); Select Committee on the Aged and Deserving Poor, Report (Parliamentary Papers 1899, Vol. VIII).
(59) Local Government Board, Annual Report for 1914/15 Part II, Housing (Cd. 8196), p.21.
(60) See W.G. Savage, Rural Housing, Fisher Unwin, London, 1915, pp.193-95.
(61) For discussion see P. Wilding 'Towards Exchequer Subsidies for Housing 1906-1914', Social and Economic Administration, Vol. 6 (1972) pp.3-18.
(62) Quoted, Wohl, The Eternal Slum, p.337.

CHAPTER III

THE INTER-WAR YEARS:
THE ECONOMY, POPULATION, HOUSEHOLDS AND HOUSING

The First World War and English Housing

What until 1939 was termed the 'Great War' was an immense event for the British economy and British society. The scale on which it was fought was something new. The American Civil War and the Franco-Prussian War, especially the former, had given a foretaste of the scale on which war could be waged by industrial powers equipped with railway transport, but they had had little impact on British thinking. The war developed into a huge conflict fought by massed armies (and to a lesser extent massed navies and air forces), which had to be supplied on a corresponding scale with munitions of war and stores of all kinds. To do this the Ministry of Munitions ran a very large organization indeed. There was a complete change of scale in the size of the Government machine and in public perceptions about what Government could do. Tax rates were raised to hitherto unthought of heights. Direct controls over the production, sale, distribution, and prices of essential goods were widespread and effective by 1918. Most of the controls went soon after the war, and the size of the government machine was reduced, but there was no going back to 1914.

The scale and severity of the war brought political changes. The horrors of war produced a widespread desire for a better world when the war was over, and the means of controlling resources developed in the war seemed to offer the way of bringing it about. There was as a result a strongly collectivist flavour to the thinking about a better Britain after the war, which influenced plans and thinking about post-war housing policy.

54

In the later years of the war and immediately after it, fear of socialist or communist forces (or "Bolshevism" from 1917 onwards) was a strong influence in the direction of collectivist policies to meet, at least part way, the interests of urban workers. Before 1914 there had been talk in many countries of socialist parties not fighting 'capitalist wars'. This had not come about in 1914, but the prospect that it might happen was a powerful stimulus to the government to use direct controls to keep down the prices of essentials and restrain "profiteering". When the Communist government took Russia out of the war in 1918 the fear of labour unrest that would impede the conduct of the war was strengthened. At the end of the war much of central Europe was convulsed by revolution; and fears of unrest were not lacking in Britain. Such fears exerted a strong influence on what was considered politically acceptable and what was not.

The war was the cause both of a very substantial worsening of housing shortages, and the form taken by the shortage. House building came to a virtual halt early in the war, which had a far greater effect than did destruction of houses by enemy action. The number destroyed was small, for the bomb loads carried by the Zeppelins and then the Gotha aircraft were light; and the bombardment of coastal towns (Hartlepool, Lowestoft and Scarborough) by naval gunfire could cause only local damage. The effect of the war on housing shortages can be gauged by the fact that the increase in the housing stock between the 1911 and 1921 Censuses was under 300,000, whereas the number of potential households increased by an estimated 1,100,000 (see Tables III.5 and III.9 below). Of the difference of 800,000 households, 200,000 were accommodated by a reduction in the number of vacant dwellings, but the others had to be accommodated through more sharing, including newly married couples living with in-laws instead of being able to set up on their own.

The increase in sharing between 1911 and 1921 came on top of an already high level of sharing in 1911. This sharing, by about 1,150,000 households out of a total of 7,950,000 (1), was attributed primarily to inability to afford a whole house, and so was not the expression of a shortage in market terms. But wartime changes increased the number of households that could afford separate accommodation. The inter-action of rent restriction and

55

inflation had forced rents sharply downwards in
real terms and relative to incomes, and thereby
raised the effective demand for housing at the
controlled rents. In 1924, which may be taken as a
year when both the immediate post-war boom and then
the slump had passed, the general price level was
some 90% higher than in 1914 (2) and the average
weekly earnings of manual workers appears to have
risen by about approximately 5% more than this (3).
The increase in controlled rents allowed in 1919
and 1920 amounted to 40% above the July 1914 level,
so that rents that were subject to control were
about 25% lower in real terms in 1924 than they had
been at the outbreak of war. Such a reduction in
rents in real terms was sufficient to increase
substantially the number of households that could
afford a house to themselves. Part at least of the
pre-1914 lack of effective demand for separate
housing was thereby transformed into a demand that
at going rents was effective but un-met. The pervasive housing shortage caused in the ways described was the background to all the housing policies in the inter-war years, and was a very powerful influence on the policies pursued.

The British Economy in the Inter-War Years

The key question here about the economy in
the inter-war years is how far the course of the
economy can explain why investment in housing and
the number of new houses built ran so much higher
than in the two decades before 1914. A housing
boom might be considered to have been due in the
1920s or early 1930s even had there been no fundamental changes since before the war; but the size
of the boom was something altogether new. How far
the course of real incomes contributed to the boom
is a question of some importance; so too is the
contribution of interest rates and the supply of
credit.
The end to hostilities was followed by a boom
as demands that had gone un-met during the war came
onto the market. The boom provided jobs for most
of the ex-Servicemen as they were demobilized and
for former munitions workers, but the rise in
prices was very rapid indeed. Between 1918 and
1920 prices, as measured by the consumers' expenditure deflator, rose by 27% (4); 1920, however, saw
the peak of the boom, and it was followed by a
slump in which prices, incomes, output and employ-

ment all fell steeply. Monetary and budgetary
policies in 1920 were strongly deflationary, but
the slump was world wide; policy within Britain
aggravated the slump but did not cause it. When
the world economy came out of the slump so did
economic activity in Britain; but in contrast to
the rest of the world, unemployment in Britain did
not fall below levels which before 1914 had been
experienced only at the low point of the trade
cycle. Persisting high unemployment remained a
feature of the British economy until the outbreak
of war in 1939, and indeed beyond. This is not the
place to discuss at length the causes of the high
unemployment in the inter-war years, but the fact
of it merits note in the present context, as it
makes the housing boom all the more remarkable;
unemployed men could not buy houses, nor could they
pay the rents that would make building to let a
remunerative proposition. The income support
arrangements for the long term unemployed in the
inter-war years made "means testing" a term of
opprobrium, disliked and detested just as the Poor
Law had been by previous generations.

Notwithstanding the high level of unemployment, it is important to emphasize that the numbers
in employment rose fast. Total civil employment
in 1938 was almost 1½ million more than at the peak
of the post-war boom in 1920, even though there
were nearly 1.7 million more unemployed (5). The
growth of the working population (employed and
unemployed) was almost entirely the consequence of
the growth of the working age population, not an
increase in the proportion of the population of
working age seeking employment, for in the inter-
war years the working age population expanded more
rapidly than ever before (or since).

Within this growth in total employment, there
was a change in the structure of employment.
Employment in the professions, banking and
insurance, and public administration expanded fast;
so too did employment in electricity supply and (in
the 1930s) public transport. These so-called
"sheltered occupations" (in the sense of not being
exposed to the pressures of international competition in the way in which the textile, ship-building
and coal mining industries were exposed, for
example) offered secure employment that enabled
people working there to consider house purchase in
a way that those employed in more vulnerable occupations could not. This contrast between employ-

ment growth in the secure and expanding services, industries, and occupations on the one hand, and the vulnerable industries on the other, goes a considerable way to explain why the demand for housing was so strong in times when unemployment was so high. The growth of salaried employment also merits note. Salary income as a proportion of wages and salaries combined was estimated at 26% in 1920 compared with 25% in 1913, but 33% in 1938 (6). This growth of salaried occupations strengthened the demand for housing, and particularly house purchase, for salary earners in general were less at risk to unemployment and suffered fewer cuts in pay in the later 1920s and early 1930s than did wage earners, though salary cuts were by no means unknown (7). The average increase in pay is shown in Table III.1, along with gross domestic product in total and per person employed.

Table III.1 - The Growth of Output and Earnings in the United Kingdom in the Inter-War Years

(Index numbers: 1924 = 100)

	Gross Domestic Prod.		Weekly Earnings	Consumers' Expenditure Deflator	Real Earnings
	Total	Per Person Employed			
1913	104.2	94.3	51	53	96
1920 (a)	101.6	86.5)	)	)	
(b)	97.6	88.4)	142)	136)	104
1921	85.7	87.6			
1924	100.0	100.0	100	100	100
1929	112.2	105.4	100	96	104
1932	106.6	104.9	94	87	108
1937	134.1	115.4	102	89	115
1938	132.3	113.6	106	91	116

Rates of Increase (per year)

1924-29	+2.2	+1.0	...	..	+0.8
1929-37	+2.3	+1.1	...	..	+1.3
1924-37	+2.3	+1.1	...	..	+1.1

Note: 1920(a) includes, and 1920(b) excludes, Southern Ireland.

Source: Feinstein. National Income, Expenditure and Output 1972, Tables 8, 51, 57, 59, 61 and 65.

The severity of economic fluctuations in the
inter-war years makes assessment of the underlying
trend particularly difficult. If, however, one
follows Matthews (8) and takes 1924, 1929 and 1937
as the nearest that can be got to comparing like
with like, the trend rate of growth of GDP in real
terms is estimated at 2-2½% a year in total, and
just over 1% a year per head of the employed population. These were rather faster rates of growth
than were achieved between the mid-1870s and 1914.
Output per man/year appears to have been only about
3% to 4% higher in 1924 than in 1913 once allowance
is made for the exclusion of Southern Ireland, but
the increase in output per man/hour was much
greater. There were large reductions in hours of
work in 1919 and 1920. The normal working week had
been about 54 hours before 1914, but in the 1920s
and 1930s, 46-48 hours were usual (9). The exact
effect on total hours worked is uncertain, but the
reduction can hardly have been much less than 10%.
If so, the increase in output per man/ hour was
about 15%, a respectable enough increase by all
past standards, all the more so for a decade that
included both the Great War and the post-war slump.
Real earnings changed in the same way as output per
head between 1913 and 1924. For the rest of the
1920s, earnings ran level in money terms while
prices fell slowly. In the Depression, earnings
fell on average by 5% to 6%, but prices fell twice
as much. In the recovery the gain in real earnings
was not only retained but slightly enlarged.

The distribution of incomes is relevant to
ability to pay for housing, as well as changes in
the average. Changes in income distributions are
difficult to summarize, and there are exceptions to
virtually any generalization. It would be generally agreed, though, that during and just after the
war, differentials between earnings in skilled and
unskilled manual work narrowed appreciably; and
that otherwise there was not much re-distribution
except at the expense of the very highest paid
(10). During the inter-war years differentials
tended, if anything, to widen again, but not by
enough to reverse all the narrowing that had previously occurred. Such changes went some way
towards reducing the gap, which had been extremely
wide in Edwardian and Victorian times, between what
decent housing cost to provide and what people in
low paid employments could afford. Greater regula-

rity of employment also contributed; with the
decline of casual work (except in the docks),
hawking and street trading, semi-employment and
under-emloyment diminished, with a much clearer
cut distinction between being in full-time work or
out of work altogether. Outright unemployment as a
cause of poverty was susceptible to remedy in a way
that under-employment was not.

The other aspect of the economy in the inter-
war years that requires comment in a history of
housing policy is interest rates. The connection
between the housing boom of the 1930s and the
"cheap money" policy has attracted much interest
from economists; but by any standard other than
that of the 1920s, money in the 1930s was not
particularly cheap, as may be seen from the rate of
interest on Consols, the longest consistently
defined series for long-term interest rates.

Table III.2 - Yield on Consols:
Inter-War Years and Pre-1914

1875-84	(Av)	3.1	1931	4.4
1885-94	(Av)	2.9	1932	3.7
1895-1904	(Av)	2.7	1933	3.4
1905-14	(Av)	3.1	1934	3.1
1915-19	(Av)	4.3	1935	2.9
1920-23	(Av)	4.8	1936	2.9
1924-29	(Av)	4.5	1937	3.3
1930		4.5	1938	3.4

Source: B.R. Mitchell and Phyllis Deane,
           Abstract of British Historical Statistics, p.455.

In comparison with the half century before
1914, long-term interest rates in the 1930s were
not particularly low. But in the 1920s they were
exceptionally high, to a degree that was without
precedent in a period when the price level was
moving downwards. Interest rates rose during World
War I when very large amounts were borrowed without
the direct controls that enabled World War II to be
financed as a "3% War". Interest rates were kept
high after the war, first to restrain the post-war
boom and then, when the slump had gathered force,
to keep up the exchange rate in order first to
facilitate a return to the gold standard at the
pre-war parity and then to support that parity
(11). The departure from the gold standard in 1931
removed the need for a dear money policy to protect

the exchange rate; but interest rates came back only to where they had been before 1914.

Population and Households in the Inter-War Years

The very rapid increase in the population of working age that was referred to in the previous section means that the population of household-forming age rose just as fast. The increase in the adult population in 1921-31 (see Table III.3 below) was the largest ever. The fall in births reduced the rate of growth of the population in total, but not until well into the 1930s did it begin to affect the growth of the adult population. By then an increase in marriage rates was under way which more than offset any slackening in the growth of the adult population (married and unmarried together). At this time household formation took place predominantly through marriage, so the rise in marriage rates was very important for the demand for housing. Table III.3 shows the total population, the adult population and the married population. The last is represented by the female married population, as the 1939 estimate of it is more reliable than for the male married population (12).

Table III.3 - The Main Population Totals for England and Wales and Their Rates of Change

(thousands)

	Total Population	Population Aged 20 and over	Female Married Population
1911	36,071	21,683	6,630
1921	37,887	23,883	7,590
1931	39,953	26,997	8,604
1939	41,460	29,129	9,666
Increase ('000 a year)			
1881-91	303	192	48
1891-1901	353	286	80
1901-1911	354	295	91
1911-21	182	220	96
1921-31	207	311	101
1931-39	188	267	133

Source: 1939 figures from Registrar-General's Statistical Review of England and Wales, Text Volume for 1938 and 1939 (published 1947), Tables XCIV, XCVa and XCVb.

The increase in marriages in the inter-war years was sufficiently important for household formation to be shown in more detail so as to bring out the sharpness of the contrast with the twenty years before 1914.

Table III.4 - Marriages in England and Wales 1891-1938

		Number ('000)	Per thousand unmarried males aged 15 or over	Per thousand unmarried females aged 15 or over
1891-1900	(Av)	239	53.6	44.9
1901-1905	(Av)	260	52.3	43.7
1906-1910	(Av)	268	50.9	42.6
1921-25	(Av)	301	55.3	42.3
1926-30	(Av)	304	53.9	41.0
1931-33		312	53.4	41.6
1934-38		354	60.2	47.0

Source: Registrar-General's Statistical Review of England and Wales 1973, (Population), Tables C.1 and D.1.

That marriage rates were higher for men in the 1920s than in the pre-war decade but not for women is explained by the large number of men of marriageable age killed in the War. But in the 1930s male and female marriage rates increased by approximately equal amounts. This was the beginning of a rise in marriage rates through earlier marriage and more marriage that was to continue until the early 1970s, with powerful effects on the demand and need for housing.

That the increase in marriages was instrumental in the rapid rise in the number of households in the inter-war years is not in doubt, but the total increase in households can be estimated only approximately. As there was no census in 1941 owing to the war, there must be considerable uncertainty about an estimate of the number of households in 1939. In 1921 housing shortage kept down the number of couples that could live as separate households, which makes the census total of households in 1921 difficult to interpret. In the 1931 Census Housing Report (13) the number of households as enumerated in successive censuses for 1861 to 1931 was compared with the household-forming population, which showed that in 1921 there

were some 300,000 to 400,000 fewer households than
would have been expected from the relationship that
would be seen to have held in 1861-1911 and re-
appeared in 1931. The explanation, according to
the 1931 Census Housing Report ".... is not very
far to seek .... However great the pressure may be
upon members of existing families to establish
themselves as separate families in independent
homes, it cannot materialize in the formation of
new family units without separate houseroom in
which a separate family existence may be secured.
In 1921 this indispensable element of new family
increase was deficient". It is highly probable
that most of this shortfall of separate households
in 1921 relative to what would have been expected
consisted of young recently married couples. Certainly the 1951 figures, also affected by a war-
induced shortage of housing, suggest that this is
likely to have been so. For purposes of analysis,
therefore, it is useful to introduce the concept of
"potential households", comprising households as
enumerated plus married couples living in someone
else's household. The 1931 Census provided information about household composition only in selected
wards in Camberwell and Sheffield (for studying
overcrowding), but in conjunction with the 1951
data can be used to make an approximate estimate.
The 1951 data are also the basis of the estimate of
the number of households in 1939. The method cannot be described in full here for reasons of space;
but it depends on the household headship rates (14)
calculated for 1951 being applied to the 1931 and
1939 populations analysed by age, sex and marital
status, with allowance for married couple headship
rates in 1951 being depressed by housing shortages.
The estimate of 11,750,000 households in 1939 made
by this method is higher than previous estimates.
Bowley, for instance (15) worked back from the
Registrar-General's projection (published in 1935)
of 11,150,000 households in 1941 (16). This was
the first ever estimate of the future number of
households in this country, but since it did not
foresee the rise in marriage rates in the 1930s
(Table III.4 above) it was far too low.
Table III.5 shows the estimates of households
and potential households. Average household size
is calculated from the population in private households; this under-states "true" household size,
because men and women enumerated in places other
than private residences (e.g. patients in hospital,

63

visitors staying in hotels) even though usually
resident in private households were not counted in
the private household population. Not until 1961
could this distinction be drawn according to place
of usual residence.

Table III.5 - Households and Population in England and
Wales 1911-39

('000)	1911	1921	1931	1939
Whole population	36,070	37,887	39,952	41,460
Population in private households	34,606	36,180	38,042	39,480 (a)
Households	7,943	8,739	10,233	11,750
Married couples without own household	200	550	350	250
Potential households	8,143	9,289	10,583	12,000
Persons per household	4.36	4.14	3.74	3.36
Persons per potential household	4.25	3.89	3.59	3.29

Note: (a) Assumed to be in same proportion to whole
             population as in 1931.

Source: See text for method of caluclation.

In the period covered by Table III.5, the
increase in the number of 'potential' households is
a better measure of the effect of population change
on the demand for housing than is the increase in
the number of actual households, as being less
influenced by housing shortages. Whereas between
1891 and 1911 the number of households increased by
an average of about 95,000 a year, between 1911 and
1921 the increase in the number of potential households averaged about 115,000 a year, between 1921
and 1931 130,000 a year, but in 1931-39 175,000 a
year. In the inter-war years the increase in
households did not result simply from the growth of
the total population as the increase in the number
of households in the nineteenth century had done,
but was much more complex. It stemmed from the
combined effect of the changing age structure of
the population, an increase in marriage rates, and
the beginning (as far as can be judged) of a rise
in headship rates among widows. In this the inter-
war years resemble the 1950s and 1960s, not the
decades before 1911.

The contrast with pre-1914 is to be seen also in household size. There was no material change in average household size in the half century before 1911, but between 1911 and 1939 average household size fell by between one-fifth and one-quarter. This decline was to go much further in the post-war years; but whereas then a major cause was (as we shall see) a large increase in the number of one-person households as more and more widows and widowers continued on their own as independent households, in the inter-war years the fall in birth rates was the main cause. Of women married in 1870-79, 51.6% had six or more live born children, but of women married in 1900-09, only 19.1% did so, and of women married in 1920-24, 9.3% (17). The consequence was a large fall in the number of large households, as Table III.6 shows.

Table III.6 - Households Analysed by Size in England and Wales 1911 and 1931

(thousands)

Number of Persons in Family	1911	1931	Change
1	423	689	+266
2 or 3	2,816	4,700	+1,884
4 or 5	2,584	3,251	+667
6 or 7	1,375	1,169	-206
8 or more	745	424	-321
Total	7,943	10,233	+2,290

Source: Census of England and Wales 1931, Housing Report and Tables, p.xiv.

Corresponding figures are not available for the later 1930s. But the 1951 Census (see next chapter) shows that the reduction in the number of large households continued after 1931. Smaller families and the decline in employment of residential domestic servants led to a reduction in the demand for large houses, and in crowding. But the exceptionally rapid growth (by all past standards) in the number of households meant a faster growth in the demand and need for houses in total.

New Houses: Number, Location, and Standards

We now consider how that demand and need was met. In the inter-war years, unlike before 1914, the Government collected and published regular statistics of houses completed. The figures were published for years ending 31 March (and subsequently half-years ending 31 March and 30 September). Houses built by private enterprise with state assistance are distinguished from those built without assistance. As well as building for owner-occupation and for letting by private land-lord, "private enterprise" included what in the inter-war years were termed "public utility housing societies" and would now be known as housing associations. The chronology is sufficiently important for the totals completed to be shown year by year for the whole period.

Table III.7 - Annual Totals of Houses Completed:
England and Wales

(thousands)

Year (a)	Local Authorities	Private Enterprise with State Assistance	Private Enterprise without Assistance	Total
1919/20	0.6			
1920/21	15.6	12.9)	)	
1921/22	80.8	20.3)	53.8 (b))	251.8
1922/23	57.5	10.3)	)	
1923/24	14.4	4.3	67.5	86.2
1924/25	20.3	47.0	69.2	136.9
1925/26	44.2	62.8	66.4	173.4
1926/27	74.1	79.7	63.9	217.6
1927/28	104.0	74.5	60.3	238.9
1928/29	55.7	49.1	64.7	169.5
1929/30	60.2	50.1	91.7	202.1
1930/31	55.9	2.6	125.4	183.8
1931/32	70.0	2.3	128.4	200.8
1932/33	56.0	2.5	142.0	200.5
1933/34	55.8	2.9	207.9	266.6
1934/35	41.6	1.1	286.4	329.1
1935/36	52.4	0.2	272.3	324.9
1936/37	71.7	0.8	273.5	346.1
1937/38	78.0	2.6	257.1	337.6
1938/39	101.7	4.2	226.4	332.4

Table III.7 (continued)

Notes: (a) Figures refer to twelve months ending at
31 March.
(b) Ministry of Health estimate of 300,000 up to
September 1922; and recorded number of 23,800
in the six months to March 1923.

Source: Statistical Abstract of the United Kingdom
No. 76 (Cmd.4233) Table 30; No. 83 (Cmd.6232),
Table 33.

In the first five years after the end of the
war only 340,000 houses were completed, which was
well below the rate needed to keep up with household formation, (Table III.5 above), let alone make
any impact on the shortage that had accumulated
during the war. There was here a sharp contrast
with what was to happen in the five years after
1945, when very different policies were pursued.
But from 1925/26 onwards the number of houses
completed year by year compared very favourably
with the rate of completions in the boom at the
turn of the century. The difference was equal
approximately to the average number of dwellings
completed for local authorities in 1925/26 to
1932/33. This is not absolute proof that the local
authorities' house building was a net addition to
what private enterprise would have built on its
own, but nevertheless tells heavily against a
simple 'crowding out' hypothesis. When the number
of dwellings completed passed 200,000 in 1926/27
this was for the first time ever. It may be true
that a building boom of turn of the century proportions was due in the later 1920s, following the
slump that had set in well before 1914. Nevertheless, house building in the later 1920s deserves
more attention than it has so far received, being
overshadowed by the boom of the 1930s.

The boom of the middle and late 1930s, however, left the already high rate of building in the
previous eight years far behind. The number of
houses built year by year in 1934-38 was not
exceeded until the mid-1960s, and the number built
for private owners was never reached again. The
highest subsequent total of houses completed for
private owners in any one year was 213,000 (England
and Wales) in 1968, 73,000 less than the 1934 peak
and 50,000 less than the 1934-38 average. The boom
of the 1930s is therefore a very notable feature in

British housing history. It has attracted a great deal of interest from economists, primarily as what at first sight was seen as the principal means by which the "cheap money" policy pursued in the 1930s contributed to the recovery of the British economy from the Depression (18). The way in which financial and monetary circumstances in the 1930s enabled the building societies to attract the money to finance the boom will be discussed in some detail in Chapter VI, but in the light of subsequent history there are other questions to be asked, notably how houses could be supplied in such quantities at prices low enough to be afforded without either direct or indirect subsidy. The subsidy provided by the Housing Act 1923 was abolished in 1929; tax relief was given on mortgage interest, for reasons discussed later in the chapter, but the starting point of tax relief on interest and liability to tax on the assessed rental value of owner occupied houses was high enough for the tax reliefs to be of little or no importance to all but a small proportion of households.

A key question is therefore what happened to house prices? Information is available about building costs, and contract prices for council houses; but for house prices as such, the material from which to construct suitable measures lies in the records of building societies, and it is greatly to be hoped that societies will preserve their records and allow historians access to them. Until this work has been done, the best available evidence is the average new advance made by building societies, converted to average prices by the advance-to-price ratios provided by the Halifax Building Society (the largest society) (19). It is available only for 1930 onwards, and is shown in Table III.8 along with average contract prices for council houses and building costs.

Table III.8 suggests that in the early 1930s house prices came down with building costs and the general level of prices, and in the later years of the decade did no more than rise in line with prices generally. The measure of house prices is much less secure than would be desirable, but there is no sign of any marked rise in house prices during the boom, nor any mention of it in contemporary comment. The absence of such a rise in house prices during so strong a boom is very noteworthy. During the inter-war years the nineteenth

Table III.8 – House Prices and Building Costs 1930-38

	Average New Advance (a)	Percentage Deposit	Implied Average Price Amount	Index	Average Contract Price for Council Houses (b) Index	Building Costs (c)	General Price Level (d)
1930	470	20.6	590	111	117	111	110
1931	474	21.2	600	113	114	107	105
1932	444	18.2	540	102	105	102	102
1933	446	15.8	530	100	100	100	100
1934	447	12.8	515	97	100	100	100
1935	452	15.1	535	101	103	102	101
1936	458	16.9	550	104	108	106	101
1937	464	14.4	545	103	122	112	105
1938	464	14.6	545	103	126	114	106

Note:

(a) Excludes advances over £1,000, few of which are likely to have been for owner-occupied houses. Source: Chief Registrar of Friendly Societies.

(b) Prices of 3 bedroom houses without parlours. Source: J.R. Jarmain Housing Subsidies and Rents, Stevens, London, 1948: Appendix 1.

(c) Feinstein, National Income Expenditure and Output, Table 63. Source: Maywald.

(d) Consumers'expenditure. Source: Feinstein, Table 61.

century tendency, discussed in the previous chapter, for the price of housing to rise distinctly faster than prices generally, was in abeyance. A fall in building costs, due mainly to a fall in costs of building materials (20) contributed, but there is little doubt that the main reason was the very large increase in available building land. The earlier rise in the price of housing relative to the general price levels was attributed in Chapter II to constraints on accessibility; but in the inter-war years these constraints were set aside for the time being by a combination of developments in transport and the absence of any strict control over land use. These developments in transport began before 1914 but did not have their full effect until later, especially the electrified railway, the motor bus, and the electric tram. The inter-war years were the heyday of public transport; for although private cars were becoming more numerous, car ownership was not widespread enough to have much influence on the relationship of place of residence and place of work. The motor bus had a very powerful influence; so too, especially around London, did the electrified railway, the London Passenger Transport Board's (and its predecessor bodies') system to the north of the Thames, and Southern Electric to the south. The result was an extremely rapid spread of suburban housing. For a full discussion of suburban growth around London, reference may be made to the work of A.A. Jackson (21). Similar developments occurred around the other English cities, though of course on a much smaller scale. Between 1931 and 1939 the population of outer London increased at a wholly unprecedented rate averaging 116,000 a year (22). Suburban house building was by no means only for people who still worked in town centres and formerly lived there. There was a substantial growth of employment in the suburbs themselves, also facilitated by the revolution in transport in that the growth of road transport enabled factories to be located in suburban sites some way from railways.

Planning policies and land use control exerted very little restraint over the inter-war growth of the suburbs. The rate at which land was built on was far higher than anything before or since. The rate of transfer of land from farming to urban uses is estimated at 62,000 acres a year (net) in 1931-39, compared with 22,000 acres a year in 1922-26 and 52,000 acres a year in 1926-31 (and 39,000 a year in 1945-75 (23)). Suburban growth on this scale had come by the end of the 1930s to be condemned as "sprawl", and policy was moving in favour of policies of containment. The first steps in setting up the London Green belt were taken in 1938; and in 1939 the report of the Royal Commission on the Distribution of the Industrial Population (24) came down very strongly in favour of restraint on the suburban growth, especially of London. These were the policies that were to carry the day after the war, with consequences that will be discussed later in this book. Here we note their inter-war origins, and how they were the outcome of conditions indispensable to the housing boom.

Suburban growth not only permitted an increase in the quantity of housing, but a large step up in quality as well. The esteem in which suburban semi-detached houses are held has been subject to ups and downs, but if they are compared with the terraces built before 1914 the improvement is clear. A rise in standards of housing was partly the result of policy. The tone was set by the Tudor Walters Report (25), the report of a Committee that was one of several parts of the preparations for post-war reconstruction, and imbued (as were such committees in World War II to an even greater degree) by the view that after such a war conditions must be better than they had been before it. Tudor Walters recommended three bedrooms as the standard for families (unless they were very large); provision for heating in all rooms; an inside lavatory; and a bathroom. On the very important subject of density, a maximum of twelve houses to the acre was recommended, which meant building semi-detached or in short terraces. These were much higher standards than found in pre-1914 building for the "working class" market by private enterprise (26). Most of these recommendations were incorporated in the 1919 Housing Manual (27), the first of a long sequence giving guidance to local authorities about design and standards of subsidized housing. Its space recommendations were rather higher than those made by Tudor Walters; but on the other hand although a fixed bath was required, it could be either in a separate bathroom or the scullery. At the time the usual practice was to cook meals in the living room, with washing, washing up, and bathing (in a portable galvanized iron bath) done in the scullery. But the trend was towards doing more of the cooking in the scullery, upgrading it in effect to a kitchen. Subsequent Housing Manuals and other guidance to authorities reduced the space standards, and with them the standards of layout, in order to reduce costs (28); but even so, the houses built for local authorities were much higher in standard than those built for "the working classes" before 1914. In particular, three bedrooms remained the standard, and so did a fixed bath. Large numbers of the pre-1914 houses had two bedrooms only, and no bath.

At the other end of the scale far fewer really large houses were built for private owners in the inter-war years than before 1914. The increasing difficulty of recruiting and retaining domestic servants and higher wages to be paid to them made large houses more expensive in real terms to run than before 1914 and with the trend towards smaller families, fewer rooms were needed. By far the commonest type of house built for private owners was the ubiquitous three bedroomed semi-detached house; detached houses and terrace houses were less common, but not rare. A separate bathroom and inside lavatory were always provided; they were not compulsory by law, but houses would have been extremely hard to sell without them. Houses built in the inter-war years were designed to be easier to run than those built a generation earlier, particularly through being wired for electric appliances, fitted with hot water systems and with conveniently planned kitchens (29). One sees here the combined effects of technical progress, particularly in development of household electrical appliances, and systems for combining water heating with room heating; and substitution of capital for labour. Some of the capital was in the house itself; some of it was in portable appliances (vacuum cleaners, for example).

The Balance Between Dwellings and Households, Housing Shortages, and Housing Conditions

Household formation and the demand side of the housing system, and the response from the supply side may now be brought together to show how the balance changed between the number of households and the number of separate dwellings, and what this balance implied about the number of households without a dwelling to themselves. In this context

we look at crowding which, as will be shown, was
closely connected with sharing; and very briefly at
the number of dwellings that were slums or lacked
what subsequently came to be known as the "basic
amenities". Table III.9 shows the number of
'structurally separate dwellings', the concept
introduced in the 1921 Census and ever since the
basis of official statistics of the housing stock.
The concept in use in 1911 and earlier was somewhat
different, especially in counting blocks of flats
as one "house" and including as "houses" some
premises that would not have been counted as
private residences in 1921 and subsequently. The
1911 Census collected sufficient information about
buildings, however, for re-classification according
to the 1921 definition to be possible. The 1921
and 1931 figures are census enumerated totals of
dwellings, as published. The 1939 figure is an
estimate, in which the main sources of uncertainty
are the number of houses demolished or going out of
use for reasons other than slum clearance; and the
conversion gain.

Table III.9 shows clearly not only how severe
was the worsening of the balance between households
and dwellings between 1911 and 1921, but also how
limited was the improvement between 1921 and 1931.
Not until 1924/25 did the number of houses built
(Table III.8) come anywhere close to the increase
in the number of households and not until 1925/26
were enough houses built to allow any reduction in
the accumulated shortage. The shortfall of dwellings relative to potential households probably
reached a peak at about 1,500,000 in 1925. Between
then and 1939 the shortfall diminished to about
500,000. But throughout the inter-war years the
housing situation was characterized by shortages,
even though they were of diminishing severity in
the 1930s. For reasons discussed at the beginning
of this chapter, the shortage was expressed to a
far greater extent than before the war as an excess
of demand at prevailing prices relative to supply.
This was a key feature of the inter-war housing
situation, with a pervasive effect on policy.

One aspect of the shortages that can be
studied from the available statistics is crowding.
A distinction can be drawn between ordinary sized
families living in part of a house and large
families in ordinary sized houses as causes of
crowding. The amount of crowding increased between
1911 and 1921, as would be expected from the

Table III.9 - Dwellings, Households, and Sharing: England and Wales 1911-1939

(thousands)	1911	1921	1931	1939
All dwellings	7,691	7,979	9,400	11,500
Vacant Dwellings: Furnished }	430	219	115	Not known
Unfurnished }			161	Not known
Total households	7,943	8,739	10,233	11,750
Potential households including married couples living with others (a)	8,140	9,290	10,580	12,000
Excess of actual households over all dwellings	252	760	833	250
Excess of potential households over all dwellings	450	1,310	1,180	500
Sharing				
Separate households sharing	1,150 (b)	1,732	1,959	930/1,010 (c)
Sharing households, including married couples without own households and those with whom they live.	1,550	2,830	2,660	1,430/1,510
Sharing households including married couples, etc. as % of all potential households.	19	30	25	12/13

Notes: (a) See Table III.5 and accompanying text.
       (b) Estimate.
       (c) Lower figure assumes the same number of vacant dwellings as in 1931, higher figure assumes 100,000 more vacant dwellings than in 1931. The average number of sharing households per shared dwelling as enumerated was 2.30 in 1921, 2.32 in 1931 and 2.30 in 1951. In view of this constancy over thirty years, the same number may be taken to have applied in 1911 and 1939.

increase in the number of sharing households, but between 1921 and 1931 the number of crowded households fell to less than what it had been in 1911, notwithstanding the much greater excess of dwellings over households in 1931. If the criterion for 'crowded' is taken to be more than 1½ persons per room (increasingly used as an indicator of crowding in the inter-war years though never official policy (30)), the number of crowded households was 1,293,000 in 1911, 1,423,000 in 1921 and 1,174,000 in 1931.

The fall in crowding was however primarily the result of the reduction in the number of large households (shown in Table III.6). The proportion of households comprising 8 persons or more that lived at densities exceeding 1½ persons per room rose from 65% in 1911 to 72% in 1931; for households comprising 6 persons or 7, the proportions were 26% and 28% (31). It was the fall in births that had reduced the number of crowded households, not an improvement in the supply of housing. The extent to which crowding was due to sharing can be estimated for 1931, because for the first time information was collected about the size of sharing households and the number of rooms they occupied. The national figures were estimates, derived from a special study of the census enumerations for Manchester; not until 1951 was a full tabulation made.

Table III.10 - Crowded Households in England and Wales, 1931

(thousands)	Sharing Households		Households not Sharing	
	Over 1½ but not over 2 persons/room	Over 2 persons /room	Over 1½ but not over 2 persons/room	Over 2 persons /room
Size of Household				
1 or 2	76	-	9	-
3 or 4	92	59	49	9
5 or 6	69	72	196	50
7 or 8	21	41	203	72
9 or 10	2	7	52	61
More than 10	-	-	8	26
Total	260	179	517	219

Source: Calculated from Tables XVII and 6 of Census of England and Wales 1931, Housing Report and Tables.

There was no survey in the later 1930s that
produced information about density of occupation
with which the 1931 Census figures could be
compared. Some different but nevertheless valuable
information was produced by the surveys carried out
by local authorities in 1936, as required by the
Ministry of Health under powers conferred by
Section 1(1) of the Housing Act 1935 (32) to determine how many houses in their areas were overcrowded by the statutory definition in the Act
(33).

The findings of the 1931 Census about overcrowding were a major reason why the 1935 Housing
Act included specific provisions on the subject.
Sharing was the principal cause of the most extreme
overcrowding; the Registrar-General's estimates,
derived from the special study made of the
Manchester Census data just referred to, indicated
that some 50-55,000 of the households living at
densities greater than 3 persons per room were
sharing households living in one room or two. The
others comprised 28,000 households with 10 or more
members living in three-roomed dwellings. By 1935
the census was out of date, and in any case the
Housing Act provided a standard for overcrowding
that was much more complicated than just a specified number of persons per room. The statutory
standard was a severe one, even for its time:
overcrowding existed if the persons present
exceeded the "permitted number", which was 2 if the
house had one room, 3 if it had two, 5 if it had
three, 7½ if it had four; if it had five rooms or
more, the number was 10 plus 2½ for each room above
five; rooms of less than 110 sq.ft. in area were
counted according to a special scale. In working
out the "permitted number", children under 10 years
of age counted as half a "unit", and babies under
one year of age did not count at all. A family
consisting of a married couple, children aged 9 and
6, and a baby aged 11 months living in two rooms
would not, therefore, be overcrowded so long as one
of the rooms were 110 sq.ft. or more in area and
the other more than 70 sq.ft. The survey found
341,554 dwellings to be overcrowded; given the
definition of 'dwelling', which counted sub-
lettings as separate 'dwellings' for this purpose,
the same number of households was overcrowded. Not
all authorities submitted returns in time for
publication; scaling pro-rata to population gives
an estimated total of 345,000. Households of 4

"units" or more comprised 30.4% of the overcrowded
households; households of six "units" or more comprised 161,000, 47% of the total. Owing to the
differences of definition these figures are not
readily comparable with the 1931 Census figures in
Table III.10, but since over 200,000 of the households living at densities of over 2 persons per
room in 1931 comprised seven persons or more, there
is little doubt that between 1931 and 1936 there
was a further reduction in the number of overcrowded large households.

The other aspect of unsatisfactory housing in
the inter-war years was unfitness in physical
terms. Its origins were discussed in the previous
chapter, and unless there was extensive deteriora-
tion of houses in the war years and the 1920s
(impossible to check in the days long before a
house condition survey had been thought of), the
houses built to low standards in the 1870s and
before constituted the bulk of the slum problem in
the inter-war years. Clearance of unfit houses had
a history that reached back to the Torrens and
Cross Acts of the 1860s and 1870s; but here as in
much else the inter-war years saw a complete change
of scale. In the 1920s slum clearance activity was
on a small scale only, in view of the severity of
the housing shortage. The financial basis for a
larger slum clearance programme was provided by the
special subsidies provided by the Housing Act 1930
for housing built to re-house people displaced by
slum clearance (34); the stimulus in policy terms
was applied by the combination of the ending by the
Housing (Financial Provisions) Act 1933 of the
subsidy for building for general needs and the
retaining it for slum clearance, and the government's call to local authorities (Ministry of
Health Circular 1331, April 1933) to submit programmes for the clearance within five years of
unfit housing within their areas. The original
programmes submitted (35) provided for a total of
267,000 houses to be demolished or closed. They
were subsequently added to, and by March 1939
totalled 472,000 (36). As became very clear in the
1950s and 1960s, local authorities' returns of
unfit houses are frequently strongly influenced by
their views about how many such houses they can in
fact deal with, and so cannot be treated as if they
were 'objective' measures of the number of unfit
houses. The figure of 472,000 therefore cannot be
regarded as anything other than the lowest possible

figure for the number of unfit houses as of 1933.
There is information about the condition of
houses in individual areas in the 1930s (37), but
not on a national scale. National survey information is, however, available for 1947; since so few
new houses were built between 1939 and 1947, and
even small scale building work was strictly controlled, the 1947 information probably gives a
reasonably reliable picture of conditions at the
end of the 1930s. The information refers to
possession of a fixed bath, hot and cold water
supply, and a wash hand basin. Whether or not
there was an inside WC was not included in the
inquiry (38). A piped water supply was also
included in the enquiry.

Table III.11 - Facilities and Amenities of Dwellings in 1947

Proportion of households with:	All	Pre-1918 Dwellings	Post-1918 Dwellings
Piped water supply	97	90	99
Fixed bath in bathroom	55	36	93
Hot water supply to sink, bath and hand basin	36	..	..
Hot water supply to sink	51	..	..

Note: Figures for hot water supply refer to Great
Britain; the others to England and Wales.

Source: The British Household, Tables 36, 37, 39, 40,
42 and 43.

Of the pre-1914 dwellings still standing in
1947 and hence at the end of the 1930s, 10 percent
did not have a piped water supply (mainly in rural
areas, but shared standpipes were not unknown in
the poorer parts of towns). Many of the 270,000
houses demolished as unfit in the 1930s are likely
to have had no piped water supply; and most are
highly likely to have had neither a hot water
supply nor a bathroom. How many of the pre-1918
dwellings had hot water supplies or bathrooms
installed during the inter-war years is not known,
but the contrast between pre-1918 and post 1918
dwellings is clearly shown.

Resources and Policy

That far more resources went into house building in the inter-war years is not in dispute, nor is the fact that from the later 1920s onwards housing conditions improved in a way that they had not done before. The key questions from the standpoint of a history of housing policy are how far this was the consequence of policy, and how far the result of other changes, above all the great increase in the supply of housing land made possible by developments in transport. Finality cannot be achieved, but some comments may usefully be made. It is useful first to show gross fixed investment in dwellings, which ran at higher levels from the mid-1920s onwards than it had done even in the strongest of the pre-1914 housing booms.

Table III.12 - Gross Fixed Investment in Dwellings

	Investment in Dwellings (£m, 1938 prices)	% of Gross Domestic Product	% of Total Gross Fixed Investment
1898-1903	71	2.3	20
1921-23	68	2.0	21
1924-28	120	3.2	30
1929-32	130	3.1	31
1933-35	183	4.0	39
1936-38	174	3.6	30

Source: Feinstein, National Income, Expenditure and Output, Tables 1, 39 and 40.

The picture shown by gross fixed investment in dwellings is (as would be expected) very similar to that of the number of houses completed (see Table III.8), though not exactly, in part due to the difference in timing between work done and completions, but also to differences of source. The proportion of gross domestic product devoted to housing rose in the 1930s to levels that were wholly without precedent, and not reached again until the mid-1960s.

Public expenditure on housing in selected years is shown in Table III.13.

Expenditure on subsidies for local authority housing rose year by year. With the exception of the subsidies payable under the 1919 Act (discussed

Table III.13 – Public Expenditure on Housing 1920-38

	Exchequer Subsidy (£m)	Rate Fund Subsidy (£m)	Capital Expenditure (£m)	Total (£m)	Total as % of all Public Expenditure	Local Authority Expenditure as % of all LA Expenditure
1921	4.1	1.4	86.7	92.2	6.4	22.0
1923	8.2	1.3	28.4	37.9	3.7	9.2
1926	9.5	2.8	64.1	76.4	6.9	16.6
1928	12.2	2.8	56.4	71.4	6.5	14.8
1931	14.2	3.5	50.2	57.9	4.9	12.5
1934	15.6	3.8	41.1	60.5	5.7	11.2
1936	16.6	4.2	54.8	75.6	6.4	12.8
1938	17.7	5.2	74.8	97.7	6.2	15.1

Source: A.T. Peacock and J. Wiseman, The Growth of Public Expenditure in the United Kingdom, Princetown University Press, Princetown, 1961, Tables A-15, A-18 and A-23.

in Chapter VII), the subsidies were all of the form of specified annual sums, of which payment commenced when the house was completed. Changes in rates of subsidy, or abolition of subsidy, applied only to houses built after the operative date; subsidies already in payment continued undisturbed. The growth of the local authority housing stock therefore led to a corresponding growth of expenditure by the Exchequer on subsidies and of contributions from local authorities' general rate funds. For this reason expenditure on subsidies tended to grow relative to capital expenditure on housing. This tendency came in for much criticism in later years, but was the inevitable consequence of subsidies depending on the total size of the local authorities' housing stock and capital expenditure depending on additions to it. In the inter-war years housing was a substantial element of public expenditure, both nationally and locally.

As will be shown in Chapter VII, the subsidies and rate fund contributions covered about one-third of the current costs of local authority housing. Rents were aligned in broad terms with controlled rents charged under the Rent Restrictions Acts plus a premium for the much higher quality of the accommodation. The 1936 survey of rents showed the average to be 7s 4d a week, compared with about 6s a week for controlled tenancies. These rents were equivalent to 11½% and 9½% respectively of average weekly earnings of adult men in manual work, whereas in 1912 rents (excluding rates) had been equivalent to 13-14% of average earnings. Rent control and inflation had forced rents down in real terms, and subsidies had been set on that basis. De-controlled rents (discussed in detail in Chapter VIII) were on average similar to council house rents, but for a generally much poorer standard of accommodation. Subsidies therefore brought housing of post-war standards within the reach of households that unaided could only afford pre-1914 "working class" housing.

As before 1914, rates added substantially to housing costs. For 1937/38 the Ministry of Labour's survey of household budgets provided fairly detailed information (39). For tenants included in the survey (manual workers and lower paid salaried workers) rates averaged £7 to £8 a year. At this level rates were the equivalent in round terms of an ad valorem tax of about 40% on rented housing, rather more than in the years

81

immediately before World War I, when rates appear
to have been equivalent to a tax of about 30-35%
ad valorem. Rates averaged about 3½% of household
expenditure (and by implication of household
income); and were equivalent to about 4% of average
earnings of adult men in manual work, rather higher
than before 1914. The causes of these rate burdens
lay in local authorities' expenditure, which grew
fast. Their current expenditure averaged 6.4% GDP
in 1924-28 and 7.1% in 1934-38, compared with only
4.5% in 1913 (40). Locally financed expenditure,
i.e. net of central government grants, rose from
3.2% of GDP in 1913 to 4.2% in 1924-28; it fell
back to 3.9% in 1934-38, but only as a result of
the grant to offset the full de-rating of agriculture and 75% de-rating of industry in 1929. De-
rating was for the purpose of assisting industry
and agriculture, and the grant to replace the rate
revenue lost as a consequence could obviously do
nothing for domestic rate payers. In the circumstances of the time (notably a severe housing
shortage and rent control that permitted the
landlord to recoup rate increases from the tenant
where rates were paid by the landlord) there was
little prospect of any of the burden of rates being
shifted from tenants to landlords via lower rents.
As before 1914, so in the inter-war years, the
system of local government finance raised housing
costs substantially.

Rates were of course paid by owner-occupiers
as well as tenants. The average rate poundage was
11s 6d, in 1937/38 more than double the rate at
which income tax was levied on the assessed rental
value of owner-occupied houses (Schedule A). The
standard rate of income tax was paid only by
minority even of owner-occupiers. When the average
weekly earnings of adult men in manual occupations
in industry were equivalent of £180 a year, the
starting point of income tax liability (if all
income was from employment) for married couples
with no children in 1937/38 was £225; for a married
couple with two children £375. Even then a reduced
rate of 1s 8d in the £ (8.3%) was payable on the
first £135 of taxable income. Except for people
with substantial investment incomes, income tax was
not of any real consequence until £500 was reached;
and only about 800,000 people had incomes higher
than this (41). Taxing owner-occupiers on the
rental value of their houses was an outgrowth of
nineteenth century, even eighteenth century,

methods of tax collection, not the result of a considered decision of Parliament to tax 'imputed income' from house property. The definition of Schedule A income was very similar to rateable value, though in practice in the inter-war years linked more closely to actual rents (42). The revaluation that was made for Schedule A in 1935 was to prove the last. With the charge to income tax on the assessed rental value of owner-occupied housing went tax relief on mortgage interest, not as a special relief but as the result of one of the general principles of the income tax, that costs incurred in producing income could be set off against income in assessing liability. In terms of the mechanics, though, the first step was taken towards converting tax relief on mortgage interest into a special relief. Normally a borrower paid interest net of income tax on the interest, but from 1925/26 onwards a special arrangement was made by which interest due to building societies was paid to them in full, without deduction of tax. To balance, the borrower was enabled to set interest due to building societies against his own income for tax purposes. This was the procedure until the beginning of mortgage interest relief at source in 1983. The arrangement was helpful to the building societies. But its fiscal effect was not immediately great. There is no contemporary estimate of the cost of the relief; but since in 1945 the cost is officially estimated at £10 million only (43), the cost in the late 1930s could hardly have been more than £8 million to £10 million a year, which is small compared with the totals of subsidies for local authority housing which averaged £22 million a year in 1936-38.

Tax relief, and the special arrangements with building societies, do not therefore seriously qualify the conclusion that the private enterprise housing boom of the 1930s was something that government applauded but did not sustain financially. Private house building in the 1920s, in contrast, was supported by a very substantial amount of subsidy. About 400,000 houses were built with subsidy (excluding dwellings built for housing associations with the local authority subsidies), about 40,000 under the Housing (Additional Powers) Act 1919, and 360,000 under the Housing Act 1923. In the years from 1924/25 to 1927/28 (that is to say before the rate of subsidy was reduced), one-half of all houses built for private owners were

built with the subsidy (Table III.7).   The subsidy
was £6 a year for 20 years (reduced to £4 in 1927),
which could be taken as a capital sum of   £70 (£50
after 1927) if the recipient chose.   £70 was about
one-sixth to one-seventh of the cost of houses of
the type for which the subsidy was available.   The
working of this subsidy has never been studied in
any detail; we do not even know what proportion of
houses were subsidized by the lump sums and what
proportion by annual payments.   This lack of
interest is to be regretted, as the 1923 Act
subsidy is the only instance of subsidy to private
owners (owner-occupiers and landlords alike) in the
history of British housing. How high the number of
houses built for private owners ran in the middle
and later 1920s, notwithstanding dear money, was
remarked on earlier in this chapter.   The subsidy
payable under the 1923 Act could well have been an
important part of the explanation; but it is not
possible to be sure in the absence of a study of
who bought houses, and the prices they paid, with
and without subsidy.   The subsidy was reduced in
1927, and ended in 1929, on grounds of the fall in
building costs. The coming to office of the Labour
government in 1929 led to the reduction in the 1924
Act subsidy to local authorities provided for by
the previous government being countermanded, but
the ending of the 1923 Act subsidy was left to take
its course.

On a very long view, the inter-war years stand
apart from the rest of more than a century and a
half of English housing history from the early
nineteenth century to the end of the 1970s as being
the great exception from the faster rise in the
price of housing than in prices generally.   The
rise in the price of housing in real terms in the
century before 1914 was explained in the previous
chapter in terms of pressure of urban populations
against limited accessible land. But in the inter-
war years the coming to fruition of innovations in
transport was combined with the absence of more
than loose controls over land use. The combination
of railway electrification, the motor bus, the
shorter hours of work greatly increased the amount
of accessible building land.   The results were
almost universally condemned as "sprawl", and by
the end of the 1930s articulate opinion was
strongly in favour of stricter land use controls.
The reaction to suburban house building in the
1930s was the basis of the much stricter land use

controls in the 1950s and 1960s. The implicit judgement was that the costs of suburban expansion greatly outweighed the benefits. This judgement was never effectively challenged; but due attention should, in the present author's view, be given to the advantages conferred by the inter-war building boom. An extremely large housing deficit in numerical terms was much reduced, by houses built to much higher standards than before 1914, at prices which if anything fell relative to the general level of prices. In such circumstances, the proportion of housing needs that could be met only with the aid of subsidy was not very great. When housing costs again rose faster than prices, the need for subsidy would become greater.

In most other respects however, the inter-war years were the precursors of three decades after 1945 rather than a period set apart. The inter-war years saw the beginning of a major change in the demographic side of housing demand and need. The number of separate households formed from a given adult population began to rise so that the growth of the adult population ceased to be the main demographic influence on housing. Large scale slum clearance began in the inter-war years; so too did the growth of owner-occupation (see Chapter V for the figures) and public and governmental interest. The inter-war years also saw, of course, the beginning of large scale building of houses by local authorities with subsidy from central government, and of rent restriction in peace time. Both are discussed in some detail in subsequent chapters. Here the point to be made is that in the inter-war years they were to a much greater extent separate and separable policies than they subsequently became. The present author would not share the view expressed by, among others, Daunton (43) that not only was there nothing inevitable about the emergence of subsidized council house building, but that its explanation lay in private landlords being regarded as expendable for political reasons both by the Conservative party and by the Labour and Liberal parties. This contention harks back to the pre-1914 controversies discussed in the previous chapter. The view was that Conservative strategy was to seek to defend the interests of large property-holders by allying to those interests the interests of a large number of small property-holders; and that for this purpose owner-occupiers were considered much more advantageous than private

85

landlords. Labour, the argument runs, could readily take over the Liberals' poor view of landlords for which it had reasons of its own. With Conservatives favouring owner-occupation and Labour municipal housing, the private landlord was bound to be squeezed out. But in reading the post-1919 history in the light of the pre-1914 controversies (and especially Offer's influential interpretation of them) (44), it is important to have regard both to what the war did to building costs and to price expectations, and to how severely it aggravated housing shortages. With building costs rising rapidly at the end of the war but expected to fall, private enterprise would not be likely to build for letting. Anybody who invested in houses when prices were temporarily high would be unable to charge rents that would give a return on his investment when faced with competition from others whose houses were built later after prices had fallen. If house building for renting was not to be deferred until after costs and prices had fallen, the Exchequer would have to carry the loss. That was the basic reason why house building with Exchequer subsidy began in 1919; it left as an open question what would happen after prices and costs had fallen. The 1919 policy did not, as we shall see in Chapter VII, last until prices and costs had fallen and then stabilized; it was curtailed and then terminated on purely financial grounds at a time when housing shortages were greater than at the end of the war, and still worsening. The Housing Act 1923 then provided a temporary subsidy for building by private enterprise and local authorities alike. The decisive steps in making local authority housing a permanent part of the British housing scene and on a large scale were the 1924 subsidy legislation (Housing (Financial Provisions) Act 1924) sponsored by the first Labour government, and that legislation being retained and implemented by the 1924-29 Conservative government. The 1924 Act provided for permanent subsidies for local authorities, and extended to 1939 the subsidy payable to private owners under the 1923 Act; but within a few weeks of the Act becoming law, the 1924 Labour government fell, and was succeeded by a Conservative government (Baldwin's second administration) with a large Parliamentary majority. The significance in practical terms of the 1924 Act would thus depend on the policy of the Conservative government. The Act

was left on the Statute Book, and it was used very
extensively. This was when local authority house
building with Exchequer subsidy became a permanent
part of housing policy in Britain. Baldwin's own
views appear to have been important here (see
Chapter VII) in a way hard to reconcile with the
"expendable landlords" thesis.

Equally hard to reconcile with that thesis is
the actual history of rent restriction (see Chapter
VIII). Newly built houses and flats were exempted
from 1919 onwards, and in the 1930s (and probably
in the 1920s as well) large numbers of houses and
flats were built for letting by private landlords,
who were entitled to the subsidies described above
as available for owner-occupation. It is possible
to contend that if rent restriction had in fact
ended in 1925 as the 1923 legislation envisaged
instead of being prolonged by Baldwin's administration, new building for letting by private enterprise would have increased still further; but it is
not self-evident. With income tax relief on
mortgage interest so much less important than it
subsequently became, plus the Schedule A charge to
income tax on the rental value of owner-occupied
houses, the tax system in the inter-war years did
not favour owning as against renting in the way
that it did in the 1950s and later. The Rent
Restrictions Acts were principally a response to
housing shortages. Those shortages were the most
potent single influence on housing policy in the
inter-war years. By the later 1930s they were
waning, and the private enterprise housing boom had
begun to weaken (see Table III.8 above for the
figures). But well before the boom could end,
World War II caused a return of housing shortages.

Notes and References

(1) Estimated by working back from 1921 by reference to the number of households and occupied dwellings.

(2) Measured by the consumers' expenditure deflator given in Table 61 of C.H. Feinstein, National Income, Employment and Output of the United Kingdom 1855-1965, Cambridge University Press, Cambridge, 1972. The weighting of the official Cost of Living Index made it unsuitable as a measure of changes in the general price level in this period.

(3) Feinstein, National Income, Employment and Output, Table 2.1 p.34, and Table 65.

(4) Ibid, Table 61.

(5) Ibid, Tables 57 and 59.

(6) Ibid, Table 21, based on the work of A. Chapman and R. Knight.

(7) A.L. Bowley (Ed.) Studies in the National Income, Cambridge University Press, Cambridge, 1942.

(8) R.C.O. Matthews 'Some Aspects of Pre-War Growth in the British Economy in Relation to Post War Experience', Manchester School, 1964.

(9) Department of Employment, British Labour Statistics Historical Abstract, HMSO, London, 1972, Table 35, 38 and 39, but see also G. Routh, Occupation and Pay in Great Britain Cambridge University Press, Cambridge, 1965.

(10) G. Routh, Op. cit.

(11) S. Howson, 'The Origins of Dear Money', Economic History Review, 1974.

(12) The principal source was the National Register, an emergency enumeration of the civilian population shortly after the outbreak of war. Nearly all married women were in the civilian population at this date, but many married men were in the Forces and so not included in the National Register.

(13) Census of England and Wales 1931, Housing Report and Tables, Chapter 5 ("Abnormal Character of the 1921 Private Household Situation").

(14) A 'headship rate' is the ratio of heads of household to all members of a defined group. A headship rate of 80% for widows aged 70-79, for example, means that of widows aged 70-79

living in the private household population, 80% were household heads. Headship rates are a key concept in demography as applied to housing.

(15) M. Bowley, Housing and the State, Allen and Unwin, London, 1945.

(16) Census of England and Wales 1931, Housing Report and Tables, p.lviii.

(17) D.V. Glass and E. Grebenik, 'The Trend and Pattern of Fertility in Great Britain', Papers of the Royal Commission on Population, Vol. VI (1954) Part 2, Table 16.

(18) See for instance W.F. Stolper, 'British Monetary Policy and the Housing Boom', Quarterly Journal of Economics 1951-52; G.P. Braae, 'Investment in Housing in the United Kingdom' Manchester School, 1964; and E.T. Nevin, The Mechanism of Cheap Money, University of Wales Press, Cardiff, 1955. For a more sceptical view, see H.W. Richardson, Economic Recovery in Britain 1932-39, Weidenfeld and Nicholson, London, 1967.

(19) Nevin, Cheap Money. Table XLVIII.

(20) H. Richardson and D.H. Aldcroft, Building in the British Economy Between the Wars, Allen and Unwin, London, 1968.

(21) A.A. Jackson, Semi-Detached London, Allen and Unwin, 1973.

(22) Census 1951, Report on Greater London and Five Other Conurbations, Table A on p.xxvi; and Registrar-General's Statistical Review of England and Wales 1939, Part II, Table E.

(23) R.H. Best in A.W. Rogers (Ed.) Urban Growth, Farmland Losses, and Planning, Wye College of the University of London, London, 1978.

(24) Cmd. 6153 (1940).

(25) Building Construction: Report of a Committee appointed to consider questions of Building Construction in connection with the Provision of Dwellings for the Working Class (Cd.9191; 1918, Vol. XIV).

(26) M. Swenarton, Homes for Heroes, Heinemann, London, 1981.

(27) Local Government Board, Manual on the Preparation of State Aided Housing Schemes, 1919.

(28) See W.V. Hole, 'Housing Standards and Social Trends' Urban Studies, 1964.

(29) For a further discussion, see J. Burnett, A Social History of Housing 1815-1970, David

and Charles, Newton Abbott, 1978.

(30)   Note the criticism of it in the 1931 Census
       Housing Report and Tables, pp.xxxiv-xxxv.

(31)   Census of England and Wales 1911, Vol. VIII
       (Tenements), Table 1; 1931, Housing Report
       and Tables, Table 6.

(32)   See pp.iv-vii of Ministry of Health,
       Report on the Overcrowding Survey in England
       and Wales 1936.

(33)   S.2 (1) (b), and Sch. 1.

(34)   See Chapter VII for full discussions.

(35)   Published by Ministry of Health in
       Particulars of Slum Clearance Programmes
       Furnished by Local Authorities, (Cmd.4535,
       1934).

(36)   Ministry of Health Annual Report for 1938/39
       (Cmd.6089), p.82.

(37)   See in particular M.J. Elsas, Housing and the
       Family, Meridian Books, London, no date.

(38)   The enquiry was conducted in the first
       instance to collect information for the
       Ministry of Works about domestic water
       heating appliances. P.G. Gray (of Social
       Survey) The British Household, Central Office
       of Information, 1947.

(39)   The information on rates was extracted from
       it by J.R. Hicks and U.K. Hicks and published
       by them in J.R. Hicks and U.K. Hicks, The
       Incidence of Local Rates in Britain,
       Cambridge University Press, Cambridge, 1945.

(40)   Peacock and Wiseman, Growth of Public Expen-
       diture, Tables A-2 and A-18.

(41)   Annual Abstract of Statistics 1938-50,
       Table 271.

(42)   See J.R. Hicks, U.K. Hicks, and C.E.V. Leser,
       The Problem of Valuation for Rating,
       Cambridge University Press, Cambridge, 1944,
       p.69 for Schedule A valuations and rating
       valuations in the inter-war years.

(43)   M.J. Daunton, House and Home in the
       Victorian City, Arnold, London, 1983,
       Chapter 12.

(44)   A. Offer, Property and Politics 1870-1914,
       Cambridge University Press, Cambridge, 1981.

CHAPTER IV

FROM WORLD WAR II TO THE 1970s

World War II and British Housing

The Second World War, like the first, was the cause of a severe shortage of housing. In contrast to World War I, the damage done by air attack between 1940 and 1945 was severe. The number of houses destroyed by enemy action was officially estimated at 218,000, of which 81,000 had been built between the wars. These losses were heavily concentrated in Greater London (which bore the brunt of the V1 and V2 attacks in 1944-45, as well as air raids in 1940-41) and to a lesser extent the large provincial cities. Another 250,000 houses were, according to official estimates, so badly damaged as to be uninhabitable (1). Priority was given to repairing those houses that could be repaired fairly quickly, and those that were too badly damaged for that had to be left. Numerically more important, though, than the 450,000 or so houses destroyed or made uninhabitable by air attack were the houses not built owing to the war. House building was brought to a virtual halt at the outbreak of war, apart from completing houses already at an advanced stage of construction. The labour force in the building and civil engineering industry was run down from 1,264,000 in 1938 to 623,000 in 1944 (2) in order to provide manpower for the armed forces and for production of munitions of war. Those that remained in the industry were employed mainly on construction work for the forces, and to a lesser extent for the war industries; and in repairing damage caused by air attack. The number of houses completed between mid-1939 and mid-1945 was only about 190,000, compared with perhaps 1¾ million in the absence of

war, even allowing for the boom tailing off. The
housing stock at mid-1945 is estimated at about
11,350,000, of which 250,000 were uninhabitable
owing to war damage. The number of usable houses
was thus reduced by about 400,000 between mid-1939
and mid-1945 (by changes of use and miscellaneous
losses as well as enemy action).

The number of households, in contrast, continued to grow fast, particularly if there are
included the potential households that could not
set up on their own owing to the housing shortage.
The number of households at mid-1939 was estimated
in the previous chapter at 11,750,000, plus 250,000
married couples living as part of someone else's
household, or 12,000,000 potential households altogether. The number of households at mid-1945 was
estimated (by means of an interview survey carried
out by the Government Social Survey in May, June
and July 1945) (3) at 12,227,000. "Household" was
defined in the way that had by then become standard
(and has remained so); and hence did not include
married couples sharing with in-laws. How many
such couples there were was not reported, and is
exceedingly difficult to estimate from the data
published; the concept itself is ambiguous as
applied to the circumstances of 1945, when so many
men were in the forces. Did a married woman living
with her parents when her husband was away in the
forces count as a "concealed married couple household"? For present purposes the answer is 'yes',
on the ground that when the husband came home there
would be a couple with no home of their own. The
number cannot be directly estimated from the 1945
survey. The 1947 survey (4), however, estimated
that about 7.4% of households included a married
son or son-in-law of the housewife, which would
imply between 900,000 and 950,000 married sons and
sons-in-law. Since the 1951 Census showed there to
be a small number of older married couples living
with households headed by sons and sons-in-law, the
higher figure of 950,000 is considered the better
figure for all married couples living with others.
The number of married couples living with in-laws
is likely to have been fairly similar at mid-1945
and in 1947, so the total of separate households
plus 'concealed' married couples in 1945 can be put
at 13.2 million, in round terms. That figure compares with an estimated 12.0 million at mid-1939
and 14.0 million at the time of the 1951 Census.
The number of sharing households can be estimated

92

from the 1945 survey at 2,050,000. Where married
couples lived as members of another household, both
that household and the household with which they
lived are taken to have been sharing. Table IV.1
brings together the estimates of dwellings and
households in 1939 and 1945.

Table IV.1 - Estimates of Dwellings, Households,
            and Sharing in 1939 and 1945

(million)

	1939	1945	Change
Dwellings	11.5	11.1 (*)	-0.4
Separate households	11.75	12.25	+0.5
Potential households (including married couples living with others)	12.0	13.2	+1.2
Separate households sharing	0.9/1.0	2.1	+1.1
Households sharing, including married couples living with others and those they live with	1.4/1.5	4.0	+2.5
Sharing households including married couples, etc. as % of all potential households	12/13	30	...

Notes: (*)   Excludes dwellings so badly damaged as to be
              uninhabitable.

At the end of the war the shortfall of dwellings relative to potential households was about 2
million. This was the largest shortfall ever; in
1921 it was about 1.3 million, and at its post-
World War I peak was probably about 1.5 million.
Nearly 4 million potential households shared in
1945. This was the situation in which the government of the day declared in its statement of post-
war housing policy that its first objective of
housing policy was the provision of "a separate
dwelling for every family that wishes to have one"
(5).
Other effects of the war made the objective
extremely hard to achieve. The British economy was
very fully mobilized for the war effort, far more

93

so than either Germany or the United States. In 1942, 1943 and 1944 public current expenditure on goods and services absorbed some 54% of gross national product (6), and capital investment came virtually to a halt except in the industries closely concerned with the war effort. This extreme of concentration on the war effort meant that at the end of the war there were widespread shortages of almost everything, of plant and machinery just as much as of consumer goods of all kinds. As a claim on resources the provision of houses was but one claim among many. More pressing than all the domestic demands was an urgent need to export more; world shortages of materials and food had driven up the price of British imports and reduced the purchasing power of the income produced by the overseas assets that still remained in British ownership; large quantities of such assets had been sold in the early part of the war to pay for imports. The official estimate was that exports 75% greater (by volume) than in 1938 were required if needed imports of food and raw materials were to be afforded. The priorities that this situation imposed for Britain in the post-war years were summed up by the Chancellor of the Exchequer, Sir Stafford Cripps as: ".... our own consumption requirements have to be the last in the list of priorities. First are exports ...., second is capital investment in industry, and last are the needs, comforts and amenities of the family" (7). Housing was in the last of Cripps' categories.

The war had inevitably generated inflation, though remarkably little given the intensity with which the economy was devoted to the war effort and much less than in World War I. The price level, as measured by the consumers' expenditure deflator (8) was 56% higher in 1946 than in 1939, compared with the doubling of prices that took place between 1914 and 1918; over two-thirds of the price increase took place in the first half of the war between 1939 and 1942. On the average, earnings in manual occupations more than kept pace with the rise in prices; between 1938 and 1946 the increase was some 10-15%, according to which of the price indexes is used. Salaries, particularly the higher salaries, increased less in percentage terms than did wages, thus narrowing the pre-tax spread of real income (9), and they were more severely affected by the war-time increases in income tax.

At a time when wages had risen in real terms

(even if there was not much to spend them on) rents
in real terms were pushed sharply downwards. The
same had happened in World War I, as described in
the previous chapter. In World War II, though, the
sharp cut in rents in real terms took place in two
distinct ways, instead of only one as in the
previous war. The Rent and Mortgage Interest
(Restriction) Act 1939 was one of a batch of Bills
hurried through in preparation for war in August
1939 when the outbreak of war was seen to be imminent; in World War II there was no waiting for the
equivalent of the 1915 rent strikes. This Act
froze rents other than for local authorities'
houses at their September 1939 levels. For some 3
million dwellings these were 1914 rents plus 40%.
The rise in the general price level meant that
rents frozen at 1939 levels in money terms were by
1946 some 33-36% lower (according to which index is
used) in real terms. The war also produced a sharp
reduction in real terms in rents of local authority
houses. With hardly any new building during the
war, very little capital expenditure was incurred,
and with interest rates kept low and with much of
local authority debt consisting of long term loans,
loan charges rose hardly at all in money terms, and
so fell sharply in real terms. As a result, local
authority rents rose no more in money terms than
needed to cover costs of upkeep and management.
Chapter VII gives the figures in detail. Rents
averaged about 7 shillings a week in 1938/39, and
7s 6d in 1945/46. In real terms (measured by the
consumers' expenditure deflator) there was a reduction of about 33%. In both the private and public
rented sectors, therefore, rents were reduced by
about one-third in real terms. This was rather
larger than the reduction in real terms between
1914 and 1924. Not only was there no post-war
increase in controlled rents after World War II as
there had been in 1919 and 1920, there was no post-
war slump and fall in the price level. The forcing
down of rents in real terms as a result of war-time
inflation was to have long-lasting effects on
tenants' attitudes and expectations about what rent
levels were reasonable.

Also important for housing policy was the way
in which the war changed public opinion and attitudes in an egalitarian direction, with much
increased support for reliance on action by government in preference to markets. The war economy had
been run by direct controls (10), with financial

policy having only a subsidiary function (11). With this reliance on centralized controls had gone allocation policies of highly egalitarian character. There is no doubt at all that this was what opinion at the time wanted (12). To fight the war very large numbers of men and women had to be mobilized in the forces and the war industries. They were urgently needed; so their views counted. Equality of sacrifice was the watchword, and rationing as a way of allocating scarce goods was highly popular; the notion that wealth could buy advantages was highly unpopular. "Rationing by the purse" was for long a by-word for unfairness stemming from the uneven distribution of wealth; "queue jumping" was equally a term of opprobrium. Both go with a body of concepts about distributing goods and services by reference to need and equity in which income and wealth have no part. The main shift of opinion towards the political Left went further in World War II than in World War I, partly indeed as a consequence of what happened after World War I. That the ghost of Lloyd George was one of the reasons for the defeat of Churchill in the 1945 General Election is something of a commonplace. The sweeping victory of the Labour party in that election was the consequence of the shift to the Left of opinion during the war, and that shift of opinion had a long-lasting effect as well on policies advocated by the Conservative party and pursued by Conservative governments.

The British Economy from 1945 to the 1970s

The course of the economy was a strong influence both on the private demand for housing and on the housing policy of governments, and so should be summarized before house building and household formation are discussed. It is necessary to emphasize at the outset that from the late 1940s to the early 1970s the rise in output was uniquely rapid if compared with past performance of the British economy, even if it appeared disappointingly slow in comparison with the Western European countries and (at times) the USA. The impression to the contrary is derived from concentrating too much on the troubles of the 1970s. The period from 1945 to the late 1970s can in fact be divided into three sub-periods of very unequal length: post-war reconstruction, which merged into re-armament; the two decades of sustained though uneven growth from 1952

or 1953 to 1973; and the years after 1973 when
growth was slower, inflation higher and unemployment worse. At the time of writing we are far too
close to the events of the third sub-period to be
able to judge objectively whether the 1970s saw a
marked deceleration in the long-term rate of growth
of the British economy as the 1870s did (and if so
why?)

At the end of the war and in the immediate
post-war years, recollections of the boom of 1919
and 1920 and then the severe slump were still
vivid. The Second World War had lasted longer than
the First and the concentration of the economy on
the war had been much greater, so that the backlog
of unmet demand at the end of the war was far
larger. But memories of the 1919-20 boom and the
belief that the hectic nature of the boom had been
the main reason for the ensuing slump were a major
reason for relying on war-time controls to restrict
the rate at which the backlog of demand came
through into the economy, so as to avoid a dis-
orderly scramble. This policy had a considerable
measure of success, helped of course by aid from
the USA under the European Recovery Programme
(termed "Marshall Aid" after the US Secretary of
State at the time). The effect of World War II on
the British economy was far from over, however,
when the outbreak of hostilities in Korea led to
the decision to undertake large scale re-armament.
Re-armament, especially by the United States, and
stock-piling of strategic materials set off a
renewed boom in commodity prices and for a time
revived and exacerbated the inflation that had
resulted from World War II but which was beginning
to die down. In the "reconstruction" years between
1946 and 1952 wage earners generally retained the
increase in real income that they had secured
during the war, and indeed improved their position
slightly. But for the whole population, consumption per head in real terms did not return to the
1938 level. In contrast to wages, salaries and
still more so incomes from interest, rents, and
dividends, had not kept up with prices during the
war and had made up very little of the lost ground
by 1952. The way in which personal consumption was
the residuary legatee of the economy at this time,
after exports and investment, can be seen in the
contrast between the 23% increase between 1938 and
1952 in real gross domestic product and the 3% in
real consumers' expenditure. The rate of infla-

tion, though, was fairly modest, given the pressure
of excess demand. In this the controls achieved
their object; there was no repetition of the boom
of 1919-20. Likewise there was no repetition of
the slump of 1920-21. Different opinions may be
held about how far the avoidance of such a slump
was the result of better management by governments
around the world. But the absence of a post-war
slump kept at bay the risk that house building
would be sharply cut on purely financial grounds,
notwithstanding the housing shortages, as it had
been in 1921. Limitations on real resources led to
the amount of house building being restricted; but
the number of houses built in the six years after
May 1945 far exceeded, as we shall see, the number
built in the six years after November 1918. 1952
saw the beginning of the end of excess demand for
virtually everything at home and abroad. Shortages
of particular goods remained, but generally falling
pressures of demand, especially for food and raw
materials, permitted the ending of most of the war-
time controls in the next two years. Food rationing ended in 1954, and so did building licensing.

It is convenient at this stage to summarize
the main indicators of the growth of output and
real incomes. The terms of trade are included
because changes had a strong effect on the
resources available in the Bitish economy.

Comparison of the rates of growth of gross
domestic product in total and per person employed
that are shown in Table IV.2 with the inter-war
years (Table III.1) and the sixty years before
1914, leaves no doubt about economic growth in the
later 1940s, the 1950s, the 1960s and the early
1970s having been much more rapid than in any
previous period of comparable length in British
history. This is important not only for what it
implies about the demand for housing and the resources available to meet it, but also for whether
the housing policies pursued were imimical to economic growth through absorbing funds that might
otherwise have been invested in industry and trade,
reducing labour mobility, and perhaps in other
ways. This is a question, though, that is better
discussed in the concluding chapter than here. The
measures of output shown in Table IV.2 do not pick
up the way in which the average number of hours
worked per week fall and the length of paid holidays increased, so that output per man/ hour rose
distinctly faster than output per man/ year.

Table IV.2 – Main Indicators of Output and Real Income 1946-79

	Gross Domestic Product Total (£ million, 1980 Prices)	Gross Domestic Product per Person Employed (a) (£, 1980 Prices)	Real Disposable Income per Head of Population (£, 1980 Prices)	Real Earnings of Manual Workers (Gross) (b) (Index, 1952 = 100)	Terms of Trade (1963 = 100)
1946	(88,260)	(3,840)	(1,335)	94	101
1952	98,852	4,226	1,397	100	85
1958	115,841	4,750	1,633	119	95
1963	135,636	5,500	1,943	136	100
1968	160,605	6,465	2,121	155	100
1973	187,037	7,464	2,574	185	91 (c)
1979	203,053	8,002	2,842	189	99

Rates of Change (% per Year)

1946-52	+1.9	+1.6	+0.7	+1.0	...
1952-58	+1.9	+1.9	+0.7	+2.9	...
1958-63	+3.4	+2.6	+3.5	+2.7	...
1963-68	+3.4	+3.3	+1.7	+2.7	...
1968-73	+3.1	+2.9	+3.9	+3.5	...
1952-73	+3.1	+2.7	+3.0	+3.0	...
1973-79	+1.3	+1.1	+1.6	+0.3	...

Notes: (a) There is a break in the series in 1959, which is allowed for in the rates of change. See source for explanation of the break. GDP is expenditure series.

(b) April figures in 1952 to 1968; New Earnings Survey in 1973 and 1979, revalued by index of retail prices.

(c) 1972 value was 104.

Source: Economic Trends Annual Supplement, 1985 Edition pp.13, 18 and 99; Annual Abstract of Statistics 1985 Edition, Table 2.1. Link back to 1946 from Feinstein, National Income Expenditure and Output Tables 5, 10, 55, 57; 61, 64 and 65.

The trend rates of increase are not the only measure of the performance of the economy. Stability is also important, and here also the record was better not just than in the inter-war years but also than the sixty years before 1914. Freedom from anything other than short departures from full employment until the 1970s also was favourable to an improvement in housing conditions. The demand for housing was further reinforced by the increase in the proportion of married women in paid employment. Between 1951 and 1976 the proportion of married women aged 20-24 in paid employment rose from 36.5% to 54.6%; at ages 25-44 the proportions were 25.1% and 56.3%; and at ages 45-59 21.5% and 61.3% (13). The effect on the total labour force was largely offset by the reduction in the number of boys and girls in paid employment owing to the raising of the school leaving age and the larger numbers remaining at school beyond the school leaving age and in full time higher or further education. But unlike the earnings of sons and daughters who within a few years would have gone to set up homes of their own, wives' earnings could be reckoned on for paying for housing, and in the 1960s and 1970s were increasingly regarded as such by building societies and other lenders for house purchase.

With the rapid growth (by all past British standards) of output and real income went a rise in the price level. In contrast to the early 1920s there was no post-war slump, and hence no fall in the price level to reverse even partially the increase in prices during the war. The war-time price increase thus became built into the economic system, and thereafter prices continued to rise. This inflation was a constant source of concern to governments, and a cause of reluctance at times to take action that would appear as deliberately putting up the cost of living, whatever the merits considered in isolation. Nevertheless, it is important to emphasize that the history of prices was not one of continuous acceleration of the rate of rise. As Table IV.3 below shows, the average rate of increase in prices in 1957-62 was lower than in 1952-57; and was lower in 1962-67 than in 1952-57. Not until the very end of the 1960s did the rate of inflation accelerate; and the 1970s were without parallel as a decade of peace-time inflation. That up until 1968 at any rate inflation was not accelerating is very important because

Table IV.3 - Interest Rates and the
Rate of Rise of Prices: 1948-79

	Consols (%)		Treasury Bills (%)		Increase in Prices (Annual Average in Brackets)	
1948	3.2)		0.5		7.6)	
1949	3.3)		0.5		3.0)	
1950	3.5)	3.6	0.5		2.9)	6.3
1951	3.8)		0.6		9.0)	
1952	4.2)		2.1		9.4)	
1953	4.1)		2.3)		3.1)	
1954	3.8)		1.8)		1.7)	
1955	4.2)	4.4	3.7)	3.5	4.6)	3.6
1956	4.7)		4.9)		5.0)	
1957	5.0)		4.8)		3.6)	
1958	5.0)		4.6)		3.2)	
1959	4.8)		3.4)		0.6)	
1960	5.4)	5.4	4.9)	4.4	0.8)	2.5
1961	6.2)		5.1)		3.3)	
1962	6.0)		4.2)		4.2)	
1963	5.6)		3.7)		2.0)	
1964	6.0)		4.6)		3.2)	
1965	6.4)	6.3	5.9)	5.2	4.8)	3.3
1966	6.8)		6.1)		3.9)	
1967	6.7)		5.8)		2.4)	
1968	7.4)		7.0)		4.8)	
1969	8.9)		7.6)		5.4)	
1970	9.2)	8.7	7.0)	6.5	6.4)	6.6
1971	9.1)		5.6)		9.4)	
1972	9.1)		5.5)		7.1)	
1973	10.9)		9.4)		9.2)	
1974	15.0)		11.4)		16.1)	
1975	14.7)	13.4	10.2)	9.9	24.2)	16.2
1976	14.3)		11.1)		16.5)	
1977	12.3)		7.5)		15.8)	
1978	11.9		8.6		8.3	
1979	11.4		13.1		13.4	

Note: (*) Year-on-year increase over previous year.
Source: Annual Abstract of Statistics; Economic Trends Annual Supplement.

101

it affects the interpretation put on the rise in interest rates. The trend of interest rates was very definitely upwards. Chapter I explained why interest rates are so important for the finance of housing, and this rising trend of interest rates was a fundamental reason for the problems faced in housing finance by successive governments in Britain and indeed in many other countries as well. It is therefore worthwhile to show interest rates year by year, as the chronology is important both to any conclusions about the causes of the upward trend, and for the way in which the course of interest rates helps explain the development of policy on subsidies, rents, and tax relief. Long-term interest rates are represented by the rate on 2½ percent Consols; short-term rates by the Treasury Bill rate. To use these may appear slightly old-fashioned, but they have the merit of a constant definition, and in view of the way in which financial markets work are reasonably representative both of the changes in long-term and short-term interest rates, and of their height in nominal terms. The year-on-year rate of rise of the general price level is represented by the Index of Retail Prices and its predecessors.

In view of the course of price inflation, the upward trend of interest rates in the 1950s and 1960s was not in any simple way the consequence of inflation. In the early and mid-1950s it probably owed much to the ending of the direct controls which enabled the war to be financed as a "3% war" and then to increasing reliance on monetary policy as the means of restraining inflation. Also considered important at the time was London's position as a financial centre, and the function of sterling as a reserve currency was probably important as well, making British interst rates subject to the exigencies of international capital flows and "confidence". The 7% bank rates in 1957, 1961 and 1965 are examples; by 1967 in order to create the same sort of impact, an 8% bank rate was necessary; and at the end of 1973, 13%. The amount of internationally mobile money grew, and by the 1970s had become very large indeed. Developments in the technology of money transmission and the dismantling of exchange controls increased the ease with which this money could flow from one financial centre to another and made interest rates increasingly volatile. Some of this volatility is averaged out in the annual average interest rates shown in Table IV.3; the large and rapid swings in interest rates came to pose financial problems for housing in the 1970s over and above those posed by the upward trend. Such was the inflation in the 1970s that notwithstanding the high nominal rates, 'real' rates (in the sense of the interest rate minus the annual rate of inflation) were negative in real terms, as we shall see in Chapters VI and VII.

Population and Households from the 1940s to the 1970s

To introduce the discussion of that part of the demand and need for housing that stemmed from the increase in the number of households, the number of "potential" households is compared with the total population and the adult population. "Potential households" are preferred to actual households as a measure of demand and need, owing to the way in which housing shortages forced so many couples to live with in-laws in the 1940s and 1950s. From 1951 onwards "potential households" include lone-parent families living as part of someone else's household, but there is no information with which to estimate their number in 1939 or earlier.

By all past standards the increase in the adult population from 1951 to 1981 was slow; but relative to the increase in the adult population the increase in the number of households was rapid. In the three decades the adult population increased by 12.9%, whereas the number of potential households increased by 31.6%. In absolute terms there was an increase of almost 4.5 million in the number of potential households, compared with an increase of 4.05 million in the adult population. If the same relationship between the growth of the adult population and the number of households had applied in 1951-81 as in 1911-31, there would have been an increase of about 1.9 million households, little more than 40% of the actual increase. If the 1931-51 relationship had applied in 1951-81, the increase in households would have been about 75% of the actual increase. There was thus a radical change in the relationship between the growth of the adult population and household formation that was fundamentally important for the demand side of the housing system.

Table IV.4 - Total Population and Households in
England and Wales 1939-81

(thousands)

	Total Population	Population Aged 20 and over	Potential Households
1939	41.460	29,129	12,000
1951	43,758	31,362	14,194
1961	46,196	32,340	15,426
1971	49,152	34,152	17,144
1981	49,634	35,414	18,680

Increase (thousand a year)

1911-21	182	220	115
1921-31	207	311	129
1931-39	188	267	178
1939-51	192	186	167
1951-61	244	98	123
1961-71	296	181	172
1971-81	48	126	154

Source: See Chapter III for estimates for 1939. 1951 population figures are from census; 1961, 1971 and 1981 are mid-year census-based, taken from for Households, see Department of the Environment, Housing Policy Technical Volume, Chapter I, Tables I.5 and I.8 for 1951 and 1961; Housing and Construction Statistics 1969-79, Table 99; and 1981-Based Estimates of Numbers of Households.

Two distinct elements can be distinguished in this changed relationship between the adult population and the total of households: marital status and headship rates. Earlier marriage and more marriage result in more household formation, other things being equal; so too do higher divorce rates, because over four-fifths of divorced men and women head households, so that for every 100 married couple households that dossolve between 160 and 170 successor households are formed. Headship rates are separate; they are defined as the proportion of members of a specified group, e.g. widows aged 70-79, who head households. Increases in headship rates were a very important part of the growth in the number of households after 1945. An approximate calculation to show their importance is in Table IV.5. It is no more than approximate, because it uses the headship rates derived from the 1951 Census (14) to analyse the effect of changes in headship rates between 1931 and 1961. The 1951 headship rates have to be used here because the data needed to apply the headship rates calculated for 1961, 1971 and 1981 were not collected in earlier years. For 1961-71 and 1971-81, the headship rates for those years were used to estimate the increase in the number of households that was due to headship rate changes.

Table IV.5 - Analysis of Increase in Potential
        Households 1931-81

(thousands)

	Total Increase	Growth of Adult Population	Change in Age/Marital Status Composition	Change in Head-ship Rates
1931-39	1,420	950	350	120
1939-51	2,010	1,000	775	235
1951-61	1,230	440	510	280
1961-71	1,720	820	330	570
1971-81	1,540	575	255	710

Source: Derived from Table IV.4 by methods described in the text.

Growth of the adult population by itself accounted for only two-fifths of the increase in the number of households between 1951 and 1981, compared with all the increase in households before 1914. That the slowing down of the growth of the adult population that resulted from the fall in births that began just before World War I did not result in a slower rate of increase in the number of households, was due partly to marital status and partly to headship rates. From the 1930s to the 1960s, earlier marriage and more marriage led to increase in the number of potential households (all married couples count as "potential households", whether or not they actually have their own households). In the 1970s the rise in marriage rates was reversed, for reasons that at the time of writing are in doubt, but the effect on the number of households was more than offset by the rise in the number of divorces; there were 1,390,000 divorced men and women in England and Wales according to the 1981 Census, compared with 480,000 in 1971, and 265,000 in 1961 (15).

A closer look is called for at the changes in headship rates that explain arithmetically 1.3 million of the increase in the number of households between 1961 and 1981, well over one-half of the total increase. The headship rates are only descriptive statistics, of course; a higher headship rate cannot be said to "cause" the number of households to rise. They are nonetheless very useful descriptive statistics, in that they pinpoint which of the categories of men and women came increasingly to live as independent households instead of living as part of a household headed by someone else. Table IV.6 shows the change in headship rates among young and middle aged never-married men and women, and among widows and widowers. This comparison can be made only for 1961, 1971 and 1981; the 1951 data are less detailed and not comparably defined.

Table IV.6 - Selected Headship Rates:
             England and Wales 1961-81

(percent)	.... Men			...... Women		
	1961	1971	1981	1961	1971	1981
Never-Married						
20-24	2.8	7.3	11.3	3.7	9.0	12.6
25-29	9.0	16.4	29.5	9.1	19.7	30.4
30-34	14.7	22.5	37.8	13.8	25.6	40.0
35-37	20.9	24.5	39.3	18.8	28.7	41.4
40-44	28.3	29.6	42.9	27.4	31.3	44.0
Widowed (includes divorced)						
60-64	84.9	85.5	86.3	89.0	90.4	91.0
65-69	78.8	84.0	87.7	86.1	89.5	91.4
70-74	75.1	81.1	87.7	81.2	86.8	90.7
75 and over	64.5	73.4	81.9	67.5	77.5	83.2

Source: Department of the Environment from census
          tabulations.

Much higher proportions of never-married men and women headed households in 1981 than in 1971 or 1961; and many more widows and widowers continued to live as independent households instead of going to live with someone else. In these ways the number of never-married men and women under age 45 that headed households was some 570,000 higher in 1981 than if 1961 headship rates had continued; and the number of widows and widowers heading households was about 350,000 higher. Between 1951 and 1981 the increase in the number of households that was due to higher proportions of widows and widowers maintaining their own households was about half a million.

There are several possible explanations, none of them mutually exclusive, for the rise in the proportion of widows, and to a lesser extent widowers, living as independent households. One group of explanations would emphasize rising real income (for pensions rose as fast as earnings after the early 1950s); better health; and for those elderly people who were becoming frail, better services (including housing with the services of a warden) that enabled them to go on living longer in their own homes instead of having to go to live with relatives. An alternative explanation would place more weight on young families allegedly being less willing to have elderly relatives live with them. With the exception of sheltered housing provided by local authorities, which may well have enabled some elderly people to live as separate households instead of having to go into old peoples' homes, it is safe to conclude that the increase in the proportions of widows and widowers keeping their households going originated from the demand side of the housing system, and was not the response to an increase in the supply of housing, which would have been different had the growth in the supply of housing been less. Widowed survivors of married couple households are already in their own homes. Most owner-occupiers above retirement age own outright and so have a free choice of whether to stay on or not. Widows of tenants renting from private landlords have always had, under the Rent Acts, a right of succession to the tenancy on the death of a tenant who had security of tenure under the Acts. Tenants of local authorities had virtually the same degree of security in a dwelling of some kind (not necessarily the same dwelling, as some local authorities have at times

required widows left on their own in family dwellings to move to something smaller), for there were
no reported instances of a local authority requiring a widow or widower to leave a tenancy to go and
live as part of someone else's household. The
increase in the number of widow and widower households can thus be regarded as a demand-determined
change (with the exception of sheltered housing
which accommodated about 150,000 widowed households
in 1976) (16) to which the supply side of the
housing system had to adjust.

That is not true, however, of single people
(in the sense of never-married). They can only
form separate households if they can get separate
accommodation. The rise in the proportion of
single men and women heading separate households
was thus a process very different from the rise in
headship rates among widows and widowers. The way
in which single people came to occupy an increasing
proportion of the remaining housing let by private
landlords and began to appear among owner-occupiers
and local authority tenants in the 1970s, is discussed in the next chapter.

That the exceptional rise, by historical standards, in household formation in the 1950s and
1960s was basically the consequence of the equally
exceptional rise in real incomes is an intriguing
possibility, which is given further credence by the
fact that the trend can be discerned, although at a
slower rate, in the inter-war years when the rate
of growth of real incomes was considerably higher
than in the years before 1914, even though lower
than in the 1950s and 1960s. The further rapid
rise in headship rates in the 1970s, however, casts
doubt on an explanation in terms of real incomes
because after 1973 the rise in real incomes slowed
down abruptly. Time-lags before the slowing of the
rise in incomes affected behaviour may perhaps
explain the continuing rise in headship rates in
the 1970s, notwithstanding the check to the rise in
incomes. One explanation of the rapid increase in
the number of households that can be rejected,
though, is that the number of households is determined simply by the increase in the number of
houses. Such an explanation is not compatible with
the fact that a substantial part of the increase
came about through widowed survivors of married
couple households staying on longer as independent
households. Nor is it compatible with the very
high marriage rates in the post war years when

housing was extremely short. The number of potential households increased by about 4.5 million in 1951-81, and the number of actual households by 5.1 million; but the housing stock increased by 6.6 million (see Table IV.12 below). Such figures are incompatible with the proposition sometimes advanced that the relationship between households and dwellings is merely circular (17).

Notwithstanding the scale of the rise in headship rates, its importance as an influence on the demand for housing was for long under-estimated. Although with hindsight there can be seen to have been a definite rise in headship rates (probably among widows for the most part) between 1931 and 1951, both the Registrar-General in the Housing Volume of the 1951 Census (18) and Cullingworth (19) concentrated on how close to the enumerated number of households in 1931 was the hypothetical number calculated by applying 1951 headship rates to the 1931 population. In fact this result was largely the consequence of so many more married couples not heading their own households in 1951 than in 1931, but at first sight it was consistent with the apparent stable relationship between adult population and households discovered when the 1931 Census results were analysed (20).

With the 1951 evidence misinterpreted, the reality of rising headship rates was not appreciated until the 1961 Census results became available and even then the rate of increase tended to be understated. In his report on the 1951 Census, the Registrar-General projected an increase in the number of households in England and Wales averaging just under 90,000 a year between 1951 and 1965, and 80,000 a year in 1965-75 (21). In arriving at those figures, the proportion of married couples living as concealed households was taken to fall as housing shortages diminished, but otherwise headship rates were projected to remain unchanged. Cullingworth made very similar assumptions; the highest of his four estimates (published in 1960) had all married men heading households in 1978, but other headship rates no different from in 1951, though he observed that a shortfall of married households relative to his estimates more than offset by an increase in other headship rates was "not beyond the bounds of probability" (22). His highest assumption resulted in an estimate of 16,012,000 households in England and Wales in 1978 and an increasae between 1951 and 1978 averaging

109

111,000 a year. Estimates and projections made in the early 1960s when the 1961 enumerated total of households was known, but the individual headship rates were not, still under-estimated heavily, again as a result of making insufficient provision for the rise in non-married headship rates. Needleman's (23) maximum estimate for 1980 was 16,992,000 households in England and Wales; he assumes, for instance, 70% headship rates for widows and widowers aged 60 and over; in the event the 1981 values were 83% and 81% (see Table V.9 below). Similarly, Paige (24) made projections of 18,421,000 households in Great Britain (i.e. including Scotland) in 1975, with an average annual increase of 141,000 households in 1960-75. Miss Paige, writing in a collected volume of forecasts that were not in general characterized by reticence or undue caution, stated that the assumption that in 1990 only 16% of all adult population (defined as all persons aged 20 or over plus married men and women aged 16-19) would be neither household heads nor the wives of household heads was a maximum assumption; yet already in 1971 the figure was only 16.6%. Official views likewise under-estimated the growth in the number of households: the <u>National Plan</u>, for instance (published in 1965) put the increase in the number of households in the United Kingdom in the following 10 years at an average of 140,000 a year (25). That UK figure corresponds to 120,000 a year approximately in England and Wales, whereas the out-turn was probably about 180,000 a year. Over-estimation of the growth of the number of households was certainly not a reason for setting the very ambitious target of 500,000 houses a year. That the rise in headship rates was under-predicted for so long and by so much by knowledge-able analysts underlines how little was really known about the reasons for it.

One of the consequences of the increase in the number of widows and widowers living on as independent households, and of many more never-married men and women living independently, was a large increase in the number of one-person households. Table IV.7 shows the size distribution of households.

Very large households became increasingly rare. Whereas in the inter-war years and before 1914 overcrowding was the aspect of the match (or mis-match) between size of dwelling and size of household that aroused concern, in the 1950s, 1960s and 1970s, 'under-occupation' attracted more and more comment. Table IV.7 shows why. The reasons for the increase in the number of one-person households have already been referred to. Earlier marriage and the increasing proportion of single people leaving their parents' homes increased the number of middle-aged couples on their own.

Table IV.7 - Households Analysed by Size: England and Wales 1931-81

(thousands)

	1931	1951	1961	1971	1981
Number of Persons in Household					
1	689	1,403	1,960	3,002	3,849
2	2,240	3,627	4,383	5,267	5,696
3	2,460	3,312	3,354	3,151	3,016
4	1,980	2,491	2,681	2,790	3,205
5	1,271	1,259	1,294	1,338	1,289
6 or 7	1,169	822	785	794	573
8 or more	424	202	186	169	79
Total	10,233	13,118	14,640	16,510	17,906

Notes: 1961,1971 and 1981 figures exclude households with no members present on census night. For this reason the totals are not the same as in other tables that show total households.

Source: Census of England and Wales: 1951, Housing Report and Tables Table 2; 1961, Housing Tables, Table 4; 1971, Housing Tables, Table 4; 1981, Housing and Households, Table 2.

New House Building: Totals, Types and Standards

For purposes of record, because that record will need to be referred to on many occasions in the discussion of policy, the number of new houses started year by year is shown in an Annex of this chapter. Here a summary is more convenient, and insight into the profile through time is enhanced by showing "net new building", defined as the number of houses built less the number demolished or closed. Very little replacement building was

111

done for private owners. The private housing
market never had a mechanism for replacing old
houses by new (as distinct from replacing old
houses by commercial buildings), and investigations
in the 1960s into the possibility of developing one
proved fruitless, as we shall see later in this
chapter. Replacement building was a function of
public authorities. New building to rehouse people
displaced by slum clearance was not always one for
one; where sharing was common (especially in
London) more than one dwelling was needed for each
demolished, whereas in some of the towns of the
north of England in the late 1960s and early 1970s
the opposite was true, as some of the dwellings to
be closed were vacant and occupiers of some of the
other dwellings could find fresh accommodation for
themselves. Nevertheless, over the long term, one-
for-one is not too misleading as an approximation,
not just for slum clearance, but for other demolitions as well.

Table IV.8 - Net New House Building,
            England and Wales 1946-79

(thousands, annual averages)

	Public Sector	Private Owners	Both Sectors	Total Built Both Sectors
1946-50	131 (a)	31	162	169
1951-55	155	62	217	250
1956-60	51	135	186	259
1961-65	28	184	211	299
1966-70	56	188	244	343
1971-75	19	162	195	276
1976-79	89	130	219	255

Note: (a) Demolitions in 1946-50 are approximate esti-
              mate only.

Source: See Housing Policy Technical Volume, Table I.12
         for summarized figures of slum clearance and
         other losses from the housing stock.

During the 1970s, emphasis on the number of
houses built came to be derided as a "numbers
game". But given how severe was the housing
shortage at the end of the war (see Table IV.1
above) the number of houses built was for many
years an extremely important matter.

The first observation to be made about the number of houses completed is that in the immediate post-war years the number was much greater than in the corresponding period after World War I. In the six years from 1919/20 to 1924/25 (inclusive), 475,000 houses were completed; but in the six years 1946 to 1951, the figure was more than twice as great at 1,017,000. Of these 116,000 were "prefabs", houses assembled from factory-made parts with an expected life of 15 or 20 years. Even if these are excluded from the comparison as being a technical innovation not available in 1919 and onwards, the number of houses built in the six years after 1945 was still about 400,000 more than in the six years after 1918, notwithstanding the low priority given to housing relative to exports and manufacturing investment. The comparison does not support the view that better results would have been achieved if controls had been ended in 1946 as they were in 1919. It also shows the benefit from expenditure on housing not having to be cut on purely financial grounds (as opposed to limited supplies of labour and materials) in the way it was in 1921.

In 1945-51 building by public authorities predominated, as a matter of policy by the government of the day, with just over four-fifths of all houses completed being for public authorities. The Conservative government that took office in October 1951 did not share its Labour predecessor's view about building for local authorities being more efficient and equitable than building for private owners, but it nevertheless relied heavily on public authorities for its "300,000 houses a year" drive. 939,000 houses were completed for the public sector in 1952-56, more than in any quinquennium before or since. That 871,000 houses were added to the housing stocks of local authorities and new towns (the other 68,000 were for housing associations and for public bodies in their capacity as employers) in the first five years of Conservative post-war government may appear surprising in the light of subsequent political history, but it is a fact nevertheless. The government wanted houses built by anybody that could get them built, local authorities included. By the end of 1953, new building for local authorities had increased the size of their housing stock to practically double what it had been at the outbreak of war; new building during this time for

113

private owners was only a quarter of a million,
compared with almost 1½ million for public authorities. This was the time when, as Table IV.8 shows,
their house building was for the purpose of adding
to the stock. Subsequently it came to be mainly
building for replacement though never (if the
country is taken as a whole) exclusively so.

Types and standards of houses and flats built
must be considered as well as numbers. In view of
how controversial much of the building of flats
subsequently became, it is useful to show the
number and sizes of houses and flats that were
built. At the time of writing it appears to be
widely assumed that most of the building was of
flats, but at Table IV.9 shows, that was not so.

Table IV.9 - New Dwellings Built by Local Authorities in England and Wales 1946-79

(thousands a year)

Bedrooms	..... Houses			... Flats and Maisonettes ...			All Dwellings
	1	2	3 or more	1	2	3 or more	
1946-50	2	12	85	3	5	3	110
1951-55	4	39	93	10	22	6	170
1956-60	6	22	49	14	20	7	119
1961-65	8	14	35	22	22	8	110
1966-70	7	17	48	32	30	12	145
1971-75	6	12	34	28	16	6	102
1976-79	5	15	38	29	13	4	104

Note: This table includes new towns but not housing associations and public departments, and also excludes the
116,000 "pre-fabs", so the totals differ from those
in Table IV.8.

In the post-war decade when shortages were the
dominant influence, local authorities built mainly
houses. Out of 1½ million dwellings, including the
"pre-fabs", 1½ million were houses and only ¼ million flats and maisonettes. Of the houses, three-
quarters were with three bedrooms (85% in 1946-50).
In conditions of severe shortage, families were
given priority. The increase in the number of two-
bedroomed houses and flats built in the early 1950s
was not really a change of policy in this respect,
but rather a part of the policy of giving greater

emphasis to quantity in conditions where building materials (notably imported timber) were very short. After the mid-1950s, policies changed. By the mid-1960s as many flats as houses were being built. Nearly half of the flats had one bedroom only. They were intended for older people, who were very numerous among households displaced by slum clearance. The same explanation applies to the building of more two bedroom flats and houses: large numbers of the households displaced were couples whose children had grown up and left home, for whom a two-bedroomed house or flat was considered suitable. Flats were, however, by no means wholly, or even mainly flats in tower blocks, as Table IV.10 shows.

Table IV.10 - Storey Heights of Flats Built by Local Authorities

(percent)

Storeys	2-4	5-9	10 or more	All Flats	All Flats (Annual Average)
Year of Tender Approval					
1953-59	78	13	9	100	45,000
1960-64	62	10	28	100	61,000
1965-69	58	16	26	100	79,000
1970-74	90	8	2	100	46,000
1975-79	97	3	-	100	47,000

Source: Calculated from various issues of Housing Statistics and Housing and Construction Statistics.

Of all flats in tenders approved in 1953-79, 15% (220,000 out of just under 1.5 million) were blocks of ten storeys or higher; 26% (380,000) in blocks of five storeys or higher. High rise building was a fashion with a fairly short life: such flats were few before the early 1950s, and the number of flats in blocks of five storeys or more in tenders for subsidy reached a peak in 1966; the number approved the following year was almost 20% lower, so that building of high rise flats was clearly already in decline at the time of the Ronan

Point disaster, when a gas explosion in a tower block in the London Borough of Newham caused a partial collapse in which six people were killed (26). The reputation of high flats was diminished still further as a result. In the early 1970s, the number of tenders approved for subsidy was down to under 1,000 a year, and by the middle of the decade hardly any were being built. The reasons for the growth in popularity with local authorities of high rise flats have been discussed in some detail by Cooney (27) and Dunleavy (28), and there is no need to repeat that discussion here, though it will be touched on when the supply of land for house building is being considered. It is important to emphasize, though, that flats and tower blocks were not synonymous, nor were tower blocks and "mass" housing, in Dunleavy's use of the term. Nor was "industrialized" or "system" building, the results of which attracted a growing volume of criticism in the 1970s and still more in the 1980s, confined to high rise blocks of flats.

Both high rise building and "industrialized" building contributed much to the falling reputation of local authority housing in the later 1970s and beyond, so it is worth considering here why for a time so much use was made of them. It is important to keep the distinction clear: "system" building was for the most part novel, but flats were not. Industrialized methods were seen as the way to get both higher quality and larger quantity. It was not in the late 1950s and early 1960s cheaper than "traditional" building, but by using off-site prefabrication made much less use of many of the building industry crafts, a most important attraction at a time when these craftsmen were in very short supply with their shortage regarded as the main limitation on output. Statistics of industrialized building were kept only from 1964; in that year 21.0% of dwellings in tenders approved for subsidy were classified as industrialized (29), followed by a rise to a peak of 42.6% in tenders approved in 1967, but after that there was a decline: the proportion was 24.4% in 1973, 17.5% in 1975 and in 1979 only 3.5%. In the later 1970s the reputation of industrialized building deteriorated. Some of the dwellings developed serious faults, in particular water penetration (30). To which systems they applied, and just how many dwellings were affected is, at the time of writing, not yet known. Industrialized building was by no means used only for flats and maisonettes: in 1967, the peak year, the proportion of houses in tenders approved for local authorities that were built by industrialized methods was exactly the same as the proportion of flats.

In many ways the increase in building of flats is more in need of explanation than the increased use of industrialized building. Flats and maisonettes were not novelties like industrialized building; there was plenty of experience with them, and that experience showed that they were less popular than houses, certainly with families. That building flats, particularly high flats, was not a least cost method of providing housing was fully appreciated at the end of the 1950s (31), and the high cost of building high was recognized by the special subsidies provided under the 1956 legislation (32). So what explanation can be advanced for large scale building of flats, notwithstanding what Dunleavy engagingly terms the "rationality deficit"? (33) Flats and maisonettes were built in order to squeeze more dwellings into a given site area than if houses were built, so policy about land use is the most likely place to look for explanations. New building to high densities maximized the proportion of former slum-dwellers who could be rehoused on the sites from which they came, and kept to a minimum the number to be rehoused in estates at the edge of the built-up area. Sites near city centres had advantages from being close to places of work and places of entertainment and shops. But equally important were the obstacles in the way of building at the edges of built-up areas.

The way in which suburban growth in the 1930s engendered strong objections to urban "sprawl" was discussed in the previous chapter, and in the postwar years these attitudes carried the day in planning policy. This point will be considered in some detail in connection with land prices and house prices. Here it is important to note that in the later 1950s when most of the bombed sites in the cities had been built on, these attitudes were strongly reinforced when in the later 1950s and early 1960s rapidly rising birthrates held out the prospect of the population growing by 8 million or more by the early 1980s, and by another 8 million, at least, by the end of the century. If population growth on this scale were housed by building outward from the towns, rural land would be built

117

on at an unprecedented rate. The alternative to building outward appeared to be building upward; the preference for houses as against flats, it could be argued, belonged to different times and could not be accommodated in the changed conditions. Widely held opinions of this kind reinforced the objections of residents of outer London to building there to rehouse people displaced by slum clearance in inner London, residents of Warwickshire and Worcestershire to rehousing from Birmingham, and residents of Cheshire to rehousing from Manchester. The way local authority boundaries were drawn exacerbated these conflicts, which sometimes had a party political edge in clashes between Labour county boroughs and Conservative counties. In any assessment of gains and losses from local authority flat building and responsibility for it, the importance of rural conservation, green belts, and "good agricultural land" should not be overlooked or understated while imprecations are heaped on the urban local authorities and their architects. Just how important the environmentalist pressures were, though, must at this stage be remitted to future historians.

Mention should also be made here of the policies followed on housing standards in the sense of space and equipment. World War II, like World War I, led to a raising of standards of new houses built for public authorities. The vision of a better Britain after the war was again a major reason, even though the increase in standards after World War II was less spectacular than that after World War I. Standards for new houses to be built after the war were considered by one of the many committees that were set up in the later years of the war to advise and plan for post-war Britain. The Dudley Committee (34) which reported in 1944, recommended higher standards both of space and of fittings. In place of the 750-850 sq.ft. for three-bedroomed houses built in the inter-war years from 1923 onwards, Dudley recommended a minimum of 900 sq.ft. and a proper bathroom on the same floor as the bedrooms, in contrast to pre-war practice which sometimes had baths next to the scullery (and now and again in it) to save the cost of an upstairs hot water system. In houses designed for five persons or more, two WCs were to be required. Fitted kitchens replaced the pre-war scullery, as having to cook in the living room on a coal fired range became less and less popular and cooking in the kitchen with gas or electricity was preferred (to cook in the kitchen with solid fuel would require a room too large to provide in an inter-war or post-war family house). The Committee's recommendations were given effect by the official Housing Manuals of 1944 and 1949. The effect of these increases in standards on costs was considered in detail by the Committee of Inquiry into the Cost of House Building (35), which estimated that the cost of a three-bedroomed house built to 1947 standards in 1938/39 would have been £518, compared with the actual average cost of £380 for three-bedroomed houses built in 1938/39; the cost of the increase in standards between pre- and post-war building was thus put at about 35%. Not all of this was the consequences of more space; higher standards of fittings were also important.

So large an increase in standards and costs soon came under pressure when the amount of capital made available for house building was being tightly held down and housing shortages were so severe. In the early 1950s there was a strong shift of emphasis towards quantity rather than quality. Although this shift of emphasis is generally associated with the Conservative government's "300,000 houses a year" drive, it began before the change of government. Circular 38/51 (issued on 28 April 1951) made the second WC in five bed-space houses optional, and authorized the building of such houses with less than the 900 sq.ft. minimum area provided that the size of individual rooms did not fall below the standards set in 1944 and 1949. The process was taken a stage further in November 1951 (after the change of government) when Circular 70/51 encouraged local authorities to use the specimen designs in "Houses 1952" (published by the Ministry of Housing and Local Government), which included three bedroom five bed-space houses with a floor area (including out-buildings) 150 sq.ft. less than in houses completed in 1951, with about two-thirds of the reduction being in circulation space (hall, passages, stairs, landings) and one-third in storage space. The building of three-bedroomed four bed-space houses (i.e. with two of the bedrooms large enough only for one person) and two-bedroomed houses was also encouraged. The new government took up and gave greatly added impetus to what was already an emerging policy. The quality of the houses built to the reduced space standards was strongly criticized. The reduction in circulation space was held to have produced cramped and dark halls and stairs; and maintaining the floor area of the rooms concealed a reduction in the amount of usable space because the rooms were of such awkward shapes (36). There was little further change during the 1950s.

In the 1960s there was a swing back to emphasis towards quality. Housing standards were again considered by the Central Housing Advisory Committee, which in 1961 published its report Homes for Today and Tomorrow, generally referred to by the name of the Chairman of the sub-committee that produced it, Sir Parker Morris. The report referred to the social changes that had taken place in the 1950s, to the rise in incomes and living standards, including the possessions that people had in their homes, and concluded that housing standards should be raised in order to meet these new circumstances. Higher space standards and a second WC were recommended; but the principal change was the much increased emphasis given to heating, both of living rooms and of bedrooms. This was new; the development of central heating made such standards achievable at reasonable cost (made easier still in the 1960s by the reduction in the cost, relative to prices generally, of gas and oil). The Parker Morris report was addressed to public and private sector alike. The initial response of the government of the day was to give mild encouragement to local authorities to adopt Parker Morris standards for their new houses, and charge rents for them that reflected the qualtiy of the accommodation offered (37).

The Labour government that took office in 1964 went further in putting the Parker Morris recommendations into effect in the public sector. This decision was the more noteworthy because it was taken at a time when a substantial rise in the number of houses built year by year was intended. The Parker Morris report estimated that building to the standards recommended would raise the cost of a two-storey five bedspace house by about 11%, by coincidence about the same proportionate change (though of course in the opposite direction) as that made in 1951-52. In the same White Paper (38) that announced that the government would expect local authorities to incorporate the Parker Morris space and heating standards also stated that the government's first objective was to reach half a million houses a year by 1970 (as compared with 383,000 in the UK in 1964). The Parker Morris standards were made mandatory for local authorities in 1967. When the number of houses built was increased in the early 1950s, quality had had to take second place to quantity; but in the mid-1960s the government of the day sought both higher quality and a larger quantity. As mentioned above, industrialized system building was seen as the means by which this was to be achieved.

Standards of housing built for private owners must be considered more briefly. Table IV.11 shows that there was an increase in the proportion of new houses that were detached and a reduction in the proportion built in terraces. There is little information about densities of houses built for owner-occupiers; if (as is likely) detached houses were built closer together, there is nothing in the changes in the mix of house types shown in Table IV.11 that is inconsistent with the widespread impression that houses built in the 1950s, 1960s and 1970s were packed closer together than houses built in the 1920s and 1930s.

Table IV.11 - Types of Owner-Occupied Houses According to When They Were Built

(percentages)

	1919-40	1940-64	1965-72	1973-76
Detached	23.2	30.2	41.7	53.7
Semi-detached	55.5	40.8	43.2	29.2
Terrace	21.3	29.0	15.2	17.1
Total	100.0	100.0	100.0	100.0

Source: National Dwelling and Housing Survey, 1977.

There were changes in the equipment and fittings installed in houses built for private owners. As with the public sector, the principal change in this respect was central heating. Before 1960 this was rare, but in houses built in 1973-76 for private owners, 85% had central heating (39). By the later 1970s gas, electric, and oil-fired central heating (especially gas) had become so common that the coal industry began to advertise in the house-building trade press to persuade developers to build houses with chimneys so that owners would have the choice of putting in coal fires if they wished. Better fitted kitchens became increasingly common, and an advertised selling point for new houses; and the number of electric power points was increased to provide for the much larger range of electrical appliances now used in the home. Comparisons between Parker Morris standards in the public sector and the standards of houses built for sale to private owners are not easy to make, not least because the latter are not specifically designed for stated numbers of occupiers, hence the space standards cannot really be applied. But those authorities that in 1974/75 bought new houses from developers (authorized as a special measure because the government of the day wanted as rapid an increase in the supply of houses for letting by public authorities as could be got, and the slump in demand to buy houses made developers interested in selling to local authorities) frequently found that they often did not meet in full Parker Morris standards other than for space. They were generally popular with tenants nevertheless (40).

Quality in the sense of standards of workmanship and of materials used is very hard to measure or even judge. There appears to be some tendency to look back to a past when standards of workmanship were higher and better materials were used, but when, nevertheless, contemporary comment was full of complaints about how low standards had fallen compared with a still earlier era. Building for private owners did not, though, experience anything like the troubles that arose in the public sector with some forms of industrialized building. Improved protection was given to purchasers of new houses by making registration with the National House Building Council (NHBC, formerly National House Buildiers Registration Council) in practice virtually obligatory. Registration involved inspection while construction was in progress and when complete, with compensation for defective work from the Council's own funds if the builder had gone out of business in the meantime. The government negotiated in 1967 an agreement whereby building societies and local authorities would make loans for the purchase of new houses only where the house had an NHBC certificate, a semi-private purchaser protection scheme (only semi-private because the responsible Minister obtained the right to appoint the Chairman of NHBC) where such protection was considered to be greatly needed in view of the frequency with which firms in the building trade went out of existence. Agreement was, perhaps, more readily reached on a voluntary arrangement because the government of the day let it be known that it was prepared to contemplate statutory action if voluntary arrangements were not agreed.

Replacement and Renovation of Older Houses

Replacement was touched on above in connection with "net new building". The slum clearance programme of the 1930s was suspended at the outbreak of war, and remained effectively in abeyance until the mid-1950s. In the circumstances of shortage, an unfit house was better than none. But at the end of 1953 the government of the day decided that the much increased building programme had reduced shortages sufficiently to allow the slum clearance programme to be resumed (41). As in 1933, local authorities were required to submit estimates of the number of unfit dwellings together with programmes for dealing with them (42). As in the 1930s, the subsidy to local authorities for building houses for general needs was abolished (in 1956), with building to rehouse people displaced by slum clearance still subsidized. The slum clearance campaign of the 1950s, 1960s and early 1970s was fought on the same terrain as in the 1930s in much the same way. The geographical concentration was very similar, and so was the number of dwellings closed year by year. From the beginning of the 1960s to the early 1970s it ran at some 60,000 to 70,000 a year (see Table B of the Annex to this chapter) notwithstanding attempts by the government in the later 1960s to achieve a faster rate of clearance. Ministry of Housing and Local Government Circular 93/69 called for returns from local authorities of the numbers of unfit houses to be dealt with in the next four years, and said: "Ministers hope that wherever the local situation requires it these programmes will show a steadily increasing pace of clearance over the four year period". Dwellings demolished under slum clearance powers had to be unfit and not capable of being made fit at reasonable expense. The definition of unfitness was tightened in 1954 (43) by the removal of the reference to "standards of housing of the working classes in the district", and in 1969 (44) by inclusion of bad internal arrangement (such as

123

dangerous stairs) as a ground for unfitness; but basically the concept remained as it had been in the inter-war years and even earlier, that of a dwelling so defective as to be unsuitable for living in. The statutory definition (45) of an unfit house was one that is so far defective in one or more of the following respects as not to be reasonably suitable for human habitation in that condition: repair; stability; freedom from damp; natural lighting; ventilation; water supply; drainage and sanitary conveniences; facilities for preparing and cooking food and disposing of waste water; and internal arrangement.

Between 1955 and 1975, 1.3 million dwellings were demolished under slum clearance powers. If the small number of dwellings demolished between 1945 and 1955 are included, then nearly 20% of pre-1914 dwellings still standing in 1945 had been demolished by 1975, and almost 30% of pre-1890 dwellings, as it was the oldest dwellings that were most likely to be demolished. A distinction can be drawn between houses that were unfit by the standards of 1954, or even 1930, from the day they were built, and those that deteriorated into unfitness. Of the defining conditions for unfitness, all but repair picked out dwellings that had been built to standards that in the twentieth century were looked on as unacceptably low. There were many streets of such houses next to each other, and area clearance schemes to remove them were the central core of slum clearance in the 1930s and again in the 1950s and 1960s. Clearance of such areas was inherently a finite task, and by the mid-1970s it was a greatly reduced task. In retrospect it is not difficult to see why the amount of demolition and replacement should thus begin to decline. But that was not what was foreseen in a decade or so previously: the early and middle 1960s looked beyond the clearance of slums towards the replacement of houses that were not unfit in the technical sense just described, but regarded as not worth improving. In its statement of policy in 1963, the government stated that it wanted to see: "a vigorous drive launched for the redevelopment of the depressed residential areas just as soon as each town has cleared the worst of its slums and overtaken its present housing shortage" (46). Renewal of the outworn areas was considered to be a task for private enterprise with local authorities frequently having to assemble land (using their

124

powers of compulsory purchase, which private
developers did not, of course, possess) and to help
in rehousing tenants who had been living in low
rented houses and needing assistance with the rent
of a new house. Just how such redevelopment would
work had not been studied when the policy was
announced, though the government promised to amend
the law if that were found to be necessary to allow
redevelopment to go ahead (47). The next government considered in 1965 that "up to 2 million" new
houses were needed to replace houses that were not
yet slums but not worth impoving (48) but did not
have anything to add to what its predecessor had
said about how to organize replacement of obsoles-
cent housing. The estimate of the number of houses
that were not unfit but which nevertheless ought to
be replaced was derived from the age of the housing
stock. The Labour government's National Plan said
in 1965: "Most houses are out of date, even if they
are not entirely worn out, by the time they are 80
years old, and if it were not for the chronic and
persistent shortages one would expect most houses
of that age to be replaced as the normal thing"
(49). This view about the replacement of older
housing was widely held in the early and middle
1960s and gave rise to very high figures for the
number of houses that 'ought' to be replaced, and
hence the number of new houses 'needed'. Such
figures for replacement building were what lay
behind targets of 500,000 new houses a year, not
very large increases in the number of separate
households.

In the event, the number of dwellings demolished and replaced year by year declined as
clearing slum areas came to an end. Replacement of
fit but old houses never gathered pace. One major
reason was financial: two detailed studies by
private developers (50) showed that such redevelopment could not produce a commercially adequate
return on the investors' outlay if the new houses
built were of modern standards and let at rents the
present occupiers could afford. The Halliwell
Report, which referred to an area of 19th century
housing in Bolton, estimated the return at just
over four percent. As was pointed out by McKie
(51), this was less than the Victorian "five percent philanthropists" reckoned to get; in the 1960s
as in the 1860s, the rents that the occupiers of
poor housing could afford were not enough to cover
the cost, including a commercial return, of better

housing. But just as important as a stumbling block if compulsory redevelopment of fit though old housing had been attempted in the 1960s, was the progressive transfer of older housing to owner-occupation. Most pre-1914 houses had been built for renting; but in 1938, 24% were owner-occupied (52); by 1960 the proportion had risen to 41% (53) and in 1977 some 60% of the remaining pre-1914 dwellings were owner-occupied (54). Compulsory redevelopment would affect large numbers of owner-occupiers, many of whom lived in older and poorer houses because that is what they could afford. How they would fare if their houses were demolished, even with compensation equal to market value, appears never to have been really considered. The way in which replacement of older but not unfit houses would work appears not to have been at all well thought out when it was discussed in the early 1960s. The doctrine, such as it was, seems to have been borrowed from slum clearance, modified only by private enterprise instead of local authorities doing the replacement building, apparently for rent. In the event, of course, the ideas were never put to the test. In the 1970s the impetus went out of slum clearance; so compulsory clearance and replacement of fit though old houses never came to be tried.

The transfer to owner-occupation of older housing was probably one of the reasons why opposition to the clearance even of unfit houses increased, for the underlying presuppositions of slum clearance could be applied only with considerable difficulty to owner-occupied housing. The working doctrine had grown up when unfit houses were let by private landlords, who could be regarded as making profits from activities that were against the public interest, and hence not entitled to compensation for being compelled to desist from letting accommodation that was so far defective as not to be reasonably suitable for human habitation any more than someone prevented from selling contaminated food that was for human consumption. That was the rationale of the rule that site value should be the basis of compensation. This rule was modified for the benefit of householders who in the war and early post-war years of housing shortages bought houses that were subsequently represented as unfit; but not until 1969 did owner-occupiers receive market value compensation for houses condemned as unfit, and even then there were exceptions (mainly to prevent rented houses from being transferred hurriedly to owner-occupation to benefit from the additional compensation). Even market value compensation would leave the displaced owner-occupiers in difficulties if a fit house would cost considerably more and their financial circumstances did not enable them to borrow sufficient to purchase one.

Resistance by owner-occupiers, though, was far from being the whole explanation of the falling away of slum clearance. Another major part of the explanation was the diminishing esteem in which much new local authority house building was held, houses built by the less satisfactory industrialized methods as well as tower blocks. To replace nineteenth century unfit housing by such dwellings could be derided as being no more than 'new slums for old'. There was documented evidence to show that residents of areas to be cleared as unfit and redeveloped were often far from enthusiastic and sometimes hostile to what was being done, supposedly for their benefit (55). A policy that to start with had a strong admixture of moral fervour was running out of supporters by the mid-1970s; "pensioning off the bulldozer" had by then become a catch phrase. The ideas of the early 1960s about making a start on demolishing older but fit houses once the slums had been dealt with had been forgotten.

Only at a late stage were demolition and replacement seen as an alternative to renovation of houses. Until the 1970s they ran in parallel. The use of powers under the Public Health Acts and the Housing Acts to compel the owners of unfit houses to make them fit, included putting in proper drainage, sanitation and water supply when these were lacking, and carrying out necessary repairs has a history that reaches back to the 1870s. Such work was entirely at the owners' expense, and what the owners could afford was a constraint of some importance on how vigorously the powers of compulsion could be used. The use of powers to compel owners to bring houses up to the standard of fitness for habitation, must however be distinguished from measures to promote improvement to standards higher than this. Such measures are, with only limited exceptions, an innovation of post-1945 housing policy. The earliest instance of grants to private owners towards the cost of improvement of houses they owned was the grants for the improvement of farm cottages under the Housing (Rural Workers) Act of 1926. It was used only in a small way, with about 20,000 applications for grants approved (56). In the opinion of the Departmental Committee on Housing, which reported in 1933, one of the principal reasons was that: ".... the initiative of application rests with the private owners. However willing the authority may be .... it is often difficult to induce owners to make applications for the assistance which the authorities are empowered to grant" (57). These words remained true when improvement grants became much more generally available. The Committee (known from the name of its Chairman as the Moyne Committee) advocated compulsory purchase by local authorities of houses for which clearance was inappropriate but which needed work to bring them to fitness which the owners could not or would not carry out. The recommendation was not acted on, and acquisition of houses by local authorities for improvement did not appear as a policy in the 1960s and 1970s.

The first post-war landmark in policy on grants to private owners for the improvement of houses was the Housing Act 1949, which made such grants available in all areas, as a matter of local authorities' discretion. The Housing and House Purchase Act 1959 introduced the "standard grant" that could be claimed by house owners (whether owner-occupier or private landlord) from local authorities as of right, provided that:

i)   before the work the house was lacking one or more of the basic amenities (58);
ii) when the works are finished all the basic amenities would be present; and
iii) the house must have a useful life of 15 years or more.

There was a further change of policy announced in 1968 in the White Paper Older Houses into New Homes (59), and enacted into law by the Housing Act 1969. The grants available were made very much larger, and most of the restrictive conditions previously attached to grants were withdrawn (in particular a minimum length of time for which the owner must either himself live in the house where grant aided work has been done or let it to a tenant). Local authorities were empowered to declare General Improvement Areas, in which they could spend up to

£100 per house on environmental improvements in order to encourage owners of houses there to improve them. The 1969 Act was followed by a substantial increase in the number of grants approved (see Annex, Table C at end of chapter). There was a further large increase following the Housing Act 1971 which raised the proportion of grant to approved costs in the "assisted areas" of the country (60) temporarily from one-half to three-quarters for work completed before June 1974. The number of grants approved then fell away sharply. The Housing Act 1974 introduced a series of restrictions to reduce the chance of grants being paid towards the cost of work that would otherwise have been done entirely at the owners' expense. The exclusion of second homes was pro-bably of minor importance; but the exclusion of dwellings with rateable value above £300 was much more important, and so was the reintroduction of the requirement repealed in 1969, for repayment of the grant if the dwelling was sold within three years. The stepping up of public expenditure on improvement at the end of the 1960s cannot, on the evidence available, be seen as a switch from slum clearance forced on the government by the pressures to limit public expenditure. At the time the Housing Act 1969 was being passed, the government was calling on local authorities to increase the rate at which unfit dwellings were cleared. There appear to have been two main reasons for the policy of increasing the amount of grant-aided improve-ment. One was the evidence that the number of unfit houses was much greater than had previously been supposed. The other was that they were far less concentrated. The returns of numbers of unfit dwellings collected from local authorities had been criticized as untrustworthy (61) and the national total derived from them unreliable, because com-parison of individual authorities' figures showed that inconsistent criteria had been applied. In 1967 the first House Condition Survey was carried out to provide an estimate based on uniform criteria, and the results were published in 1968. The total of 1.8 million unfit houses that it showed was nearly twice as great as the total obtained by adding the figures returned by local authorities, and nothing like so heavily concen-trated in the industrial cities and towns. For many unfit houses area clearance was not the remedy; and if demolition and replacement were the only way of tackling unfit houses, unfitness would be around for an unconscionably long time. So greater emphasis on improvement followed logically. Another influence was the work of economists, notably Needleman (62), in applying the theory of discounting to decisions about how much would be worth spending on renovating an old house rather than demolishing and replacing it. At the 8% test rate of discount that was then deemed appropriate for appraisal of nationalized industry investments, this analysis showed that the amount that could justifiably be spent on an old house to give it a further life of 30 years was a large fraction of the cost of replacing it by a new house with a life of 60 years. This analysis appears to have been a major reason for raising the maximum amount of discretionary improvement grants (63), from one-half of £800 approved cost to one-half of £2,000.

Local authorities also increased very substantially the amounts they spent on improvement of their own houses. In the later 1960s and the early 1970s this was primarily on modernizing and upgrading houses built in the inter-war years, but in the middle 1970s urban authorities purchased houses from private owners with a view to improving them, in numbers running into the tens of thousands a year. By the end of the decade emphasis had begun to shift towards remedying defects that had become apparent in houses and flats built by industrialized methods.

The total number of improvement grants paid to private owners can be estimated from grants approved (Annex, Table C) at about 120,000 in 1949-59, about 700,000 in 1960-69; 650,000 in 1970-74 and 330,000 in 1975-79. In the thirty years from 1949, some 1.8 million houses belonging to private owners were improved with the aid of grants, compared with 1.5 million demolished, out of a total of about 7.4 million pre-1914 dwellings still in being in 1949. All had to have all the standard amenities when the work was complete. Some may have had them beforehand, and there is no way of knowing how many. That improvement grants made a sizeable contribution to the reduction in the number of dwellings lacking standard amenities is not in doubt. Some two-thirds to three-quarters of the grants to private owners went to owner-occupiers (64), and in this way improvement grants probably operated as a subsidy that enabled considerable numbers of households with only moderate incomes to enter owner-occupation. Large amounts of improvement work were done without the aid of grants. By comparing the net reduction in the number of dwellings lacking amenities with the number of demolitions and the number of grants (65), the number of houses previously without a bath, but where one was installed without the aid of a grant between 1951 and 1976, can be estimated at about 1 million; and about 2½ million houses had one or more of the amenities installed without a grant. An estimate can also be made of the number of houses and flats that had central heating installed, an improvement that was not usually grant aided. The Government Social Survey estimated that in 1960 about 800,000 houses had central heating (66), whereas in 1977 about 4½ million houses and flats built in 1960 or earlier did so (67). Of this total, about 3.3 million were owner-occupied, 0.8 million rented from local authorities, and 0.4 million rented from private landlords. Some 3.7 million dwellings that did not have central heating in 1960 had had it installed by 1977. Three-fifths of all owner-occupied houses built in the inter-war years had central heating in 1977, as did two-fifths of owner-occupied houses built before 1914. Very substantial amounts were evidently spent in the 1960s and 1970s in modernizing privately owned houses built in the inter-war years and before 1914. This was the mechanism by which obsolescence of older houses was dealt with, not demolition of old (but not unfit) houses and their replacement by new.

Households, the Housing Stock, and Housing Conditions

The increase in the number of households, new building, replacement, and improvement can now be brought together to analyse changing housing conditions, with particular reference to households unsatisfactorily housed. There are three aspects of unsatisfactory housing: insufficiency, the consequence of there being too few dwellings in relation to households; physical condition (unfitness, lack of amenities, poor repair), and mis-match (dwellings unsuitable for the people that live in them but suitable for others). Insufficiency of dwellings and consequent sharing may be discussed first; for this purpose the changing total of households must be compared with the housing stock. This balance was shown in Table IV.1 for 1945, and can be carried forward to 1981. This is not a wholly straightforward calculation, owing to problems with the census estimates of the stock of dwellings as compared with the recorded changes in the stock of dwellings through new building, conversions, and demolitions. The source of the difficulties was applying the concept of a separate dwelling to accommodation in what were once large one-family residences but since adapted for occupation by two households or more. How much adaptation qualified for counting as structurally separate was hard to define and still harder to apply in census practice. There is evidence that both in 1951 and in 1961 separate dwellings were over-counted. In 1971 instead of counting separate dwellings directly, the number was worked out from answers to questions in the census on sharing of rooms and access, but in the absence of a post-enumeration check of the kind published for 1966 and 1981, it is not known how well this procedure worked; the definition counted bed-sitting rooms as separate dwellings, but they were taken out from the official census-based dwelling stock estimate. An amended estimate is therefore used in Table IV.12 for the stock of dwellings in 1951 and 1961. Treating as shared accommodation units that in the census were counted as separate increases the number of sharing households, of course (68). Owing to these adjustments the figures are approximate only.

There are a number of uncertainties about the figures, including in 1981 whether some of the "concealed lone-parent families" were in reality non-married couples with child(ren) (69), and any effects of the change of definition in 1981 of a separate household (70), but the broad outlines of the change in the balance between the stock of housing and the demand and need are fairly clear. New building between 1945 and 1951 plus repair of war-damaged houses was sufficient to keep up with the increase in the number of households, and probably to permit a very small reduction in the number of households (including "concealed" families) having to share. This was in marked contrast to what happened after World War I when shortages worsened right up to 1925.

In the next two decades the stock of housing was increased by substantially more than the number

Table IV.12 - Households, Dwellings and Sharing in England and Wales 1945-81

(thousands)

	1945	1951	1961	1971	1981
Total dwellings	11,100	12,330	14,545	17,024	19,086
Vacant dwellings	(...)	138	314	676	795
Separate households	12,250	13,259	14,724	16,709	18,336
Concealed married couples	950	750	538	280	159
Concealed lone-parent families	(200)(a)	185	164	155	184
Potential households	13,400	14,194	15,426	17,144	18,680
Balance between dwellings and potential households	-2,300	-1,850	-900	-120	+410
Sharing households	2,050	2,200	1,060	780(b)	455(c)
All households and concealed families without a dwelling to themselves (d)					
Number	4,350	4,070	2,460	1,650	1,140
Percentage of all potential households	32	29	16	10	6

Notes: (a) Pro-rata to married couple concealed families.
(b) Census enumerated figure for 637,000 plus 130,000 bed-sitting rooms not counted in the census as sharing.
(c) Enumerated figure of 274,000, adjusted for the 40% understatement of non-self-contained accommodation indicated by the post enumeration survey.
(d) Includes the households with whom "concealed families" live.

Source: Housing Policy Technical Volume, Tables I.5 and I.14;
Housing and Construction Statistics 1973-83 Table 2; and
Department of the Environment, 1981-Based Estimates of the Number of Households

of households. Nevertheless, not until the later
1960s did the balance between dwellings and potential households return to what it had been in 1939.
In that sense it took twenty years to make good the
effects of the war on English housing, and there is
here the reason why shortages affected housing
policy so powerfully and for so long. By 1971 the
housing stock had become larger in proportion to
the number of households than it had ever been
before; and the number of sharing and "concealed"
households smaller, both absolutely and in proportion to the total number of households. But there
were still not sufficient houses to achieve the
1945 objective of "a separate dwelling for every
family that wishes to have one" (71), if "every
family" is taken to mean "every household". In the
1970s the change in the balance between housing and
households was only modestly smaller than in 1961-
71, no small achievement in what was, as we shall
see, a very turbulent decade for housing finance.
Table IV.12 shows changes in the balance, and not
whether at any stage there were "enough" dwellings.
Included among the potential households without a
separate house or flat to themselves are some that
live that way from choice, e.g. couples looking
after elderly parents, or deserted young mothers
going back to their parents; but on the other side
of the balance the housing stock includes second
homes and holiday accommodation (about 215,000 in
1981, including accommodation with people present
at the census) and housing empty while undergoing
repair or other work (180,000). In 1981 there was
probably broad equality, in national terms, between
the number of houses and flats available and the
number of households living independently or
wishing to do so (though not counting of course
single people wishing to set up house on their
own). That would imply shortages in some areas.
During the 1970s the number of households recorded
as homeless increased year by year even though the
housing stock was increasing faster than the number
of households. Why this should have been so is
considered in Chapter IX.

With the reduction in sharing went a fall in
the number of households living in crowded conditions. The point was made in the previous chapter
that crowding could be caused by large households
having to live in ordinary-sized dwellings and
ordinary-sized households in parts of dwellings.
By the 1970s crowding caused by sharing had fallen

to low levels, as Table IV.13 shows.

Table IV.13 - Crowded Households
(More than 1½ Persons per Room) 1931-81

(thousands)	Sharing	Not Sharing	Total
1931	439	735	1,174
1951	233	431	664
1961	107	308	415
1971	47	179	226
1981	9	100	109

Source: Census of England and Wales: 1931 Housing Report and Tables, Table VIII; 1951 Housing Report, Table 2; 1961 Housing Tables, Table 4; 1971 Housing Tables, Table 3; 1981 Housing and Households, Tables 2 and 3.

Overcrowding in the statutory sense became too uncommon to measure by means of surveys. The number of overcrowded households was found by the 1936 survey to be some 345,000; in 1960 the number was estimated at 81,000 (72), and since then has not been measured. From the similarity with the number of households living at densities of over two persons per room, the number had probably fallen by 1971 to about 30,000-40,000 and in 1981 to under about 20,000.

Even by the standards of the 1930s, statutory overcrowding was a very low standard indeed, and by the 1960s was obsolete as a measure of whether a household was short of space. Much more commonly used was the "bedroom standard". This standard was developed by the Government Social Survey for use in the 1960 housing survey. It had no statutory force, but would seem to correspond with what most households considered proper. The 'standard' number of bedrooms was:

(a) one for each married couple;
(b) one each for other men and women over age 20;
(c) one for each two persons of the same sex aged 10 to 20;
(d) one for any person aged 10 to 20 and a child under 10 of the same sex;
(e) one for any person aged 10 to 20 not paired as in (c) or (d);
(f) one for each two of any remaining children;
(g) one for any remaining child.

A "bedroom" was any room used for sleeping (whether designed for the purpose or not); and all such rooms counted irrespective of size, a matter of some difficulty as some houses have a small bedroom that is little more than a box room where there would not be space for separate beds for two children. The census results are not analysed in terms of the bedroom standard, but data from the General Household Survey for 1971 and 1981 can be compared with the 1960 Housing Survey.

Table IV.14 - Households and Bedroom Standard by Tenure:
England and Wales 1960, 1971 and 1981

(thousands)

	1960	1971	1981
Fewer Rooms than Standard			
Owner-occupiers	360	290	300
Local Authority Tenants	470	380	340
Other Tenants	770	320	110
All Tenures	1,600	990	790
Equal to Standard or One Above			
Owner-occupiers	4,320	5,680	6,660
Local Authority Tenants	2,860	3,600	4,030
Other Tenants	3,470	2,560	1,740
All Tenures	10,650	11,840	12,430
Two or More Above Standard			
Owner-occupiers	1,310	2,260	3,270
Local Authority Tenants	200	650	730
Other Tenants	660	700	450
All Tenures	2,170	3,610	4,450

Source: 1960 from The Housing Situation in 1960, Tables 14 and 72; 1971 from General Household Survey Introductory Report (HMSO 1973) Table 5.23, 1981 from General Household Survey, with household totals from the census (household present with usual residents, living in permanent buildings.

There was a sharp fall in the number of households with fewer bedrooms than standard; the fall in the number of such households renting from private landlords was, in all probability, mainly the consequence of reduced sharing. Large households were particularly likely to be local authority tenants, and some of them were accommodated in standard three-bedroomed houses and not the four-bedroomed houses needed to meet the standard.

For many years, unsatisfactory housing caused by mis-match of size of household to size of house meant crowding. But in the post-war years as the number of one-person and two-person households grew fast (Table IV.7) and family-size houses remained the type most commonly built, the situation of householder with a larger house than he (or more commonly she) could conveniently manage began to attract interest. Three-bedroomed houses occupied by one man or woman alone or a married couple by themselves were by far the most frequent instances of households with two more bedrooms than the standard. This is usually the result of the family cycle: many couples move into a three-bedroomed house before their first child is born; many years later the children grow up and leave and the couple are again on their own, and later on there is only the widowed survivor. The number of older couples, and widows and widowers living as independent households grew fast in the 1950s, the 1960s and the 1970s, and hence too did "under-occupation". The higher proportion of married couples becoming owner-occupiers fairly soon after getting married has also increased the number of couples who are for a time in a three-bedroomed house on their own. "Under-occupation" was for the most part neither involuntary nor a problem, though the number of elderly people who would have been better off with a smaller and easier to run home was probably not negligible.

From sufficiency of separate dwellings in number and size we may turn to their facilities and amenities. The first national information about households lacking basic amenities was collected by the Government Social Survey in 1947. For 1960 and 1964 subsequent surveys provide the information, and for 1971 and 1981 the House Condition Survey. In 1976 and 1981, unlike 1971, there were separate surveys for England and Wales; rather than go into the complicated and disputed question of how comparable the Welsh survey figures were with the English, separate figures for England in 1971 (extracted from the survey for that year) are shown for comparison with the 1981 English House Condition Survey. The so-called "basic amenities" were included throughout, that is to say a fixed bath or shower in a bathroom; inside WC, sink, wash hand basin; and a supply of hot and cold water to the bath, wash hand basin and sink. A ventilated food store was included with the amenities until the later 1960s, when it was dropped as obsolete in view of the spread of ownership of refrigerators. Presence of a piped water supply was included in the 1947 and 1960 surveys, and the 1961 Census; by the time the contents of the 1971 Census and the House Condition Survey were being settled, however, a piped water supply was so near to being universal that no question about it was asked. As well as the water supply, bath, WC, wash hand basin and sink, details are given of the proportion of houses without electricity or gas lighting. This is another example of something that by the 1970s had come to be taken for granted but which many households at the end of the war were without. Table IV.15 brings together these survey data.

If dwellings where one or more of the basic amenities were absent were neither more nor less likely to be shared than other dwellings (a reasonable enough assumption at first sight), than the proportion of households lacking one or more of the 'basic amenities' fell from about 64% in 1947 to only 5% in 1981. In absolute terms the number of such dwellings fell from about 7.3 million in 1947 to about 1.0 million (England and Wales figures). As late as 1947, one-eighth of households lived in houses with neither gas nor electricity, and so depended on oil lamps for light. By 1960 such conditions were virtually at an end; so too was dependence for water supply on a standpipe outside the dwelling or, in country areas, a well.

Resources, Costs, Finance and Policy

Before commenting on the policies pursued and on the course of public expenditure on housing, it is useful to show the changes in gross fixed investment in dwellings, both absolutely and as a proportion of gross domestic product. The figures are taken from the national income accounts, as revised in 1984 to include in gross investment in

Table IV.15 - Households Lacking Specified Services and Amenities

(Thousands)

	1947 (a)	1960	1964	1971/1971(b)	1981
Fixed bath or shower (in bathroom in 1971 and 1981)	5,300	3,210	2,478	1,630/1,621	573
Inside WC	...	2,080	1,582	1,790/1,737 (e)	479
Wash hand basin	5,200	4,560 (c)	3,596	2,043/2,034	567
Sink	...	360	312	84/77	74
Hot water supply to bath, hand basin and sink	8,000	... (d)	193	2,374/2,365	729
Piped water supply	900	180	...	.../...	...
Electricity	2,000	570	...	.../...	...
Both electricity and gas	1,500	40	...	.../...	...
All households	12,570	14,422	14,828	17,100/16,137	18,066

Notes: (a) Total 12,570,000 (interpolated from the 1945 and 1951 figures in Table IV.12).
(b) First figure refers to England and Wales, the second to England. The figures for England are taken from the report of the 1981 House Condition Survey.
(c) Probably not wholly comparable with 1947, as in 1947 the question referred to a wash basin in a bathroom.
(d) Information about lack of each individually but not about any one of the three.
(e) Outside the building; previous surveys counted WCs attached to building with those inside the building.

Source: 1947: The British Household, Tables 37, 39, 42, 43 and 48.
1960: The Housing Situation in 1960, Tables 38, 30, 40 and 42.
1961/64: The Housing Survey in England and Wales, 1964, Table 4.2.
1971 and 1981: English House Condition Survey 1981.
Figures refer to all dwellings, including those vacant.

dwellings all private expenditure on house improvement, not just (as hitherto) that aided by grants. The "price relative" for gross fixed investment in dwellings is also shown, that is to say the movement in its unit cost relative to the general price level.

Table IV.16 - Gross Fixed Investment in Dwellings in the United Kingdom

(1970 = 100)

| | Percent of Gross Domestic Product at Current Prices (a) | | | Total (Both Sectors) in £ million at 1970 Prices | (b) Price Relative for Investment in Dwellings |
	Private Sector	Public Sector	Total		
1936/38	...	...	3.2	975	78
1948-51	0.5	2.3	2.7	690	114
1952-55	1.2	2.3	3.6	985	119
1956-59	1.6	1.3	2.9	940	110
1960-64	2.1	1.2	3.3	1,295	105
1965-67	2.3	1.8	4.1	1,925	102
1970-74	2.5	1.5	4.0	1,980	112
1975-79	2.6	1.5	4.1	2,035	123
1954	1.4	2.3	3.8	1,080	115
1958	1.5	1.1	2.7	880	109
1964	2.3	1.5	3.8	1,595	107
1968	2.5	1.9	4.3	2,135	101
1970	2.1	1.6	3.6	1,870	100
1972	2.7	1.3	4.0	2,095	104
1976	2.7	1.8	4.5	2,125	125
1979	2.7	1.2	3.8	2,010	122

Notes: (a) The percentages are of gross domestic product at market prices to facilitate comparisons with other countries (Chapter IX), hence the difference from the figures for 1936-38 in Table III.12, which is a percentage of GDP at factor cost.

(b) 'Price' of investment in dwellings relative to 'price' of gross domestic product.

Source: Feinstein, National Income Expenditure and Output, Tables 3, 39, 40, 61 and 63; Economic Trends Annual Supplement (1985 Ed.) pages 8, 13, 48 and 59.

The figures for gross fixed investment in
dwellings should be read in conjunction with the
number of houses built (Appendix Table A). In the
1970s investment in improvement of houses became
much more important relative to new building. Even
so, in volume terms the peak in the mid-1970s was
no higher than in the building boom of the 1960s,
if anything a little lower. Public sector investment in housing had three peaks; the late 1940s and
early 1950s, the mid 1960s, and the mid 1970s, for
reasons that will be commented on in the discussion
of policy.

For the financing of housing, both public and
private, prices are important as well as volume,
and Table IV.16 shows that there were marked
changes in the price of house-building work relative to the general level of prices. There was
first a sharp rise in building costs during the war
years, which in Table IV.16 is reflected in the
comparison between 1936-38 and 1948-51. Between
1938 and 1947 building costs increased in real
terms by about 35% (73), and unlike the increase in
building costs between 1913 and 1920, was never
fully reversed. By the early 1960s building costs
had fallen back by about 10% in real terms compared
with 1947-48, but that still left them some 20%
higher than before the war. Just why the fall in
productivity in the war years was never made good
lacks a wholly convincing explanation, unless it is
to be found in there being no post-war slump like
that of 1920-22 to force the reversal of cost-
increasing changes in ways of working. In the
1960s the trend of building costs was only slightly
downwards in real terms, if that. The construction
boom of the early 1970s then brought about an
increase of about 30% in building costs relative to
the general price level between 1970 and 1974, and
only about a third of this was subsequently
reversed.

These changes in building costs do not wholly
explain the fact that house prices rose, taking one
year with another, significantly faster than the
general price level. This tendency, which in previous chapters was shown to have been strongly
present in the half century before 1914 but in
abeyance in the inter-war years, re-asserted itself
after 1945, is of the utmost importance for the
history of housing finance and policy. The facts
must first be recounted, and then possible explanations reviewed.

Table IV.17 - House Prices and Building Costs

	House Prices (New Houses)	General Price Level (a)	"Real" House Prices	House Building Costs (b)	"Real" Building Costs
1956-60	2.6	2.5	0.1	1.9	-0.6
1960-65	8.1	3.5	4.4	4.4	0.9
1965-70	6.2	4.9	1.2	5.2	0.3
1970-75	19.1	13.1	5.3	15.3	1.9
1975-79	16.3	13.6	2.4	15.0	1.2

Notes: (a) Gross domestic product deflator.
           (b) Index number of price of house building materials and of average earnings in the construction combined in proportions 2:1.

Source: House prices are at mortgage approval stage. Housing and Construction Statistics 1969-1979, Table 104; Housing and Construction Statistics No. 14, Table I; and Housing Statistics No. 24, Table 50.

There thus appears to have been a rise in new house prices in real terms averaging about 2.9% a year between 1956 and 1979, whereas building costs are estimated to have risen by about 0.9% a year. This increase in building costs is an imprecise figure, since it does not bring to account any extra costs associated with 'labour only' sub-contracting, or increase in non-wage costs borne by employers, and does not allow for any increase in building industry productivity either. Moreover, the house price series in Table IV.17 measures simple average prices, and so includes the effects of any changes in the mix of house types and changes in quality as well as true price increase. To separate true price increase is difficult, but the Department of the Environment's 'mix adjusted' price index calculated from the building society mortgage survey (74) indicates that shifts in the mix of dwellings sold raised the average price of new houses by a little under 1% a year between 1969 and 1979. Some allowance should be made for improvements in the quality of new houses other than in size and type, but from what is known about the cost of central heating half a percent a year is the most that would seem plausible. The implication is that the faster rise in house prices than in building costs was not due entirely to changes in the type, size and quality of dwellings built, and in the 1960s and 1970s there was an increase in the 'true' price of new houses of about 1% a year, or perhaps a little more, relative to costs.

The difference between the increase in house prices and the increase in costs could be taken up in higher profit margins (not included in the measure of costs), higher land prices, or of course both. Profit margins have never been reliably measured for house building, not least because nearly all the listed companies that build houses for sale to private owners have other activities that are included indistinguishably in their published figures for profits and turnover. It would be very surprising if higher profit margins were the whole of the explanation, and the movement of land prices suggests that it was not. The course of land prices in real terms is shown in Table IV.18.

Table IV.18 - Index of Prices of House Building Land

(1970 = 100)

	Actual Land Prices	Land Prices In Real Terms		Actual Land Prices	Land Prices in Real Terms
1963	46	64	1972	190	160
1964	52	70	1973	295	233
1965	58	74	1974	293	201
1966	62	75	1975	202	109
1967	63	74	1976	202	95
1968	73	82	1977	214	88
1969	91	98	1978	261	97
1970	100	100	1979	370	120
1971	113	103			

Note: The 1970 index number of 100 corresponds to £908 a plot.

Source: Housing Statistics No. 23, (1972),Table V; Housing and Construction Statistics No. 8,(1973) Housing and Construction Statistics 1969-1979, Table 3. Prices in real terms measured from the gross domestic product.

There was clearly a connection between the movement of land prices on the one side and the amount of house building and the rate of rise of house prices. The check to the building boom in 1965-66 was associated with a temporary halt to the rise in land prices, which resumed when in 1967 and 1968 building picked up again, followed by a further check as house building fell in 1969 and 1970. The housing boom in the early 1970s was accompanied by a rise in land prices even greater than that in house prices; and at the end of the 1970s the rapid rise in house prices was accompanied by another rise in land prices, even though there was little increase in building. That the relationship was subject to a time-lag was partly due to the lag between prices being agreed and the transaction reported, but there was probably some genuine element of lag as well, because sellers do not adjust their prices immediately according to whether sales are easier or more difficult to make. The received theory has land values being determined by demand, with the price of house building land being determined by what house buyers will pay for houses in a particular place, less the cost of building them. By this reckoning land prices are a measure of the intensity with which demand for building land presses against supply, but without themselves being a cost of production or other influence on house prices. This theory of rising land prices being a consequence and not a cause of rising house prices has however an important limitation: owners of saleable land have expectations about the price they ought to be able to get, and are normally able to take the land off the market if that price cannot be got, which can produce a ratchet effect on land prices. The course of land prices shown in Table IV.18 is consistent with such a ratchet keeping up the price of land when the demand drops moderately as in 1965-66 and 1969-70, being broken only by a slump as severe as that in 1974. Such a process depends on the supply of building land being fairly short, as indeed does the combination of a longer term rise in house prices relative to building costs and a rise in land prices in real terms.

The rise in land prices in real terms (60% in the fifteen years from 1963-64 to 1978-79 taken as a whole) suggests strongly that land supply relative to the demand may have been important in explaining the way house prices rose relative to the general price level in the 1950s, the 1960s and the 1970s, as rents had done before 1914, but with the inter-war years being the exception to this

144

long-term trend. The great increase in the supply of accessible land in the inter-war years was attributed to developments in public transport; for too few households owned cars for the private car to have much effect on the location of housing in the 1930s. But in the 1950s, 1960s and 1970s, the potential effect of car ownership was far greater. From 1.9 million private car licences current in 1948, about the same number as in 1938, the number rose to 3.5 million in 1955, 8.9 million in 1965 and 13.7 million in 1975.

The spread of car ownership on this scale might have been expected to increase the amount of accessible land very greatly indeed. Moreover around London, where sheer size and density limited more severely than elsewhere the number of people who could travel to work by car, there were further extensions to the electrified railway system in the 1950s and the 1960s. Yet the price of housing rose in real terms as it had done before 1914.

The most obvious place to look for explanations of why the post-1950 developments in transport did not work as those in the inter-war years had done is the controls over land use, which were far stricter than in the inter-war years. The Town and Country Planning Act 1947 gave local authorities (the counties and the county boroughs) very far-reaching powers to control land development of all kinds. These powers included refusal of permission for change of use (for instance building houses on land hitherto used for other purposes), and to attach such conditions as were considered appropriate (for instance about number of houses to be built and plot sizes). Local authorities were to draw up development plans (subsequently "structure plans" under the Town and Country Planning Act 1968). The statutory powers themselves, of course, were only a mechanism; what mattered was the way in which they were used. Their use was stongly influenced by the widely held opinion that considered that the suburban development in the inter-war years constituted undesirable "sprawl" that should be restricted closely. The much enhanced dependence on British agriculture during the war years gave added support for a policy of not allowing good agricultural land to be built on, and in the 1950s and 1960s preservation of "good agricultural land" attracted support as well from interests concerned primarily with amenity. By the 1970s, amenity (by then termed "the environment")

145

had become an acceptable reason in its own right for opposing development.

An important particular instance of the policy of restricting suburban development was the extension of the London green belt and the provision for green belts around most of the provincial cities and towns of any size. When in 1955 the government encouraged local planning authorities to designate green belts (Ministry of Housing and Local Government Circular 42/55), the policy was implemented effectively to prevent "sprawl" and preserve access to the countryside. As well, of course, the green belts intensified shortages of building land within and close to the cities and towns. The green belt policy attracted strong support; there was vigorous opposition to any proposal to build in green belts, for whatever purpose and regardless of whether the land that would be built on was green in any sense other than the metaphorical. To assess the balance of advantages of post-1945 policy would require an assessment of many imponderables, and is not attempted here. But in a history of housing policy it is appropriate to draw attention to the probable effect of green belts and other restrictions in contributing to the resumed rise in the price of housing relative to prices generally, and (as noted above) to the policy of building to high densities by local authorities.

The post-1945 increases in the price of land for house building brought land values back into politics again. As was mentioned in Chapter II, land values and land taxation were the subject of acrimonious controversy in the half century before 1914. Interest in the subject waned in the interwar years. But the 100% development charge (a tax at the rate of 100% on the difference between the value of sites as developed and the value in the previous use) imposed by the Town and Country Planning Act of 1947 was one among many expressions of the egalitarian sentiments described earlier in this chapter, that post-war reconstruction should not generate windfall gains for owners of land. How to prevent this was a subject studied in some detail during the war (75). The development charge was repealed in 1953; but the surge in land prices in the early 1960s led to a fresh attempt to tax increases in land values specifically through the Land Commission and Betterment Levy. The Betterment Levy was repealed and the Land Commission was abolished following the change of government in

1970; but the leap in land prices in the early
1970s led the Conservative government to introduce
the Development Gains Tax, replaced by its Labour
successor with the Development Land Tax and Community Land scheme. For a critical account of
these measures, reference may be made to the work
by Professor Prest (76).

The rise in the price of house building and of
building land relative to the general price level
was a powerful reason for the rise in public expenditure on housing. The other was the prolonged
upward trend of interest rates that is depicted in
Table IV.3. Between them they exerted strong
upward pressure on public expenditure on housing
that was alleviated only when capital expenditure
on public sector housing was falling, as in the
middle and later 1950s, the end of the 1960s and
the beginning of the 1970s, and the end of the
1970s. Table IV.19 shows the main expenditure
totals, together with tax relief on mortgage
interest. United Kingdom figures are shown rather
than for England and Wales so that the Central
Statistical Office's published tables can be used.
The figures are not wholly comparable throughout
owing to incomplete coverage of some of the lending
transactions in the earlier years. The figures for
expenditure on subsidies are comparable, however;
1953/54 is shown because it was the peak year for
capital expenditure during the "300,000 houses a
year" drive; 1971/72 as the year immediately before
the drastic reform of subsidy policy in 1972; and
1973/74 to show the way in which expenditure had
already risen sharply before the change of government in 1974.

Most notable, and central to the policy issues
discussed in Chapters VI and VII was the increase
in subsidies, both in the strict sense and including tax relief. In money terms the increase in
housing subsidies and tax relief between 1949/50
and 1979/80 was sixty-fold; in real terms the
increase was rather over seven-fold. Why this
should have occurred in three decades when fast
rising real incomes might have been expected to
increase greatly most people's ability to afford
adequate housing is a key question in any account
of housing policy after 1945. Investment in public
sector housing, on the other hand, was little
higher in real terms in 1979/80 than in 1949/50.
When juxtaposed with the increase in subsidies and
tax relief such figures for capital expenditure

147

Table IV.19 - Public Expenditure on Housing in the United Kingdom Selected Years 1949/50 to 1979/80

	Subsidies (Central and Local)	Rent Rebates Allowances	Tax Relief and Option Mortgage Subsidy	Total Subsidies, etc.	Investment in Public Sector Housing	Improvement Grants	Total	Total at 1970 Prices	Loan Transactions and Housing Associations and other (net)	Inclusive Out-turn Prices	Total 1970 Prices
1949/50 (a)	56	-	(15)	71	252	...	323	740		323	740
1953/54	80	-	(25)	105	398	1	504	945	17	521	975
1955/56	78	-	(35)	113	347	8	468	820	75	543	950
1960/61	143	-	70	213	278	12	503	755	62	565	845
1965/66	174	-	135	309	619	16	944	1,185	144	1,088	1,370
1971/72	334	-	328	662	760	48	1,470	1,315	125	1,595	1,430
1973/74	432	199	561	1,192	1,278	164	2,634	2,040	445	3,079	2,385
1975/76	1,089	292	974	2,355	2,426	79	4,860	2,500	582	5,442	2,810
1979/80	2,263	538	1,631	4,432	2,072	154	6,658	2,065	1,213	7,871	2,440

Note: (a)   Great Britain

Source: Annual Abstract of Statistics: 1938-1950, Table 52; 1960, Tables 41, 43 and 44; 1963 Tables 40, 42 and 43;
          1967, Tables 38, 39 and 40; 1974, Table 40; and 1983, Table 3.6. Tax Relief from House of Lords Official
          Report 25 January 1979, Written Answers (some year's interpolated) and Housing Policy Technical Volume,
          Table IV.18. Revaluation to 1970 prices by gross domestic product deflator, from Economic Trends Annual
          Supplement, 1985 Edition, pp.8-15.

occasioned a very substantial amount of criticism. The change in the proportions of subsidy and capital expenditure was sometimes attacked as showing more concern for those already well housed (who benefited from the subsidies) at the expense of those who needed to be better housed (and who would benefit from capital expenditure). This was a gross over-simplification. Capital expenditure financed from loan (for reasons discussed in Chapter I) results in an annual flow of loan charges; and the higher the interest rate the higher are the loan charges.

High nominal interest rates, caused partly but not entirely (at least until the 1970s) by inflation caused serious financing problems, owing to the way in which they interacted with financial systems that grew up in days when the value of money was much more stable and hence nominal interest rates were lower. The ordinary fixed interest rate mortgage (including one where the interest rate is variable but where at any given interest rate payments are level) is a device for spreading a large payment (of which house purchase is an important example) over a long period. The rationale of paying for rented housing with long term loans is similar: the rents will come in over a long period and provide the wherewithal to repay the loan. An even spread in money terms over a long period of time provides an even spread in real terms in line with ability to pay if the price level is fairly steady and the nominal interest rate low; when prices and money incomes are rising fast and nominal interest rates are high, it no longer does so. In such circumstances fixed interest loans produce a heavy concentration of expenditure in real terms in the early years of the loan, that is to say in the years immediately following purchase for the owner-occupier, or in the early years of the life of a rented house. Such a heaping up of costs in real terms in this way re-opens, for a time, the gap between costs of housing and ability to pay that rising real income might be expected to have narrowed or closed. The higher the nominal interest rate, the wider the gap to start with; the faster the rise in money incomes and prices, the more quickly it narrows. This effect of high nominal interest rates, variously termed "front loading" or "the time path problem" came to be felt increasingly seriously in the 1960s as interest rates rose, but the much faster inflation and far higher nominal interest rates in the 1970s produced a complete change of scale.

This "time-path" problem afflicted most western countries in the 1960s and 1970s and not just Britain, and was quite separate from uncertainty and risk arising from unstable interest rates and varying rates of inflation. The time-path problem would have existed even in an economy where the rate of rise of prices and money incomes bore a fixed relationship to each other and to nominal interest rates; but such stability was rarely found in the period studied; the reality was one of instability, and in the absence of subsidy or other assistance with housing costs householders would, as a consequence, have been subject to considerable financial risks. An increase in interest rates from 10% to 13%, for example, would have raised the repayment on a 25 year mortgage by 23.8%, and the loan charges on a 60 year loan by 29.7%. Such changes were large in relation to any likely increase in income; interest rate flexibility that was innocuous (from the householder's point of view) when a half percentage point change within a year was the most that was to be expected, was a great deal more risky when the increases could be much larger. An important aspect of assistance with housing costs was the way in which this interest rate risk was shared between the householder (whether tenant or mortgagor) and the tax payer. Tax relief on mortgage interest resulted in a division of (generally speaking) between 70:30 and 65:35. Subsidies that took the form of £x a year for y years (see Chapter VII) put all the risk on the tenant, unless a rate fund contribution was made. The Housing Finance Act 1972, with its provisions (described in Chapter VII) about how rents were to be determined irrespective of costs, put none of the interest rate risk on the tenant, and all of it on the national and local taxpayer in proportion varying between 90:10 and 75:25. The Housing Rents and Subsidies Act 1975 split the interest rate risk in proportions 66 (to the Exchequer) :34 (tenants and rate fund) on debt incurred after the beginning of 1975/76 and 33:67 on debt incurred before that date. Another name for 'risk sharing' in this context is 'open-ended'. Open-ended assistance arrangements were probably the only way in which effective assistance with housing costs could have been provided in conditions like those of the

1970s; and a strong case could be made for the view
that it was only through such open-ended arrangements that the improvement in housing conditions of
the 1950s and 1960s could have continued in the far
less favourable economic conditions of the 1970s.
But the cost in terms of public expenditure and
foregone tax revenue was high. How subsidy policy
coped with these problems is the theme for Chapter
VII.

Policy on subsidies followed in general from
broader considerations of policy, particularly on
house building. The dominant influence on housing
policy in the decade after the end of the war was
scarcity, the sheer shortage of nearly every kind
of housing almost everywhere. The significance in
policy terms of these shortages, moreover, was much
enhanced by the inclusion of housing among those
areas of life where planning for post-war included
the promise of better things. The formal expressions of these sentiments was in the White Paper
Housing. It was published by the Conservative
'caretaker' government that held office between the
break-up of the Coalition and the announcement of
the results of the general election in 1945, but
reflected policies that had emerged under the war-
time Coalition. It stated that the government's
first objective was that there should be "a
separate dwelling for every family that wishes to
have one" (77). This was novel as a statement of
policy, and went much further than the provisions
of the pre-war Housing Acts about unfit houses and
over-crowding. In the circumstances of the time it
was not just an aspiration: it was something that
was thought to be within the power of governments
to deliver. If it was not delivered, then it would
be held against the party forming the government of
the day as something it had failed to do, not as
the outcome of impersonal and anonymous market
forces or as being inherent in the human condition.

The main consequences of scarcity were two:
the emphasis on house building, particularly
numbers of houses built; and protection of tenants
against a weak bargaining position, hence security
of tenure and rent control for tenants of private
landlords. Control at 1939 rents was another
matter; in 1945 rents at 1939 levels in money terms
were nearly 35% lower in real terms, and by 1951
50% lower. Nevertheless, rents were left alone
until 1954. Whether there were any moves within

the 1945-51 Labour administrations to raise controlled rents has not so far emerged from any of
the studies of government policies in this period.
But about policy on house building there are no
such doubts. The house building programme was cut
substantially in 1947 and again in 1949 (78), and
was given a priority below exports and investment
in manufacturing industry. But the change of
government in 1951 was followed by a much higher
priority being given to house building. The scale
of the increase in house building after 1951 in
numbers completed or in capital expenditure as a
proportion of gross domestic product has already
been referred to. It is easy to forget that this
increase took place, as an act of policy (for the
amount of house building was at the time controlled
by licencing) at a time when re-armament was at its
peak, and when the balance of payments was in heavy
deficit. The Conservative party's 1951 election
manifesto had said that "our target remains 300,000
houses a year" and that the priority accorded to
housing would be second only to national defence"
(79), but such an imprecisely drafted pledge,
particularly in making no mention of any specific
year, can hardly by itself explain the priority
given to a large increase in house building at a
time of great economic difficulty, early in the
life of the Parliament. As well as making the
materials available, the government increased
housing subsidies to offset the increase in
interest rates that had been caused by the new
government's re-activation of bank rate as an
instrument of economic policy. The Exchequer
subsidy was raised from the £16.10s a year payable
under the 1946 Act to £24.15s, explicitly to offset
the effect of higher interest rates on the loan
charges generated by new house building. This
action deserves more attention than it has generally received for it was the only occasion on which
local authority house building was fully shielded
against the effects of the increase in interest
rates to restrain inflation. On subsequent occasions the response of successive governments to the
effects of increases in interest rates on housing
was very different. How and why the decision to
protect the finances of housing in this way was
taken in 1952 has attracted little comment. The
only history of the 1951-55 government, that by
Seldon (80), describes the subsidy increase virtually without comment, with no reference to whether

152

the Treasury opposed it, and if so how strongly and
how and why it was over-ruled. The answers to
these questions must for the time being be left
until official papers for the period have been in
the public domain long enough to be studied by
historians. The same is true of whether there were
misgivings within the Conservative government of
1951-55 about the large number of houses built by
local authorities. On the face of things, though,
the desire for as many houses as possible as
quickly as possible led the government to use whatever instruments were available to that end; and
the most powerful of them all, in the circumstances
of the time, were the local authorities.

There is a similar uncertainty, until the
records become available, about what looks like a
shift of policy in the opposite direction in
(approximately) 1954 to 1958. As noted above, the
government announced in 1953 its intention to
resume slum clearance, but from 1954 onwards new
house building by local authorities was continuously reduced; the subsidy on new house building
for general needs (as distinct from slum clearance
and certain other 'special needs') was reduced and
then in 1956 abolished. In the same year the
government announced policies on rent control in
the private sector that were enacted by the Rent
Act 1957. This Act (see Chapter VIII for details)
was more far reaching than any of the inter-war
reforms of the Rent Restrictions Acts. The reduction in local authority house building other than
for slum clearance, and "decontrol by movement" in
the private rented sector with powers for further
block decontrol, have together the appearance of
being the separate parts of a coherent policy that
saw the function of the public sector as slum
clearance only, with "general needs" building to
let a function of private enterprise (since owner-
occupation as the alternative to local authority
building for general needs lay a further decade
ahead). But alternatively, these measures could be
seen as a sequence of cuts for local authority
house building for short-term public expenditure
reasons, together with recognition that since there
had been and would not be any falling back of the
general price level towards pre-war levels, 1939
rents could not be continued, and the length of the
delay in taking action made the increase, when it
came, all the larger. A question of some importance is how far the government of the day relied

on the large scale of building in the early 1950s
having so diminished housing shortages as to
prevent a withdrawal from building for general
needs by local authorities and reductions in
security of tenure in the private rented sector
from being unduly risky. The last direct estimate
of the number of vacant dwellings and the number of
households was that provided by the 1951 Census,
which showed between 700,000 and 750,000 more
households than dwellings. Five years of new
building had increased the housing stock by about
1.2 million, net of demolitions. The Registrar-
General's household projections implied an increase
of about 570,000 households in the same period, so
even if the projection had been correct instead of
under-stating heavily, there would still have been
a net deficit of dwellings relative to households
in 1956. Whether such considerations carried any
weight in the decision, however, is something that
must await the release of the relevant papers.

If the measures of 1956 and 1957 did form a
concerted strategy of reduced reliance on subsidized building and renewed reliance on private
enterprise for rented housing, then that strategy
lasted three years at the most. The Conservative
party's 1959 election manifesto included a pledge
that no further measures to decontrol rents would
be taken in the next Parliament. In the public
sector as well, the early 1960s saw a change of
policy. The Housing Act 1961 brought back subsidies for building for general needs and local
authorities were encouraged to build. House
building by local authorities was already increasing fast when in 1965 a housing target of 500,000
houses a year (in all tenures together) by 1970 was
announced by the government of the day. The opposition countered by calling for 500,000 by 1968.
Although new building could be sustained at anywhere near these levels for more than a very short
period only by large scale clearance and rebuilding, there was no conflict between government and
opposition over a very high level of house building
being needed. The use of industrialized building
methods, and high rise buildings, were not matters
of party controversy. The early 1970s, however,
saw a heightening of party controversy, notably
over subsidy policy.

Housing tenure is discussed in some detail in
the next chapter. Here it is sufficient to note
that until council house sales emerged as a subject

of party controversy in the late 1960s, owner-occupation was not in practice a matter of controversy between the parties. The Labour party's attitude to owner-occupation had generally been one not of opposition but lack of interest. The housing issues that stirred Labour were to do with renting. Conservatives of course had long championed owner-occupation on both housing and political grounds. Neville Chamberlain's biographer quotes him as having written (in 1920) that 'with house purchase every spadeful of manure dug in, every tree planted, converted a potential revolutionary into a citizen' (81). Such was the strength of demand for owner-occupation in the inter-war years, and the backlog of demand left from the war years and the immediate post-war years, that there was no occasion for any very sweeping measures to encourage owner-occupation. From the end of the war until end of the 1950s, verbal encouragement sufficed. One widely quoted example was Eden's calling in 1946 for a 'property owning democracy'. His biographer, though, considered that this was a phrase without substance, as " .... Eden sought to appear vaguely progressive but not as extreme in this respect as Macmillan or even Butler. This meant cliches about property owning democracy" (82). The one measure in the 1950s that directly encouraged owner-occupation did so at the expense of renting from private landlords, not renting from council. The Housing and House Purchase Act 1959 provided for loans from the Exchequer to building societies for lending for the purchase of pre-1919 houses. It was part of a policy to promote improvement of older houses, but by making them more readily saleable it could only accelerate the transfer of houses out of private renting into owner-occupation. During the 1960s the fiscal treatment of owner-occupation was changed from indifference to active support, with both parties taking part. The Conservative administration repealed the Schedule A charge on owner-occupiers in 1963; the Labour administration excluded owner-occupied houses when a capital gains tax was introduced in 1965, provided the option mortgage subsidy to complement tax relief in 1967, and retained tax relief on mortgage interest when most other reliefs on interest were withdrawn from individual taxpayers in 1969. These changes are described in detail in Chapter VI. They are mentioned here to show that the fiscal support for owner-occupation that was put in place of the 1960s had bi-partisan support, even if the council house sales controversy might suggest otherwise. Powers to sell council houses had existed since the inter-war years; powers to sell them on special terms, as distinct from being subject to the ordinary duty on public authorities to get the best price for property sold, dated from 1952; but only in the later 1960s did council house sales become a specifically Conservative policy on housing tenure.

Table A - Houses Started and Completed:
         England and Wales 1946-79

(thousands)

	Started		Completed	
	Public Sector	Private Sector	Public Sector	Private Sector
1946)			92 (b)	30
1947)	287 (a)	102 (a)	122 (c)	40
1948	133	17	186 (d)	31
1949	153	30	147	25
1950	159	19	146	27
1951	164	25	150	21
1952	213	50	177	32
1953	227	81	219	61
1954	190	104	221	88
1955	154	124	173	110
1956	133	116	149	120
1957	124	122	146	123
1958	99	133	117	124
1959	125	164	103	146
1960	105	176	107	162
1961	104	181	98	170
1962	115	178	112	163
1963	138	192	102	168
1964	151	239	126	210
1965	148	202	141	206
1966	158	185	152	198
1967	178	225 (e)	170	193
1968	160	190	159	214
1969	145	158	151	173
1970	125	157	145	162
1971	115	195	130	180
1972	103	214	103	184
1973	96	199	90	174
1974	124	96	112	130
1975	154	137	138	140
1976	156	138	140	138
1977	122	122	147	128
1978	98	141	119	134
1979	72	125	93	120

Table A (continued)

Notes: (a) Includes houses started in April-December 1945.
        (b) Including 71,000 temporary houses
        (c) Including 34,000 temporary houses.
        (d) Including 11,000 temporary houses
        (e) Inflated by "technical starts" made to avoid
             Betterment Levy.

Source: Annual Abstract of Statistics: Housing Statistics;
         Housing and Construction Statistics

Table B - Houses Demolished or Closed under Slum Clearance
Powers: England and Wales 1955-79

(thousands)

1955	24.4	1968	71.6
1956	34.3	1969	69.2
1957	44.5	1970	67.8
1958	52.6	1971	70.1
1959	57.6	1972	66.1
1960	56.6	1973	63.6
1961	62.0	1974	41.7
1962	62.4	1975	52.4
1963	61.4	1976	51.5
1964	61.2	1977	41.8
1965	60.7	1978	34.5
1966	66.8	1979	33.3
1967	71.2		

Source: Housing Statistics (for the figures to 1971);
and Housing and Construction Statistics
(various issues).

Table C - Number of Dwellings in Respect of Which
Improvement Grants Were Approved

(thousands)

	Private Owners	Housing Associations (a)	Local Authorities	Total
1949-54 (Av)	2.9	...	0.4	3.3
1955-59 (Av)	39.0	...	4.8	43.8
1960-64 (Av)	86.1	...	36.0	122.1
1965	85.2	...	37.8	123.0
1966	77.5	...	30.2	107.7
1967	82.6	1.7	28.8	113.1
1968	81.1	2.1	31.0	114.2
1969	76.4	3.2	29.4	108.9
1970	110.5	4.1	42.0	156.6
1971	130.2	6.2	61.1	197.5
1972	208.4	6.8	104.0	319.2
1973	238.0	5.1	117.9	361.0
1974	149.3	5.3	77.3	231.9
1975	84.5	5.3	37.1	126.9
1976	72.8	13.9	39.0	125.6
1977	68.5	19.8	37.6	125.8
1978	62.3	14.7	50.9	127,8
1979	64.7	19.0	52.3	135.9

Note: (a)   Included with private owners before 1967.

Source: 1949 to 1976 from Housing Policy Technical
          Volume, Table X.27.
          1977 to 1979 Housing and Construction Statistics,
          No. 32, Table 29.

Notes and References

(1) Ministry of Reconstruction, Housing, Cmd.6609 (1945), para.34.
(2) Central Statistical Office, Statistical Digest of the War, Table 9.
(3) Social Survey, Population and Housing in England and Wales mid-1945 (by Geoffrey Thomas.
(4) Social Survey, The British Household by P.G. Gray (Central Office of Information, 1947) Table 19.
(5) Ministry of Reconstruction, Housing, Cmd.6609 (1945) para.4.
(6) C.H. Feinstein, National Income, Expenditure and Output of the United Kingdom 1855-1965, Cambridge University Press, Cambridge, 1972, Table 2.
(7) Quoted in J.C.R. Dow, The Management of the British Economy 1945-1960, Cambridge University Press, Cambridge, 1964, p.35.
(8) Feinstein, National Income, Expenditure and Output, Table 61. The official cost of living index is unsuitable as a measure because as an act of policy the index was kept stable from 1941 onwards by changes in subsidies. The London and Cambridge Economic Service estimated the increase in retail prices at 49%. The difference is due to the heavier weighting of heavily subsidized basic foodstuffs in the LCES index.
(9) G. Routh, Occupation and Pay in Great Britain 1906-60, Cambridge University Press, Cambridge, 1965.
(10) See W.K. Hancock and M. Gowing, The British War Economy, HMSO 1949; and D.N. Chester (Ed.) Lessons of the British War Economy, Cambridge University Press, Cambridge, 1951.
(11) See R.S. Sayers, Financial Policy 1939-45, HMSO London, 1956.
(12) P. Addison, The Road to 1945, Cape, London, 1979, Chapter 8; and A. Calder The People's War, Cape, London, 1969.
(13) Department of Employment, British Labour Statistics Historical Abstract (HMSO 1972), Table 109; Social Trends 1979 Edition, Table 5.3.
(14) Census of England and Wales 1951, Housing, Table BB.
(15) Census 1981, Historical Tables England and

Wales, Table 5.

(16) Estimated from Tables 8.2.2 of A. Hunt The Elderly at Home, HMSO for Office of Population Census and Surveys, 1978.

(17) This definition depends on the British definition of "separate household". In the USA and France, however, a household is defined as all persons living in a separate dwelling. In Germany and the Netherlands, a separate household is defined in substantially the same way as in Britain.

(18) Census of England and Wales 1951 Housing Report p.(xxviii).

(19) J.B. Cullingworth, Housing Needs and Planning Policy, Routledge and Kegan Paul, London 1960, pp.16-20.

(20) See page   above.

(21) 1951 Census, Housing Report, Table BE.

(22) Cullingworth, Housing News, p.45.

(23) L. Needleman, 'A Long-Term View of Housing', National Institute Economic Review, November, 1961. Needleman's calculation used headship rates defined as in the 1951 Census, and the 1981 percentages given were calculated on the same basis.

(24) D.C. Paige 'Housing' (Table 12.2) in W. Beckerman (Ed.) The British Economy in 1975, Cambridge University Press, Cambridge, 1965.

(25) The National Plan, Cmd.2764 (1965), Chapter 17, para.11.

(26) For full dsetails, see Ministry of Housing and Local Government, Report of the Inquiry into the Collapse of Flats at Ronan Point, Canning Town, (HMSO, London 1968).

(27) E.W. Cooney, 'High Flats in Local Authority Housing in England and Wales since 1945', in A. Sutcliffe (Ed.) Multi-Storey Living: The British Working Class Experience,. Croom Helm, London 1974.

(28) P. Dunleavy, The Politics of Mass Housing in Britain 1945-1975, Oxford University Press, Oxford, 1981.

(29) See Housing Statistics No.24 (and other issues) for the interpretation of "industrialized" which followed Ministry of Housing and Local Government Circular 76/65.

(30) In 1972 the Ministry of Housing and Local Government distinguished 93. Housing Statistics, No. 24 Table 18.

(31) See P.A. Stone, Housing, Town Development and Land Costs, Estates Gazette, London, 1963; and Needleman, 'A Long-Term View of Housing'.

(32) See Page 333 below.

(33) Dunleavy, Mass Housing, p.99.

(34) Design and Dwellings, Report of the Sub-committee on the Design of Dwellings of the Central Housing Advisory Committee (Chairman the Earl of Dudley). The Central Housing Advisory Committee was a statutory body, provided for by the Housing Act 1935. It worked through sub-committees, to which could be appointed members with specialist knowledge of the subject under reference.

(35) Usually referred to by the name of its Chairman as the Girdwood Committee. Its First and Second Reports were published by the Ministry of Health 1948 and 1950, and its Third Report by the Ministry of Housing and Local Government in 1952.

(36) See A.W. Cleeve Barr, Public Authority Housing, Batsford, 1958, for a detailed review of changes in the standard of local authority housing down to the mid-1950s.

(37) Circular 13/62, which acknowledged that the time was difficult because the country was engaged in a financial struggle, but never-theless "there will be a demand for better houses as prosperity grows" (para.11).

(38) The Housing Programme 1965 to 1970 (Cmd.2838, 1965), para.29.

(39) National Dwelling and Housing Survey, (Depart-ment of the Environment 1929).

(40) Department of the Environment, Housing Development Directorate, A Survey of Tenants' Attitudes to Recently Completed Estates (HMSO 1976).

(41) Housing: The Next Step, Cmd.9333, (1953).

(42) Published in Ministry of Housing and Local Government, Slum Clearance, Cmd.9593 (1955).

(43) Housing Repairs and Rents Act, 1954 s.9 and Sch.5.

(44) Housing Act 1969, s.71.

(45) Housing Act 1957, s.4. The 1957 Act was a consolidating Act that made no substantive changes in the law.

(46) Housing, Cmd.2050 (1963), para.161.

(47) Cmd.2050, 1963, paras.70-72.

(48) The Housing Programme 1965 to 1970, Cmd.2838 (1965).

(49) The National Plan, Cmd.2764 (1965) p.171.
(50) The Fulham Study by the Taylor Woodrow Group
      (1963) and the Halliwell Report by Hallmark
      Securities Ltd. (1966).
(51) R. McKie, Housing and the Whitehall
      Bulldozer, Institute of Economic Affairs,
      1971, p.31.
(52) Estimated from data in Appendix D of Valua-
      tion for Rates 1939 the Report of the Depart-
      mental Committee on Valuation for Rates (the
      Fitzgerald Committee), published in 1944.
(53) Housing Policy Technical Volume, Table I.23,
      derived from P. Gray and Russell, The Housing
      Situation in 1960, Table 18.
(54) National Dwelling and Housing Survey, (DoE
      1929).
(55) See, for example, N. Dennis, People and Plan-
      ning, The Sociology of Housing in Sunderland,
      Faber, London, 1970.
(56) Ministry of Health, Central Housing Advisory
      Commitee, Rural Housing.
(57) Departmental Committee on Housing, Report,
      Cmd.4397 (1933) para.101.
(58) Inside WC, fixed bath or shower, wash hand
      basin, supply of hot and cold water to bath,
      sink and wash hand basin, and ventilated food
      store.   The food store was removed from the
      list in 1969 and a sink added.
(59) Cmd.3602 (1968), Old Houses into New Homes.
(60) The "Development Areas" and "Intermediate
      Areas" scheduled for   selective investment
      incentives   and other aids to regional job
      creation.
(61) Cullingworth, Housing Needs, pp.51-52.
(62) L. Needleman, The Economics of Housing,
      Staples Press, London, 1965.
(63) Old Houses into New Homes, (Cmd.3602)
      paras. 9 and 23, (1968).
(64) An analysis by tenure was published in
      Housing Statistics (e.g. No. 9, (1968),
      Table 26 and No. 24, (1972), Table 28); and
      Housing and Construction Statistics (e.g.
      No. 14 (1975) and No. 32 (1979) Table 29).
(65) See Housing Policy Technical Volume (HMSO
      1977) Chapter I para. 83 for an example of
      this kind of calculation.
(66) P.G. Gray and R. Russell, The Housing Situ-
      ation in 1960, Table 46, (Government Social
      Survey 1962).

(67)   National Dwelling and Housing Survey, (DoE, 1979).

(68)   According to the Quality Check on the 1966 sample census (which used a sample drawn from the 1961 Census records) the 1961 Census over-stated the number of separate dwellings by about 2% as a result of counting house-holds' living quarters in buildings occupied by several households as separate dwellings even though they were not sufficiently self-contained to qualify.   P.G. Gray and F. Gee (of Government Social Survey) Quality Check on the 1966 Sample Census in England & Wales (HMSO 1972), but working back from 1971 by new building plus conversion gains less demo-litions suggest that the over-count in 1961 was about one-half as great as this. The net increase in dwellings between 1951 and 1961 as estimated from new building, demolitions and conversions was very similar to the net increase in dwellings as shown by comparing the census totals, so if there was an over-count in 1961 there was an over-count of similar size in 1951.   Such an over-count would explain what is otherwise a baffling feature of the 1951 Census, the very large increase in the number of small dwellings compared with 1931.   500,000 more dwellings with 3 rooms or fewer were enumerated in 1951 than in 1931. But very few small dwellings were built in the early post-war years, nor do many small dwellings appear to have been built in the 1930s.   The number of flats provided by conversion between 1931 and 1951 can be estimated at about 280,000, and not all of them were necessarily with 3 rooms or fewer.   An over-count of about 200,000 dwel-lings in 1951 would explain the discrepancy. For estimating the change in the balance between dwellings and households, 200,000 are taken off the 1951 Census-based total of dwellings and 100,000 off the total in 1961. On the basis of the average ratios of sharing households to shared dwellings in 1951 and 1961, the number of sharing households is raised by 330,000 in 1951 and 170,000 in 1961 compared with the enumerated total.

(69)   That the National Dwellings and Housing Sur-vey (Department of the Environment, 1979, Table 2.1) showed the number of concealed

married couples at 149,000 and concealed lone-parent families at 104,000 suggests that this may be so; for in the survey non-married couples are more likely to have described themselves as 'married' than in the census.

(70)   Individuals who catered for themselves and so would have been counted as separate households according to the 1971 definition (substantially the same as that in use since 1861) if applied correctly would be counted as members of a multi-person household if they shared the use of a living room or sitting room. The purpose was to bring the definition into line with what was considered to be the practice in earlier censuses, but in the absence of a check on how the definition was applied in 1971, there must inevitably be some uncertainty here.

(71)   See note (5) above.

(72)   Gray and Russel, Housing Situation in 1960, Government Social Survey 1962, p.70.

(73)   The Girdwood Committee (see reference (35) above) estimates that unit costs rose by 140% between 1938 and 1947. The general price level rose by some 75-80%. Feinstein, National Income, Expenditure and Output 1972, Table 61.

(74)   'A new index of average house prices' Economic Trends, October 1982.

(75)   The "Uthwatt Report", Final Report of the Expert Committee on Compensation and Betterment, Cmd.6386 (1942).

(76)   A.R. Prest, The Taxation of Urban Land, Manchester University Press, Manchester, 1981.

(77)   Cmd.6609 (1945), para. 4.

(78)   K. Morgan, Labour in Power 1945-1951, Oxford University Press, Oxford, 1984.

(79)   The text may be conveniently consulted in F.W. Craig, British General Election Manifestos 1918-1966, Political Reference Publications, Chichester, 1970.

(80)   A. Seldon, Churchill's Indian Summer, The Conservative Government 1951-55, Hodder and Stoughton, London, 1981.

(81)   K. Feiling, The Life of Neville Chamberlain, Macmillan, London (1970 Edition) p.86.

(82)   D. Carlton, Anthony Eden, Allen Lane, London 1981, p.281.

CHAPTER V

THE GROWTH OF OWNER-OCCUPATION AND OF LOCAL AUTHORITY HOUSING

The Tenure of Households and of Dwellings

In this section estimates are made of the tenure of the housing stock and of households. The difference between the two is important, particularly for measuring the size of the private rented sector. When a house is let in rooms to (for example) five households, there is one privately rented dwelling, but five households renting from a private landlord. When an owner-occupier or local authority tenant sub-lets part of his house, the tenure of the house remains 'owner-occupied' or 'rented from a local authority' as the case may be; but the occupier of the sub-let part is classified as renting from a private landlord. The relationship of dwellings to households in the owner-occupied and local authority sectors is practically one-to-one. It is scarcely possible for different parts of the same house to be owned by different people, owing to legal problems about who would be responsible for what; and local authorities in the period studied did not provide accommodation let in rooms. But lettings by private landlords of parts of houses were extremely common, though becoming less so with the passage of time. 'Private rented sector' and 'private landlord' are here defined by exception as everything other than owner-occupation and renting from local authorities and new towns and renting from housing associations. In particular, 'private landlords' include employers, among them government departments like the Ministry of Defence and public corporations such as the National Coal Board. In Chapter VIII the changing size of the different sub-sectors within the 'statistical' private rented sector is discussed.

Here only housing associations are separately considered.

Tenure was not asked about in the census until 1961. Reasonably good information was however collected about housing tenure in England and Wales in 1938 by the Ministry of Health for the Fitzgerald Committee (1), and from this source was derived the estimate of the tenure of the housing stock in 1939, as shown in Table V.1. For the next point in the time series reliance is placed on the 1953/54 Enquiry into Household Expenditure (2), with the housing stock worked forward from the census. From this Enquiry the proportion of households in England and Wales that were owner-occupiers could be estimated. For local authority tenancies the proportion was published only for Great Britain, so it was necessary to make an estimate for 1953 by working forwards from 1939 and backwards from 1961. The principal problem is the number of requisitioned houses. The power to requisition houses derived from war-time Defence Regulation powers, exercisable in principle by the central government, but in practice by local authorities on its behalf. There is some ambiguity about the numbers, for the figures published quarterly in the Housing Returns referred to 'properties', which were often occupied by more than one family. The Housing Returns show 76,000 properties requisitioned at mid-1953 (3); but how many dwellings this represents is uncertain. There is therefore an element of approximation about the estimate of tenure in 1953. For 1961, 1971 and 1981 the census is the source; but since the census could only record the tenure for households that were present, there is necessary some uncertainty about the tenure of vacant dwellings, and of second homes and holiday lettings. The published official estimates have been used, however, and tenure of households inferred from tenure of dwellings.

The figures in Table V.1 are shown to the nearest thousand and the first decimal place of percentages to avoid accumulating rounding errors; but they are not, of course, anywhere near as precise as that. The margins of error are important in the discussion that follows of the sources of the growth of the stock of owner-occupied dwellings. Here it is important to emphasize the distinction between the tenures of households and the tenures of dwellings. When extreme shortages

168

Table V.1 - Estimates of the Tenure of Dwellings and Households in England and Wales 1939-1981

(thousands)

A. Dwellings

		Owner-occupiers	Rented Local Authority or New Town	Rented from Housing Association	Rented from Private Landlord	All Tenures
1939	Number	3,790	1,180	6,530		11,500
	(Percent)	(33.0)	(10.3)	(56.7)		(100.0)
1953	Number	4,400	2,400	5,945		12,745
	(Percent)	(34.5)	(18.8)	(46.6)		(100.0)
1961	Number	6,460	3,528	4,557		14,545
	(Percent)	(44.4)	(24.3)	(31.3)		(100.0)
1971	Number	8,866	4,803	160	3,195	17,024
	(Percent)	(52.1)	(28.2)	(0.9)	(18.8)	(100.0)
1981	Number	11,180	5,465	403	2,038	19,086
	(Percent)	(58.6)	(28.6)	(2.1)	(10.7)	(100.0)

Source: Author's estimates for 1939 and 1953; Ministry of Housing for 1961 (England and Wales component of the estimate for Great Britain published in Housing Statistics No. 1 (1966), Table III) 1971 and 1981 from Department of the Environment, Housing and Construction Statistics, 1971-1981, Table 101.

Table V.1 - Estimates of the Tenure of Dwellings and Households in England and Wales

(thousands)

		Owner-occupiers	Rented Local Authority or New Town	Rented from Housing Association	Rented from Private Landlord	All Tenures
B. Households						
1939	Number	3,720	1,160	6,870		11,750
	(Percent)	(31.7)	(9.9)	(58.4)		(100.0)
1953	Number	4,345	2,370	6,865		13,580
	(Percent)	(32.0)	(17.5)	(50.6)		(100.0)
1961	Number	6,329	3,429	4,966		14,724
	(Percent)	(43.0)	(23.3)	(33.7)		(100.0)
1971	Number	8,438	4,712	155	3,399	16,704
	(Percent)	(50.5)	(28.2)	(0.9)	(20.3)	(100.0)
1981	Number	10,579	5,328	396	2,033	18,336
	(Percent)	(57.7)	(29.1)	(2.1)	(11.1)	(100.0)

Source: For 1939 see text. 1961 from Housing Statistics modified to agree with amended estimate for the housing stock. 1971 and 1981 from Housing and Construction Statistics.

of housing obliged large numbers of households to share, there were many more households than dwellings rented from 'private landlords' (in the all-embracing sense). As shortages eased and sharing was reduced, the number of households renting parts of dwellings fell, and hence the size of the private rented sector as measured by households fell more than it did as measured by dwellings. In the three decades (almost) between mid-1953 and 1981, the number of dwellings in the private rented sector excluding housing associations (probably with about 100,000 dwellings in 1953) fell by about 3.8 million, but the number of households fell by 4.7 million. This contrast is considered more fully in Chapter VIII with reference to how far the reduction in the number of lettings of parts of dwellings was the result of a fall in the supply of such lettings and not just the consequence of many fewer households being obliged by sheer shortage of separate dwellings to rent a part of a dwelling. Certainly the persistence in the private rented sector in the 1960s and 1970s of phenomena associated with excess demand does not appear compatible with a fall of 900,000 in the number of households relative to dwellings in the sector unless the supply of lettings of parts of houses was contracting as well.

The increase in the local authority housing stock came predominantly from new building, less (in 1971-81) an offset from sales. This was not so of owner-occupation, where sales of formerly rented houses and flats (mainly houses of course) were almost as numerous as new building and at certain periods more so. The changing number of sales of formerly rented houses is an extremely important part of the history of the growth of owner-occupation during the period studied, so the chronology of the transfer of houses from renting to owner-occupation is worth commenting on in some detail. It is, moreover, an aspect of the history of English housing that is different from that of most other countries. In the European countries, and in the USA also, the housing built in the nineteenth century for urban wage earners was predominantly in blocks of flats. In England other than in parts of London, in contrast, it was terrace houses. Under all legal systems owner-occupation of terrace houses is much simpler than of flats, and as a consequence most of the pre-1914 housing stock of France and Germany is still rented at the time of writing, whereas in England in 1981 nearly 70% was owner-occupied (4). As a starting point estimates of the components of change in the stock of owner-occupied housing may usefully be shown. These estimates are approximate only, with net sales for owner-occupation of dwellings formerly rented from private landlords being derived as a residual. Because it is derived in that way it includes the effect of any errors in the estimated totals of owner-occupied and privately owned rented dwellings, and in the other components of change. The tenure of houses demolished or closed, or acquired by local authorities before demolition is a particular weak spot. Nevertheless, likely errors are not sufficient to call into question the broad conclusions about the relative importance of building and purchase of formerly rented housing in the growth of owner-occuption.

Table V.2 - Components of the Growth of the Stock of Owner-Occupied Dwellings: England and Wales

(thousands)	1939-53	1953-61	1961-71	1971-81	1939-81
Totals					
New Building	+315	+865	+1,780	+1,405	+4,365
Purchase from private land-lords	+505	+1,245	+850	+825	+3.425
Purchase from public authorities	neg	+20	+60	+325	+405
Other (net) - mainly slum clearance and other demolitions	-210(a)	-70	-285	-240	-805
Total Net Change	+610	+2,060	+2,405	+2,315	+7,390

Notes: (a) Includes war losses.

Source: New Building from Chapter IV, Annex Table A; purchases from public authorities from Housing and Construction Statistics (various issues).

One may first note from Tables V.1 and V.2 that the course of owner-occupation from the end of the 1930s was in no sense one of continuously onwards and upwards: the proportion of the housing stock owner-occupied in 1953 was only slightly higher than in 1939; and in 1950 it was probably slightly lower, if anything (5). The policy of the 1945-51 Labour governments that the new houses built should nearly all be council houses was discussed in the previous chapter. Sales for owner-occupation of formerly rented houses appear to have gathered pace towards the end of the 1940s, not in the war or immediate post-war years (6). Between 1953 and 1961, however, sales are estimated to have averaged some 150,000 - 160,000 a year. This estimate depends on the estimate of owner-occupied dwellings in 1953 not being too low, but of that there is no evidence or suggestion. For the later 1950s, the inquiry into the effects of the 1957 Rent Act (7) provides independent evidence.

This inquiry found that between 1957 and 1959 rounds of interviewing there had been a net shift from renting to owner-occupation of 1.4% of comparable 'accommodation units' in London and 1.9% in the rest of England and Wales (8), which amounted to 185,000 in total. As the interval between the rounds of interviews was 19 months, the equivalent annual rate was just under 120,000. That figure did not include accommodation not covered by the survey because the Rent Act did not apply to it (agricultural dwelling houses (320,000) and dwellings rated with business premises (350,000)) (9) and also excluded 300,000 dwellings occupied rent free in 1957. There is no wholly reliable way of estimating the number of sales for owner-occupation of such dwellings; with the same proportionate rate as for other dwellings, the equivalent annual rate would be 11,000. The total net rate of transfer from the private rented sector to owner-occupation in 1957-59 thus appears to have been in the region of 130,000 a year. Transfers from owner-occupation to renting (which could include temporary lettings) were estimated at 10,000 a year, so the total of houses transferred from renting from private landlords to owner-occupation was equivalent to about 140,000 a year. The number of sales to sitting tenants can be estimated from the survey at about 65,000, so sales with vacant possession were running at about 75,000 a year. Comparison with the average annual rate of transfer in 1953-61 as a whole suggests that the rate in 1957-59 was slightly lower than before 1957, an interpretation which is given some support by evidence for the 1960s.

The 1964 Housing Survey (10) re-surveyed all the dwellings included in the 1960 survey, and so could estimate the number that were rented in 1960 but owner-occupied in 1964. The survey estimated that there were 440,000 dwellings that were owner-occupied in 1964 but rented from private landlords in 1960 (11). Since the interval between the surveys was just under 4½ years, the average annual rate was about 100,000 a year. A calculation for 1961-66 by the same method as in Table V.2 would give an estimate of an annual rate of transfer of 90,000 houses a year from renting to onwer-occupation. The two estimates would be consistent if the annual rate of sales was slowing down in the early 1960s, and this appears to have been so. An annual rate of 100,000 a year in 1961-64 would imply an average of just under 80,000 sales a year in 1964-71; and the calculation for 1961-66 would also imply about 80,000 sales a year in 1966-71. The estimates of what happened in the 1960s to sales out of renting for owner-occupation are important for interpretations of the effect of policies on rents and security of tenure, as we shall see in Chapter VIII.

The principal interest in the estimate of sales in the 1970s is that although it was expected that sales would slow down as more and more of the most saleable dwellings had been sold, no such fall in the rate of sales is to be seen in the figures in Tables V.1 and V.2. That again is an important point for assessing the effects of policies in the 1970s to encourage "down-market" lending, and for the way in which policies to facilitate access to owner-occupation contributed to reduction in the private rented sector.

The timing of the transfers of houses from renting to owner-occupation raises intriguing questions about what was their effect on the number of new houses built for private owners. Up to a point formerly rented houses put on the market with vacant possession are an alternative to new houses. The number of new houses built for private owners in the middle and late 1950s (Chapter IV, Table A) was not high in view of how few had been built in the 1940s and the early 1950s. At the very end of the 1950s and in the 1960s when the number of sales out of the private rented sector was beginning to decline, new house building for private owners rose sharply. This is not enough to prove cause and effect, of course; but the very slow increase in house prices for most of the 1950s (12) is consistent with the total supply of houses for sale from all sources (including formerly rented houses) being distinctly more ample relative to demand in the 1950s than in the 1940s, or the 1960s.

The private rented sector was diminished not only by sales for owner-occupation but also by slum clearance. The history described in Chapter II made it inevitable that the private rented sector would bear the brunt of slum clearance. The total number of dwellings in the private rented sector demolished under slum clearance powers or for other reasons, or acquired by local authorities for demolition, was between 1939 and 1981 about 1.5 million or a little more. Wartime losses due to air attack would bring the figure to between 1.6 and 1.7 million. Nearly 30% of the stock of dwellings rented from private landlords in 1939 had by 1981 been demolished or destroyed. This again is a fact of great importance for any conclusions about whether different policies could have produced a different evolution for the private rented sector after 1945, and about the reasons why the private rented sector in Britain diminished at a much more rapid rate than in most other countries.

Households and Their Tenure: Local Authority Tenants and Owner-Occupiers in the Inter-War Years

From the changes in the tenure of the English housing stock we turn to the way in which the circumstances of households were associated with tenure. Who were the households that came into the local authority sector as it grew in size? Who were the households that made up the demand side of the great expansion of owner-occupation? Not until the 1960s was much information collected on these subjects, though the material from which much might be discovered for earlier years probably lies in the records of local authorities and of building societies. In this section the immediately available information about local authority tenants in the inter-war years is brought together, and added to the even sparser information about owner-occupiers.

The information about local authority tenants
is very limited. The 1931 Census Housing Report
included information about family size and number
of rooms in the London County Council's Becontree
Estate, and estates in Birmingham, Liverpool and
Manchester (13); but apart from that, all that is
available is a small amount of local survey
material and analyses published by the London
County Council of the occupations of their tenants.
Table V.3 shows this analysis for 1938, and for
comparison the corresponding analysis published for
1912. The figures were re-classified as far as
possible according to the "socio-economic groups"
used in official surveys and the census from 1961
onwards. The re-classification is only approximate
as some of the occupations are ill-defined in the
original sources such as "checker" and "sorter",
and there were occupations in 1912 such as "horse
keeper" and "lamplighter" that had gone out of
existence by 1961.

The features of note shown by Table V.3 are
first the low proportion economically inactive, and
second the high proportion of tenants with stated
occupations that did manual work. In 1938 pen-
sioners and widows were only 7.6% of all tenants;
and if those with no occupation are taken to have
been economically inactive (highly likely) the proportion was still only 8.5%. There is here, as
will be shown later in the chapter, a very sharp
contrast with the proportion of tenants not economically active (i.e. in employment or seeking work)
in later years. Of those tenants with classifiable
occupations, four-fifths were in manual occupations
in 1912 and nine-tenths in 1938.

At this time, local authorities' statutory
powers and duties to provide houses were in terms
of "housing of the working classes" (and remained
so until 1949). That is a vague term, and not
necessarily the same thing as manual employment.

Information about the incomes of tenants at
this time is likewise sparse, and limited to a
small number of local studies. The findings from
one such study about the tenants' income is summarized in Table V.4.

Average earnings of all adult men in full-time
manual work at this time were 65s a week (14), so
on the whole the tenants of the LCC's Watling
Estate were drawn from among the better paid manual
workers. A very similar conclusion was shown by
Young's study of the Becontree Estate (15). Thirty

176

Table V.3 - Occupations of Tenants of London County Council
Houses and Flats 1912 and 1938

	...... 1912		...... 1938	
	Number	% of all Classifiable by occupation	Number	% of all Classifiable by occupation
Managerial, professional, intermediate non-manual	178	2.2	720	1.1
Junior non-manual	1,571	19.6	6,906	11.0
Skilled manual, including foremen	2,852	35.6	26,202	41.7
Semi-skilled manual and personal service	2,058	25.7	16,358	26.1
Unskilled manual	1,345	16.8	12,603	20.0
Armed forces	15	0.2	...	....
Pensioners	73	...	3,975	....
Miscellaneous un-classifiable occupations	511	...	1,745	....
Widow	-	...	1,370	....
No occupation	-	...	639	....
Total	8,603		70,518	

Source: London County Council, Housing of the Working
Classes 1855-1912, pp.158-59; and Housing
Estate Statistics for 1937/38, Table K.

Table V.4 - Average Weekly Earnings of the Chief Wage
Earners According to Size of Family and Number
of Earners: Watling, 1936

	Proportion of all Families (%)	Average Earnings of Chief Wage Earner
Small families (2 to 4 members)		
One earner	44.0	£3.16.0.
Two or more earners	8.5	£3.3.9.
Large families (5 members or more)		
One earner	26.0	£4.0.0.
Two or more earners	21.5	£3.10.4
Total	100.0	£3.12.3

Source: R. Durant, Watling: A Social Survey,
King, London, 1939, Table VI, p.124.

percent of the families in Miss Durant's study
sample had more than one wage earning member, a
proportion not very different from that among all
local authority tenant households in the 1970s.
    A fair generalization would seem to be that
"general needs" council house building in the
inter-war years provided primarily for better-paid
manual workers plus some clerks, and only in a
small way for retired people and others not in the
labour force. Slum clearance, though, was different: 280,000 houses were built under slum clearance powers before 1939, and in many instances the
slum clearance estates became stigmatized as
"rough" (16) and their occupiers sometimes shunned.
An extreme example was the well-known affair of the
"Cuttleslowe walls", where an estate built by
Oxford City Council in north Oxford had seven foot
high walls topped with revolving steel spikes to
keep the residents away from an adjacent private
estate (17). The occupiers of slum clearance
estates were the subject of one hostile stereotype,
the tenant who would use the bath to keep the coal

in.   A contrasting stereotype, though, the council
tenants too well off to need the subsidy, had
become well established in the early 1930s, barely
a decade after subsidized council housing.   The
Committee on Local Expenditure in 1932 wrote in
their report:

> "It is freely stated that there are con-
> siderable numbers of municipal tenants who
> are not in need of subsidized accommodation.
> We have not ascertained how much truth there
> is in this contention, but we think that the
> matter is one which requires careful and
> immediate investigation by every local
> authority" (18).

These two hostile stereotypes of local authority
tenants were to have a very long life, and the fact
that they did so is of interest in a history of
housing policy.   For the prevalence of such stereotypes connote the existence in some quarters of a
resentment of housing to let at subsidized rents
and an ill-will towards it that did not exist
towards (e.g.) the National Health Service or state
education.
        Information about owner-occupiers in the
inter-war years is very sparse.   Very little use
has thus far been made of building societies'
records, and it is to be hoped that records of
mortgage advances in the inter-war years could be
used to study the incomes and other circumstances
of purchasers, and the prices they paid. Here and
now, however, the only information is that published by Sir Harold Bellman from the records of
the Abbey Road Building Society (a large London
society and one of the precursors of the Abbey
National Building Society).
        There must inevitably be some doubt about how
representative in this respect the Abbey Road
Society was of building societies generally.   But
since, as a London society, most of its business
was done in south-east England where the proportion
of salaried occupations was higher than elsewhere,
it is unlikely to have done a higher proportion of
its mortgage business with wage earners than
societies operating elsewhere in England.   If its
percentages are applied, rather riskily, to all
societies, then the number of advances made to wage
earners rose from about 65,000 in 1931 to 125,000
in 1936, an increase of over 90%.   That house

179

Table V.5 - Occupations of Mortgagors with the Abbey Road Society in the 1930s

(percent)	Up to 1930	During 1931	During 1932	During 1933	During 1934	During 1935	During 1936
Professional	4.4	4.0	4.1	3.3	2.4	3.1	3.0
Independent (except professional)	15.5	13.2	17.9	14.3	12.6	11.9	13.7
Salaried	16.7	15.7	16.3	14.2	12.1	12.3	10.7
Clerk	7.3	7.3	7.4	7.6	16.8(a)	7.7	6.9
Wage earner	34.8	40.8	31.0	41.2	43.3	49.4	50.5
Labourer	0.6	0.6	0.5	0.8	0.9	1.2	1.3
Miscellaneous (b)	20.7	18.4	22.8	18.6	11.9	14.4	13.9
Total	100.0	100.0	100.0	100.0	100.0	100.0	100.0
(All building society advances, thousand)	.....	(162)	(159)	(197)	(238)	(241)	(252)

Notes: (a) "Increase due mainly to block transfer of mortgages from large public utility undertaking".

(b) "Largely composed of married women ....not gainfully employed.

Source: H. Bellman, 'The Building Trades' (pp.429-430) in British Association Britain in Recovery, Pitman (London), 1938. Figures for advances by all building societies are those published by the Chief Registrar of Friendly Societies.

purchase on mortgage became more common among wage earners, particularly the better paid, during the 1930s seems well established; but beyond that it is not possible to be at all definite.

Owner-Occupiers and Local Authority Tenants in the 1950s and the Early 1960s

A certain amount of information about housing tenure in relation to households' income and occupation was provided by the report of the Enquiry into Household Expenditure 1953/54, but not until the early 1960s was there survey information about such matters as housing tenure and the size and composition of households, and ages of household head. The published tables from the Enquiry into Household Expenditure analysed tenure in full only according to ranges of household income. For the separate groups of occupations the only distinction drawn was between owner-occupiers and all tenants. Given the interest in the circumstances of council tenants, in view of the great growth of the local authority housing stock in the late 1940s and the early 1950s, the analysis of income and tenure is shown here.

Table V.6 refers to the United Kingdom, not to England and Wales, hence the difference from Table V.1 in the proportions of households in each of the tenures. Nevertheless, the picture it shows would apply to England and Wales as well. In the lowest ranges of income local authority tenants were comparatively under-represented, and even in the highest range of incomes, over £20 a week, the proportion of council tenants was only a little below the average for all ranges. What was said above about council tenants in the 1930s was still broadly true of the early 1950s: they tended to be drawn from the better paid manual occupations, with only a small proportion of retired people and others not in paid employment. Of owner-occupiers, 37% were in manual occupations and 48% in other paid employment or self-employment (19). The proportion of 48% is not at variance with what was shown in Table V.5 for purchasers with building society mortgages. Nevertheless, income for income, people in non-manual occupations were more likely to be owner-occupiers: among households earning £14-£20 a week, for instance, 55% of households headed by an employer or manager were owner-occupiers, 54% where the head was in a profes-

181

Table V.6 - Household Income and Tenure 1953/54

(percent); average number of earners per household in brackets

Weekly Income	Owned Outright	Owned on Mortgage	Local Authority Tenants	Other Tenants	All Tenures
Weekly Income					
Under £3	18.9 (0.06)	3.7 (0.29)	12.3 (0.20)	65.1 (0.09)	100.0
£3 but under £6	22.8 (0.30)	5.2 (0.58)	14.4 (0.56)	57.6 (0.52)	100.0
£6 but under £8	15.2 (0.75)	6.2 (0.97)	18.1 (0.98)	60.5 (1.05)	100.0
£8 but under £10	11.4 (0.86)	11.0 (1.15)	24.4 (1.19)	53.3 (1.20)	100.0
£10 but under £14	11.2 (1.24)	18.3 (1.41)	24.4 (1.57)	46.1 (1.55)	100.0
£14 but under £20	14.6 (1.66)	23.5 (1.70)	20.8 (2.23)	41.1 (2.28)	100.0
£20 or over	24.2 (1.83)	24.3 (2.12)	18.3 (3.36)	33.2 (2.62)	100.0
All ranges of income	15.4 (1.10)	15.4 (1.53)	20.6 (1.63)	48.6 (1.36)	100.0

Source: Report of Enquiry into Household Expenditure, Tables 40, 41, 42, 43 and 44.

sional, teaching, or clerical occupation; and 28% in a manual occupation. This association between tenure and social class (if defined in terms of occupation) independently of income was to be observable long after 1953/54, notwithstanding the rise in the proportion of owner-occupiers generally.

The housing surveys in the early 1960s financed by the Rowntree Trust and then the official survey in 1964 provide a fuller account of the characteristics of households in the three main tenures. The main features are summarized in Table V.7.

In the early 1960s local authority housing was still primarily the tenure of families with children, of large families in particular. 'Children' were defined as being aged 15 or under, so by 1962 or 1964, those boys and girls born at the end of the war would no longer count as children, and would add to the number of 'large adult households' (which can comprise a married couple, a sixteen year old son or daughter, and a child aged 15 or under). Nearly 70% of local authority tenant households appear to have been 'family' households in this sense; 'the small adult households' in the local authority sector were, in all probability, couples in their forties and fifties whose children had grown up and left home, as childless couples were rarely allocated council houses at this time. The proportion of older households in the local authority sector was still smaller than in owner-occupation and renting from private landlords, but had risen a long way compared with 1938 and (on the evidence of the information about income (Table V.8)) since 1953 as well. Small dwellings primarily for older people, continued to attract subsidy when general subsidies for building by local authorities were stopped in 1956 (20). That the proportion of local authority tenant households with no member earning was lower in the early 1960s than for the other tenures merits note; for, as we shall see, there was here a very marked change in the 1960s and 1970s.

The relationship between income and tenure changed in the decade after 1953/54, as Table V.8 shows.

Compared with 1953/54 the main change by 1963 was the increase in the proportion of local authority tenants in the lower ranges of income. Housing for old people was one of the reasons. The

Table V.7 – Age and Occupation of Household Heads and
Types of Household by Tenure in the Early 1960s

(percent)

Age	Owner Occupiers	Local Authority Tenants	Tenants of Private Landlords	All Tenures
Under 30	7	6	15	9
30-39	19	18	16	18
40-49	20	26	15	20
50-59	22	20	19	21
60-69	17	18	20	18
70 or over	14	12	16	14
All Ages	100	100	100	100

Occupation	Owner Occupiers	Local Authority Tenants	Tenants of Private Landlords	All Tenures
Administrative, managerial, professional	18	3	7	11
Small employers, shop-keepers, farmers	8	1	4	5
Clerical and shop assistants	9	7	7	8
Skilled manual workers and foremen	31	44	33	35
Semi- and unskilled manual, personal service	10	24	21	17
Retired and unoccupied	23	19	24	23
Unclassified	1	2	3	2
Total	100	100	100	100
Proportion with no earners (%)	20	16	24	20

Table V.7 – Age and Occupation of Household Heads and Types of Household by Tenure in the Early 1960s (continued)

(percent)

Household Type	Owner Occupiers	Local Authority Tenants	Tenants of Private Landlords	All Tenures
Individual under age 60	3	2	7	4
Small adult households	14	7	17	13
Small families	22	22	18	21
Large families	10	19	9	12
Large adult households	23	26	20	23
Individuals aged 60 and over and couples of whom at least one was 60 or over	27	23	29	27

Source: J.B. Cullingworth, English Housing Trends, Bell, London, 1965, Tables 5 and 6 (the 1962 Rowntree Survey); Government Social Survey, The Housing Survey in England and Wales (HMSO 1967), Table 2.31.

Table V.8 - Tenure and Household Income 1963

(percent)

Weekly Household Income	Owners with Mortgage	Outright Owners	Local Authority Tenants	Other Tenants	All Tenures	All Tenures as percent of Total for all Incomes
Under £6	2	21	29	48	100	8
£6 but under £10	6	33	23	38	100	10
£10 but under £15	12	20	28	40	100	15
£15 but under £20	23	14	30	33	100	19
£20 but under £25	26	13	29	32	100	16
£25 but under £30	31	15	30	24	100	12
£30 but under £40	34	17	27	22	100	11
£40 or over	40	27	15	18	100	8
All income ranges	22	19	27	32	100	100

Source: Family Expenditure Survey, Report for 1963, Table F.

other, it is reasonable to believe, was the resumption of slum clearance transferring substantial numbers of other households with low incomes from private sector to public sector tenancies.

The growth of owner-occupation between 1953/54 and 1963 was least in the lowest ranges of income (as would be expected), but otherwise was fairly uniform across all ranges of income. Further insight into the growth of owner-occupation is provided by the tenure proportions within each age group, that is to say the data on ages of household heads in Table V.7 re-presented "the other way round".

Table V.9 - Housing Tenure by Age of the Household Head: England and Wales 1964

Age	Owner Occupiers	Local Authority Tenants	Other Tenants	All Tenures
Under 30	32	15	53	100
30-39	46	24	30	100
40-49	44	31	25	100
50-59	46	23	31	100
60-69	40	23	37	100
70 and over	42	20	38	100
All ages	42.5	23.3	34.2	100.0

Source: The Housing Survey in England and Wales, Government Social Survey 1967, Table 2.31.

That the proportions of owner-occupiers were very similar in all age ranges from 30-39 upwards is consistent with large numbers of owner-occupiers having acquired their houses for ready money at low prices. Not many households buy a house on mortgage for the first time at full market prices at ages above 45; and the 1960 Housing Survey found that 59% of owner-occupiers aged 50-59 owned outright, as did 77% of those aged 60-69 (21). If the growth of the number of owner-occupiers in the 1950s had been primarily as a consequence of purchase on mortgage by people who moved to the houses they bought (as was so in the 1960s and 1970s), the increase would have been concentrated in the younger age groups, which would have led to the proportions of owner-occupiers in the 30-39 and 40-49 age groups in 1964 being much higher than in the 50-59 age group and higher. This is not what the 1964 survey showed (and the 1960 survey gave a very similar result in this respect).

Not all of the growth of owner-occupation in the 1950s and early 1960s was the result of a preference by households for that tenure: the 1960 survey (22) found that of owner-occupiers with mortgages, some 21% said that they would have preferred to rent rather than buy; and among households where the household head had a net income of £10 or less (some 20% of all mortgaged owner-occupiers) the proportion was 27%. The rapid transfer of dwellings away from renting and into owner-occupation in the 1960s that was described above thus left a considerable number of households with no option but to buy, even though they would have preferred to rent. 21% of owner-occupiers with mortgages was equal to about 600,000 households, one-tenth of all owner-occupiers. As will be shown later in this chapter, survey questions on tenure preferences in the later 1970s gave very different results. The 1960 evidence of a substantial number of owner-occupiers that would have preferred to rent is important, though, in showing how recent is the near-universal preference for owner-occupation that by the late 1970s had come to be regarded as axiomatic.

Owner-Occupiers and Tenants in the 1960s and 1970s

Table V.1 showed that in the two decades after 1961 the number of owner-occupiers in England and Wales rose by some 4.25 million; tenants of local authorities and housing associations (the "social sector") by about 2.2. million (23); whereas the number of tenants renting from private landlords fell by about 2.8 million. What changes in the characteristics of owner-occupiers and tenants went with these changes in the number of households is considered here. The comparison is for the most part between 1960 and 1977 (the year of the National Dwelling and Housing Survey) (24) rather than 1981, because by 1981 sitting tenant purchasers of houses from local authorities were numerous. These were a distinct group and for the most part became owner-occupiers as a consequence of a major change of policy in 1979, and are best excluded from a discussion of what happened in the 1960s and 1970s. Sales of council houses in the early 1970s were numerous in relation to what had gone before, but not on anything like the scale of 1979 and subsequently.

As we shall see, the demand for owner-occupation increased strongly. Much of this demand was met, but the characteristics of owner-occupiers did not materially change. What <u>did</u> change was the proportion of households with these characteristics that were owner-occupiers. Throughout the period under discussion, house purchase on mortgage remained something for households with reasonably stable incomes sufficient to make the required payments without aid other than tax relief (or option mortgage subsidy). It was not the tenure, therefore, for households with only low or intermittent earnings, or no earnings at all. The only numerically important group of owner-occupiers without sizeable earnings were retired people who had paid off their mortgages during their working lives. But with more and more of the households with sizeable and stable earnings becoming owner-occupiers, those households that were tenants were increasingly those with only low earnings, or no earnings at all. It will be argued that the survey information for the later 1970s shows that a selection process was at work, whereby owner-occupiers were selected for low unemployment risk, better health, and even marital stability (an important matter when for many couples house purchase depended on the incomes of both husband and wife). As more and more households that met these criteria became owner-occupiers, tenants were to an increasing extent those that did not. An essential aspect of the way this process worked was that except for sitting tenant purchasers (from private landlords in the 1950s and early 1960s and public authorities at the end of the 1970s) few people bought a house on mortgage at ages above the mid-40s, and most were younger than this. The explanation lies of course in the wish by both borrowers and lenders for the mortgage to be paid off before the borrower (mortgagor) retires from employment. In consequence, the age distribution of owner-occupiers at a time when their number is expanding will be very different if the expansion comes mainly from purchase by moving households that buy at market prices rather than by sitting tenant purchase. These aspects of the dynamics of the growth of owner-occupation can be illustrated by comparing the age distribution of owner-occupiers in 1960 and 1977. Household heads aged 30-39 in 1960, for example, were approximately the same people as the household heads aged 45-54 in 1977 (not exactly, owing to migration as well as the two year discrepancy, which is unavoidable owing to the years when the surveys were carried out).

Table V.10 - Numbers and Proportion of Owner-Occupiers in 1960 and 1977

Age Range		Proportion of House-holds that were Owner-Occupiers		Number of Owner-Occupiers	
1960	1977	1960	1977	1960	1977
...	Under 25	...	31	...	250
...	25-34	...	60	...	1,800
20-29	35-44	30	65	370	1,740
30-39	45-54	40	58	1,080	1,680
40-49	55-64	43	51	1,180	1,550
50-59	65-74	46	50	1,300	1,380
60-69	75-84	45	47	1,000	650
70-79	85 or over	41	43	550	110
80 or over	...	32	..	130	...

Source: 1960 figures worked out from Tables 14 and 26 of The Housing Situation in 1960; and scaled from England and Wales to England by reference to the census. The 1977 figures are for England and were taken from the National Dwelling and Housing Survey (NDHS).

The growth of owner-occupation was heavily concentrated in the younger age groups. A very high proportion of households buying their first house do so with a mortgage: in 1971 the proportion was about 94%, according to the Movers Survey (25). The Building Society Mortgage Survey has consistently shown the proportion of first-time purchasers with building society mortgages who were aged 45 and upwards to be under 10%. The proportion was 9.0% in 1970, 7.5% in 1973, 7.8% in 1977. The reasons were referred to above; as a consequence the growth of owner-occupation was concentrated in the younger age groups, with the higher age groups little affected apart from the increase that occurred as entrants to owner-occupation grew older with the passage of time.

When looking at the way in which the characteristics of owner-occupation households differed

190

Table V.11 – Proportion of Owner-Occupiers According to Age and Marital Status of the Household Head, England 1977

(percent)

Age of Household Head	Married Men	Widowed Men	Widowed Women	Separated and Divorced Men	Separated and Divorced Women	Single Men	Single Women
Under 30	56.0	....	....	45	15	22.3	13.3
30-44	68.5	....	46	46.5	33.3	48.3	40.4
45-59	58.8	39.4	45.9	39.8	38.2	43.0	51.7
60-69	55.6	42.5	44.8	.... }	45	43.1	48.0
70-79	54.3	44.3	41.2	.... }	} 39		
80 and over	57.3	48.3	40.3	.... }		45.4	45.4
All Ages	60.7	43.7	42.8	40.3	33.2	36.7	39.5
Total of Owner-Occupiers							
('000)	7,034	239	955	102	177	269	311

Source: National Dwelling and Housing Survey.

from tenants, it is convenient to begin with marital status. As Table V.11 shows, owner-occupation was pre-eminently the married couples' tenure. In consequence, the great rise in the proportion of married women in paid employment (26) had more effect on owner-occupier households' income than on tenants' incomes.

The lower proportion of owner-occupiers among divorced, separated and widowed men and women than among married couples had a number of causes, some of them plainly selection effects, others whose nature is still uncertain at the time of writing. Couples that married young were much more likely to be tenants than other couples (27), and couples that marry young are much more likely to separate (28). Work by Murphy and Sullivan, though, has shown that even when age at marriage is allowed for, owner-occupiers divorced less frequently than did tenants (29). That the proportion of owner-occupiers among widows and widowers was lower than among couples was partly the result of heavier mortality among tenants, who were therefore more likely to be widowed. The difference in mortality rates was discovered from the OPCS Longitudinal Study which took a 1% sample from the 1971 Census, to which were linked subsequent registrations of births and deaths. Table V.12 shows the findings about mortality in relation to social class and tenure.

Table V.12 - Mortality by Social Class and Tenure 1971-75 Among Men Aged 15-64

(standardized mortality ratios)

Social Class	Owner-Occupiers	Local Authority Tenants	Renting from Private Landlords
I	79	99	93
II	74	99	104
III - non-manual	79	121	112
III - manual	83	104	99
IV	83	106	100
V	98	123	126

Source: P. Goldblatt and A. Fox, 'Household Mortality from the OPCS Longitudinal Study, Population Trends No. 14, 1978.

A 'standardized mortality ratio' is the ratio of the actual number of deaths in a particular population to the number that would be expected if the population being studied was subject to the same age-specific mortality rates as the whole population. 'Social class' in medical statistics is defined in terms of occupation, so when occupation is held constant death rates were distinctly higher among tenants than among owner-occupiers, just as were unemployment rates. The association between tenure and mortality may presumably be interpreted by higher death rates being associated with poorer health, poor health leading to lower earning power, and low earning power leading to renting rather than owner-occupation. A mechanism of selection, or self-selection (or of course both) for health risk appears to have been at work, which left those householders with poorer health and most at risk of unemployment little choice but to be tenants, which meant increasingly local authority tenants.

Unemployment rates also differed between tenures in a way that could not be explained by regional differences in unemployment rates and in housing tenure, or by differences in the occupations of tenants and owner-occupiers. Table V.13 shows this for 1977.

A higher proportion of tenant household heads in the occupations where unemployment was comparatively high was thus only a small part of the explanation of why the proportion unemployed was so much higher among tenants than among owner-occupiers. Unadjusted, the difference was 6.5 percentage points for local authority tenants and 4.0 for other tenants; after adjustment for occupation the differences were 5.1 percentage points and 3.3, that is to say about four-fifths as great as the difference before allowing for the variations in unemployment with occupation. A finer classification of occupations might, of course, increase the calculated proportions of the difference that was due to occupation as opposed to tenure as such. Nevertheless, the distinction is clearly marked, and would seem to show that in the 1970s people most at risk to unemployment were most likely to be council tenants and least likely to be owner-occupiers. We can rule out as an explanation owner-occupiers being obliged by unemployment to sell up and become tenants or unemployment causing them to be dispossessed as a result of court action

193

Table V.13 - Unemployment Rates Among Heads of Household
            According to Socio-Economic Group and Tenure:
            England 1977

(percent)

	Owner Occu- piers	LA and HA Tenants	Tenants Renting from Private Landlords	All Tenure
Professional occu- pations, employers, managers	1.3	5.7	3.7	2.0
Intermediate and junior non-manual	2.6	6.3	6.9	3.9
Skilled manual (incl. foremen and own account non- professional)	2.5	8.3	5.4	4.9
Semi-skilled	4.4	8.8	8.3	6.9
Unskilled	6.1	16.4	10.9	12.9
All Occupations	2.4	8.9	6.4	4.8
Average, if proportion of heads in each occupation were the same in all tenures	2.7	7.8	6.0	4.8

Source: NDHS

for mortgage possession; such evidence as there is
(30) about the number of moves from owner-occupation to renting (whether from a private or public
landlord) and the reasons for moving suggests that
such moves are too few in total to have been a
major explanation for the much lower unemployment
rate among owner-occupiers. Likewise, greater
difficulties faced by local authority tenants in
making long distance moves (31) cannot contribute
much to explaining the difference in unemployment
rates between owner-occupiers and local authority
tenants, for the proportion of owner-occupiers
making long distance moves for reasons to do with
employment was too low for a similar frequency of
moves by council tenants to have had an appreciable

effect on the number of tenants unemployed. The implication is that a selection effect was at work, by which householders least at risk to employment were most likely to become owner-occupiers, with the others having little choice but to be tenants. Increasingly they were local authority tenants.

During the 1960s and 1970s the proportion of local authority tenants with no member earning increased very sharply. At the beginning of the 1960s (see Table V.7 above) a smaller proportion of local authority tenant households were headed by someone classified as 'retired and unoccupied', or had no member in paid employment. But by the late 1970s the oppposite had become true, with a much higher proportion of local authority tenant households than of owner-occupier households having no member earning.

Table V.14 - Households According to Number of Earners

(percent)

	None	One	Two	Three or More	All House- holds
Owner-Occupiers					
1962	17	45	28	9	100
1978	19	30	40	11	100
Local Authority Tenants					
1962	11	34	33	22	100
1978	30	30	28	12	100
All Tenures (*)					
1962	16	42	29	13	100
1978	25	30	35	10	100

Note: (*) In 1978 owner-occupiers, local authority tenants and tenants renting unfurnished from private landlords.

Source: 1962 from J.B. Cullingworth, English Housing Trends, Table 6; 1978 from Family Expenditure Survey in Housing and Construction Statistics No. 32, Table XXII.

The increase in the proportion of local authority tenant households with no earning member was
much greater than could be explained just by the
increase in the total number of households in the
population with retired heads as a result of the
ageing of the population, and the much higher
proportion of widows and widowers continuing to
live as independent households after their
partner's death. Further confirmation of this is
given by the analysis of the tenure of households
receiving National Assistance (Supplementary
Benefit after the end of 1966). The distinction
between recipients above and below pensionable age
was not drawn in official figures before 1960, but
it is an important distinction and is the reason
for including 1965 and 1967 figures to allow for
the replacement of National Assistance by Supplementary Benefit. This change was intended to
(among other things) end the "poor law" reputation
of National Assistance; if it succeeded, the impact
could reasonably be expected to be greatest on the
take-up of benefit by older people who could
remember old days of the Poor Law, the Boards of
Guardians (32) and the Relieving Officer.

The contrast between the way in which householders of pensionable age receiving benefit were
divided between the public and private rented
sectors in 1960 (in proportions 37:63) and in 1976
(70:30) shows how building for older people and
slum clearance had increased the number of older
people who were local authority tenants. Equally
striking was the increase in the number of tenants
below pensionable age receiving National Assis-
tance/Supplementary Benefit, whose number virtually
trebled between 1960 and 1976. More divorces and
separations and higher unemployment increased the
number of households below pensionable age
receiving Supplementary Benefit; as a result of the
selection process commented on above and allocation
of local authority tenancies according to need, 80%
of the increase in the number of such households
were local authority tenants. Since the Supplementary Benefit (and before that National Assistance)
scales included rent in full (33) (except where the
accommodation is adjudged in excess of the claim-
ant's needs, which hardly ever arose with local
authority tenants), the proportion of tenants that
had the whole of any increase in rent paid for them
rose from one-eighth in 1960 to one-fifth in the
mid-1970s. There were further increases in the

Table V.15 - Tenure of Householders Receiving
Supplementary Benefit: Great Britain

(thousands)

		Local Authority Tenants	Other Tenants	Owner Occupiers	All Households (Excl. rent free)
1954		291	917	144	1,352
1960					
Above	pensionable age	338	565	139	1,042
Below	pensionable age	168	165	38	371
Total		506	730	177	1,413
1965					
Above	pensionable age	477	517	178	1,172
Below	pensionable age	222	158	45	425
Total		699	675	223	1,597
1967					
Above	pensionable age	698	622	299	1,619
Below	pensionable age	279	192	63	534
Total		978	814	362	2,159
1970					
Above	pensionable age	855	568	825	1,748
Below	pensionable age	331	177	74	582
Total		1,186	745	398	2,330
1976					
Above	pensionable age	894	385	300	1,579
Below	pensionable age	495	174	109	778
Total		1,389	559	409	2,357

Source: National Assistance Board, Annual Report for 1954, Cmnd.9530 (1955); Annual Report for 1960 Cmnd.1730 (1962), p.17; Annual Report for 1965, Cmnd.3042 (1966), Table 7 Ministry of Social Security Annual Report 1967, Cmnd.3693 (1968), Tables 38-40; Department of Health and Social Security, Annual Report 1970, Cmd.4714 (1971), Tables 120-122; Social Security Statistics 1976, Tables 34.63 and 34.65.

1980s, but that is beyond the period that this book covers.

Proportions of households do not tell the whole story when the total of tenant households was growing fast; the absolute numbers are important as well. In 1962, there were in England and Wales about 3,150,000 earning and 400,000 non-earning households who were local authority tenants; in 1969 about 3,500,000 earning and 950,000 non-earning households; in 1978 about 3,800,000 earning and 1,650,000 non-earning households. Between 1962 and 1978 there was a net increase of about 1,900,000 in the number of local authority tenant households; of this net increase about 650,000 were households with at least one earner, and 1,250,000 were households with no earning member. This increase in the number and proportion of households was the inevitable outcome of a policy of allocating local authority tenancies according to assessed need, for absence of a regular earner in the household is obviously an extremely common reason for a household having an income too low to afford adequate housing, in conditions when an ever-increasing proportion of those households with sufficient income to have a choice of tenure chose owner-occupation.

By the 1970s owner-occupation had become the preferred tenure of all but elderly household heads and other householders not in the working population. This preference was extremely important not just for the demand to rent from local authorities but for the private rented sector as well. The preference for owner-occupation is outlined in Tables V.16 (preferred tenure by current tenure) and V.17 (preferred tenure according to age and occupation). The information about preferences is taken from the General Household Survey for 1978 and refers to household heads. It is therefore to be preferred to the rather more widely quoted figures (including 70% of people preferring owner-occupation) from the survey carried out in 1975 by the British Market Research Bureau for the Building and Civil Engineering Economic Development Council (34), which were not confined to household heads.

That only a negligible proportion of owner-occupiers with mortgages expressed a preference for renting is significant because they are likely to be much more recent entrants to owner-occupation than are outright owners; very few new entrants to owner-occupation come in without a mortgage. The

198

Table V.16 - Expression of Tenure Preference by Heads of Household 1978

(percent)

Actual Tenure	Rent from Council	Rent Privately	Rent but no Preference about from whom, or from other Source	Owner-Occupation	Other or Undecided	Total
Outright owner	8	1	2	84	4	100
Own on mortgage	1	-	-	97	1	100
Rent from local authority	43	2	5	49	2	100
Rent with job or business	15	4	3	76	2	100
Rent with housing association	16	12	13	56	3	100
Rent from private landlord, unfurnished	23	12	12	47	6	100
Rent from private landlord, furnished	11	7	4	74	4	100
All tenures	19	2	3	72	3	100

Source: General Household Survey 1978, Table 4.27

Table V.17 - Tenure Preference According to Age and Occupation of Household Head

(percent)

	Preferred Tenure				
	Rent from Council	Rent Privately	Rent from other Source or Undecided	Owner-Occupation	Other or not Stated	Total
Age of Head						
Under 25	9	3	3	85	1	100
25-29	5	1	-	93	1	100
30-44	6	1	1	91	1	100
45-59	17	1	3	77	2	100
60-69	31	4	4	58	3	100
70 or over	39	5	9	41	6	100
Occupation						
Professional	1	-	1	96	2	100
Employers, managers	3	1	1	94	1	100
Intermediate non-manual	3	1	1	93	1	100
Junior non-manual	11	1	2	84	2	100
Skilled manual, etc.	11	1	1	85	1	100
Semi-skilled and personal service	21	2	3	73	2	100
Unskilled	34	3	5	56	2	100
Not economically active	36	4	7	48	5	100

Source: General Household Survey 1978, Tables 4.23 and 4.25.

increase in owner-occupation in the 1960s and 1970s
was the response to an increase in demand, very
isolated exceptions apart, not a willy-nilly
adjustment to a reduced supply of rented accommodation. Table V.16 also shows clearly that the
preference for owner-occupation was far from being
just a preference against renting from local authorities. One cannot over-emphasize the fact that
during this period the preference for owner-
occupation was substantially stronger as against
renting from private landlords than against renting
from local authorities. This preference for owning
as against renting from private landlords was
extremely important, as we shall see in Chapter
VIII, in explaining the reduction in the private
rented sector.

Table V.17 shows that the age profile of
preference for owner-occupation was clear cut as
the age profile of actual owner-occupation (Table
V.10 above). Many older people who had first set
up home when renting was the majority tenure
retained the preference for renting when younger
people preferred to own. There was also a clear
connection between occupation and preference for
owning, though it should be noted that in all
groups other than the economically inactive a
majority preferred owner-occupation. The way in
which the change in the actual tenure proportions
(as distinct from preference) was related to
occupation is shown in Table V.18. To use census
information to make the comparison, 1981 must be
included, which brings in the effect of the council
house sales policy introduced by the new government
in 1979. But because out of the total increase in
the owner-occupied housing stock between the 1971
and the 1981 Censuses, only about 0.2 million came
from council house sales between May 1979 and the
1981 Census, nearly all of the change shown in
Table V.18 depicts the 'ordinary' growth of owner-
occupation. "Chief economic supporter" in 1961 and
household head in 1981 are not identical, but are
close enough to allow the comparison to show the
broad picture of how housing tenure changed for
each of the socio-economic groups.

The proportion of householders in all socio-
economic groups that were tenants of private landlords fell sharply and the proportion of owner-
occupiers rose. The rise in the proportion of
owner-occupiers was however least among unskilled
manual workers. The unchanged proportions of local

Table V.18 - Housing Tenure and Socio-Economic Group in England and Wales 1961 and 1981

(percentages)

	.... 1961			.... 1981		
	Owner Occupier	Local Authority Tenants	Other Tenants	Owner-Occupier	Local Authority Tenants	Other Tenants
Employers and managers	67	7	26	82	7	11
Professional occupations	69	6	25	87	4	10
Intermediate non-manual	60	11	28	77	11	13
Junior non-manual	51	17	32	66	18	16
Foremen and skilled manual employees	37	32	31	56	35	9
Semi-skilled manual employees	29	32	39	42	42	16
Unskilled manual employees	22	39	39	31	56	13
Working on own account (excluding professional)	57	11	32	70	17	13
Total of above	43	24	32	62	25	12

Note: Percentages do not always add to 100 owing to rounding.

Source: Census of England and Wales 1961, Household Composition Tables, Table 4;
         Census 1981 Household and Family Composition England and Wales, Table 16.

authority tenants in the non-manual occupations were a marked contrast with the rise in the proportion of local authority tenants among households headed by semi-skilled and unskilled manual workers. These changes, alongside the rise in the proportion of local authority tenant households with no earning member, were viewed by some observers with concern as "social polarization" between the tenures and (a more extreme contention) taking local authority housing in the direction of "welfare housing" on the (alleged) American model. Something of the sort was probably inherent in a situation where owner-occupation is the preferred tenure and financially within the reach of a high proportion of households that are in steady employment. So long as owner-occupation grew mainly by open market purchase, the rate of movement in the direction of "polarization" would be slow and the local authority housing stock would continue to grow, though slowly. Much more rapid change could occur if council houses were sold to sitting tenants, but that is outside the period this study covers.

Within the period, however, the growth of owner-occupation led to a slowing down in the growth of demand for council housing and hence to a fall in the size of the increment to the local authority stock demanded year by year and in the pressure of demand for tenancies. The war years and post-war conditions resulted in a demand for tenancies far greater than the number available, and a demand by local authorities to build many more houses than the number for which central government was able to provide the resources and funds. In such conditions fairness in allocating a limited supply was all-important in maintaining public confidence, and where "queue jumping" was anathema. There was for long a strong flavour of the wartime ideas of "fair shares" and "wait for your turn". There were from time to time pressures for reform so as to give more weight to 'social' needs and less to housing needs and time on the waiting list. The best discussion of these issues was in Council Housing Purposes, Procedures and Priorities, Ninth Report of the Housing Management Sub-Committee of the Central Housing Advisory Committee (HMSO for Ministry of Housing and Local Government 1969), usually known as the Cullingworth Report. Most of this report consisted of advice about the various categories of housing need for which local authorities might cater, and about balancing the conflicting claims of households in different kinds of 'need'. That the local authorities could not meet all the demands in them, it was taken for granted in the Report's discussion. The first signs of change came at the end of the 1960s and in the early 1970s when, particularly in the north of England, many local authorities found that the supply of dwellings for re-letting was rising and the demand falling, so that long queues were no longer the order of the day. The surge of house prices in 1972 and 1973 and the leap in interest rates cut down the supply of re-lets as fewer tenants could afford to move away to buy, and added to the demand for tenancies. But in the mid- and later 1970s, when a fresh building drive augmented by purchases of houses had added to supply, the "difficult to let" problem reappeared, and on a larger scale. Instead of almost any council dwelling almost anywhere being gladly taken by households that had been waiting a long time, there were unpopular types of dwellings and unpopular estates that would be refused by many prospective tenants. This was novel, and the working doctrine and principles that guided councils and their officers were ill-suited to managing in such conditions. The doctrine and principles had been evolved in the conditions of shortage just referred to. Some local authorities responded by widening the range of households to whom they would let accommodation that their priority clientele were little interested in, including experiments with 'over the counter' letting. In these conditions the local authorities' demand to build diminished.

Other Aspects of Housing Tenure in the 1960s and 1970s: Council House Sales and Housing Associations

Council house sales were not numerous enough in the period studied to make much of a contribution to the change in the tenure pattern discussed above, but from the late 1960s onwards they generated a great deal of party contention. That was not always so, however, and a brief look at the history of policy on sales is of interest for that reason. Under the Housing Acts sale of houses built with subsidy required the consent of the Minister (originally the Minister of Health, then the Minister of Housing and Local Government, and after 1970 the Secretary of State for the

Environment). In this respect sales of council
houses differed from sales of land and buildings
used in the provision of other local authority
services, which were governed by the ordinary rules
about obtaining the best price for assets disposed
of, and only disposing of them when the service for
which they were used could better be provided in
other ways. Selling council houses to save the
Exchequer subsidy (always discontinued on sale) was
advocated as early as 1932 by the Committee on
Local Expenditure (35), though as far as is known
nothing came of it. In 1952 the Minister gave a
"general consent" to the sale of council houses,
subject to conditions about the price (36). For
pre-1939 houses the price was to be at least 20
times the annual rent; for post-war houses the
price was to be not less than cost. This "cost
floor" (as it subsequently came to be termed)
remained part of the rules governing council house
sales, and served to prevent subsidized building
for sale in the guise of building for letting. The
1952 Circular required that the terms of sale
should include a right of 'pre-emption', that the
local authority should have the right to buy back
the dwelling at the original disposal price if the
purchaser should move away within 5 years. The
condition was imposed, in the words of the
Circular, to prevent "profiteering" (37). The next
Circular on the subject, Circular 5/60, renewed the
general consent to sales on the terms of the 1952
Circular, but reiterated that these were minima
that should not be regarded as the norm, coupled
with an admonition against selling at "sacrificial"
prices and to consider carefully the effect that
sales would have on the ability of authorities to
accommodate poorer families at rents within their
means. A Conservative government, of course,
issued this Circular. Inflation made the 1952
minimum prices obsolete for sales of post-war
houses, and Circular 24/67 replaced them with a
general consent to sell at prices up to 20% below
market value provided that there was a 5 year pre-
exemption condition. The discount was rationalized
by the pre-emption condition making the property
less valuable than it would have been had it not
been encumbered by such a condition. In the
absence of a market in houses subject to such
conditions, though, whether a 20% discount really
did accord with the reduction of the market value
could not be tested. This Circular was issued by a

Labour government; comparison of its terms with the Circular issued in 1960 shows that council house sales had not yet become a source of contention between the parties to any great degree.

That stage was soon reached, though. Conservatives won control of many major local authorities in 1967, notably Greater London and Birmingham, and in those two authorities in particular embarked on selling council houses as a matter of party policy. The following year Circular 42/68 restricted sales in any one year in Greater London, the West Midlands, Manchester and Merseyside conurbations (considered to be the areas where shortages of housing were greatest) to one-quarter of one percent of local authority's housing stock in any one year. The incoming Conservative government in 1970 revoked this restriction and gave a general consent to sales at discount of up to 30% subject to an 8 year pre-emption condition (Circular 54/70).

A brief reference to housing associations is called for in a history of policy on housing tenure in the post-war years and particularly the 1960s and 1970s. The nineteenth century origins of housing associations were discussed in Chapter II. In 1914 they probably owned about 50,000 dwellings, of which nearly 40,000 were in London. In the inter-war years housing associations were enabled to build with subsidies broadly similar to those available to local authorities. The total number of houses and flats they built in the inter-war years can be estimated at about 24,000 (38). Housing associations continued to be active in the post-war years, when as well as what had come to be known as the "traditional" housing associations, "industrial" housing associations, that is to say associations set up to provide housing to let to workers in particular industries, became more prominent. The Coal Industry Housing Association was an example. The "traditional" housing associations had close working relationships with the local authorities, as indeed they had always done since the Metropolitan Board of Works provided them with sites. Loans from local authorities were their main source of finance for capital expenditure, and the authorities normally obtained in return the right of nomination to a proportion of the tenancies. They received subsidies on the same scale (per dwelling built) as did local authorities and provided for much the same kind of household

except, perhaps, by accommodating a higher proportion of older people than the local authorities did
before the end of the 1960s.

In the early 1960s came a major innovation of
policy: the Housing Act 1961 provided for the
financing of experimental 'cost rent' and 'co-
ownership' societies, and the Housing Act 1964 set
up arrangements for financing such societies on a
much larger scale. It set up the Housing Corporation to make loans to housing societies from a fund
of £100 million borrowed from the Exchequer, and
exercise the supervision appropriate. The expectation was that finance would be provided in proportions two-thirds from building societies and one-
third from the Corporation. These 'new style'
housing societies were seen as an alternative to
owner-occupation and subsidized public sector
renting, an attempt to avert a continuing move
towards a state of affairs where the only alternative to owner-occupation was subsidized housing to
rent plus a fast diminishing private rented sector.
The Scandinavian example seems to have been particularly important (39).

There were high hopes in the early and mid-
1960s of 'new style' housing societies; but neither
type made any real headway. Cost-rent housing was
quickly made financially unworkable by high
interest rates: the rent required to cover the
outgoings was so high that virtually anyone who
could afford it could afford the mortgage outgoings
to buy a house, with the added advantage that
morgage interest attracted tax relief whereas rent
(of all kinds, cost-rent housing included) did not.
Only 1,600 'cost-rent' houses were built. Co-
ownership lasted somewhat longer, not least because
as a species of owner-occupation it attracted tax
relief on mortgage interest (Finance Act 1963) and
option mortgage subsidy (Housing Act 1967). Co-
ownership was a cross between renting and owner-
occupation: what distinguished it from renting was
that members leaving after five years were entitled
to receive a capital payment based on the appreciation in value of houses owned by the society. When
house prices rose as fast as they did in the early
1970s though, such a payment was unattractive
compared with the full capital appreciation that
the owner-occupier received. There was no real
financial advantage compared with owner-occupation
other than the low deposit (six months rent) and
absence of the need to raise a mortgage individu-

ally. By the early 1970s, the impetus behind co-
ownership societies was spent.

Then came a very radical change in the financing of housing associations and the amount of their
activity. The Housing Act 1974 provided financial
arrangements that enabled housing associations to
build houses, and improve older houses, on a large
scale notwithstanding the high interest and rapid
inflation, overcoming them by sheer weight of
subsidy. Under the Housing Finance Act 1972 rents
of housing association dwellings were determined
through the 'fair rent' system (40), which would
avoid the disparities that there could have been
between rents for similar dwellings charged by
different associations if historic costs were used
as the basis for setting rents. That part of the
cost of new houses or flats (or of improvement
work) that could not be paid for, through loan
charges, from 'fair' rents (after deducting costs
of upkeep and management), was met from a capital
grant, the 'Housing Association Grant'. This
arrangement in effect wrote off a large part (often
as high as three-quarters, and even more in London)
of the capital cost, so as to leave to housing
associations only what they could service from fair
rents. Since their rent income was fixed from
outside and the extent to which they could cross
subsidies from the 'profit' on older houses built
at lower historic cost varied so much from one
association to another, there was a need for a last
resort source of revenue, which was provided by
Revenue Deficit Grant which was payable at the
discretion of the Department of the Environment.
Such a subsidy system necessarily carried with it
very detailed control over housing associations'
capital expenditure, exercised partly by the
Housing Corporation and partly by the Department of
the Environment. The contribution to public sector
house building that was made by housing associations grew fast during the 1970s, both absolutely
and relative to the public sector as a whole.
Housing associations were also active in buying
older property for modernization and conversions.

Concluding Observations

The principal theme of this chapter has been
how rapidly owner-occupation increased, both
absolutely and as a proportion of all households
and of the housing stock. But, as the chronology

208

summarized in Table V.1 makes amply clear, to think
of the course of owner-occupation having been
'onwards and upwards' ever since the end of World
War I would be greatly in error. In the decade
from 1939 there was little net increase in the
number of owner-occupiers compared with an increase
of around 600,000 in the number of local authority
houses; and from the late 1940s to the very end of
the 1950s the resumed growth of owner-occupation
came much less from the revival of new building for
sale to owner-occupiers than from a very large
number of sales for owner-occupation that had
previously been rented from private landlords. It
was the transfer of houses from the private rented
sector, not new building for private owners, that
made owner-occupation the largest of the tenures by
the end of the 1950s. During the 1950s and 1960s,
encouraging owner-occupation had the practical
effect less of reducing the number of households
that wanted local authority tenancies than of
hastening the transfer of houses (and some flats)
from private landlords to owner-occupiers. In
considering whether this transfer really did add to
the pressure of demand for local authority housing
(the implicit assumption of those that argued that
different policies on rent control would have
permitted substantially less building in the public
sector) regard must be had to where the purchasers
from landlords of vacant houses for owner-occupation would otherwise have gone. Most would have
had to rent; for the houses sold by landlords were
for the most part at the cheapest end of the market
(most had been built before 1914), so that it is
very unlikely that there would have been much more
new building for owner-occupation in the absence of
sales. If so, then the demand for local authority
tenancies would have been very little less than it
actually was. And given the preference for owner-
occupation rather than renting, it could be argued
that the pre-1914 housing stock that was not unfit
provided better service if owned by its occupiers
than if it remained rented.

If this argument is correct, competition
between owner-occupation and local authority
housing was minimal until at least the later 1960s
and probably the early 1970s. Both grew by housing
people formerly catered for by accommodation let by
private landlords.

In the 1950s, as in the 1920s and 1930s, those
who looked with disfavour on a growing local

authority housing stock and preferred provision of
housing to be by private enterprise, tended to look
less to owner-occupation than to a revival of the
private rented sector. Disadvantages of owner-
occupation were discerned not only from the political Left but from the political Right. An
example may be seen in the contention (in a booklet
published by the Institute of Economic Affairs)
that " .... it would have been a much more sensible
sort of society in which they (i.e. marginal first-
time house purchasers) had been able to leave that
specialized business (management and upkeep of
houses) to a landlord, and rent a house in a free
market" (41). This was a judgement that heavily
under-estimated the growth in the preference for
owner-occupation, but had the merit of recognizing
that owner-occupation and the private rented sector
were rivals. In such circumstances encouraging the
growth of owner-occupation and stimulating the
private rented sector were contradictory aims of
policy. Not until the private rented sector had
diminished a very long way did encouraging owner-
occupation provide a way of obviating a further
rapid growth of public sector renting, and that
stage was not reached until the very end of the
1970s. The revival of new building for letting by
private enterprise as an alternative to public
sector building, whether in the inter-war years or
in the 1940s, 1950s and 1960s would have depended
either on subsidized building for rental by private
owners, or on higher pricing all round for housing,
with rents raised sufficiently and standards
lowered if necessary for a commercially acceptable
return to be obtained from the rents that could be
got from the housholds that in the 1950s became
council tenants. Why British housing policy did
not take the second of these courses is a reasonably straightforward question to answer, though as
we shall see in Chapters VII and VIII, measures
were taken in the second half of the 1950s that
appeared to be pointing in that direction. But why
subsidized housing for renting in Britain was
almost entirely in direct ownership of public
authorities whereas in most other countries subsidies to private owners have been used very extensively is a much more difficult question to answer.

Notes and References

(1) Ministry of Health, Departmental Committee on Valuation for Rates, Report on Valuation for Rates 1939, Appendix D (published in 1944).

(2) Report published by Ministry of Labour and National Service, 1956.

(3) Ministry of Housing and Local Government, Housing Returns 30th June 1953

(4) General Household Survey, 1981, (unpublished table).

(5) In the Housing Policy (1977) Green Paper (Cmd.6851), p.14, the number of owner-occupied dwellings in 1951 was estimated at 3.9 million, 31% of the stock.

(6) See Chapter VI, Table 2.

(7) Ministry of Housing and Local Government, Rent Act 1957, Report of Enquiry, Cmd.1246, (1960)

(8) Cmd.1246, (1960), Tables 2(a) and 2(b).

(9) Cmd.1246, (1960), p.11.

(10) Government Social Survey, The Housing Survey in England and Wales, HMSO, 1967.

(11) Housing Survey in England and Wales, Table 6.5.

(12) Chapter VI, Table 2.

(13) Census of England and Wales 1931, Housing Report and Tables, pp.xlv-1, and Appendix Table M.

(14) British Labour Statistics Historical Abstract (Department of Employment, London, 1972) Table 38 gives 64s.6d. as an average wage in 1935 for men in manual work in industries covered by the census of production.

(15) T. Young, Becontree and Dagenham, Becontree Social Survey Committee, London, 1934.

(16) For examples see J. Tucker, Honourable Estates, Gollancz, London, 1966.

(17) J. Collison, The Cuttleslowe Walls, A Study in Social Class, Faber, London, 1963.

(18) Committee on Local Expenditure, Report, Cmd.4200 (1932), para.96.

(19) Report of Enquiry into Household Expenditure, HMSO 1967, Tables 25, 26, 27, 28 and 29.

(20) See Chapter VII.

(21) Government Social Survey, P. Gray and R. Russell The Housing Situation in 1960, Table 26.

(22) Ibid., Table 27.

(23) The number of housing association tenants in 1961 can be estimated, by working back from 1971, at about 100,000.

(24) For details of this survey, see Department of the Environment, National Dwelling and Housing Survey, (HMSO, 1979).

(25) Housing Policy Technical Volume 1977, Chapter 7, Table VII.1.

(26) See page 100 above.

(27) On the evidence of the 1976 Family Formation Survey carried out by the Office of Population Censuses and Surveys. See A.E. Holmans, 'Housing Careers of Recently Married Couples', Population Trends No. 24, (1981)

(28) K. Dunnell, Family Formation 1976, (HMSO for Office of Population Censuses and Surveys), 1979.

(29) M. Murphy, communication.

(30) Housing Policy Technical Volume, Chapter 2, Table II.39.

(31) G.A. Hughes and B. McCormick, 'Do Council Housing Policies Reduce Migration?', Economic Journal, 1981.

(32) Boards of Guardians were dissolved in 1929 and their responsibilities (and their staff) transferred to Public Assistance Committees of the counties and county boroughs. Means-tested assistance to people above working age was "nationalized" by the National Insurance Act 1946.

(33) This was the system that was in force until the introduction of Housing Benefit in 1983.

(34) British Market Research Bureau, Housing Consumer Survey, National Economic Development Office, London, 1977.

(35) Committee of Local Expenditure, Report, Cmd.4200 (1932) para.97.

(36) Ministry of Housing and Local Government, Circular 64/52.

(37) Circular 64/52, paragraph 6 (2).

(38) The number of houses built by private enterprise (which before 1945 included housing associations) under the Housing Acts 1924, 1930 and 1935.

(39) Department of the Environment, Housing Associations a Working Paper by the Central Housing Advisory Committee, HMSO, 1971, pp.53-54. See Chapters 3 and 4 for a description of cost-renting and co-ownership societies.

(40) See Chapter VIII for detailed discussion.
(41) N. Macrae, <u>To Let</u>, Institute of Economic
      Affairs, London, 1960, p.37.

CHAPTER VI

FINANCE OF OWNER-OCCUPATION

The previous chapter outlined the increase through the years in the number of owner-occupiers, and who they were in terms of income, age, occupation and type of household. This chapter discusses the way in which that growth of owner-occupation was financed, the terms on which it was financed, and support for owner-occupation from public funds. For reasons discussed in Chapter I, finance is far more important for the purchase of houses and housing than for any other goods and services bought by households, so policy on house purchase finance is very important. Sources of finance for house purchase and rates of interest must necessarily take a history of housing policy some way into the history of money, finance, and banking generally, and brings the recent part of such a history into contact with questions of national economic policy. A major theme must be how the arrangements for housing finance coped with high and rising interest rates, and then in the 1970s very unstable interest rates. The institutions, practices and usages of house purchase finance had grown up in conditions when the price level was fairly stable and interest rates low (at least by the standards of the 1960s and 1970s), and so too had the ways of thought of both borrowers and lenders. The way in which house purchase finance adapted to higher interest rates in Britain was strongly influenced by the extent of the dependence of the housing market for finance on a single class of specialist financial intermediaries, the building societies. From the 1920s onwards, the building societies were the principal lenders for house purchase, and taken as a group dominated the

214

British housing market in a way that had few, if
any parallels in other countries. The savings bank
system in Britain was closely linked to the State,
and channelled the funds invested into government
(including local government) debt. The commercial
banks, again in contrast with other countries, took
little interest in house purchase finance for
nearly all the period studied, apart from bridging
loans and house purchase loans to their employees.
Long-term loans to ordinary customers for house
purchase were very few. Why the British banks
should have kept away from the housing market in
this way until the 1980s is a question that belongs
more to a history of banking; but the fact of their
not seeking business in the market for house
purchase loans was extremely important for it left
the building societies with no effective rivals for
most of the time. The main groups of lenders other
than the building societies were the local authorities and the insurance companies. English local
authorities were first empowered to make loans for
house purchase in 1899 (by the Small Dwellings
Acquisition Act) and, as we shall see, there were
times when they made house purchase loans on quite
a large scale. But they were never a real
challenge to the building societies. Insurance
companies likewise never lent on a large scale for
house purchase. Private loans, often arranged by
solicitors with funds to invest on behalf of
clients, are widely considered to have been an
important source of funds for house purchase before
1914 and in the inter-war years, but no estimate
has ever been made of the number of such loans.

Table VI.1 below brings together such estimates as can be made of the number of house
purchase advances outstanding during the period
covered by the present history. It begins with
1939, as not until then is there a satisfactory
estimate of the total owner-occupied housing stock
with which to compare the number of loans. Before
then, all that can safely be said is that the
number of outstanding house purchase loans by
building societies was lower in relation to the
total owner-occupied housing stock, before 1914
much lower. Not until 1960 can an estimate be made
of the proportion of the owner-occupied housing
stock that was mortgaged, and hence the total of
house purchase loans.

Rather more than one-third of the owner-
occupied housing stock was mortgaged to building

Table VI.1 - Owner-Occupied Dwellings and Outstanding Loans: England and Wales

(thousands)

	Total Owner-Occupied Dwellings	Total Mortgaged Dwellings	Building Societies	Local Author-ities	Insurance Companies	Banks	Other
1939	3,790	...	1,370	100	...	...	...
1953	4,400	...	1,630	110	...	...	...
1961	6,390	3,250	2,350	260	200	...	440
1971	8,660	4,690	3,510	460	340	...	380
1977	10,170	5,790	4,540	680	330	170	70

Sources: Totals of owner-occupied dwellings from Table V.1.

Totals of mortgaged dwellings: 1961 calculated from Housing Situation in England and Wales, Table 26 (50.9%); 1971 from General Household Survey, 1977 National Dwelling and Household Survey with estimate for Wales. Building society mortgages: total outstanding less 5% for Scotland and Northern Ireland, less 4% for advances on dwellings not owner-occupied in 1939, 2% in 1953, and 1% in 1961, 1964 and 1971. Local authorities and insurance companies: deduced from outstanding debt, pro-rata to building societies, modified by difference between average size of new advance compared with building societies.

societies as security for house purchase loans in
1939; about the same proportion in 1961; but 40% in
1971, and 45% in 1977. The figures for outstanding
advances by "banks and other" (mainly "other"
before 1971) are residuals, and so less secure than
the estimate of loans by building societies,
insurance companies, and banks. But they are
sufficient to show that although private loans were
still numerous at the beginning of the 1960s, by
the later 1970s they had almost died out as
building societies had expanded. In view of the
way in which building societies came to be the main
source of house purchase loans, their growth must
be studied in considerable detail, including the
amounts lent and borrowed, their interest rates,
and sources of funds. Lending by local authorities
and insurance companies is studied more cursorily.

Building Societies:
The Transformation in the Inter-War Years

It was in the inter-war years that building
societies came to be an important part of the
housing system in England, as the main source of
finance for the boom in house building for owner-
occupation that was described in Chapter III. But
they had a history that can be traced back to the
last quarter of the eighteenth century. For
present purposes, though, it is not necessary to
review their history as far back as that, or even
to say much about their nineteenth century history,
for even then their activity was on too small a
scale to have any significant impact on housing.
Their history that far back is much more a part of
social history, particularly that of friendly
societies, than of the history of housing. As
friendly societies they became subject to the
jurisdiction of the Friendly Societies Registry,
which continued to be the agency that regulated
them long after they had grown into quite different
organizations, and indeed continues to do so to
this day. The history of the replacement of the
original 'terminating' society (a society which
came to an end when all the members who had joined
with a view to purchasing a house had been enabled
to buy them) by the 'permanent' building society
(still part of the name of some of the older established building societies), and the legislation of
1836, 1874 and 1894 may be studied in the standard
histories by Cleary (1) and Ashworth (2). The

point of emphasis here is that in the decade before 1914 the building societies activity even in total was small in scale compared with the size of the housing system. Their total assets in 1900 were some £60 million, of which £46 million was out on mortgage; in 1910 these totals had grown to £76 million and £60 million respectively, and in 1913, building societies had total assets of £65 million, of which £61 million was out on mortgage (3). The sharp drop in total assets between 1910 and 1913 was the result of the failure of the Birkbeck Building Society in 1911. This society had been run more like a bank than a building society (4) with very little of its funds invested in mortgages, so its collapse left total lending on mortgage by building societies, as distinct from their total assets and liabilities, little affected. Not all the mortgage advances were on owner-occupied houses at this time, or even on houses at all. There were numerous individual instances of loans on security of commercial property (5), but no aggregate figures. Some inferences about building societies' lending can be made, though, from the analysis of outstanding loans in 1911 by size of amount advanced that was published by the Chief Registrar of Friendly Societies (6). This showed 51.0% of mortgage balances consisting of amounts of £500 or less, 19.1% £500 to £1,000, 20.9% £1,000 to £5,000, and 3.6% consisting of advances of more than £5,000. Mortgages on properties re-possessed by the lending society, or twelve months or more in arrears, made up the rest of the total. When the average price of new houses, including land, was probably about £300 (7), very few mortgages on owner-occupied houses would be anywhere near £500. So of the £60 million in total that building societies had out on mortgage in the years immediately before 1914, it is likely that well under £30 million was advanced on security of owner-occupied houses. The number of mortgages on owner-occupied houses could hardly have been more than 100,000 to 150,000 and may well have been less.

The total number of separate dwellings in 1911 was just under 7.7 million and owner-occupied houses are supposed to have been about one-tenth of the total. So the proportion of owner-occupied houses mortgaged to building societies before 1914 was much smaller than it became in the inter-war years. The main reason was lack of demand to borrow for house purchase. Over one-half of build-

ing societies' lending appears to have been to
landlords on security of houses to let, or on
property other than houses. Competition for mortgage business was a recurring theme, and if there
had been a strong demand for mortgage money to
purchase houses for owner-occupation, there would
have been no occasion to make more speculative
investments. But although the scale of building
societies' activity before 1914 was small by all
subsequent standards, many of the basic principles,
concepts and doctrines that influenced the societies' activities when they were many times larger,
had their origins in the days when they were more a
part of the friendly societies'movement than of the
housing system. The concept of the building society
as a mutual organization, not carried on for
profit, in which the funds of the investing members
are lent to borrowing members was particularly
influential, and long after 1914 gave building
societies' operations a flavour different from that
of a commercial financial institution borrowing in
the cheapest market and lending in the dearest.
Instead the working principle (however difficult to
apply in practice) was that of an equitable balance
between the interests of borrowers and investors.
Likewise, encouraging saving on grounds of the
moral and social advantages of thrift and facilitating home ownership as something desirable in
itself, are aspects of building society thinking
that had origins before 1914. Until well into the
1970s the building societies styled themselves
collectively as "the building society movement", an
expression originating in the pre-1914 world of the
friendly societies. Not until the mid-1970s did
the building societies come to style themselves
instead the "building society industry". A record
that covers the 1920s is essential in order to show
when the break with pre-1914 levels of activity
took place, and to put into proper perspective the
building societies' contribution to financing the
housing boom of the 1930s. The number of new
advances and the number of advances outstanding
were not recorded until 1928 though the amount
advanced on mortgage each year and the amount of
mortgage debt outstanding were tabulated by the
Chief Registrar of Friendly Societies from the
annual returns that building societies were
required by statute to make. Table VI.2 shows
gross advances in money terms (revalued to constant
prices), the number of advances (from 1928

onwards), and the net increase in shares and deposits (also revalued to constant prices) as the measure of the funds attracted by building societies.

Table VI.2 - The Growth of Building Society Activity
         1913 to 1939

	..... New Advances		Mortgage Advances Outstan- ding (a) ('000)	Net Increase in Shares and Deposits (£m at 1924 prices)
	Number ('000)	Amount (£m at 1924 prices)		
1913	...	17	...	...
1919	...	14	...	7
1921	...	16	...	6
1923	...	32	...	17
1925	...	50	...	22
1928	116	61	554	44
1930	159	95	720	63
1932	159	94	869	58
1933	197	121	949	33
1934	238	147	1,067	59
1935	241	153	1,180	48
1936	252	162	1,295	54
1937	241	153	1,392	57
1938	232	151	1,478	48

Note: (a) At end of year.

Source: Reports of the Chief Registrar of Friendly Socie-
         ties, tabulated by Building Societies Association
         in Compendium of Building Society Statistics,
         Tables B2 and B3. The price index used to revalue
         to 1924 prices was the consumers' expenditure
         deflator from C.H. Feinstein, Table 61.

In the immediate post-war years building societies' lending was no greater in real terms than before the war. But in 1923 a considerable increase is discernible, which continued right through the 1920s. The intake of funds by building societies and the amount they lent was much higher in the 1930s than even the later 1920s; but undue concentration on the building societies' contribution to financing the housing boom of the 1930s can easily lead to too little account being taken of how much larger, compared with before 1914, their activities had become in the 1920s. Any explanation of how the building societies were able to attract so much more money from investors in the inter-war years than before 1914 must therefore not focus exclusively on the effects of 'cheap money' and on the Depression making investments in company shares unattractive. Likewise the increase in lending began in a modest way in the early 1920s, but had gathered considerable pace by the later 1920s.

The figures for gross lending in the 1930s were probably inflated by the inclusion of loans for purposes other than buying a fresh house, in particular to replace an existing loan by a fresh loan at a lower rate of interest. Building socie- ties with an ample supply of funds were willing to make new loans to pay off old mortgage loans taken at higher rates of interest (8), as interest rates were declining and building societies were well supplied with funds. Variable rate mortgages were still far from being general, and some societies allowed their mortgagors a rebate on the interest on loans that had been taken at interest rates higher than were currently charged to new borrowers (9), in order to avoid the replacement of those loans by loans from other societies. But such arrangements were not universal, and the number of loans repaid leaves no doubt that the recorded totals of new loans were inflated by such re- financing loans. Estimating their number is too complex for the calculation to be set out here, but the over-statement is put at 17,000 advances in 1933, 10,000 in 1934, 5,000 in 1935, and 12,000 in 1936. The corrected totals of new advances are therefore estimated at: 1933, 180,000; 1934, 228,000; 1935, 236,000; and 1936, 240,000.

Before these estimates of new loans can be compared with the number of houses completed, comment is called for about what proportion of them were advances for the purchase of houses for owner- occupation, and then about what proportion of the advances for house purchase were for new houses. There is little information about either, and in the absence of figures collected from building societies generally, it is necessary to make use of the figures published by Bellman for the Abbey Road Building Society. Bellman stated that of the mortgages by the Abbey Road Society, 99.8% were on private dwelling houses, and 92.8% were to owner- occupiers (10) which leaves 7% of the mortgages as being on rented property. Some further evidence,

this time for all societies, is the analysis
published by the Chief Registrar of Friendly
Societies of size of mortgage, which distinguished
the number and amount of mortgages of £1,000 or
more. At the prices prevailing in the 1930s,
£1,000 was a very large amount to advance on an
individual house; the median price of houses on
which the Abbey Road Society made advances in 1933
was about £620; only 10.2% were priced above
£1,000, and the proportion above £1,500 (probably
reasonable figure for the price of houses on which
a £1,000 mortgage might be advanced) was only 3.1%
(11). So it is reasonably safe to reckon on a high
proportion of advances of more than £1,000 being to
finance houses built for letting. In 1928 advances
of £1,000 or more were 6% of the total by number
and 21% by value; in 1933-37, 4½% by number and 21%
by value. On this evidence, and that provided by
Bellman, it is reasonable to take 93% to 95% (by
number) of all building societies' advances in the
1930s as being for house purchase.

On the proportion that were for the purchase
of new houses, recourse has to be had once again to
Bellman:

> ".... an analysis of the Abbey Road
> Society's advances during 1932 show (sic)
> that they were about equally divided between
> new properties not previously occupied and
> properties changing hands. Admittedly, this
> particular year cannot, for reasons of
> policy which tended to give old properties a
> special prominence, be taken as evidence of
> normal conditions, but nevertheless, such a
> high proportion of older properties might
> not have been expected" (12).

The implication is that one-half of advances being
on new houses was lower than 'normal', but that the
'normal' proportion of advances on second-hand
houses was nevertheless substantial. For purposes
of comparing building societies' advances on new
houses with the total of new houses built, we may
therefore deduct one-third (at least) of the
advances as being on second-hand houses.

Local authorities lent for house purchase in
the 1920s and early 1930s on a considerable scale,
as is shown a little further on in this chapter.
About one-third of their loans before 1934 were on
new houses (13), and although it is not known

Table VI.3 – Comparison of Building Society Advances on New Houses with New Houses Completed for Owner Occupiers 1927-1939

(thousands)

	(A) All Dwellings Built for Private Owners	(B) Dwellings for Owner-Occupation (est.)	(C) All Building Society Advances	(D) Advances on New Dwellings for Owner-Occupation	(E) Local Authority Advances on New Dwellings	(F) Residue (B) less (D) less (E)
1926/27	151	110	96	60	10	40
1927/28	141	102	106	66	9	27
1928/29	119	86	116	72	7	7
1929/30	147	107	141	88	6	13
1930/31	133	97	159	99	3	-5
1931/32	136	92	162	101	3	-12
1932/33	151	102	159	99	2	1
1933/34	222	151	180	113	3	35
1934/35	294	199	228	143	3	53
1935/36	280	190	236	148	5	37
1936/37	283	192	240	150	4	38
1937/38	268	182	241	150	3	29
1938/39	237	161	232	145	2	14

Notes: Column (C); Calendar year figures taken to be comparable with financial year figures for new building; 1926 and 1927 projected from 1928 by reference to advances in money terms and index of building costs. Building society advances exclude replacement advances.

whether this proportion was constant from year to year, there is no evidence to support a different assumption. How many of the new dwellings built for private owners were for letting was not recorded fully, only the number with a rateable value of £26 or less (£35 in London) not for occupation by the owner. Estimation was therefore required (14). Table VI.3 brings together advances on new houses and new houses built for owner-occupation. Since the figures for advances by building societies refer to the whole of the United Kingdom (excluding Northern Irish societies, but including advances on properties in Northern Ireland by societies with head office in England, Wales or Scotland), houses completed in Scotland are included.

Very sweeping assumptions were made to construct Table VI.3, particularly the constant ratio of advances on new houses to total advances and the constant ratio of houses built for owner-occupation to total houses built for private owners, so it must be interpreted very cautiously. The values in column (F) for 1930, 1931 and 1932 show, indeed, that the ratios were not in fact constant. Nevertheless, it seems safe to conclude that in the boom years from 1933 to 1937, the building societies financed some 70 to 80 percent of new houses built for owner-occupation, a proportion that was, if anything, slightly higher than in the late 1920s. There must however be some doubt about this until estimates are made from building societies' own records. Building societies did not finance all of the boom in house building for owner-occupation in the 1930s, but they financed enough of it to be regarded as having played an indispensable part.

That was not all that the building societies did in the 1930s: they also financed building for letting on a substantial scale. The volume of lending in amounts above £1,000 suggests that building societies' lending to finance building for letting almost trebled between 1928-29 and 1936-38, most of which was probably to finance rented housing. For most of the 1930s building societies had as much money as they could lend or more, and were looking for mortgage business.

To explain how building societies could attract more money than they could lend, we look both at their interest rates and (as far as the evidence will allow) at their sources of funds. Building societies' interest rates may be compared with both long-term market interest rates (represented by Consols) and short-term rates (represented by 3 months bank bills, which had a very low default risk). These rates are compared with the rates charged by building societies on mortgages, and paid by them on shares. Building society shares are technically sums subscribed by investing members, and withdrawable at notice according to the society's rules. They are to be distinguished from "deposits" by investors who are technically creditors and not members, and as such would take precedence over shares in the event of winding up in recognition of which a lower rate of interest was paid than on shares. There were no instances of a major building society being wound up in the inter-war years; deposits became less and less important, so the rate of interest paid on shares may be taken as the rate received by the building society investors. The quoted rates were 'tax paid' rates, so an "equivalent gross rate" is shown, which was the rate that would give to an investor liable to income tax at the standard rate the same return net of tax as that offered by building society shares.

As was noted in Chapter III, interest rates in the 1930s were not particularly low in comparison with the half century before 1914; money was "cheap" only in comparison with the exceptionally dear money of the 1920s. Mortgages at 6% at a time when the price level was tending downwards and increases in money incomes were few (see Table IV.2) were very expensive indeed by the standards of the 1950s, 1960s and 1970s. Even in the middle and later 1930s, mortgage rates of 5% and 4½% were by subsequent standards high in relation to the rate of rise of money incomes and prices. The explanation lay not in the margin between the interest rates paid by building societies and the rate they charged to borrowers, but in the rates paid to investors. In the 1920s, the rate paid by building societies was approximately the same as the yield on Consols, but the latter was subject to tax and the former tax paid; for the investor liable to tax at the standard rate, building society shares gave a yield about 1 percentage point higher than Consols. When the general level of interest rates fell in 1932 and the next three years, rates paid by building societies came down later and by less; the interest rates offered by building societies therefore became increasingly

Table VI.4 - Building Society and Government Interest Rates
             1930-38

(percent)

	Consols	3 Month Bank Bills	Mort-gages	Shares	Share (Equiva-lent Gross Rate)
1930	4.5	2.6	5.82	4.65	6.00
1931	4.4	3.6	5.87	4.62	6.13
1932	3.7	1.9	5.87	4.52	6.03
1933	3.4	0.8	5.57	3.95	5.27
1934	3.1	0.8	5.44	3.80	4.90
1935	2.9	0.6	5.21	3.64	4.70
1936	2.9	0.6	4.97	3.45	4.53
1937	3.3	0.6	4.87	3.38	4.51
1938	3.4	0.6	4.82	3.37	4.65

Source: Rates of interest on mortgages and building society shares are as calculated by the chief Registrar of Friendly Societies (i.e. interest received or paid as a percentage of the mean of balances at the beginning and end of the year) and tabulated in Building Societies Association Compendium of Building Society Statistics. Rates on Consols and bank bills from B.R. Mitchell and Phyllis Deane, Abstract of British Historical Statistics, Chapter XV, Tables 8 and 10.

advantageous relative to competing rates, and so the amount of money seeking investment with them increased. That the building societies could attract money more readily in the 1930s is thus simply explained. Less easily explained is the increase in their receipts during the late 1920s and in 1930 and 1931 (see Table VI.2). The increase in receipts in 1930-31 can, perhaps, be explained by investors seeking safety in the Depression, but the increase during the 1920s cannot be explained in this way.

In the inter-war years the building societies attracted money in larger individual amounts from more substantial investors than they formerly did. The only figures about the size distribution of investors' individual holdings thus far published are those for the Abbey Road Building Society published by Bellman. Table VI.5 summarizes the Abbey Road Society's figures for 1913 and 1932.

Table VI.5 - Size of Abbey Road Building Society Share
Accounts 1913 and 1932

	.... 1913			.... 1932		
	Number ('000)	Amount (£'000)	Amount (%)	Number ('000)	Amount (£'000)	Amount (%)
£100 or under	5.8	127.1	21.8	40.8*	1,562	6.7
£100-£250	1.1	176.5	30.3	19.3	3,209	13.7
£250-£500	0.4	145.3	25.0	13.7	5,024	21.4
£500-£1,000	0.1	88.8	15.3	8.7	6,050	25.8
£1,000-£2,500	(a)	34.5	5.9	3.5	5,173	22.1
Over £2,500	(b)	10.0	1.7	0.7	2,415	10.3
Total	7.5	582.1	100.0	86.7	23,442	100.0

Notes: (a) 25
(b) 3
* Excludes accounts of under £1, most of which were opened by borrowers to comply with the Society's rules.

Source: Sir H. Bellman **The Thrifty Three Million**, Abbey Road Building Society, London, 1935, Tables E and F, pp.177-78.

To compare the figures for 1932 with those for 1913, the rise in prices of about 60% (see Table III.1) has to be allowed for. £250, which is a fairly generous interpretation of the upper boundary of 'small savings' in 1913 (it was about three years average pay), corresponded to £400 in 1932. 48% of the total invested with the Abbey Road Society in shares in 1913 was in holdings over £250, whereas in 1932 67% was in holdings of more than the equivalent sum at 1932 values. Almost a third of the total in 1932 was in holdings of over £1,000. Bellman observed (15):

"Before the war building societies on the investment side were .... essentially institutions catering for the smaller type of capitalist, i.e. predominantly the wage earning class. Probably small shopkeepers and others of similar social status utilized their services, but the wage earning class, together with an increasing proportion of the lower middle class, no doubt formed the bulk of the membership".

227

In the inter-war years, however:

> ".... the movement, without in the least discouraging or inconveniencing the very modest capitalist, has tended to attract the savings of a somewhat more substantial type of investor" (16).

These "somewhat more substantial" investors tended to be more sensitive to changes in interest rates. The building societies had changed from "thrift institutions" of the friendly society type into specialist financial intermediaries (though that term was not invented until the 1950s) that competed in the market for investible funds, even though building society chairmen still quoted Samuel Smiles on formal occasions.

That the fall in the general level of interest rates made building societies' rates very competitive and attracted interest sensitive money helps explain several important aspects of building societies' actions during these years. The amount of money on offer tended to exceed the investment opportunities on offer, with the result that there was keen rivalry between building societies for mortgage business. When the amounts of money offered to them were greatly in excess of what they could lend on mortgage, as in 1933, the societies limited the amount of new money they would accept from investors. The pressure of money seeking investment and the consequent competition for mortgage business was the origin of most of the struggles within the building society world in the 1930s, notably the attempts to secure acceptance of a "code of ethics" that would regulate competition (17) and especially dissuade societies from taking on risky mortgage business that would in time result in losses that would harm the reputation of the whole building society movement, including the more cautious societies as well as those that had taken the risks and incurred losses. In retrospect, the pressures on the building societies in the 1930s do not look very different from those experienced by many other industries in those years: demand fell short of the capacity of the industry to supply, with consequent opportunities for buyers to gain by playing off one seller against another. To form price agreements, or agreements to share the market, or both, was a common defensive response in many industries: the code of ethics and then (in 1939) the Building Societies Association's recommended rates agreement can be seen as the form this defensive response took in the building society "industry".

But an inevitable question is why interest rates were not reduced further, to reduce the embarrassment of unwanted money on offer from investors and to generate more business from house buyers. None of the published histories of individual building societies, or of the 'movement' address themselves to this question, and until a much needed history of a major building society in the inter-war years has been written from its own records that sets it firmly in the context of the housing market, only surmise can be offered. By far the most likely explanation, though, is the influence of ideas and concepts carried forward from the friendly society days of building societies being mutual organizations carried on for the benefit of both investing and borrowing members. Such concepts engendered opposition to a policy of forcing down the rates paid to investing members when any that withdrew their money and left could be replaced easily by money borrowed from other investors. Mortgage rates of 5% to 6% were time-honoured, and the borrowing member was being fairly treated if those were the rates he had to pay. Such ideas would make building societies' interest rates rigid downwards. Moreover a view that the lower market interst rates would not last (quite a common belief) may well have reinforced a reluctance to move building society interest rates downwards.

The building societies in the inter-war years were encouraged by the government of the day, but until the end of the 1930s the only tangible assistance that they received (or needed) were the special arrangements for tax relief on mortgage interest discussed in Chapter III. That they could finance so large a boom without any more assistance than that must be considered due to conditions on the supply side of the housing market. These were discussed in Chapter III, besides which reference may be made to Ball's stimulating comments on the subject (18). In 1938-39, though, legislation (The Building Societies Act 1939) was needed to extricate the movement from potentially embarrassing difficulties over the way in which some of them had financed the purchase of new houses from builders (19).

Lending for House Purchase by Local Authorities in the Inter-War Years

The contribution of central and local government to encouraging house building for owner-occupation went further than encouraging the building societies. As well as the lump sum subsidy payments under the Housing Act 1923 (discussed in Chapter III), house purchase lending by local authorities underwent a complete change of scale in the inter-war years. It was much smaller than house purchase lending by building societies, but was never wholly negligible and in the middle of the 1920s was of considerable importance. Local authorities were first given powers to make house purchase loans by the Small Dwellings Acquisition Act of 1899. It was a purely permissive power, and before 1914 little use was made of it. Nor was it much used in the years immediately after the war, but changes made by the Housing Act 1923 were followed by much more activity. The maximum price limit and the maximum percentage advance under the 1899 Act were increased, and a new power given (subsequently consolidated into the Housing Act 1925) to lend for the purchase of new houses. Year by year figures for the number of advances begin with 1934, but a total was published of advances made since 1919 (20) and there were published figures for house purchase advances in money terms (21) from which the numbers of advances made year by year may be estimated.

At its peak in the later 1920s, house purchase lending by local authorities was equal to between one-quarter and one-third of that by building societies. A higher proportion of local authorities' than of building societies' advances, though, were for the purchase of second-hand houses: up to the middle of 1934/35 there were a total of 113,000 loans under the Small Dwellings Acquisition Acts for the purchase of second-hand houses, and 57,000 under the Housing Acts 1923 and 1925 for new dwellings (22). The reduction of local authorities' house purchase lending in the early 1930s and its subsequent low level can probably be explained in large part by the ready supply of building society money. The Housing (Financial Provisions) Act of 1933 gave local authorities further powers to guarantee building society loans, and the Ministry of Health sought to persuade local authorities to use this power rather than make loans themselves.

Table VI.6 - House Purchase Lending by Local Authorities
1919-39

	Amount (£ million)	Number ('000 estimated)
1919/20 to 1922/23	0.3	under 1
1923/24	0.7	between 1 and 2
1924/25	6.0	13
1925/26	10.7	23
1926/27	14.4	31
1927/28	12.4	27
1928/29	9.0	19
1929/30	7.9	17
1930/31	4.8	10
1931/32	3.9	8
1932/33	3.1	6
1933/34	4.2	9
1934/35	4.6	10.2
1935/36	6.9	14.4
1936/37	5.0	11.5
1937/38	4.6	10.6
1939	3.0	7.2

Source: Figures for amounts lent in 1933/34 and earlier years are from Local Taxation Returns, with the number of loans estimated. The figures for 1934/35 to 1938/39 are from the Housing Return Table VIII.

The building societies had supported this scheme as they had more money than they could lend; and in the years 1933/34 to 1938/39 nearly 27,000 building society advances were made under local authority guarantee (23). Local authorities direct lending for house purchase in the 1930s fell well short of replacing earlier loans that were paid off: at the end of the financial year 1930/31 the amount of debt outstanding was just under £49 million, but at the end of 1938/39 £36.4 million only remained outstanding. Table VI.6 shows that about £35 million of new advances were made during these eight years, which means that some £48 million was paid off. This was less, in proportion to debt outstanding, than redemptions of building society mortgages, but still high enough to suggest that considerable numbers of fixed interest mortgage taken in the 1920s were paid off so that they could be replaced by new mortgages at lower rates.

Building Societies and the Housing Market in the Post-War Decade

In the war years there was little for building societies to do. As we saw in Chapter IV house building stopped at the outbreak of war apart from finishing houses that were already at an advanced stage of construction, so that financing the sale of new houses, which had been their main business in the 1930s, quickly came to an end. Between the beginning of 1940 and the end of 1944 they made 220,000 loans, less than one year's lending in the 1930s. During the five years the total of loans outstanding fell by 165,000, so 385,000 loans (a quarter of the total outstanding) were paid off. At the end of 1944 building societies' holdings of cash and investments (nearly all government debt of one kind or another) amounted to £236 million, 29.7% of total assets, compared with £68 million (8.8% of total assets) five years earlier (24). Building societies had become for the time being one among several channels through which war-time savings were attracted into investment in government debt.

There was not much more for the building societies to do in the immediate post-war years. As was mentioned in Chapter IV, new building for private owners was held down tightly by direct control as a matter of policy, so until new building gathered pace from 1953 onwards, the business for building societies lay mainly in financing moves from one owner-occupied house to another, and the transfer of houses from private landlords to owner-occupation. The available statistics do not allow this process to be depicted as clearly as one would like, owing to new advances being inflated by re-financing transactions (25). Net lending has therefore to be used as the measure of activity by building societies. This is far from wholly satisfactory but until work with building society mortgage records produces more firmly based figures, it is better than nothing in a period that is distinctive in the history of the market for owner-occupied housing.

The notable feature of the house price history depicted in Table VI.7 is the way in which house prices rose very sharply at a time when the number of transactions (as inferred from advances less repayments) was low, but levelled off and then fell when the amount of market activity increased.

Table VI.7 - Building Society Advances Compared with House
          Prices 1938-1954

	New Advances Less Advances Repaid ('000)	Net Lending (£ million)	Index House Prices (1970 = 100)
1938	86	51	12.0 (a)
1945	-23	11	23.8
1946	-2	67	28.7
1947	22	93	37.1
1948	23	104	42.3
1949	52	117	41.2
1950	65	106	42.6
1951	71	98	44.9
1952	75	105	44.2
1953	100	133	40.9
1954	125	178	39.7

Note: (a) 1934/39
Source: Advances and lending from reports of Chief Regis-
         trar of Friendly Societies, tabulated in Building
         Societies Association, Compendium of Building
         Society Statistics, (1982) Tables B.1 and B.2
         House Prices: Department of the Environment from
         data from Board of Inland Revenue. See Housing
         Policy Technical Volume, (1977), Chapter 4, Table
         IV.2

House prices rose fast during the war years.
Figures derived from information collected by the
Inland Revenue in the course of administering stamp
duty (the source of Table VI.7) and published in
the Report of the Inter-Departmental Committee on
the Selling Price of Houses (26) show that the
increase was more marked in the later part of the
war years: there was an increase of 34% up to the
first quarter of 1943, but an increase of 41%
between then and the first quarter of 1945. As
Table VI.7 shows, between 1945 and 1948 there was a
further increase of between 75 and 80%. In view of
the very small number of house purchase advances in
the war years, the large increase in house prices
can only be interpreted as the result of an
imbalance between a small demand and an even
smaller supply. The number of advances ran higher
in 1948-51 than in 1945-47, which argues strongly
against the slackening of the rise in house prices
having been anything to do with the demand side of

the market, and the number of new houses built for
private owners in both sub-periods was too small to
make much difference to the balance between supply
and demand. Much the same argument would apply to
the fall in house prices between 1952 and 1954.
The course of house prices and of the number of
building society loans therefore suggests strongly
that most of the estimated 500,000 sales for owner-
occupation between 1939 and 1953 of houses formerly
rented from private landlords (Table V.2 above)
took place not in the war years and immediately
after but in the later 1940s and early 1950s. An
increase in the supply of houses coming onto the
market from this source could explain first the
halt to the rise in house prices and then, in the
early 1950s, the fall. The number of new houses
completed for private owners did not rise
materially until 1953.

Financing the change of ownership of houses
that were already owner-occupied, the transfer to
owner-occupation of houses formerly let by private
landlords, and the small number of new houses built
for sale did not use up all the money the building
societies could readily have raised from investors.
The "cheap money" policies of the government of the
day kept the general level of interest rates low,
so that building society interest rates that were
very low by the standards of any other time (2½%
tax paid on shares) were nonetheless very competitive. There was competition for mortgage business,
and limits on the amounts accepted from investors,
for the last time during the period covered by this
book.

Building Societies from the 1950s to the 1970s: Interest Rates and the Attraction of Investment Funds

By the mid-1950s, the conditions in which
building societies operated had changed decisively.
The principal change, and the dominant feature of
the next two decades, was the sustained upward
trend of interest rates. The increase in interest
rates and how far it was associated with inflation
were discussed in Chapter IV, where it was shown
that up to the very end of the 1960s the ever-
rising interest rates could not be explained simply
by worsening inflation. In discussing how building
societies responded, it is important to recall that
only gradually did those parts of British financial

markets concerned with house purchase finance become more competitive, and not until the 1970s did support for relying on price (i.e. interest rates) to allocate credit gain much ground. The banks were the largest deposit-taking financial institutions. They did not compete with each other in the interst rates they offered, and the amount they lent was subject to quantitative restriction as a result of official "requests" at various times between the mid-1950s and the later 1960s. There was little point in their competing more aggressively for depositors' funds if they could not lend out to their customers any extra funds they attracted. Nor did the building societies' other main potential competitor, National Savings, compete at all vigorously by means of interest rates. As Table VI.9 below shows, in the two decades between 1951 and 1971 the amount invested in National Savings increased by 47 percent, which was equivalent to a fall of 29 percent in real terms. In the context of the very limited price competition in financial markets that characterized the 1950s and 1960s, there was nothing anomalous about the building societies not pushing up their interest rates by the full amount that would be needed to 'clear the market' for new mortgage loans. Such a policy followed naturally and logically from the doctrine of striking an equitable balance between the investing and borrowing members, particularly as variable rate mortgages meant that rates so set as to clear the market for new loans would have to be paid by existing borrowers as well.

The 1970s were different. The thrust of financial policy was to rely far more on controlling the money supply and allocating credit by price than on controlling the volume of bank advances by means of official "requests". In 1971 the Bank of England's policy statement <u>Competition and Credit Control</u> notified the end of reliance on "requests" to the banks and stated that instead the price mechanism would be relied on. An exception was made though, in a right that was reserved to request the banks not to raise the rates paid on deposit accounts if that was necessary to prevent undue pressure on building societies' receipts and interest rates. Obviously the government and Bank of England were concerned about the effect that free competition through interest rates would have on house purchase finance. This power, analogous to Regulation Q in the United States, was used only

once, in September 1973. Target rates of increase
in the money supply became a major part of economic
policy in 1976. And by the end of the decade
received opinion had swung against the notion of
privileges for house purchase finance and in favour
of competition on equal terms between financial
institutions and among their customers. Such
competition was among the themes of the report of
the Committee on the Functioning and Financial
Institutions (the Wilson Committee) (27). In the
building society world, there was a similar swing
of opinion against the policy of rationing mortgages in order to moderate increases in mortgage
rates and in favour of interest rates high enough
for the market for mortgage money to clear without
mortgage rationing. The Building Societies
Association's Committee on Mortgage Finance in the
1980s argued strongly for such a policy (28).

This is the background to the interest rate
policies of the building societies from 1955
onwards, when interest rates as a means of economic
control were brought back into active use after
being in abeyance for nearly a quarter of a century
(apart from a brief spell in 1952). How the
building societies' policies coped in the following
quarter century will be reviewed in some detail.
Why towards the end of the 1970s, a decade in which
interest rates reached unprecedented heights, there
should have been the swing of opinion away from the
efforts to keep the increase in mortgage rates to a
minimum and in favour of charging 'competitive'
rates for house purchase finance, will be commented
on briefly. The starting point though, is the
chronology of interest rates (Table VI.8). The
measures of the general level of interest rates
with which building societies' interest rates are
compared are the rates on Consols and Treasury
Bills. In the 1960s the interest rate on money
deposited with local authorities at 3 months
notice, usually termed the "local authority 3 month
rate" was customarily used as an indication of
money market short-term interest rates in measuring
changes in building societies' competitiveness
relative to those rates, but this market grew up
only in the later 1950s, so rates there cannot be
quoted for 1955.

In 1953 and 1954 the building societies' share
rate, grossed up to the equivalent rate for the
standard rate taxpayer, was 2.3 percentage points
and 2.7 percentage points higher than the average

236

Table VI.8 - Building Societies' Interest Rates Compared
with the General Level of Interest Rates
1953-1979

	Consols	Treasury Bills	Mortgage Rate	Share Rate	Share Rate Gross Equivalent
1953	4.1	2.3	4.55	2.45	4.45
1955	4.2	3.7	4.66	2.61	4.54
1958	5.0	4.6	6.13	3.48	6.05
1960	5.4	4.9	5.89	3.37	5.50
1962	6.0	4.2	6.61	3.70	6.04
1964	6.0	4.6	6.16	3.50	5.71
1966	6.8	6.1	6.95	4.01	6.83
1970	9.2	7.0	8.58	4.94	8.41
1972	9.1	5.5	8.26	4.88	7.97
1973	10.9	9.4	9.59	6.51	9.30
1974	15.0	11.4	11.05	7.53	19.94
1975	14.7	10.2	11.08	7.21	11.09
1979	11.4	13.1	11.94	8.43	12.04

Source: See Table IV.3 for interest rates on Consols and
Treasury Bills; building society rates from
Compendium of Building Society Statistics
Table D.1.

rate on Treasury Bills, but in 1955-59 (a span of
years that included times both of monetary restrictions and of ease) the average difference was only
1.2 percentage points. That narrowing of the
difference between the rate offered to investors by
building societies and the general level of short-
term interest rates marked the end of the years of
ample funds and competition for mortgage business.
It likewise marked the beginning of a quarter-
century in which the amount of money that the
societies had to lend fell short, by varying
degrees, of what would be needed to meet the demand
from credit-worthy would-be borrowers. Some of the
consequences of their 'mortgage rationing' are
considered subsequently. Here a look is taken at
the interest rate policies that gave rise to it.

Over the years, the rate offered by building
societies to investors rose at about the same pace
as did short-term interest rates generally. As just
mentioned, in 1955-59 the building societies' share
rate (grossed up) averaged 1.2 percentage points

more than Treasury Bill rates. In 1960-64 the
average difference was 1.3 percentage points, in
1965-69 0.7, in 1970-74 1.2, and in 1975-79 0.7
percentage points. Keeping the rate offered to
investors in line with short-term interest rates in
this way, taking one year with another, enabled the
building societies to keep the rise in their
mortgage rates below the rise in the general level
of long-term interest rates, because the gap
between short-term and long-term interest rates
widened. In 1955-59 the difference between the
rates on Consols and Treasury Bills averaged 0.5
percentage points, in 1965-69 0.8, and in 1975-79
2.8 percentage points. In 1955-59 the average
interest rate paid on building society mortgages
was 0.9 percentage points higher than the interest
rate on Consols (compared with 1.4 in 1945-49 and
1.9 percentage points in 1934-38); in 1965-69 the
two rates were approximately equal; but in 1975-79
the average rate paid by building society mortgagors was 2.0 percentage points less than the rate
of Consols. By any reckoning, house purchasers who
were able to borrow more cheaply than could the
government, were obtaining their money on very
advantageous terms. That they paid not quite 1
percent more than the government in 1955-59 but 2
percent less in 1975-79 is a measure of the extent
to which building societies were able to keep down
the price of house purchase credit when the cost of
credit generally had a strong tendency to rise.

The interest rates just referred to were lower
than would have balanced the supply of a demand for
mortgage funds. Mortgage rationing and mortgage
queues were the rule; the severity of the rationing
varied with short-term changes in the competitiveness of the rates offered to investors, but only
rarely was the degree of rationing insignificant
(in late 1967, in late 1971 and early 1972, and
late 1977 possibly), and at no time did open
competition between societies for mortgage business
re-appear. The environment in which the building
societies worked was one of more demand for
mortgages than they could meet at going interest
rates, which put all the thrust of competition
between them, and with other financial institutions, into competiton for investment funds. Most
of the post-1955 development of building societies,
including the network of branches, the widening
range of types of investment, and the much larger
amounts that could be withdrawn on demand from

ordinary share accounts can be explained in terms of competition for funds by means other than the simple paying of a higher interest rate.

The Building Societies Association's recommended rate arrangement was instrumental in the policy of setting rates at levels lower than would clear the market for new mortgage money. For reasons just discussed, building societies were able to keep down the rates of interest charged on mortgages because they raised their money by borrowing at short-term rates. To finance such a long-term transaction as lending for house purchase by borrowing on short-term might appear anomalous and risky: "borrowing short to lend long" has long been a byword for imprudent financing. In fact building societies' lending was much less 'long' than might appear. This was partly due to the stream of capital repayments coming in from regular payments of interest and principal combined, but much more important was the fact that virtually all building society mortgages were variable interest rate mortgages, so that any increase in rates paid to investors could be recouped by increases in mortgage rates. A long-term loan that is at variable interest rates has most of the characteristics of a short-term loan so long as the lender does not have to recall the capital outstanding. The standing of the building societies with investors was sufficiently strong for a 'run on the bank' to be a remote risk, so that variable interest rates on mortgages made borrowing at short-term safe, notwithstanding the rising trend of interest rates and the volatility around it. But without the recommended rate arrangement and the building societies being mutual institutions with a body of doctrine about an equitable balance between the interests of investing and borrowing members, the variable rate mortgage would have been a very onerous contract from the point of view of the borrower, since it gave the lender the right to vary the interest rate by an unlimited amount, subject only to notice. The borrower's only contractual right was to repay the loan if the increase in the interest rate was unacceptable, but to most borrowers that was obviously of no value as a safeguard. The recommended rate arrangement provided a safeguard in that the size of any increase was determined not by anonymous market forces but by the decision of men known to the public by name, meeting at a known place, date and time, and hence answerable for the decision. The recommended rate system, and the policy of holding interest rates at levels lower than would 'clear the market' for mortgage money had their critics, as we shall see. Here we only note that whether variable rate mortgages of the building society type would have been acceptable without the recommended rate arrangement should not necessarily be taken for granted.

The building societies were, moreover, subject to only mild competition in the market for their chosen source of funds: personal savings invested at short-term. Their main competitors were National Savings and the banks, and neither competed aggressively for the personal saver's funds for most of the period studied here, though as will be shown a little later in this chapter, 'personal savers' funds' did not mean small savings. A comparison may be shown between personal sector holdings of building society shares and deposits, deposits with banks, and National Savings. The figures for deposits with banks are far less comprehensive before 1963 but the figures for building societies and National Savings are comparable.

Although the growth of shares and deposits with building societies relative to personal deposits with banks attracted most comment and criticism, for most of the period it was National Savings that lost most ground. In the later 1940s and the 1950s, personal deposits with the London clearing banks rose much less than did building society shares and deposits, but to some extent that may have been a reflection of a smaller proportion of personal bank deposits being with the clearing banks. Of the sum of National Savings, building society shares and deposits, and personal deposits with the London clearing banks, building societies had 25.6% in 1938, 10.0% in 1946 and 22.0% in 1958. In the 1960s the banks kept their share of personal sector deposits, but National Savings fell back a long way. In the rapid expansion of banks' lending and deposits in 1972 and 1973, the banks increased their share, but between 1973 and 1977 the banks' share of the total dropped (from 38.2% to 31.7%) while the building societies' share rose very sharply (from 38.1% to 47.8%). This, no doubt, was the origin of the increasing volume of complaint from the banks in the mid- and later 1970s about being prevented from competing

Table VI.9 - Building Society Shares and Deposits Compared
with Other Personal Sector Liquid Assets
1938-1979

(£ million)

	Building Society Shares and Deposits	National Savings	Personal Sector Deposits with Banks (b)	Total
1938	704	1,491	560 (c)	2,755
1946	810	5,895	1,423	8,128
1951	1,265	6,103	1,675	9,043
1954	1,757	6,090	1,862	10,491
1958	2,467	6,479	2,255	11,201
1960	3,147	7,426	...	...
1963	3,941	7,758	6,237	17,936
1965	5,099	8,189	7,225	20,513
1967	6,923	8,279	8,250	23,452
1969	8,575	8,245	9,240	26,060
1971	12,020	8,975	11,015	32,010
1973	16,287	10,114	16,317	42,718
1975	22,477	10,876	19,206	52,559
1977	31,757	13,599	21,018	66,374
1979	42,442	17,636	30,340	90,418

Notes: (a) There were changes in definition and coverage during the period of the table, but as far as possible the coverage is constant, e.g. by including the Trustee Savings Banks in the end-1979 figure for National Savings. Up to 1961 (inclusive) the end of calendar-year figures were got by interpolation between the end of financial year figures.

(b) London clearing banks personal deposits before 1963.

(c) 31 March 1939.

Source: Financial Statistics December 1972, Table 88; December 1975, Table 99; August 1980, Table 10.2 Annual Abstract of Statistics, 1960, Table 334, and 1963, Table 302; Committee on the Working of the Monetary System, Report Cmnd.827 (1959), Table 22.

241

fairly with the building societies and hence losing funds to them to the (alleged) detriment of the supply of finance for commerce and industry. But the increase in the building societies' share of the personal sector's investment in liquid capital-certain assets was much less at the expense of the banks than of National Savings. That the building societies were able to provide so large a volume of house purchase loans at interest rates some way below what central government had to pay was thus due in considerable measure to the absence of strong interest rate competition from National Savings. The rates of interest offered on National Savings are a matter of government financial policy, to be determined in the process of balancing the need to keep down the interest cost of the public debt against securing the distribu-tion of the debt that will be conducive to monetary control. This highly complex subject cannot be gone into further here: how far (if at all) the very limited amounts that governments raised (net) from National Savings in the late 1950s, the 1960s and the first half of the 1970s was the result of a deliberate intent to facilitate the supply of house purchase money through the building societies, must be remitted to historians of national debt manage-ment.

An influence of some importance on the level, as distinct from the rate of increase, of building societies' interest rates was the advantage they gained by paying tax on investors' interest at the composite rate. This arrangement was not a subsidy but a form of deduction of tax at source, which had a history running back to 1894. Under the general principles of the income tax, interest would be paid net of tax at the standard rate; the recipient would have no further liability to tax (other than surtax) on the interest, and if he was liable to less than the standard rate or not liable to tax at all he could reclaim from the Inland Revenue the tax deducted. The circumstances of building socie-ties were special in that they paid fairly small amounts of interest to large numbers of investors, many of them with incomes too low to be liable to tax. To avoid the large amount of record-keeping that would be needed both by building societies and by the Inland Revenue if the standard procedure were followed, arrangements were made by which building societies made a composition settlement of income tax on investors' interest, at a rate

intended to be as far as possible the weighted
average of investors' tax rates up to the standard
rate of income tax (basic rate from 1973).
Societies offered investors a rate on which tax
liabilities at the standard rate had been compounded for, but with no entitlement to reclaim tax
if the investor was not liable to income tax or was
liable only at a rate below the standard rate
(there were reduced rates down to 1970, and again
in 1977-80). The value to the investor of the
interest rate offered by a building society then
depended on the investor's marginal rate of income
tax, and enabled the societies to offer what was in
effect a higher interest rate to standard rate
taxpayers than to other investors, a distinct
advantage if (as appears to have been so) the
better-off investors were the most sensitive to the
competitiveness of interest rates. How sensitive
to interest rates were investors with low incomes
is not known, though (as is shown below) investments of small amounts were less interest-sensitive
than large amounts in the short-term. In 1958/59
the difference between the value of the share rate
to the standard rate taxpayer and its cost to the
societies was about 1¼%: in 1968/69 it had
diminished to 1%, but in 1978/79 had widened again
to 1½%. The arrangement reduced the cost to
building societies of being competitive with market
interest rates (all of them subject to tax except
National Savings Certificates) only so long as, and
to the extent that, investors with income too low
to be liable to tax continued to invest with
building societies, which they did during the
period studied. The arrangement was criticized
from time to time as being unfair to low income
investors by depriving them of the extra income
they would have got if ordinary income tax arrangements had applied; and was criticized by the
Committee on the Functioning of Financial Institutions as discriminating in favour of the building
societies and so giving them an artificial advantage relative to their competitors, the banks in
particular.

Mention was made above about the building
societies having by the 1930s come to attract sizeable sums of money from substantial investors, and
that remained so in the 1950s, 1960s and 1970s.
They had enough dependence on interest-sensitive
"large" money for the net intake of new money from
investors to be subject to large and rapid swings

243

upward and downwards in response to changes in how
competitive were building societies' interest rates
relative to the general level of interest rates.
These swings in building societies' intake of
funds, and hence in their lending, were sufficiently important in the history of housing policy
for the mechanism to be worth describing in some
detail.

The extent to which building societies depended on "large" money may first be shown. The data
necessary were first published in the later 1970s,
but the picture they show was probably valid well
before then. Table VI.10 shows the size distribution of individual accounts with building societies. The figures were compiled from returns by
individual building societies and so do not aggregate the holdings of investors with accounts with
more than one society. For an estimate of how much
difference that makes to the estimated amount of
money with building societies that is part of a
large block, recourse will be had to a separate
source.

Table VI.10 - Share and Deposit Accounts Analysed by Size:
End-1978

Size of Balance in Account	Number of Accounts ('000)	(%)	Amount of Balances ('000)	(%)
Up to £500	14,482	53.8	1,788	4.9
£500-£1,000	3,589	13.3	2,647	7.2
£1,000-£2,000	3,503	13.0	5,005	13.6
£2,000-£5,000	3,471	12.9	11,150	30.3
£5,000-£10,000	1,492	5.5	10,587	28.8
£10,000	423	1.5	5,606	15.2
Total	26,960	100.0	36,783	100.0

Source: Building Societies Association, Mortgage Finance in
the 1980s (1979) Table B.6.

Since the Building Societies Association estimated that there were about 18 million adults with
investment accounts with building societies (29)
there was plainly some duplication within the
totals in Table VI.10 through investors having more
than one account. There are several reasons why
investors might do this: one was to improve their
prospects of getting a mortgage by establishing

themselves as savers with more than one building
society; another was to invest larger sums than any
one society would accept owing to the limit
specified by the Inland Revenue as part of the
composite rate agreement, £10,000 at the date to
which Table VI.10 referred, or £20,000 for accounts
in the joint name of husband and wife. For
evidence about the money invested with building
societies in large amounts but spread between
societies, reference may be made to the Inland
Revenue's Survey of Personal Income, which identified interest received from building societies
separately from other income. The method of
estimation and the reasons why total holdings
estimated by this method are well below the corresponding balance sheet totals were outlined in the
Housing Policy Technical Volume (30).

Table VI.11 - Estimates of Holdings of Building Society
Shares and Deposits 1978

	Number ('000)	Amount (£ million)
Under £10,000	4,635	10,095
£10,000 but under £20,000	405	5,475
£20,000 but under £50,000	155	4,375
£50,000 or more	15	1,040
Total identified	5,210	20,985

Source: Calculated from Inland Revenue Survey of Income,
1978.

The amounts invested with building societies
that formed part of holdings of £10,000 or more
thus came to a total of almost £11,000 million,
twice as much as was invested in accounts of
£10,000 or more with individual building societies.
Large holdings can be accumulated by frequent
addition of large numbers of individually small
amounts. But other information collected and
published by the Building Societies Assocation
showed that the building societies received from
investors substantial amounts that were in large
individual blocks of money, and that these were the
most interest-sensitive. How sensitive were
inflows of "large" money is shown in Table VI.12,
where inflows month by month are set alongside the
differential between the building societies' rate
paid to investors and an indicator of money market

Table VI.12 - Building Societies' Net Receipts and Interest Rate Competitiveness

	1977			1978		
	Up to £2,000 (£m)	£2,000 or over (£m)	Interest Rate Competitiveness (%)	Up to £2,000 (£m)	£2,000 or over (£m)	Interest Rate Competitiveness (%)
January	119	-6	-1.92	203	162	+2.89
February	125	100	+0.12	189	149	+1.62
March	68	158	+1.42	157	135	+1.62
April	185	314	+3.01	160	175	+0.82
May	169	366	+3.06	98	114	-0.78
June	82	246	+2.81	72	75	-1.54
July	133	211	+2.51	117	82	-0.02
August	101	225	+3.25	94	105	+0.63
September	181	306	+4.04	173	172	+0.71
October	222	393	+5.14	210	153	-0.35
November	161	417	+3.89	158	103	-1.96
December	165	281	+2.31	141	113	-0.37

Note: Interest rate competitiveness is measured by the difference between the building societies' grossed up share rate and the local authorities' 3 month rate.

Source: Building Societies Association, Mortgage Finance in the 1980s, (London, 1979), Table B.11

interest rates. That building societies' net
receipts from investors were influenced by competitiveness relative to money market interest rates
and not by competitiveness relative to the interest
rates offered by banks on ordinary deposit accounts
was shown by statistical analysis (31). A clear
cut proof that this was so was given when in
September 1973 the banks, at the request of the
Bank of England, did not raise their seven days
deposit rate when other interest rates rose in
order to assist the building societies; but there
was no discernible effect on building societies'
net receipts, which dropped in the way that would
be predicted from the difference between their
interest rates and the money market rates. Only
fairly substantial sums could be invested at money
market rates of interest. Individual investors
generally invested at such rates through banks.

Clearly the interest rate differential had
little or no effect on net receipts of money in
amounts below £2,000, but a large and rapid effect
on net receipts in individual amounts of £2,000 and
over which were too large to be saved straight out
of income. There was not an exact relationship
between changes in interest rate competitiveness
and changes in net receipts of 'large'money, but in
round terms a change of 1 percentage point in the
interest rate differential made a difference of
about £60 million a month (32) in the late 1970s.
The effect per percentage point had increased
through time at least as fast as the general price
level. The lag between change in the interest rate
differential and a change in net receipts of
'large' money appears to have been less than a
month. Such net shifts in the intake of money from
investors by building societies were small in
relation to the total amount of shares and deposits
they held; the shifts of funds were very much at
the margin. But the margin matters: variations of
£60 million a month per percentage point were quite
enough to produce very sharp swings in the amount
of building societies' lending if market interest
rates fluctuated much. Two percentage points would
make a difference of £360 million in three months,
which would finance about 35,000 advances in round
terms (33).

Fluctuations of this scale in money market
interest rates were far from uncommon, and their
severity increased. When in 1955 monetary
restraint was brought back into use to restrain

inflation after being in abeyance for almost a quarter of a century, apart from largely symbolic use in 1952, money market interest rates rose by 2.2 percentage points in seven months; and between July and October 1957, they rose by 2.8%. in three months. This continued to be the scale of increase in the rest of the 1950s and the 1960s, between 2 and 3 percentage points when interest rates were raised. But in the 1970s the amplitude and speed of the swings became far greater than anything seen in the 1960s and 1950s. Just why interest rates were so much more unstable in the 1970s than in the 1960s and the later 1950s is still the subject of controversies that cannot be gone into here. Reasons widely discussed include the large increase in the volume of funds that could be moved between financial centres across the foreign exchanges and in the speed with which this could be done ('at a flick of a computer terminal' as the phrase had it in the later 1970s); the abandonment of official "requests" to the banks as the means of influencing the volume and allocation of bank lending and reliance on prices (i.e. interest rates) instead; and the use from 1976 onwards of target rates of increase in the money supply as a prominent feature of the government's financial policy. But although the relative importance of the several contributory causes of the greater instability of interest rates may be debatable, the fact of the instability is not. Between the end of June and the end of December 1973, the local authority 3 month rate rose by 8 percentage points; between the end of December 1976 and the end of October 1977 it fell by 10 percentage points; and between the end of April 1979 and the end of February 1980, it rose by 6 percentage points. The swings in interest rates between 1955 and the end of the 1960s had no precedents more recent than before 1914, but the instability of interest rates in the 1970s was even more extreme.

This instability in money market interest rates was not matched by corresponding changes in interest rates to investors. The rationale of this policy and the effects on the housing market will be discussed in a later section of this chapter. Here it is convenient to show the swings in net receipts and the changes in interest rates to which they were associated, along with the variations in house building activity and in the rise of house prices, both of which were held (though not without

Table VI.13 - Building Societies' Net Receipts, New Lending and Private House Building Activity 1955-79

	Net Receipts (£ million, 1975 Prices)	Interest Rate Differential (a) (percentage Points)	Annual Rate			
			New Loans ('000)	Houses Started ('000)	Houses Completed ('000)	Increase in House Prices
1955 I	466	+1.21	304	122	107	..
II	494	+0.79	280	153	120	+5
1956 I	254	+0.23	244	121	122	+3
II	348	+0.55	220	120	126	+1
1957 I	390	+1.79	242	125	129	-1
II	290	+0.45	256	126	124	+1
1958 I	310	+0.43	230	128	125	+1
II	514	+2.27	256	146	132	+9
1959 I	646	+2.52	288	162	144	+1
II	560	+1.71	354	172	158	+5
1960 I	466	+0.31 (+0.62)	308	185	165	+3
II	408	+0.04 (+0.30)	322	181	172	+18
1961 I	440	+0.40	300	194	180	+7
II	392	-0.98	306	185	175	+11
1962 I	672	+0.74	286	179	175	+5
II	882	+1.73	370	193	175	+7
1963 I (b)	962	+1.57	338	168	156	+4
II	1,156	+1.48	462	231	194	+19
1964 I	1,176	+0.81	432	236	214	+13
II	902	-0.14	464	259	222	+10
1965 I	716	-0.95	360	226	221	+8
II	1,766	+0.43	404	196	206	+4
1966 I	1,554	+0.54	470	206	210	+7
II	1,070	-0.57	452	181	201	+6
1967 I (c)	2,016	+1.19	448	256	190	+7
II	2,092	+0.83	560	211	211	+7

Table VI.13 (continued)

	Net Receipts (£ million, 1975 Prices)	Interest Rate Differential (a) (percentage Points)	Annual Rate			Increase in House Prices
			New Loans ('000)	Houses Started ('000)	Houses Completed ('000)	
1968 I	1,188	-0.53	530	204	222	+5
1968 II	1,226	+0.12	466	196	222	+9
1969 I	1,414	-0.64	450	174	189	+5
1969 II	1,188	-0.85	470	160	174	+5
1970 I	1,888	-0.37	488	153	166	+4
1970 II	2,515	+1.13	592	177	174	+13
1971 I	2,548	+1.22	594	183	181	+8
1971 II	3,232	+2.81	712	231	202	+23
1972 I	3,264	+2.80	680	217	197	+32
1972 II	2,426	+0.32	682	239	176	+65
1973 I	2,932	+0.69	592	235	196	+33
1973 II	1,488	-2.91	504	196	178	+20
1974 I	656	-3.57	352	119	152	+2
1974 II	2,144	-1.39	514	93	129	+7
1975 I	3,490	-0.54	590	141	151	+5
1975 II	2,918	-0.07	710	157	151	+10
1976 I	2,912	+0.68	700	168	154	+8
1976 II	1,104	-2.43	730	141	150	+12
1977 I	2,832	+1.48	618	129	140	+2
1977 II	4,216	+3.53	858	140	142	+11
1978 I	2,290	+0.77	836	150	152	+8
1978 II	2,298	-0.23	768	164	146	+31
1979 I	2,120	-0.65	704	127	130	+25
1979 II	2,212	-2.21	726	154	139	+32

Table VI.13 (continued)

Notes: (a) Up to 1960 market interest rates were repre-
             sented by three months Bank Bills; from 1960
             onwards by local authority three months depo-
             sits. For 1960 both measures are shown, with
             the differential relative to interest rates
             on Bank Bills in brackets.
        (b) House building was held down by exceptionally
             severe weather.
        (c) The number of starts was inflated by work
             done to avoid Betterment Levy. Starts were
             inflated by 20-25,000 (40-50,000 expressed as
             an annual rate).

Source: Advances from Compendium of Building Society Stat-
         istics with 1955, 1956 and 1957 divided into half
         years by reference to amounts advanced. Receipts
         from investors (which exclude interest credited)
         from Compendium of Building Society Statistics,
         Table A.3. Revaluation to 1975 prices from Econo-
         mic Trends Annual Supplement 1983 edition pages
         19-20; starts and completions from pages 63-64.
         House prices up to 1966 from source cited in Table
         VI.7, thereafter from Building Society Mortgage
         Survey. See Economic Trends October 1982 for
         weighted index from this source for 1968 onwards.

disagreement) to have been affected by changes in
the volume of building societies' lending.
    Before commenting on the trend shown in the
Table and the fluctuations around that trend, it is
useful to look at lending in the post-war years by
other agencies.   The building societies were the
dominant source of funds for house purchase, but
did not have a monopoly. An important question
about the effect of falls in building societies'
lending (for instance in the first half of 1974,
the extreme example) is what scope there was to
turn to other sources of finance.

Finance of House Purchase by Agencies Other Than
Building Societies

    Apart from building societies, the lenders
that were of significance for house purchase were
the local authorities and insurance companies. The
pre-1945 history of local authorities as lenders
for house purchase was discussed earlier in the
chapter.   Insurance companies' house purchase

Table VI.14 - <u>House Purchase Lending by Local Authority and</u>
<u>Insurance Companies</u>

(thousands)

	Local	Authorities		Insurance Companies		
	Total	New Houses	Other Houses	Total	New Houses	Other Houses
1949/50	9	..	..	..	..	..
1950/51	15	..	..	..	..	..
1951/52	22	..	..	..	..	..
1952/53	18	..	..	..	..	..
1953/54	24	..	..	..	..	..
1954/55	39	..	..	..	..	..
1955/56	53	..	..	..	..	..
1956/57	51	..	..	..	..	..
1957/58	45	..	..	..	..	..
1958/59	42	..	..	..	..	..
1959	45	8	37	..	..	..
1960	48	9	39	..	..	..
1961	62	14	49	..	..	..
1962	53	11	42	48	..	..
1963	58	11	47	40	..	..
1964	77	19	59	45	..	..
1965	87	19	69	51	..	..
1966	46	6	40	43	..	..
1967	57	6	50	34	12	22
1968	39	4	35	42	14	29
1969	19	2	17	40	13	27
1970	44	3	41	32	9	23
1971	47	3	44	30	8	22
1972	45	2	43	25	7	18
1973	59	3	57	29	7	22
1974	75	5	71	26	6	20
1975	102	6	95	22	4	18
1976	24	1	23	17	3	14
1977	23	-(a)	23	16	3	14
1978	27	-(a)	27	17	3	14
1979	36	-(a)	36	19	3	16

Note: (a)   Under 500,

Table VI.14 (continued)

Source: Local Authorities:

1949/50 and 1950/51: Figures for lending from Local
Government Finance Statistics: 1951/52 to 1958/59
Ministry of Housing and Local Government Annual
Reports, Annex L, Table 1, 1959 onwards Housing
Statistics No. 3, Table 36(a); No. 24, Table 53(a):
Housing Statistics No. 3, Table 36(a); No. 24,
Table 53(a): Housing and Construction Statistics
No. 16, Tabl;e 40(a); No. 32, Table 41(a).

Insurance Companies:

1962/66 figures estimated by using index of new
house prices and index of second-hand house prices
(weighted 1:2) to project back to 1967 average
advance; which was then applied to the amounts
advanced as shown in Table 40 of Housing Statistics
No. 23. Advances in 1967-70 ibid, Table 51; after
1970 from Housing Construction Statistics.

lending is documented only back to the early 1960s.
The number of advances by local authorities and
insurance companies is shown in Table VI.14. As
the notes on sources show, a considerable amount of
estimation was required. The figures for lending
by local authorities refer to England and Wales;
for insurance companies the United Kingdom.
    The changes from year to year in the totals of
local authority house purchase loans reflect partly
changes in policy (usually on public expenditure
grounds), though with some tendency to increase (as
in 1961, 1965 and 1973-74) when building societies'
loans were falling. 1968-69 was the exception;
that local authorities' loans fell sharply at a
time when building societies' lending was also
falling is to be explained by cuts in public expenditure following the devaluation of sterling late
in 1967. Local authorities' house purchase loans
were not, in general, cheaper than building societies' loans. They were not subsidized, and so were
at rates of interest that covered the local authorities' borrowing costs plus costs of administration. In view of the building societies being able
to lend at interest rates that compared favourably
with those paid by the government, local authorities obviously could not undercut them. Would-be

house purchasers who were acceptable to building societies therefore had an inducement to turn to local authorities only when rationing of loans by building societies was severe, as it was in the years just referred to. Otherwise, the local authorities lent for the purchase of houses that building societies did not look on with favour, sometimes (though not always) with advances that were higher in relation to the price of the house than the building societies would offer (34).

When large reductions in local authority house purchase lending took place during the period covered by Table VI.14, they were the result of such lending being counted as part of total public expenditure for purposes of policy. This was something new in the 1960s. Formerly, local authorities' house purchase lending had been of little concern for financial policy: it was not subsidized and so made no call on taxation, and the money borrowed to finance house purchase loans was repaid out of repayments of the mortgages. For local authorities to borrow to finance house purchase loans was therefore perfectly proper. The reforms of the early 1960s initiated by the Plowden report (35) led to public expenditure being planned by central government in a comprehensive way, bringing together into one total central government direct expenditure, the National Insurance funds, and local authorities' expenditure on current and capital account. When public, political, and financial attention was focused on the total of public expenditure and then in the 1970s the public sector borrowing requirement, one cut was as good as another, £ for £, and cuts in local authorities' house purchase lending were among the easiest to make. A mechanism to give effect to them (loan sanctions) was ready to hand; the cuts could be made quickly; and since so much of the lending was on second-hand houses, any effect on output and employment was delayed and indirect. That local authorities' house purchase lending was cut in 1965, in 1968 and 1969, and again in 1975 and 1976, for general public expenditure reasons, is thus in no way surprising.

Lending by insurance companies, however, did not do anything significant to offset swings in building societies' lending after the 1960s. Over the long-term they took less and less interest in lending for house purchase. The Committee on the Working of the Monetary System wrote in 1959:

"The insurance companies prefer to finance large blocks of offices, shops, and flats; in the private house business they have usually been small in comparison with the building societies. During the credit squeeze (36), however, they greatly extended their mortgage lending on house property to meet the demand .... On the long view the companies expect their mortgage business to go down; they take opportunities brought to them but are not chasing the business" (37).

A similar response is discernible in 1965 and 1968; but by 1973 the response of insurance companies' lending to a shortage of building society mortgage money had become very small. The way in which mortgage interest rates rose distinctly less than the interest rates on government securities made house purchase lending increasingly unattractive, and commercial property development provided outlets that were more convenient as well as more profitable. In the early 1960s the insurance companies were lenders of some importance in the housing market when the building societies were short of funds. By the late 1970s they were barely significant as lenders.

Except for a brief period in 1972 and 1973, the banks did little house purchase lending in the period studied other than bridging loans and loans to their employees. The expansion of banks' house purchase lending in the 1980s, when they were actively seeking the business and advertising in the newspapers, lies outside the period that this history covers. Up until then, the British banks had been unusual in comparison with other countries, in doing so little house purchase lending. It is hard to believe that the banks' reputed preference for short-term lending (to match the short-term nature of their deposits) was at all an important part of the explanation: the average length of life of building society loans in practice was about 8 years, even though 25 years was by far the commonest term for which loans were granted; and much of banks' lending to industry and commerce was long-term in practice, if not in form. Much more important, in all probability, were the limitations on banks' lending for reasons of monetary policy. In the 1950s and 1960s such limitations followed from the then prevailing ideas of using official "requests" to banks to restrict their lending; in the 1970s controlling the growth of the money supply (liabilities of the banking system, apart from notes and coin) produced the same result. With the total of their lending restricted in this way the banks gave priority to lending to industry and commerce. The building societies, of course, did not lend to industry and commerce at all; so an informal 'division of function' existed between them and the banks, whereby the banks lent to industry and trade and the building societies lent for house purchase. This division of function appeared to satisfy both parties until the mid-1970s, when the banks began to express dissatisfaction, and in their evidence to the Committee to Review the Functioning of Financial Institutions, the banks pressed hard for what they regarded as the building societies' unfair competitive advantages to be redressed. The slower growth of bank deposits relative to building society deposits (Table VI.9) may well have been one of the reasons.

During the 1950s and 1960s, therefore, swings in building societies' lending were partially offset by lending by local authorities and to a lesser extent insurance companies, but from the mid-1970s these alternatives had become far less important. This virtual absence of competition for building societies was then quickly replaced by far stronger competition than anything experienced for well over half a century; but that lies outside the period that this book covers.

Building Societies and the Housing Market

The ups and downs of building societies' lending and the effects that they were considered to have on the housing market attracted most interest, but a comment is first called for about the long-term trend. The interest rate differentials column in Table VI.13 shows that in the first decade of active monetary policy and varying interest rates, building societies' rates offered to investors did not fully match the rise in market rates. The differential averaged +1.2 percentage points in 1955-59 but zero in 1965-69 (plus 0.3 approximately if the same measure of competitiveness had been used), but in both 1970-74 and 1975-79 the differential averaged +0.1 percentage points, so on average in the later 1960s and the 1970s, the building societies moved their interest

rates in line with the market over the medium term.
This policy was compatible with a large increase in
the number of loans. In 1936-38 the average had
been about 240,000 a year; in 1955-59 267,000; in
1960-64 359,000; in 1965-69 461,000; in 1970-74
571,000; and in 1975-79 724,000. This was a rapid
rate of increase. Since for most of the time the
demand for mortgages exceeded what the building
societies had on offer, it could be argued that a
policy of setting interest rates high enough to
balance the supply and demand would have led to
more funds being attracted, hence more loans and a
still more rapid growth in home ownership. But in
the period studied that proposition was less self-
evident than it might look. On the supply of funds
side it could not have been taken for granted that
competitors would have acquiesced in building
societies having a consistently stronger competitive advantage; they could well have retaliated.
Nor should the observed short-run insensitivity of
demand for mortgages to increase in interest rates
lead too quickly to the inference that the demand
in the longer term would have been equally insensitive, particularly on the part of marginal
purchasers. Nor should the distinction between
more mortgages and larger mortgages (if money was
more plentiful) be overlooked.

It was however the shorter-term swings in
lending that attracted most comment, and were the
basis for most of the criticisms of building societies' interest rate policies. We may first look at
the record of what appears to have been the effect
on house building and house prices, and then consider the rationale of the interest rate policy
that the building societies pursued. In Table
VI.13 six up-swings in the supply of loans can be
distinguished: 1958-59; 1962-64; 1967-68; 1970-72;
1975; and 1977. Likewise there were seven down-
swings: 1956; 1960-62; 1965; 1968-69; 1973-74;
1976-77; and 1978-79. The dating is not very precise owing to lags between changes in the numbers
of new loans approved and the number of loans
actually made, but it will suffice for present
purposes. Even a cursory glance at the number of
houses started and completed shows that in all the
periods just designated as 'up-swings' in the number of loans the number of new houses started and
completed increased, in most instances sharply; and
in the 'down-swing' periods after 1960-62, the
number of houses started and completed diminished.

The up-swing of 1962-64 was accompanies by a substantial increase in the number of houses completed
(47,000 annual rate, equivalent to 27% between the
second half of 1962 and the second half of 1964),
and an even larger increase in the number of starts
(66,000, equivalent to 34%) in the same period.
The fall in lending in 1965 and 1966 was accompanied by a considerable reduction in house building
activity; and an upturn in 1967-68 was associated
with an increase in lending (the number of advances
in the second half of 1967 and first half of 1968
was 95,000 higher, equivalent to 21%, than in the
second half of 1966 and the first half of 1967).
The surge of building society lending in 1971 and
1972 was accompanied by an increase in starts that
had no precedent: the number of loans made was
217,000 (44%) higher in the second half of 1971 and
first half of 1972 than in the second half fo 1969
and the first half of 1970, and starts were 60,000
higher (38%) in the second half of 1972 and the
first half of 1973 than in the second half of 1969
and the first half of 1970. The increase in completions was smaller, only 26,000 (15%), which was
much less than in the 1963-64 boom. When the boom
broke, house building fell with a steepness that
had no precedent more recent than the first decade
of the century. The annual rate of completions in
the second half of 1974 was 70,000 (35%) down from
the peak; starts were almost 150,000 (60%) down.

The interpretation placed on the association
between swings in house purchase loans and house
building is very relevant to any conclusions
reached about the highly controversial question of
how far, if at all, variations in the rate of rise
of house prices were influenced by swings in the
volume of lending for house purchase. For there is
no theory about the working of markets that could
explain how swings in the volume of lending could
affect quantities of houses sold and produced but
not affect house prices. That the swings in the
supply of mortgage money influenced demand in the
market for houses, and hence the output of new
housing for private onwers, was not at the time
contested. In the circumstances of Britain in the
1950s, 1960s and 1970s, a distinction could usefully be drawn between effective demand in the
market and what might be termed 'underlying
demand'. Effective demands meant willingness and
ability to buy, where ability to buy required
access to mortgage credit (other than for the

minority of purchasers able to buy from ready money). 'Underlying demand' was a function of prospective purchasers' actual and expected income, house prices, interest rates, preferences for owning as against renting (for reasons that ranged from wholly non-financial reasons such as security to financial reasons like houses being expected to keep their value and more in inflationary times) and, in the aggregate, of the demographic influences on household formation. Mortgage rationing could keep 'underlying' and 'effective' demand apart: in a housing market where house purchase credit was available, at a price, to all credit-worthy borrowers in such quantities as they could afford, the distinction would be without meaning. But, as was shown in an earlier section of this chapter, would-be house purchasers in England in the 1950s, 1960s and 1970s who were unable to obtain building society loans generally had no alternative sources to which they could turn. So reductions in building societies' lending led to the gap between underlying and effective demand opening wider. Exactly how much was unmeasurable. Since mortgage interest rates increased at the time when lending was reduced, it is likely that some potential purchasers were priced out by the increase in mortgage rates, though there were no means of knowing exactly how many. What the present author would reject as implausible, however, in the light of contemporary comment about mortgage rationing is any contention that the falls in the number of advances (e.g. in 1960, 1965, 1968 and 1974) were the consequences primarily of a falling demand to borrow. That a tightening of mortgage rationing by building societies in response to a reduced inflow of funds could have a "quite direct" effect on the pressure of demand on the building industry was noted by the Committee in the Working of the Monetary System in its Report in 1959 (38). Nor is there really any convincing reason for thinking that the house builders' organizations were barking up altogether the wrong tree when in times of rising interest rates they urged building societies to follow suit rather than rely on mortgage rationing.

The house building industry's response to changes in the amount of building societies' lending was not the same throughout the period studied. This is extremely important in any assessment of the effect of swings in lending on house prices, because it is but a truism that prices are determined by the inter-action of supply and demand, and new house building was a very important part of the balance between quantities of houses supplied and demanded. In 1959-60, in 1962-64, and again in 1967-68, the increase in effective demand to buy houses led before long to substantial increases in the quantities of new houses supplied. Between 1958 and the second half of 1960 the number of houses completed rose by 43,000 (annual rate); between 1962 and the second half of 1964 by 47,000; and between the first half of 1967 and 1968 by 32,000. In contrast, completions in 1972 were only 26,000 higher than in 1970; and the boom of the late 1970s led to an even smaller increase in the number of houses completed, only 6,000 more in 1978 than in 1977. In the late 1950s and the 1960s much more of the increase in effective demand went into additional output and less into higher prices than was to happen in the 1970s. Why this was so has yet to be explained at all conclusively: several possible reasons were suggested, none mutually exclusive, such as land with planning permission and services being ever harder to come by, the 1972-73 boom coinciding with a surge of grant-aided improvement work (see Chapter IV), causing severe shortages of building industry tradesmen, and then (in the 1970s) the losses and bankruptcies in the 1973-74 slump deterring newcomers from entering house building and deterring existing firms from expanding output to meet an increase in demand that they feared might be reversed before many of the additional houses had been completed and sold. These changes in the house building industry's response to an increase in effective demand, it will be argued, went a considerable way towards explaining why the increases in building societies' lending in the late 1950s and the 1960s were not accompanied or followed by increases in house prices on anything like the scale seen in the 1970s.

The historical record of the associations between swings in building societies' lending and variations in the rate of rise of house prices from 1955 to 1979 is shown in Table VI.13 and the house price history of the two previous decades is summarized in Table VI.7. The historical record may be examined to see whether increases, relative to trend, in building societies' lending were accompanied by or followed by increases, relative to trend, in the rate of rise of house prices. Equally imporant is whether there were instances of the rise in house prices accelerating without there being any increase in building societies' lending.

Table VI.13 shows that there were instances before 1971-73 when increases in building societies' lending to levels well above those before the preceding down-swing were accompanied and followed by more rapid increases in house prices. More rapid increases in house prices accompanied by building society lending at high levels can be seen to have occurred in 1960-61 and 1963-64, followed in both instances (but more markedly in the second) by a slackening of the rise in house prices as building societies' lending fell back. And another such episode occurred in the later 1970s, when the surge of lending by building societies in the second half of 1977 and the first half of 1978 was followed by an acceleration in the rate of rise of house prices. A more unusual instance of rapidly rising house prices was that in the later war years and the early post-war years. The amount of lending by building societies rose very fast, though from an extremely low level, and house prices increased rapidly. A further point that is extremely important in interpreting the history of increases in house prices is that the record shows no instance of an acceleration of house prices not accompanied by or preceded by a rise in building societies' lending. This fact about the historical record must be emphasized, because it implies that an up-swing of building societies lending was either an essential pre-condition for an acceleration of house prices, or caused jointly with rising house prices by some other influence. Of the eight up-swings in building societies' lending shown in Tables VI.7 and VI.13 in 1944-47, 1951-55, 1959-60, 1963-64, 1967, 1970-72, 1974-75 and 1977-78, five were accompanied or followed by an acceleration of house prices (1944-47, 1959-60, 1962-64, 1967, 1970-72 and 1977-78) and three were not (1951-55, 1967 and 1974-75). Moreover, the evidence is against there having been any marked increase in house prices during the boom of the 1930s, even though building societies had more money to lend than the market could take.

The key to interpreting this diversity in the response of house prices to up-swings in building societies' lending may be found in the truism that prices are determined by supply and demand. The way in which supply was moving, or responded to increasing demand, was far from being the same in all the eight instances just listed. As mentioned above, new house building rose rapidly in response to the increase in demand in 1959-60, 1962-64 and 1967-68, but only much more tardily in 1971-73 and less still in 1977-78. In 1952-55 new house building was rising fast as restrictive controls were first relaxed and then withdrawn, and the supply of houses for sale was augmented by sales of formerly rented houses. In 1944-47, in contrast, very few new houses were built for private owners at all. In these years, as in the 1930s, the building societies were competing for mortgage business. But whereas in the 1930s, the supply of houses for sale could repsond to an increase in demand, in 1944-47 it could not. There is nothing surprising, therefore, about competition for mortgage business being accompanied in the one instance by fast rising house prices, and in the other by house prices that were apparently steady notwithstanding the boom.

Even the half yearly figures shown in Table VI.13 are sufficient to show that in the period studied, house prices responded to an up-turn in effective demand only with a lag. For a time there was typically an increase in the number of transactions without either an increase in house prices or an increase in house building. The most likely explanation was that during the time when the amount of lending was depressed, unsold houses accumulated, some of them vacant (e.g. houses put up for sale by the executors of owners who had died, or landlords trying to sell with vacant possession houses formerly occupied by tenants who had moved away), others occupied by householders wishing to move. For a time an increase in the demand to buy houses was met from this carry-over of unsold houses, with houses selling less slowly than before but not at higher prices; but in time, the fact that houses were proving easier to sell led sellers to expect higher prices. The rise in house prices in 1975 and 1976 at rates well below the rate of inflation can probably be explained in this way; so can the comparatively slow rise in house prices in 1962, 1966 and 1970.

When the rate of increase of house prices fell back following a reduction in the number of building society loans there was likewise a time-lag. The reduction in lending in 1973 was accom-

panied by a rise in house prices at what was still
a high rate, even though somewhat less than in
1972; in the same way, house prices rose very fast
in 1979, even though the number of advances was
much lower than in 1978. Experience in those
years, when the number of loans fell, the amount of
house building fell, but house prices continued to
rise fast, was disconcerting (falling house
building and fast rising house prices appeared as
the worst of all worlds), and was held to cast
doubt on whether the volume of lending really did
influence the rate of rise in house prices. The
most likely explanation lies in past increases in
house prices affecting the expectations of sellers
about the prices they ought to get, so that if such
prices were not obtained the houses would, for a
considerable time, be left unsold. Higher house
prices combined with higher mortgage rates would
squeeze out some would-be purchasers, but those
able to pay the prices asked would take up the
mortgage money available; and the resulting transactions were the basis of the average prices
recorded. Because many sellers were able to defer
selling if the prices they were offered were not to
their satisfaction, numbers of sales responded more
quickly to a fall in the amount of mortgage money
available than did the prices at which transactions
took place, hence prices as recorded continued to
rise during 1973 even when the number of sales was
dropping. In time, the increasing difficulty of
making sales affected the prices that sellers
expected to get, which brought the rise in prices
to a halt in 1974.

The historical record, in the view of the
present author, lends no support to the contention
that in the period studied the volume of building
society lending had little or no effect on short-
run variation in the rates of rise of house prices.
There are, moreover, several published econometric
studies of the British housing market, notably by
Whitehead (39), Hadjimatheou (40), Mayes (41),
Buckley and Ermisch (42) and Nellis and Longbottom
(43). All except the last found the amount of
mortgage credit to be an important, though not all-
important, influence on the housing market. The
alternative to supplies of mortgage credit as the
suggested main explanation of short-run variation
in the rate of rise of house prices was the rate of
rise of personal income. That variations in the
rate of rise of personal income in real terms

explained most of the variation in the rate of rise
of house prices was argued for by, among others,
Boleat (44) and Bradley (45). Which of real
personal disposable income or the supply of
mortgage credit explained more of the variation in
the rate of rise of house prices might appear to be
a straightforward enough question to answer statis-
tically, but it proved not to be. The main reason
that may be suggested is the connection between
building societies' lending and the cyclical
fluctuations in the economy. What in the early
1960s was termed the "go" phase of the cycle was
characterized by reductions in interest rates,
expansionary fiscal policies (which raised post-tax
incomes), and a more relaxed attitude to pay
increases. The times at which building societies
took in exceptionally large amounts of money were
thus those when real personal incomes after tax
were beginning to accelerate relative to trend.
This coincidence in time, for reasons to do with
the cycle in the economy and economic policy, of
exceptional increases in building societies'
lending and exceptional increases in personal
income, would seem to the present author to be the
explanation of why their effects on the housing
market and house prices could not be straight-
forwardly separated.

A hypothesis that changes in real personal
disposable income were the main influence of effective demand (not underlying demand) to buy houses
has a number of problems. Most serious is that no
mechanism suggests itself by which an increase in
real incomes could make itself effective in the
market in the absence of a sufficient supply of
mortgage money. Another is that the received
theory holds that in view of how long-term is the
commitment to buy on mortgage, demand would be
governed by expected income over the long-term
("permanent income") and be little affected by
short-term variations as actual income. A more
general theoretical point is that in a decade when
belief in the importance of the money supply (most
of which is the counterpart, on the other side of
banks' balance sheets, to bank lending) as an
influence on the general price level made great
strides, there was something very anomalous about a
contention that in the market more dependent than
any other on credit, the amount of such credit had
little or no influence on the course of prices
there. To argue, as was sometimes done, that since

building societies only made loans to credit-worthy borrowers to purchase houses that were good security for mortgages their lending could not have contributed to instability in the housing market, was reminiscent of the nineteenth century monetary controversies about whether there could be an 'over-issue' of notes by the banking system so long as the banks financed only genuine trading trans-actions.

Thus far we have looked at the results of the policy of using mortgage rationing to cope with shortages of mortgage money occasioned by not following market rates all the way up when they rose, instead of following market interest rates and charging marking clearing rates for mortgages. Here we look at the rationale. The policy kept mortgage rates from being as unstable as they might have been, but at the cost of greater instability in the amount available for lending. The house builders consistently pressed the building socie-ties to put up interest rates rather than resort to severe mortgage rationing; and from their point of view that was a wholly reasonable line to take. Why then did the building societies do otherwise? Part of the explanation lies in pressure exerted by successive governments to keep increases in mort-gage rates to the unavoidable minimum. For more than thirty years, from 1948-1979, governments tried to implement an 'incomes policy' or a 'prices and incomes policy' to keep down the rate of infla-tion. Whether they were wise in adopting such policies is not a matter for discussion here; the fact that they did so meant that governments were bound to be very concerned about the rate of increase of a large item of outgoings in the budgets of millions of households. But quite apart from the concern of governments with prices and incomes policies, there were other strong pressures to restrain building societies from following rising market interest rates all the way up until mortgage rates were high enough to 'price out' enough potential purchasers for supply and demand to balance. For with variable rate mortgages, there was not one mortgage market, but two: the market for new mortgages; and those households that already had their mortgages as a result of buying houses previously. In the market for new mort-gages, potential purchasers could withdraw if interest rates rose beyond what they could afford, but households that already had mortgages obviously

could not. Nor would the increase in their outgoings be mitigated in any way if part of the
increase in interest rates was offset by house
prices rising less than they might otherwise have
done, a market response to high interest rates.
Given time, rising money incomes would reduce the
ratio of mortgage outgoings to income and hence
provide a margin within which increases in mortgage
outgoings could be absorbed, but obviously that was
not so of mortgages taken out recently. Owing to
the way in which mortgage lending was increasing, a
high proportion of borrowers had had their mortgages for only a short time: in 1973 almost 40% of
all mortgages had been running for under three
years (46). At the mortgage rates current at the
end of the 1960s (in contrast to a decade earlier)
there was little scope for mitigating the effect of
higher interest rates by lengthening mortgage terms
(which spreads the repayment over a longer period
and so keeps down the payment of interest and
principal combined) (47).

In these circumstances, how far building
societies could go in following market interest
rates upwards depended on how much financial
pressure their existing mortgagors, particularly
those who had taken out their mortgages recently,
were considered able to withstand. 1973 provides
the clearest examples; between the summer of 1972
and the autumn of 1973 the building societies'
recommended mortgage rate had risen from 8% to 11%,
which produced an increase of 23% in the outgoings
(net of tax) on a 25 year mortgage. Such an
increase was in excess of the increase in the
incomes of most mortgage holders during this time,
as average earnings rose by 18% between the third
quarter of 1972 and the fourth quarter of 1973.
The building societies appear to have decided that
the increase to 11% was the most that their
borrowers could withstand; for when market interest
rates jumped again at the end of 1973 following the
increase in oil prices and the threat of a coal
strike, the building societies did not attempt to
follow. The government of the day took pains to
make clear that it left the decision to the
building societies, and they decided to acquiesce,
at least for a time, in much reduced inflow of
money from investors and hence in their lending.

An obligation to have regard to the interests
of their existing borrowers (about four million in
the early 1970s) and not just clear the market for

new loans was inherent in building societies'
organisation and structure. Mortgagors were
borrowing members and not merely debtors with loan
agreements that gave very sweeping powers to the
lender. Striking the balance between the interests
of existing mortgage holders, investors, and would-
be new purchasers was difficult, and presented a
wholly new set of problems for building societies.
When the era of fluctuating interest rates began in
1955, nothing in building societies' accumulated
experience and working doctrine gave any guidance
about what increases in interest rates were tolerable. Great caution in discovering what was
tolerable was therefore far from surprising, hence
the gradual increase in the size and frequency of
the increases that were considered acceptable. The
increases considered acceptable were larger in the
1970s than in the 1960s, and increases in mortgage
rates larger and faster in the later 1970s than in
the earlier years of the decade: interest rates
were raised speedily by 2% in November 1978 when
market interest rates turned upwards; and the
increase of 3½% at the end of 1979 was wholly
unprecedented. That is not so say, of course, that
increases on such a scale would have been acceptable or feasible a decade earlier, let alone two.

What really were the effects of holding
mortgage rates below market levels with more severe
mortgage rationing when market interest rates rose,
and who gained and who lost are more problematical
than might appear. Whether the number of people
able to become owner-occupiers over the years would
have been greater had mortgage money been more
continuously available, though at a higher price,
is debatable. Certainly the combination of
building society interest rates that would clear
the market for new loans and mortgages with
interest rates that were variable without limit at
the lender's discretion would have made house
purchase on mortgage risky when interest rates were
as volatile as they were in the 1970s. The risks
would have been greatest for the marginal house
purchaser who could only just afford house purchase. How many of them would have been 'priced
out' of the market if interest rates had been at or
close to market clearing levels is open to doubt,
both because there was uncertainty about how
purchasers would respond to higher interest rates,
and also about what would be the mortgage rate at
which the market would 'clear'. That in turn

depended on how much more money building societies could get at higher interest rates, which would depend on, among other things, whether their competitors in the market for investible funds would retaliate. Investors obviously would have gained from a policy of higher interest rates; given the substantial amounts of 'large' money invested with building socieities, the gains to investors would by no means have all accrued to small savers whose losses in times of inflation were increasingly contrasted in the 1970s with the appreciation of house values enjoyed by people buying houses on mortgage.

That a more stable supply of mortgage money, even though at times expensive, would have been to the advantage of house builders is not in doubt. What is more arguable is whether the swings in lending did any real harm to the house building industry and the housing market before, at the earliest, the end of the 1960s. The speed with which output of new housing responded to the rise in demand in 1959-60, 1962-64 and 1967-68, argues against the capacity of the industry having been reduced or its efficiency impaired. But the increase in output between 1970 (when demand began to revive) and 1972 was smaller and more tardy, which could be attributed to the preceding slump having reduced the industry's capacity and affected its expectations adversely. Fears that a boom in demand might be short-lived could obviously be a powerful disincentive to tying up working capital in houses that would not be ready for sale until a year after deciding to start them, by which time the market might have changed completely. That happened with vengeance in the second half of 1973 and the first half of 1974, when the interest charges on capital tied up in partially complete or complete but unsold houses reached unprecedented heights. Bankruptcies among house builders resulted, including that of Northern Developments Ltd. which at the time claimed to be the largest house builder in the country. There is here the main explanation, in all probability, of why the next boom in demand produced so little additional output and hence so large an increase in house prices, second only to 1971-73.

There is a similar question about whether instability in the flow of loans caused an increase in house prices, relative to what would otherwise have happened, over a run of years, as distinct

from causing an increase in house prices that would
otherwise have been spread fairly evenly over a
number of years being heavily bunched in one or two
years. Swings in house prices like those in 1971-
73 could however force up the long run rate of rise
of house prices through a ratchet on land prices
and building costs. The ratchet would work through
the expectations of sellers, principally of land,
though perhaps sellers of labour as well. The
course of land prices was discussed in Chapter IV
above. During the 1960s land prices rose fast in
real terms in the years when the housing market was
buoyant, and levelled off when the housing market
weakened and house building fell back. The boom of
the early 1970s produced an equally exceptional
boom in land prices, which was however reversed
following the slump. The historical record is
consistent with a moderate drop in activity such as
was experienced from time to time during the 1960s
halting the increase in land prices, in real terms,
but not pushing prices any way back to where they
had been previously. That could only be done by a
slump in the housing market as severe as that of
1973-74. The most likely explanation is that
increases in prices affected sellers' expectations
about the prices they should be able to get, and
that if offers at these prices were not received,
the land was simply left on the market unsold.
Only a really severe slump could break such expectations. The effect of land prices being determined in this way was to reduce the supply of new
houses built, because only those builders who
expected to sell their house at prices high enough
to leave them with a profit, even after paying for
the land, would buy. With new house building
limited in this way, the price of houses was likely
to be higher than it would otherwise have been. So
it is highly probable that the instability of house
prices had effects, via the land market, that
resulted in house prices being higher in the longer
term then they would otherwise have been.

The surge in house prices in 1971-73 had
shorter-term effects that were harmful. Potential
purchasers who would have come into home ownership
had prices been closer to normal, were kept out.
The steep decline in advances to first-time
purchasers between 1972 and 1973 (96,000, equal to
21%) compared with only 21,000 (7%) (48) to moving
owner-occupiers, is the clearest evidence of rising
house prices working in a discriminatory way

against first-time purchasers. Furthermore, the
increase in house prices in the boom worsened the
shortage of mortgage money in the slump, because
what morgage money there was would finance fewer
transactions. In 1974 the building societies
advanced £2,950 million in new loans comprising
433,000 advances. If the average advance had
increased since 1970 only in line with the general
price level plus 3% a year (a margin more than
sufficient to accommodate increases in the quality
of houses, and any slower growth of productivitiy
in house building) the same amount of money would
have financed another 50,000 advances. This would
not have been enough to avoid a slump, but it would
have been considerably less severe. These consequences of the surge in house prices were widely
recognized at the time, and prompted much discussion of whether the surge could have been avoided.
Clearly there was no automatic mechanism for doing
so. Reasons were advanced above regarding as
implausible the contention that the volume of
demand made effective in the market through
mortgage credit had little or no effect on house
prices. The building societies in 1971 and 1972
had ample funds, they were meeting demands to
borrow from credit-worthy would-be borrowers, and
the fact that the slump did not bring with it
substantial numbers of mortgage defaults, and had
debts showed that the boom in house prices had not
been accompanied by lending on poor security, in
contrast to much of the lending by secondary banks
to the property market in the early 1970s. These
facts, though, are fully consistent with the growth
of lending having permitted a greater increase in
house prices than would otherwise have occurred,
just as there is no inconsistency between an
increase in banks' lending being on perfectly good
security yet the increase in the money supply that
was the counterpart on the other side of the
balance sheet to that increase in lending, resulting in an increase in the general price level
greater than would have happened otherwise. On the
evidence of the early 1970s there was no automatic
mechanism, particularly one derived from standards
of prudent lending, that would keep the amount of
lending in line with what the housing market would
take without an undue increase in house prices.
Ideas mooted in the 1970s about a discretionary
substitute for such an automatic mechanism will be
considered in the next section on public policy.

Government Policy and House Purchase Finance

When considering government policy and the finance of owner-occupation, a distinction may usefully be drawn between subsidies (including tax reliefs of like effect) and measures to increase the supply of credit for house purchase either in general or selectively. Subsidies and tax reliefs may be considered first. The one housing subsidy received by owner-occupiers (or builders of houses for sale to owner-occupiers) on terms similar to the local authority housing subsidies, described in Chapter VII, was under the Housing Act 1923. The subsidy under this Act on houses built for private owners was not intended as a subsidy specifically for owner-occupation. It was available on houses for letting and for owner-occupation alike, and although it appears to have been used mainly by owner-occupiers, that was the consequence of building for letting not being very profitable at the interest rates at which money could be raised, not a matter of policy. But with this one exception, the history of fiscal assistance to owner-occupation is the history of the way in which the tax system changed from neutrality between owner-occupation and renting and between owning houses and owning other assets to providing substantial fiscal support for owner-occupation.

In the inter-war years the tax system neither favoured nor burdened owner-occupation relative to renting: tax relief was allowed on mortgage interest, but income tax (Schedule A) was charged on the annual values of houses occupied (tenants, other than weekly or monthly tenants could deduct the tax they paid from their rents, but the owner-occupier obviously could not and so bore it himself). The income at which liability to income tax began was high enough, though, in relation to income generally to make the tax treatment of owner-occupiers irrelevant at the time to all but the better off householders.

This situation began to change in the 1940s and 1950s, but as a by-product of changes in taxation directed to other ends, not for reasons of housing policy. The lowering of the starting point (in real terms) of income tax liability and the rise in real incomes made the tax treatment of owner-occupation important to a much increased proportion of owner-occupiers. Tax relief on mortgage interest was given, as it always had been, at the taxpayer's marginal tax rate, and for an increasing number of owner-occupiers that rate was the standard rate of tax less earned income relief (basic tax rate from 1973 onwards). Up to 1970 the taxpayer with an income just above the starting point paid tax at a reduced rate, but in the 1970s (1977-80 excepted) tax rates started at 30% or higher. At any given interest rate, tax relief became more valuable; and the increases in mortgage interest rates made the tax relief still more important. Tax relief on mortgage interest had originally formed part of an income tax system which included a charge on the annual value of owner-occupied houses. This was not a tax on "imputed income" as a matter of deliberate policy, but a side-effect of the method used to tax rental income. To tax rents by means of taxing an assessed annual value of land and buildings, instead of charging tax on the rent ascertained to have been received, was a nineteenth or even eighteenth century method of tax administration. It was simpler than assessing tax by reference to records of rental income received, impossible to evade, and would work satisfactorily when prices, costs, and rents were fairly stable. The assessments were revised at five year intervals (usually); but by the time owner-occupation was growing fast the standard of assessment appears to have been in decline (49), to the taxpayer's advantage. The reason had nothing to do with owner-occupation, being mainly (after 1918) the consequence of rent control in causing a dearth of evidence of market rents. A revaluation for Schedule A was carried out in 1935; the next was due in 1940, but obviously could not be carried out owing to the war. Provision was therefore made (Finance Act 1940) for rents in excess of the assessed amounts to be taxed under Schedule D of the income tax. This tax on "excess rents" applied only to rents received in cash, and provided the means for taxing any increase in cash rental income without a revaluation. A distinction thus came to be clearly drawn between taxing landlords' rental income and taxing the imputed income of owner-occupiers.

A tax on imputed income from owner-occupied houses was anomalous in the context of the British tax system, however much approved of by economists before and since. The income tax was on income received in money or money's worth, out of which the tax could be paid. It was not, as a general principle, levied on 'imputed income' from assets that yielded no cash income. The Schedule A charge was reveiwed by the Royal Commission on the Taxation of Profits and Income, which reported in 1955. The Commission recommended that it should be retained, on the ground that income for income, the taxable capacity of someone who owned his own house is greater (by the amount of the rent) than that of his opposite number who has to pay rent (50). This was not a very sophisticated argument. It was a long way from the propositions about neutrality between investment in houses and other forms of investment that were advanced by subsequent advocates of taxing owner-occupiers' imputed income (51), and led the Commission to the view that the appropriate measure of the owner-occupiers' additional taxable capacity was the rent his house would fetch if subject to rent control (since that was what he would be paying if he lived in the same house as a tenant). In the mid-1950s the charge on owner-occupiers produced about £25 million (52) and by the early 1960s about £45 million a year (53), not a negligible amount by the standards of the day. Inflation had whittled away the burden in real terms of a charge based on 1935 values, which had remained in use owing to the cost of a full revaluation. But at the beginning of the 1960s a full revaluation of all property, including houses, was carried out to provide up-to-date rateable values on which to base local rates. To continue to base the Schedule A charge on 1935 values when up-to date values were available would have had no justification, but to change to the 1963 values would have meant a tripling of the amounts of tax charged (54). As a consequence Schedule A was repealed, so ending the charge on owner-occupiers, with landlords' rental income tax entirely on the amount received, instead of (since 1940) partly on the amount received and partly on the assessed value. The change was made under a Conservative government, but had the support of all three parties. When announcing in 1962 the government's decision to bring the charge on owner-occupiers to an end, the Chancellor of the Exchequer said:

"It is obvious that we could not charge owner-occupiers .... with Schedule A Income Tax on the new rating valuations. We should then be trebling or quadrupling the burden

273

of the tax on many of those who pay it.
That would be intolerable" (55).

Only for 1959/60 is there fairly detailed
information available about the Schedule A charge
on owner-occupiers, for only in that year was it
distinguished in the Inland Revenue's Survey of
Personal Incomes from the rest of Schedule A. The
number of owner-occupiers and the average amount of
their Schedule A income is shown in Table VI.15
below. The total number of owner-occupiers that
the Schedule A figures show is less than the total
shown by the housing stock statistics (Chapter V)
because large numbers of households with no significant amounts of income, apart from National
Insurance retirement pensions, were not included in
surveys of personal income because their incomes
were not regularly reviewed by the Inland Revenue.

Table VI.15 - Numbers of Households with Owner-Occupiers
Schedule A and Amount of Income

Range of Total Net Income ('000)	Total Number of Incomes ('000)	Number with Schedule A ('000)	Average Amount of Schedule A Income (£)
£180-499	7,303	1,034	20.8
£500-699	5,260	1,284	19.7
£700-999	5,147	1,721	21.0
£1,000-1,499	2,272	1,104	26.0
£1,500-1,999	448	296	36.3
£2,000-4,999	444	330	51.5
£5,000 and over	81	63	102.1
All Ranges of Income	20,955	5,832	25.0

Source: Commissioners of Inland Revenue, 105th Report
(1961-62), Cmd.1906 (1963), Tables 76 and 78.

The rules of Schedule A provided that where
the taxpayer had in a five-year period spent more
on repairs than the deduction from gross rental
value allowed in arriving at the net value on which
the charge was made, the difference could be set
against the Schedule A income as "excess maintenance". The 1959/60 survey of personal incomes
found just under 600,000 of such claims, amounting
to £23.3 million, some 17% of total incomes
assessed. Of taxpayers with total net incomes of

£2,000 or more, 35% claimed "excess maintenance" (56). Rising repair costs increased the number of taxpayers that could make "excess maintenance" claims, which meant that the yield of the tax was being eroded in money terms, let alone real terms. That a higher proportion of owner-occupiers with higher than average incomes made "excess mainten- ance" claims meant that the progression of the tax was less steep than Table VI.15 suggests.

The ending of Schedule A was one part of the process which during the 1960s turned a basically neutral tax system into one which provided substan- tial fiscal support to owner-occupation and house purchase. Another was the total exclusion of sole or main residences from liability to capital gains tax when it was introduced in 1965. This was considerably more favourable than the "roll over" relief allowed since 1951 in the United States. The other parts of the process of providing fiscal support for owner-occupation concerned mortgage interest. The first was negative, that relief on mortgage interest was left undisturbed when in 1969 tax relief on interest paid by individuals was withdrawn except on loans for defined purposes (of which purchase or improvement of houses was the main one). By this means the status of tax relief on mortgage interest became unambiguously that of a special relief, not just the by-product of prin- ciple of more general application. From 1968/69 tax relief was complemented by option mortgage subsidy, introduced by the Housing Subsidies Act 1967, as an alternative to tax relief. Its purpose, as stated in the White Paper introducing it, was,

> ".... lenders usually fix the sum they are willing to advance on mortgage by reference to the proportion of the borrowers' income needed to meet the payments on the loan. The option mortgage subsidy will reduce the annual payment a man of modest means has to make for a given sum borrowed, and as a result lenders will often be willing to advance a larger sum, or to make advances which would otherwise not have been pos- sible. In this way, home ownership will be open for many more people" (57).

To provide subsidy for those not able to benefit from tax relief was to recognize that the tax relief on mortgage interest was in substance a housing subsidy. Tax relief and option mortgage subsidy provided very similar assistance, even though the form was different; there was no sense in which the one could be said to be part of the burden of public expenditure whereas the other reduced the weight of taxation. Assistance to owner-occupiers with the interest costs of house purchase was thus open-ended (apart from the limitation to £25,000 introduced in 1974), given at rates determined by the rate of income tax. Changes in the rate of income tax had nothing to do with housing finance; but of the increase between 1973/74 and 1975/76, for example, some £140 million out of the total increase of £410 million in tax relief and option mortgage subsidy was the consequence of the basic tax rate being raised from 30% to 35%. Such an increase in an ordinary subsidy would be likely to have been discussed in terms of value for money in relation to other public expenditure; but the increase in tax relief was automatic. Since it took place as a by-product of tax increases, however, few households are likely to have noticed the benefit. The combined effects of the growth of owner-occupation, rising house prices, rising interest rates, and the abolition of the reduced rate of income tax, resulted in a quadrupling of the cost of tax relief during the 1960s, but just how costly tax relief on mortgage interest had become seems to have been little appreciated until the 1970s. It is important to emphasize that the system of fiscal support for owner-occupation that aroused increasing controversy was largely a creation of the 1960s; it was not something that had always existed.

Finance of Owner-Occupation

Table VI.16 - Tax Relief and Option Mortgage Subsidy
                1945-1979

(£ million)

	Tax Relief	Option Mortgage Subsidy	Total	Total 1975 Prices
1945/46	10	-	10	40
1950/51	15	-	15	55
1960/61	70	-	70	190
1965/66	135	-	135	305
1966/67	155	-	155	335
1967/68	180	-	180	380
1968/69	195	5	200	400
1969/70	235	10	245	465
1970/71	285	15	300	535
1971/72	310	20	330	545
1972/73	365	30	395	610
1973/74	510	50	560	790
1974/75	695	75	770	905
1975/76	865	105	970	925
1976/77	1,090	140	1,030	1,025
1977/78	1,040	150	1,190	875
1978/79	1,110	140	1,250	850
1979/80	1,450	190	1,640	990

Souce: 1945/46 to 1960/61; House of Lords, Official
          Report 25 January 1979, Written Answers,
          Col. 1729.

We may turn now to interest rates and the supply of mortgage credit. Provision of mortgage credit by public bodies and State guarantees of private loans were not of any great importance in Britain in this period, in contrast to many other countries (USA, Canada, New Zealand, for example). The history of local authorities' lending for house purchase was described in an earlier section of the chapter, and emphasis was placed on the fact that it was not subsidized lending in any sense. Local authorities had, as well, powers to guarantee mortgage advances (introduced in 1933) but they were little used. The major provision of funds from the Exchequer for lending for house purchase was under the Housing and House Purchase Act 1959, which made available £100 million to building societies for on-lending on houses built before 1919 and priced at under £2,500. £92 million was advanced before the scheme was terminated as part of a package of public expenditure cuts in July 1961. The number of loans was never reported, but given the level of house prices at the time it was probably about 70,000. Given the total amount of building societies lending in 1959, 1960 and 1961, the lending under the 1959 Act was a far from token affair. The only other instance of Exchequer loans to building societies was in 1974, but since that was closely bound up with restraining mortgage interest rates from rising, it is best considered in the context of interest rates.

As mentioned earlier, mortgage interest rates were regarded as important by governments from the standpoint of prices and incomes policy as pursued in the 1960s and 1970s. This led the government of the day in 1965 to press the Building Societies Association to delay recommending an increase in mortgage rates, and in 1966 to building society mortgage rates being referred to the National Board for Prices and Incomes for investigation and report (58). In the 1970s, the governments went further than exhortation and moral pressure and used public funds to obviate increases in mortgage interest rates that would otherwise have occurred. The first such occasion was in 1973, when in order to prevent the mortgage rate being raised to 10% (a 'double figure' interest rate for the first time in the building societies' history) a "bridging grant" was paid to building societies to enable them to keep their mortgage rate at 9½% for three months, during which time the general level of short-term

interest rates was expected to fall. To start with
the policy seemed likely to work: from a peak of
10.9% in March, short-term interest rates (represented by the local authority three month rate)
fell to 8.9% in June and July, and building societies' net receipts from investors rose to the
perfectly adequate level of £200 million a month.
But in July and August, market interest rates rose
by six percentage points in as many weeks and the
attempt to keep mortgage rates out of double
figures had to be abandoned. In September the
Building Societies Association recommended a rate
of 11%. The attempt to keep down the mortgage
rates attracted a great deal of criticism, not
least from the building society world, where
complaint about 'political interference' with
mortgage rates was vigorous; but it has to be
remembered that at this time the government was
devoting all its efforts to trying to secure
acceptance of a statutory prices and incomes policy
when the price level was under severe pressure from
the boom in the prices of food and raw materials,
so it could hardly do other than try to secure some
restraint over major items in the household budget
which were beyond the scope of the Price Code.

The circumstances were somewhat similar in
1974, when the Government lent the building societies £100 million a month for five months on condition that mortgage rates were held at 11%. In the
winter of 1973-74 the building societies had not
followed market rates upwards as was mentioned
above. They appear to have considered that 11%,
compared with 8% little more than a year before,
was as much as their borrowers could stand. But at
such a rate the building societies' interest rates
were so uncompetitive that there were strong
pressures for a further increase. To prevent this
from happening at a time when the Government was
trying to secure support for a voluntary incomes
policy (the 'Social Contract'), money was advanced
to building societies to replace some of the money
they would have attracted from investors by
offering more competiive interest rates. The
government expected interest rates to fall, so that
five months would be sufficient to see building
societies' current interest rates become competitive again, and that the loan would not be outstanding for very long. The building societies were to
make payments on the loan when their net receipts
in the aggregate exceeded £150 million a month.

One-half of any excess over this sum was to be devoted to repayments. The government's expectation proved right; only £100 million of the original £500 million remained outstanding at the end of 1974/75 financial year, and the loan had been wholly repaid by December 1975.

The £500 million loan contributed to mitigating the instability in the supply money for lending as well as avoiding a further rise in mortgage interest rates. The steep increase in building societies' lending in 1971 and 1972 and the equally steep fall in 1973 and 1974 led to suggestions for a stabilization fund which would be built up when the inflow of money to building societies was unusually large (as in 1971 and the early months of 1972) and drawn on when interest rates turned the other way and the societies' inflow of money fell. The Labour party when in opposition, expressed interest in the idea and a certain amount of support for it. In October 1974 the Labour election manifesto proposed a 'national housing finance agency' that would stabilize mortgage lending and assist first-time purchasers. The idea of a stabilization fund was a straightforward application to house purchase finance of the principle of buffer stocks, a concept that goes right back to the storing of one-fifth part of the grain crop in each of the seven good years that were to precede the seven poor years (59). On investigation, though, mortgage money appeared to be much harder to store in Britain in the 1970s than corn in Egypt in the time of the Pharaohs. The stabilization fund would be built up at times when the yields obtainable on liquid financial investments were low, certainly well below the rate that would be earned on mortgages and more likely than not below the rate paid to investors. In the second half of 1971, for example, mortgages earned 8½%, the building societies were paying 7.25% on shares, including tax at the composite rate on investors' interest, whereas money invested with local authorities at three months notice earned only 5.4% on the average. For building societies to deposit substantial sums with a stabilization fund at interest rates based on market short-term rates would be an unattractive proposition financially in such circumstances. At the rates just referred to the loss would have been about £1.9 million per £100 million per year, which may be compared with the building societies' total operating surplus of £47 million in 1971. As well as that, to have to put loanable funds into a stabilization fund over and above the additions they would make in the ordinary course of business to their holdings of liquid assets (60) was an unwelcome idea to the building societies, as it meant refusing to meet demands for loans from creditworthy borrowers when there were funds available, which ran counter to building societies' ideas of what they were there to do. The stabilization fund would also present problems for government financial management and monetary policy if invested directly or indirectly in public sector securities (as it was virtually sure to be). It would accumulate funds at the time when public debt was easiest to sell (when interest rates were falling), and run them down at the time when expectations of rises in interest rates made debt most difficult to sell. The presence of a large net disinvestor in public debt in such circumstances would make the money supply harder to control.

How far these considerations weighed with the 1974 Labour government in not setting up a new housing finance agency is not a subject to which there is any reference in the public record. Labour instead relied on the arrangement that the Conservative government had negotiated with the building societies in 1973, as extended by a further agreement negotiated in 1975.

The Memorandum of Agreement of October 1973 set out as agreed objectives:

i)   to continue to support the growth of owner-occupation;
ii)   to produce and maintain a stable flow of mortgage funds to enable the house building industry to plan for a high and stable level of house building for sale;
iii) to contribute towards the stabilization of house prices;
iv)   to maintain an orderly housing market in which, subject to (iii) above, sufficient mortgage funds are available to allow purchasers a reasonable choice of owning the sort of house they want.

To facilitate discussion between building societies and government about giving effect to these agreed objectives, the Joint Advisory Committee on Building Society Mortgage Finance was set up (61). The

working of the agreement reached in 1975 is best
described by quoting the Building Societies Associations's written evidence to the Committee to
Review the Functioning of Financial Institutions.
The evidence is in the present tense as it described arrangements in effect at the time it was
submitted (1978):

> "... the JAC assesses the amount of mortgage
> lending needed to maintain a healthy housing
> market without an undue increase in prices.
> Each six months the Technical Sub-Committee
> of the JAC estimates the amount of building
> society mortgage finance needed to meet
> these objectives. After the appropriate
> figure has been agreed by the JAC, the Asso-
> ciation takes the necessary steps to ensure
> that it is not exceeded" (62).

For discussion of the way in which these
arrangements worked, reference may be made to
Whitehead (63) and, from the building societies'
point of view, Boleat (64). In 1978 the government
of the day used the 1975 agreement to call for a
reduction of £70 million a month in building societies' lending for house purchase, for the purpose
of restraining an acceleration in the rise in house
prices that was judged to be getting under way.
The building societies complied. But there was
much criticism from within the 'industry', and the
Building Societies Association members of the Joint
Advisory Committee were very much on the defensive,
as even a cursory reading of the Building Societies Gazette in 1978 would show clearly. The
reduction in lending in 1978 did not halt the rise
in house prices, any more than did the reduction in
lending in the second half of 1972, for reasons
discussed above.

Criticisms of Government Policy on House Purchase Finance

In the 1950s and 1960s the policies just
described did not attract much controversy. High
mortgage interest rates caused complaint, and so
did the "mortgage famine" of the early months of
1965, but very little compared with the 1970s. Tax
relief on mortgage interest then became very
controversial indeed, even though the only changes
to the system were restrictive (the exclusion in

1974 of mortgages on second dwellings and the £25,000 limit). Criticism of the financial arrangements for house purchase, particularly the tax reliefs, centred on the contrast between what appeared as the huge increase in the cost of the tax relief and the fall (compared with the 1960s) in the number of new houses built, and the way in which the tax relief was distributed between income groups. Instead of financing additions to the stock of housing and thereby improving housing conditions, the system drew in, at great cost to the public purse, ever-increasing amounts of capital that might have been used to finance productive investment but instead financed no more than a turnover of ownership of the existing housing stock at ever-higher prices (65). The explanation offered for the large amount of mortgage money, and hence tax relief, absorbed in financing increases in the price of second-hand houses was that the combination of tax relief on mortgage interest, exemption from capital gains tax, and absence of any tax on imputed income from owner-occupied houses made house purchase for owner-occupation a uniquely advantageous investment. These tax reliefs and exemptions made owner-occupied houses very "tax efficient" investments, and the ability of building societies to lend at rates lower than those paid by the government enabled house purchasers to finance the purchase of an asset that appreciated in value in real terms by borrowing at a rate of interest that was negative in real terms even before tax relief was taken off. Small wonder, the argument ran, that there should be a rush to invest in houses. The theory of portfolio management predicts that investors' search for the best yields on their capital will result in the price of a particular class of asset (in this instance houses) being bid up until the expected yield (net of tax and including capital appreciation) is in line with the yields obtainable on other assets. Since dividends are subject to income tax, and realized increases in share prices subject to capital gains tax, it would be expected that house prices would be bid up relative to share prices, and that the proportion of personal wealth held in the form of houses would rise relative to shares and other assets liable to income tax and capital gains tax. The consequence would be an inflation of house prices and hence of land prices and a diversion of investible funds towards housing and away from other forms of asset. Such an all round rise in house prices conferred no benefit on the national economy, it could be argued; and the diversion of investible funds away from industry and trade could be harmful. The combination of fiscal advantages for house purchase ran counter to the ideal of neutrality, that the tax system should not favour some activities relative to others. They could also be criticized as wasteful and inequitable in giving the greatest advantage to the better-off (who could afford the most expensive houses) who were the least in need of assistance to enable them to afford adequate housing, and hence wasteful. These criticisms could be levelled against tax relief at the basic rate; all the more could they be levelled against relief at the higher rates of tax. This critique of tax relief for owner-occupation was not unique to Britain: it was pressed with vigour in the USA a well (66).

This same group of arguments was also deployed in the 1970s, with increasing vigour towards the end of the decade, against the building societies' policy of not following interest rates all the way up and rationing mortgages in response to the reduced intake of money. The recommended rate arrangement had its critics on grounds of its being a form of price fixing that restricted competition and protected inefficient building societies by setting a wider margin between borrowing and lending rates than the more efficient societies really needed. But more criticized was the policy of keeping mortgage rates lower than what would clear the market. The building societies were becoming restive about the policy, with the result that the Building Societies Association's working party on mortgage finance and policy in the 1980s recommended in 1979 that 'competitive' interest rates should be paid and charged to obviate mortgage rationing (67).

Although the lines of argument just summarized became increasingly influential in the later 1970s, there are points of substance to be made on the other side. The fundamental problem for housing finance in the later 1950s, the 1960s and the 1970s was to learn to live with rising and increasingly unstable interest rates. For owner-occupiers high nominal interest rates combined with rising money incomes produced a 'front-loading' of mortgage costs in real terms that would have caused a heavy burden in the early years of a mortgage, even if the mortgage rate could be described as negative in the sense of being less than the annual rate of rise of the price level. For the house buyer there was a world of difference between paying 11% interest at a time when prices and incomes were rising at 14% a year and paying nothing while the debt melted away at 2.7% a year (68) in a world of constant prices and incomes. Tax relief provided a partial alleviation of the burden caused by 'front-loading', and partial shielding against increases in interest rates after the mortgage had been taken. The interest of existing mortgagors in security against disruptive increases in outgoings was fully legitimate. To say merely that "they borrowed the money, didn't they" (the reputed reply of President Coolidge to expressions of concern about the effect of war debts on international trade and finance) would have been equally inadequate if applied to house purchasers with variable rate mortgages. So too was there more of a case than was sometimes acknowledge for assistance in carrying the burden generated by 'front-loading', given that this effect of high interest rates was more severe than practically any other. High interest rates, and large increases in interest rates in particular, impose costs and alter the distribution of income and wealth. The way in which they do so is less explicit than the effects of fiscal measures and hire purchase controls, both used as economic regulators in the period to which this history relates. The distributive or 'directional' effects were generally given little attention by those concerned with monetary measures and financial markets, and the costs were left to fall as they may and lie where they fall. Without tax relief a high proportion of the costs would have fallen on households buying their houses on mortgage; the tax relief shifted about 30% of the costs back onto taxpayers generally. Indexed mortgages, generally in the form of indexing with interest above the specified rate added to the outstanding debt, would provide a solution to the problem of higher though stable interest rates. But they would have their own problems in a world where interest rates, the rate of rise of prices and earning and the difference between them were unstable, and there were wide dispersions around the average rate of rise of house prices and of earnings. As was emphasized in the 1977 Housing Policy Review (69), house prices do not all rise at the same average rate, nor do earnings. Without government financed guarantees, borrowers and lenders would merely have exchanged one set of risks for another, and not necessarily smaller, set.

The obverse of the criticism quoted of the high cost of the system of fiscal support for owner-occupation was that it got owner-occupied housing through an extraordinarily troubled decade (by all past standards) without even more damage than actually occurred. The cost was high; but the number of owner-occupiers continued to grow fast, and housing conditions continued to improve. This is not to defend, of course, every detail of the policies pursued. But it is important not to lose sight of the fact that conditions of a rising trend of interest rates and increasing instability around that trend were novel, and how to accommodate to them could only be discovered by experience. To raise interest rates as little as possible was a natural outcome of the building societies' accumulated doctrine and of their structure as mutual organizations. What were the safety limits in the sense of the increases that their mortgagors could withstand could only be found out gradually and cautiously. That experience in the 1970s indicated that the safety limits were wider than had previously been thought is probably a fair inference, but it does not mean that the previous caution had been unwise. To leave in place tax reliefs that provided some protection against what were felt to be heavy burdens was similarly defensible. Without the tax relief, of course, the variations in mortgage rates that mortgagors could live with would have been less, and the risks of following market interest rates more closely would have been higher.

Notes and References

(1) E.J. Cleary, The Building Society Movement, Elek, London, 1965.
(2) Sir Herbert Ashworth, The Building Society Story, Franey, London, 1980.
(3) Figures tabulated from reports of the Chief Registrar of Friendly Societies, tabulated in Table B2 of Building Societies Association, A Compendium of Building Society Statistics (3rd Edition).
(4) Cleary, Building Society Movement, p.157.
(5) Cleary, Building Society Movement, Chapters 7, 8 and 9.
(6) Sir Harold Bellman, The Thrifty Three Million, Abbey Road Building Society, London, 1935.
(7) See page 34 above.
(8) E.T. Nevin, The Mechanism of Cheap Money, University of Wales Press, Cardiff, 1955, pp.261-62.
(9) Bellman, The Thrifty Three Million, p.135.
(10) Bellman, p.223.
(11) Bellman, Table L (p.204).
(12) Bellman, pp.216-17.
(13) Table VIII of the Ministry of Health's Housing return showed that between 1919 and the end of September 1934, local authorities had made 113,000 loans under the Small Dwellings Association Acts and 57,000 under the Housing Act 1925 (S.92). The latter were for the purchase of new dwellings.
(14) The analysis by tenure in 1938 of houses built after 1918 was made by the Fitzgerald Committee was the main source, plus an estimate of flats built.
(15) Bellman, The Thrifty Three Million, p.167.
(16) Bellman, The Thrifty Three Million, p.155.
(17) See Cleary, Building Society Movement and Ashworth, Building Society Story, for the pressures, counter-pressures, rivalries, and mutual distrust that were prevalent at this time.
(18) M. Ball, Housing Policy and Economic Power, Methuen, London, 1983, especially Chapter 2.
(19) For the fullest discussion available thus far, see P. Craig, 'The House that Jerry Built?' Building Societies, the State and the Politics of Owner-Occupation, Housing

Studies, Vol. 1 (April 1986) pp.87-108.

(20) Ministry of Health, Housing return (half yearly from 1934) Table VII.

(21) Totals of capital expenditure on small dwellings acquisition were published annually in Local Taxation Returns, subsequently Local Government Financial Statistics. The problem about using these figures is in excluding from these totals amounts repaid by local authorities to lenders. From 1930/31 onwards this was shown for all classes of authority, so no problem arose; from 1926/27 to 1929/30 it was shown for some authorities (metropolitan and county boroughs) but not others; and in 1925/26 and earlier it was not shown at all. But the amount was small in 1926/27 and can be assumed negligible in 1925/26 and earlier; and in 1926/27 to 1929/30 can be estimated for all authorities from the information for county boroughs and metropolitan boroughs.

(22) Ministry of Health, Housing returns, September 1934, Table VIII.

(23) Ministry of Health, Housing returns, September 1934 and March 1939, Table VIII.

(24) Figures from Building Societies Association, Compendium of Building Society Statistics, Tables B1, B2 and B3.

(25) Replacement of old loans by new, presumably at lower interest rates, are the only way of accounting for the number of loans terminated in a year being as high as 17% of all loans outstanding, compared with 10-12% in later years.

(26) Cmd. 6670 (1945) p.7.

(27) Committee on the Functioning of Financial Institutions, Report, Cmd. 7937 (1980), especially Chapter 14 and 27.

(28) Building Societies Association, Mortgage Finance in the 1980s (Report of a Working Party, 1979).

(29) Mortgage Finance in the 1980s, p.58.

(30) Chapter 7, paragraphs 97-98 and Table VI 33, which was estimated in the same way as Table VI.13.

(31) Housing Policy, Technical Volume Chapter 7, Annex D.

(32) Building Societies Association, Mortgage Finance in the 1980s, p.63.

(33) Funds required to maintain the ratio of

liquid assets to total assets and funds
produced by repayment of mortgages on the
houses sold would approximately offset each
other.

(34) See Housing Policy Technical Volume, 1977,
Chapter 7 paragraphs 12-17.
(35) 'Control of Public Expenditure'; Cmd. 1432
(1961). There is a large literature on the
system of public expenditure control which
grew from it, known as PESC (Public Expenditure Survey Committee, the inter-departmental
committee that ran the annual survey that
Cmd. 1432 recommended).
(36) i.e. the "squeeze" that began in 1955 and
ended in 1958.
(37) Cmnd. 827 (1959), para.248.
(38) Cmnd. 827 (1959), para.294.
(39) C.M.E. Whitehead, The UK Housing Market,
Saxon House, Farnborough, 1974.
(40) G. Hadjimatheou, Housing and Mortgage
Markets, Saxon House, Farnborough, 1976.
(41) D.G. Mayes, The Property Boom, Robertson,
Oxford, 1979.
(42) R. Buckley and J. Ermisch, 'Theory and
Empiricism in the Econometric Modelling of
House Prices' Urban Studies, Vol. 20 (1983)
pp.83-90.
(43) J.G. Nellis and J.A. Longbottom, 'An
Empirical Analysis of the Determination of
House Prices in the United Kingdom', Urban
Studies, Vol. 18 (1981) pp.9-22.
(44) M.J. Boleat, 'The Housing Market - Economic
Framework', in Building Societies Associa-
tion, House Price Determination, 1981.
(45) J. Bradley, 'House Prices - Statistical
Analysis', in Building Societies Association,
House Price Determination, 1981.
(46) Housing Policy Technical Volume, Chapter 7,
Table VII 25.
(47) See S.K. Edge, 'Repayments of Capital on
Building Society Mortgage Loans', Building
Societies Gazette, December 1967.
(48) Housing Policy Technical Volume, Chapter 6,
Appendix A, Table A.4.
(49) J.R. Hicks, U.K. Hicks and C.E.V. Leser wrote
in 1944: "Gradually as Schedule D came to
take the place of Schedule A as the most
important revenue producer, the Inland
Revenue appear to have lost interest in independent valuation and come more and more to

base Schedule A valuations on rating". J.R.
Hicks, U.K. Hicks and C.E.V. Leser. The
Problem of Valuation for Rating, Cambridge
University Press, Cambridge, 1944, p.69.

(50) Royal Commission on the Taxation of Profits
and Incomes, Final Report, Cmd. 9474 (1955),
paragraphs 826-28.

(51) See in particular J.E. Meade (and others)
Structure and Reform of Direct Taxation,
Allen and Unwin for Institute of Fiscal
Studies, London, 1978; J.A. Kay and M.A.
King, The British Tax System, Oxford
University Press, Oxford, 1978; A.B. Atkinson
and M.A. King, 'Housing Policy, Taxation, and
Reform', Midland Bank Review, March 1980.

(52) Cmd. 9474, (1955) paragraphs 827 and 849.

(53) The full year cost of abolishing the Schedule
A charge was estimated at £48 million, including 'beneficial occupation' by tenants as
well as owner-occupiers, H C Deb. Vol. 675,
col. 458.

(54) The average Schedule A value was about £25
(see Table VI.15) or perhaps slightly less
owing to households with incomes not included
in the survey of personal incomes having
dwellings of lower annual values. The
average rateable value of owner-occupier
dwellings in 1963 after revaluation, according to the Family Expenditure Survey, was
£71. Family Expenditure Survey, Report for
1963, Table P.

(55) H C Deb. Vol. 657, col.978.

(56) A.A. Nevitt, Housing, Taxation and Subsidies,
Nelson, London 1966, p.176, quoting material
supplied by the Board of Inland Revenue.

(57) Help Towards Home Ownership, Cmnd. 3163
(1966), para.2.

(58) National Board for Prices and Incomes, Report
No. 22, Rate of Interest on Building Society
Mortgages, Cmnd. 3136 (1966).

(59) Book of Genesis, Chapter 41, verses 34-36.

(60) Liquid assets (technically "cash and investments") were built up (within limits) when
interest rates were favourable and the inflow
of money good, and run down (within limits)
in the opposite circumstances.

(61) The full text of the Memorandum of Agreement
was published in House of Commons Debates,
Written Answers 16 January 1974, cols. 94-97.

(62) Committee to Review the Functioning of

Financial Institutions, Second Stage Evidence, Vol. 3, p.8 (HMSO 1979).

(63) C.M.E. Whitehead, 'What should be done with the Guideline', CES Review No. 7, Centre for Environmental Studies, London, 1979.

(64) M. Boleat, The Building Society Industry, Allen and Unwin, London, 1982.

(65) See, for instance, M. Clark, 'Too much Housing', Lloyds Bank Review, October 1977; B. Kilroy, 'Why so Priviledged?', Lloyds Bank Review, October 1979; and in more depth and with more rigour, A. Grey, N.P. Hepworth and J. Odling Smee, Housing Rents, Costs and Subsidies (2nd Edition) Chartered Institute of Public Finance and Accountancy, London, 1981.

(66) See Harvey S. Rosen, 'Housing Decisions and the US Income Tax; an Econometric Analysis', Journal of Public Economics, 1979, and references cited there.

(67) Building Societies Association, Mortgage Finance in the 1980s.

(68) 1.14 divided by 1.11 is 1.027.

(69) Housing Policy Technical Volume, Chapter 7, paragraphs 146-156.

CHAPTER VII

LOCAL AUTHORITY HOUSING FINANCE

The Origins of Exchequer Housing Subsidies and House Building under the 1919 Housing Act

The history of local authority housing, like the history of house purchase finance, includes a pre-1914 prologue but with the main action being in the inter-war years and after 1945. The origins of permissive powers for local authorities to build and retain houses for letting, first under the Housing of the Working Classes Act 1885, then consolidated as Part III of the House of the Working Classes Act 1890, were described in Chapter II. So too was the attempt to turn the purely permissive power under the 1890 Act into, in some circumstances, a duty; and the ineffectiveness in practice of these powers against a recalcitrant local authority. In the decade before 1914 there was a growing realization that if houses of a standard that was adequate according to perceptions of the time were to be let to poorer households, a subsidy would be needed, and that if local authorities were to build them on any scale, part at least of the subsidy would have to come from the Exchequer.

How soon and on what scale such subsidies would have come into being is an intriguing historical 'if'. The main barrier against the introduction of Exchequer subsidies for housing in the years before 1914 was the growth of public expenditure that was already in progress. Major innovations of policy generating substantial expenditure were non-contributory old age pensions, of which payment began in January 1909 and whose cost reached £12.5 million by 1913/14; and National Health Insurance, to which the Exchequer contributed 2d a week to the employee's 4d and the employer's 3d at a cost of £6.1 million in 1913/14 (1). Coinciding with this increase in civil social expenditure was a large increase in expenditure on the Royal Navy, from £31.1 million in 1907/08 to £48.8 million in 1913/14, primarily as a result of the battleship building race against Germany. No major new sources of revenue were in prospect: Lloyd George had already introduced the super-tax in 1909, and his land tax looked like bringing in little; and to Liberals even a tariff for revenue was anathema. In such circumstances there were strong fiscal objections to taking on new commitments to pay subsidies.

In 1913 and 1914 the most likely starting point for any Exchequer support for subsidized house building appeared to be in rural areas, where wages were acknowledged to be lowest and so the prospect of private enterprise house building at remunerative rents poorest. The governments's Housing Bill in 1914 did include provisions to authorize the Board of Agriculture to purchase land for cottage building, and to make loans to "public utility societies" (what in the 1970s and later would have been known as housing associations), without actual subsidy but at interest rates that reflected the Exchequer's credit (2). The objections raised to these proposals though, led the government of the day to drop them from the Bill in order to secure rapid passage of the rest of it, primarily to arrange for the provision of houses for employees at Rosyth naval dockyard.

Housing Bills had been introduced annually since 1911 by back-bench Conservative MPs (notably Sir A. Griffith Boscawen). The details varied, but the 1911 Bill may be taken as representative, in providing for a £1 million annual Treasury grant, half for slum clearance and half for housing in rural areas, but nothing for assistance to cities and boroughs building houses under Part III of the 1890 Act. The Bill received a second reading, but could progress no further because the government declined to move the necessary Financial Resolution (3). That this would happen was widely known, of course, so doubt can be entertained about how many of those Members who voted for the Bill did so merely as a gesture rather than out of real support for it. Plainly such interest as there was in Exchequer financing for housing before 1914 cut across party lines. The amounts proposed though, were small, and could hardly have made more than a modest addition to the small amount of house building that was done by local authorities. The number of houses built by local authorities before 1914 under Part III of the 1890 Act was about 20,000, one-sixth by the London County Council.

The 1914-1918 war (or the 'Great War' as it was known until 1939) brought about a complete change. Before discussing the way in which wartime and expected post-war conditions led to Exchequer subsidies for housing in 1919, there is an important point to note about the way in which the war had made people accustomed to government doing things on a very large scale and in a great hurry. The war was fought by massed armies (and to a lesser extent navies and air forces), which needed to be supplied on a corresponding scale with munitions of war and stores of all kinds. The organization to manufacture and transport the vast quantities of munitions and stores had to be improvised, but improvised it was, and by 1917 and 1918 the government (particularly the Ministry of Munitions) ran a very large organization indeed. A consequence was a complete change of scale in thinking about what government could organize if the need was urgent enough. The contrast between the thinking in 1918-19 in terms of 500,000 houses in three years and the 20,000 built in two decades before 1914 illustrates this. Supplying the armed forces made people accustomed to think in hundreds of thousands if not millions. What would have looked substantial in 1914 terms would have looked like the merest penny numbers in 1918.

Thinking about post-war housing policy began in 1916, when planning for "reconstruction" began. Housing had necessarily to be included: for house building had come virtually to a halt early on in the war, apart from building by the Ministry of Munitions of about 10,000 houses (4), with the result that housing shortages worsened in the way described in Chapter III. Housing was considered to be second only to rising prices as a cause of unrest, according to the Commission of Enquiry into Working Class Unrest (5), which reported in 1917. There were pressures to plan ahead, therefore, not just to wait and see what happened. Planning for post-war housing in 1917 and 1918 was dominated by there having been a large increase in building costs since 1914, with an expectation that after the end of the war prices, including building costs, would fall back to "normal". This view was put to the Ministry of Reconstruction's Housing Panel in April 1917 in a memorandum by Rowntree which said that state aid for housing immediately after the war would be needed because the cost of building would be abnormally high. "Until it becomes normal .... no appreciable number of houses will be built unless action is taken by the state", in the form of subsidy to cover the difference between the cost of building during the period immediately under consideration and its future normal cost (6). This view was stated clearly in the Panel's published report. "In the years immediately following the war, prices must be expected to remain at a higher level than that to which they will eventually fall when normal conditions are restored .... Anyone building in the first years after the war will consequently be faced with a reasonable certainty of a loss in the capital value of their property within a few years" (7). This proposition was, as far as can be seen, the basis for the widespread agreement that house building immediately after the war would need to be subsidized, probably heavily. The report recommended that a statutory duty should be placed on local authorities to build houses, with central government to act in default, which was not an empty threat in view of the house building carried out by the Ministry of Munitions during the war, and that Ministry's apparent ability to organize the production of almost anything. But whether a subsidy would be needed after building costs and prices had returned to normal was left for later consideration: it was possible to agree to large-scale subsidized house building in the years immediately following the war without conceding the case for subsidized building as a permanent arrangement, so that the breadth of support in 1918 for subsidized house building at the end of the war is not necessarily to be taken as ".... testimony to the dramatic impact of the war years in generating a new commitment to radical social change" (8).

Much more radical in their substance and their implications were the recommendations of the Tudor Walters Committee (9) about the standards of the houses that local authorities should build. These standards were a long way above those to which 'working class' housing had been built in the years before 1914. The Committee justified these recommendations on two main grounds: that there was a shortage of housing of all types, so the local authorities would not be building just for the poor; and that since a house was expected to last for 60 years, it would be false economy not to design them to standards well above the accepted minimum at the time of building, for standards would rise during their useful life. The architectural aspects of the Tudor Walters recommendations, including the layouts, have been discussed many times, most recently by Swenarton (10), so here it is sufficient to note the recommendations that three bedrooms should be the standard for family accommodation, that there should be fireplaces in each room, and that there should be a bathroom. Not only were the houses themselves to be much more spacious; a density of 12 houses to the acre was recommended, which would permit a mixture of short terraces and semi-detached houses in place of the long terraces that had been usual before 1914. These recommendations were endorsed by the Minstry of Health and made obligatory for local authorities by the Housing Manual issued in 1919 (11). Building to such standards, one can see with hindsight, would result in capital costs and hence loan charges too high to be recovered from rents without subsidy even if the abnormal element in costs caused by wartime inflation were excluded. Perhaps surprisingly, none of the sources consulted, including Wilding (12), suggest that this point was taken in 1918 and 1919.

What should be the financial terms on which local authorities would build houses for letting after the war was the subject of a prolonged struggle in 1917-19 between the Ministry of Reconstruction, the Local Government Board (subsequently dissolved and its housing responsibilities transferred to the newly created Ministry of Health), and the Treasury. For an account of this struggle the reader may be referred to Swenarton or (in less detail) Merrett (13). Here the important point to note is that funadmentally what the struggle was about was how much of a potentially open-ended liability should be borne by the local authorities and how much by the Exchequer; and what limits should be set to the Exchequer's liability. It was common ground that the extra cost of building immediately after the end of the war rather than waiting until prices and costs had to be met from subsidy; but at the time no one could say what those costs would be. Local authorities were not prepared to take on commitments that could lead to an open-ended liability falling on the rates, and for that reason the number of houses they offered to build on the financial terms offered to them in 1918 (the Exchequer to meet 75% of the deficit in the first seven years, and where the local authority's 25% share exceeded 1d rate, the Exchequer grant <u>might</u> be increased by the excess over 1d rate) was far fewer than the goverment wanted, only about 100,000 compared with the 500,000 looked for. The local authorities, with the Association of Municipal Corporations in the lead, pressed for the local authorities' financial liability to be limited to the product of a 1d rate, and this in the end the government had to concede, in order to get the houses built.

That the cost to public funds of the proposed house building programme would be very high was realized right from the start. When the Housing Bill had been introduced, the government published its estimate of the cost: 500,000 houses at an average cost of £500 to £700 each would result in capital expenditure of £250 million to £350 million; and the annual cost to the Exchequer of the subsidies was put at £5 million to £7.5 million (14). Expenditure on that scale ran directly contrary to official thinking about financial policy after the war. Finance had not been excluded from planning for 'reconstruction'. The Committee on the Currency and Foreign Exchanges after the War, generally known after its chairman (the Governor of the Bank of England) as the Cunliffe Committee, recommended (15) that as soon as possible after the end of the war, government borrowing should cease and that public expenditure should be cut to provide a surplus of revenue over expenditure out of which the floating debt could be progressively repaid. To provide this surplus public expenditure would have to be cut sharply, which meant that demands for expenditure on 'reconstruction' would have to be resisted and capital expenditure by government avoided. Why, then, was the decision taken in 1918 and 1919 to embark on a large and costly programme of subsidized housing building?

One answer to this question that has been suggested by Merrett (16) and Swenarton (17) is that fear of revolution led to the subsidized house building programme being undertaken by a government whose basic beliefs were those propounded in the Cunliffe Committee's report just referred to, and hence would jettison the house building programme along with the other reconstruction measures as soon as it appeared safe to do so. That fears of revolution were widespread in the autumn and winter of 1918 and in 1919 is not, of course, in doubt. As was mentioned in Chapter III, much of Germany was convulsed with insurrections; nearer home were the attempted local general strike in Glasgow, and then the police strike in Liverpoool with military force employed in both cities. Disaffection, and in some instances mutiny, in the army, caused by delays and perceived unfairnesses over demobilization might easily have turned into something worse. The connection between all this and the housing programme, according to Lloyd George, was that "Britain would hold out against the danger of Bolshevism, but only if the people were given confidence - only if they were made to believe that things were being done for them. We had promised reform time and time again, but little has been done. We must give them conviction that this time we mean it, and we must give them that conviction quickly. We could not afford to wait until prices went down". As to the cost, "what was that compared with the stability of the State" (18). How far Lloyd George or his Cabinet colleagues believed this is not known. But what is not in doubt is that they eagerly supported the Housing Bill, as did most of their Parliamentary supporters. Motives are usually mixed, and there is no reason to doubt the genuineness of the belief that everything should be made to make Britain a better place in which to live after so terrible a war. This is the sentiment to which Lloyd George appealed when he spoke (in December 1918 at Wolverhampton) of making the country "a land fit for heroes". He did not, in fact, speak of "homes for heroes", words often attributed to him when alleging that the ending of the housing programme was an act of cynical bad faith. Before looking at the contention that fear of revolution led the government in 1918 and 1919 to make promises that it had no intention of keeping, we may look at what happened to the housing programme begun in 1919 and known from the name of the Minister of Health (and before that Minister for Reconstruction) as the Addison programme.

The "Addison" House Building Programme and Subsidies

As is well known, the number of houses built was much smaller than intended, and the average capital cost much higher. All told, some 170,000 dwellings were built with the 1919 Act subsidy (19) compared with the 500,000 planned, and as late as March 1921 only 16,000 had been completed. As against the average cost of £500 assumed in the explanatory financial memorandum, the actual average cost, including land and site works, was just over £1,000 (20). The principal reason both for the slow progress and high costs was the pressure of demand on the building industry from industry and commerce. The efforts of local authorities and the Ministry of Health to keep down costs generally made house building for local authorities less attractive to builders than building for industry and trade at a time when, owing to wartime disruption, productivity was well below what it had been in 1914. The wartime direct control over building was ended in December 1918. In retrospect that decision has the appearance of a major mistake if the house building programme was to have any priority. The decision was taken out of fear of unemployment, lest the local authorities should not be ready with their housing programmes to get work to building contractors to employ the men demobilized from the forces (21). The strength of demand on the building industry was not generally foreseen, though the Ministry of Reconstruction argued strongly for keeping the controls.

The strong pressure of demand on the house building industry and rising costs and prices put the Ministry of Health in a very difficult position. The fact that the extra loan charges generated by higher capital costs would fall wholly on the Exchequer (except where a local authority did so little that the net current cost fell short of a 1d rate product) meant that central government had to exercise close supervision over the details of the plans and specifications, and the costs. There was great Parliamentary pressure for faster progress, and growing complaint about the cost. The Departmental Committee that reviewed the costs in 1921 concluded that due economy had been observed in acquiring land, and that nothing more could have been done "... to secure economy in connection with specifications, plans, and other-

wise of a technical nature" (22); but what the
Committee termed the absence of any "community of
interest between the state and the local authority
in securing economy" would have led to friction in
almost any circumstances. The same was true about
rents: local authorities had to set the rents
(subject to the Ministry of Health's regulations),
but at the margin all the extra income from higher
rents accrued to the Exchequer, but all the consequent odium was borne by the local authority. The
Ministry of Health's regulations (23) provided that
when first fixing rents, local authorities should
have regard to rents obtaining in their locality
for working class houses; any increases allowed by
amendments to the Rent Restrictions Acts; any
superiority in the condition or amenities of the
houses provided; and the class of tenant for whom
the houses were provided. These regulations
amounted in practice to controlled rents plus a
supplement for higher quality; and because the step
up in quality had been so large, the supplement
that could be charged could be substantial. The
Act provided that the subsidy could be reduced in
the event of failure to comply with these regulations, with a Tribunal (with two members appointed
by the Minister and two nominated by the local
authority associations) to adjudicate disagreements
between local authorities and the Ministry of
Health. The Tribunal was resorted to in well over
100 cases (24), and remained in existence until the
consolidation of housing accounts in 1935 ended the
distinctions between rents that depended on under
which Act houses had been built.

How high the rents were set, on the average,
what proportions of total current costs they
covered, and how the 1d rate contribution in
practice divided the cost between Exchequer and
local authorities should be simple enough questions
to answer, but they are not. Expenditure and
receipts in respect of houses built under the 1919
Act were first distinguished from other local
expenditure on housing in the Local Taxation
Returns for 1924/25. But the amounts summarized
there were so drawn as to debit rates on local
authority houses as a cost, and credit them as a
receipt along with rents. Not until 1933/34 were
these rates shown separately (in a footnote), so
that they could be netted out of both receipts and
payments. The amount can be roughly estimated for
1924/25, on the assumption that rate payments on

local authority houses changed pro-rata with total rate poundages. In that year rents met just under 40% of the total cost chargeable to revenue, and of the rest seven-eighths were met from the Exchequer and one-eighth from rate fund contributions. In 1933/34 rents still met just under 40% of total costs, but of the balance the Exchequer's share had diminished to six-sevenths and the rate fund's increased to a little over one-seventh. Rents were lower as a result of reductions allowed by the Ministry of health on grounds of falls in prices and tenants' income (26); loan charges were lower as a result of re-financing at lower interest rates of money raised short-term on 'housing bonds'; and the increase in total rateable value increased the amount that a 1d rate would bring in. In 1924/25 the rate fund contribution averaged about £5 12s per dwelling, which (as we shall see) was higher than the rate fund contribution required under the 1924 Act; that such a contribution would meet no more than one-eighth of the part of the cost not recovered from rents was due to costs being so high. Not only were capital costs much higher than expected, but the bulk of the money was raised at 6% to 6½%, well above the interest rates prevailing during the war. Such interest rates on top of the high capital costs made incapable of achievement the intention of the reconstruction planners that after seven years the houses should be self-financing if one-third of the capital cost was written off as being due to the exceptional post-war conditions.

With hindsight, the greatest of the ironies of the "Addison" house building programme was that not until the post-war slump began to bring down the demands on the building industry from industry and commerce could local authority house building command a sufficient share of the industry's capacity to make progess at anything like the rate hoped for; but the same slump fatally weakened support for the programme and the policy that it embodied. The slump began in the late summer or the autumn of 1920. The turning point cannot be ascertained with any precision, but the monthly unemployment percentages show clearly that the slump was well under way by the end of the year. With the worsening of the slump, pressure for cuts in public expenditure grew during the winter of 1920/21 and in the following spring. A campaign was waged by Lord Rothermere's newspapers against "waste" and "squandermania", and 'anti-waste' candidates began to do well at Parliamentary by-elections. The sheer size of capital expenditure on housing made the housing programme a prime target for the 'anti-waste' campaign, and antipathy among Conservative MPs to Addison's reputed radical views made him still more vulnerable. In response to these pressures, Addison was persuaded by Lloyd George to give up the Ministry of Health, which he did on becoming Minister without Portfolio. In November 1920, the Chancellor of the Exchequer (Austen Chamberlain) had pressed for a 20% cut in all public expenditure so as to provide £250 million for reducing the floating debt; Addison had then successfully resisted cuts in housing; but in the next six months the slump had deepened very rapidly and the housing programme could no longer be protected. That the shift of influential opinion in favour of large cuts in public expenditure on purely financial grounds, regardless of other consequences, was the basis for the decision in June-July 1921 to limit subsidized house building to completion of those houses for which tenders had already been accepted, is fully documented in the work by Wilding and (much more accessible) Swenarton. In June 1921 the Cabinet Finance Committee considered that ".... in view of the difficult financial situation there was no alternative open to the government but to decide housing questions not on merits but on financial considerations only" (26).

When questioned about consultations on the subject of reviewing housing need, Mond (Addison's successor) replied: "I consult the local authorities, but mainly I have to consult the national financial position" (27). He warned the Cabinet though, that limiting house building to houses included in contracts signed and tenders approved could not be defended as having any relation to the housing needs of the country but must be defended simply and solely on grounds of financial necessity. No return of private enterprise building was in sight (28). Nevertheless, that was the policy decided on; and in accord with the conventions of British Cabinet government, Mond had to defend the decision. He did so in terms that harmed his reputation. Referring to the housing difficulties of newly married couples, he was reported as saying ".... they should be so happy that they can enjoy living in even one room. Isn't the demand for a separate house a comparatively recent development. In China and the east generally, I understand, they continue to live under the parental roof quite contentedly" (29).

The dates are important to the view taken about the importance of the slump as the main cause of the end of subsidized house building as against the view that it was abandoned because its raison d'etre had gone once the danger of revolution had passed. The refusal of the railway and transport unions to strike in support of the miners occurred on April 15 1921 (termed "Black Friday" in trade union history). Had they struck, there would have been virtually a general strike, which at the time was widely looked upon as tantamount to revolution. That the coal strike would be defeated could hardly have been evident until well into June 1921. But Addison had left the Ministry of Health well before "Black Friday" and the Cabinet was moving towards its decision to halt the house building programme before the defeat of the coal strike. "Black Friday" and the defeat of the coal strike were the events considered to have allayed the fear of revolution. Their timing is against their having been instrumental in the loss of support for the "Addison" house building programme.

Even if the allegation that the precipitate ending of the Addison programme was the result of bad faith is regarded as not proven, there is no doubt that its ending, and the subsequent cuts in other public services, were regarded as a betrayal of promises made at the end of the war. This was long remembered; that 'the ghost of Lloyd George defeated Churchill in 1945' became something of a commonplace. But Lloyd George depended on Conservative MPs for his Parliamentary majority, and when those MPs came to cease to support the improvements and extensions of public services promised in 1918, there was little that Lloyd George could do. When the official Conservative candidate at the St. George's Westminster by-election in June 1921 was defeated by an "anti-waste" candidate, it was clear that Conservative MPs would press hard for 'economy' and that if Lloyd George was to remain Prime Minister he would have to take up the cause of 'economy', even if his colleagues and past promises had to go by the board (30). One of his responses was to set up a special committee on economies in public expenditure under the chairmanship of Sir Eric Geddes (Minister of Transport and one of the businessmen brought into the government during the war). The "Geddes Axe" subsequently became a by-word for cuts in the public services, and the ending of the 'Addison' house building programme is sometimes attributed to it. But here again dates are important: the decision to limit the programme to houses in tenders already approved was announced in July 1921, whereas the Geddes Committee was not appointed until August, and reported in February 1922. Addison's salary had been voted to him only until the end of the Parliamentary session (Parliamentary approval was needed because a Minister without Portfolio was a new position) and it was then that Lloyd George made the subsequently notorious remarks that Addison's "unfortunate interest in public health had excited a good deal of prejudice ...." and that ".... he was rather too anxious to build houses". To the present author this reads like clumsy banter on behalf of a colleague rather than "unmatched .... condescending cyncism" (31), though Addison's most recent biographers take a different view (32). Whatever might be thought of Lloyd George remaining in office in such circumstances, there is no reason to doubt that if he had resigned, an entirely Conservative administration would have been just as eager to cut; and no reason at all to think that the worsening housing shortage (see Chapter III) would have led to any resistance to the purely financial considerations that were dominating policy.

Subsidized Housing becomes a Permanent Part of the British Housing Scene: Policy and Legislation from 1923 to 1938

The decision in July 1921 to terminate the 'Addison' subsidy programme in the sense of no more houses being approved for subsidy might have been the end of council house building in England. But it was not, and a history of housing policy has to explain why. The exceptional conditions in 1918 that had generated wide support for the Addison programme no longer applied. So what does the history of policy after 1921 imply about the explanation of council house building as a measure to reduce the risk of revolution (Merrett and Swenarton), or as a consequence of sacrificing the interests of the private landlord in the interest of a strategy to protect the larger property

interest (Daunton) (33)? The 'revolution' argument
could apply only to the Lloyd George coalition
government and the Addison programme; but the
'expendable private landlords' argument is
obviously not time-limited in this way. In coming
to any conclusion about whether with a different
policy towards rents and security of tenure for
houses rented from private landlords there need
have been no substantial amount of building for
local authorities, the history of policy in the
private rented sector is as important as the public
sector. The private rented sector is discussed in
the next chapter, but some cross-references can
usefully be made.

The houses already approved for subsidy by
July 1921 went through to completion, which for a
time kept the house building industry occupied and
added to the housing supply. 83,000 houses were
completed in 1921/22 and 50,000 in 1922/23. But by
the beginning of 1923 the 'pipeline' was nearly
empty. Private enterprise house building had not
revived, so the government of the day had recourse
to subsidy. The subsidies provided under the
Housing Act 1923 were not really local authority
house building subsidies at all; they were available to private owners for houses whether built for
letting or for sale, with local authorities able to
receive them only if they could satisfy the
Ministry of Health that they needed to build (not
difficult in practice owing to pervasive housing
shortages that existed). The simplicity of the
form of the subsidy followed from the wide range of
circumstances in which it might be used: there were
no conditions or restrictions about rents, or
indeed any requirement that the houses should be
let; and the subsidy could be taken in the form
either of the £6 annual payments for 20 years, or
as a lump sum (£70). Where the lump sum was taken,
local authorities could borrow the money and pay
the loan charges on it from the £6 a year received
from the Exchequer. The Act provided that the
subsidies would be available only for houses
completed by the end of 1925. The Rent Restrictions Act of 1923 also extended rent restriction
only to the end of 1925, which suggests that the
government hoped for a rapid transition to conditions in which the state would do more in housing
that it had done in 1914. Whether things would
have turned out that way if Baldwin had not gone to
the country in 1923 and consequently lost office

can be no more than another historical 'if'. The
1923 Housing Act subsidies known from the name of
the Minister of Health as the 'Chamberlain' subsidies, were the first of what may be termed the
'classic' type of British housing subsidy, £x a
year per house for y years. Under the Housing Act
1923, x equalled 6, y equalled 20. There were to
be different values in future of x and y, especially x; but not until 1967 were subsidies paid that
were completely different in form.

The restriction of this subsidy to houses
completed before the end of 1925 was repealed by
the Housing (Financial Provisions) Act of 1924,
generally known as the 'Wheatley' Act from the name
of the Minister of Health in the first Labour
government. More important in numerical terms,
though, than extending the 1923 Act to houses built
before the end of 1939, was the new subsidy for
local authorities and "public utility societies"
(but not private owners) which ran in parallel with
the 1923 Act subsidy, with local authorities able
to choose which subsidy they wished for houses they
built. The Exchequer subsidy under the 1924 Act
was £9 a year for 40 years, or £12 10s in agricultural parishes (on account of wages in agriculture
and hence rent-paying capacity being particularly
low). The rate fund contribution was governed by
the "appropriate normal rent". The "appropriate
normal rent" was defined as the average rent
charged for pre-1914 working class houses (34), and
the rent at which the houses built with the aid of
subsidy under the 1924 Act were to be let was not
to exceed the "appropriate normal rent" unless a
rate fund contribution of more than £4 10s a year
would be needed to bridge the gap between outgoings
(including loan charges) on the one side and income
from rents and the Exchequer subsidy. In such
circumstances (in fact the normal circumstances,
until the later 1920s) the rents could be set at
whatever level might be needed to meet costs over
and above those met by the Exchequer subsidy of £9
a year and the rate fund contribution of £4 10s.
With interest rates at 5%, the 1924 Act subsidy
(and associated rate fund contribition) would cover
about 40% of the cost (35) and so requiring, in the
mid-1920s, a rent of about 7s 6d a week to cover
the remainder of the costs. Average controlled
rents of pre-1914 houses were about 6s a week, so
the £4 10s rate fund contribution (when set against
costs net of the Exchequer subsidy) rather than the

'appropriate normal rent' was in most places the main influence on the level of rents actually charged in the early years of the subsidy.

In complete contrast to both the 1919 Acts, the subsidy provided by the 1924 Act was intended to be permanent. No time limit was set, though the rates of subsidy (and those under the 1923 Act as extended) were required to be reviewed every two years. On the strength of the subsidy being permanent, Wheatley negotiated with the building industry trade unions relaxations of their apprenticeship rules so as to make possible an increase in the number of building industry craftsmen. A building programme of 63,000 to 95,000 houses in 1926, rising to 150,000 to 225,000 in 1934 or 1935 was envisaged (36). These were not totals of houses that the Ministry of Health had the machinery to "deliver", but rather what the 1924 Labour government expressed its wish to see, and wished the industry to be able to provide. What methods (if any) Wheatley intended to use to get the number of houses built annually up to 90,000 in 1925/26 or 225,000 in 1934/35, or even anywhere near these totals is unknown. The 1924 Act (in the First Schedule) specified these figures, with a power (but not an obligation) to discontinue the subsidy if the number of houses built fell short of two-thirds of these totals.

But although the Housing (Financial Provisions) Act of 1924 was the first Labour government's main piece of legislation, that government fell within a few weeks of the Act having received the Royal Assent, and at the ensuing general election a Conservative goverment was returned with a large majority. What would be the practical effect of the 1924 Act thus depended on a Conservative government. If they adhered to the policy announced in 1923, the logical implications would be outright repeal. In the event, however, the 1924 Act was left in effect. The Prime Minister (Baldwin) approved of Wheatley's Act, according to his biographers (37), and he spoke in emphatic terms of the importance of dealing with the housing shortage. The way in which the Act was administered by the 1924-29 Conservative government has not thus far been studied in any detail. So we do not know whether the Minister of Health had a policy about the number of dwellings to be approved for subsidy and whether it 'rationed' them between authorities, and if so according to what criteria.

Nor do we know much about how local authorities decided about how many houses to build, how they allocated them, or indeed whether there were more would-be tenants than there were tenancies available. The general impression is that during the 1920s the central government's attitude was largely passive: it did not seek to spur the local authorities into doing more but neither did it seek to restrain those that wanted to build. But until the subject has been properly studied, that is no more than an impression. The Conservative government and its Parliamentary majority could have repealed the 1924 Act in 1925, before the number of commitments for subsidy exceeded a few thousand. But they did not. Credit (or responsibility) for local authority housing becoming a very large going concern in the inter-war years thus lies as much with Baldwin's 1924-29 administration as with any other. There is a strong case for regarding 1925 as the year when local authority house building on a substantial scale, for letting at subsidized rents, became part of the established practice of British society, not 1919. Only if the housing shortage which moved Baldwin is considered to be the consequence of treating landlords as expendable can the 1924-29 government's policy be explained in Daunton's terms.

The rates of subsidy under the 1924 Act were required to be reviewed every two years. In December 1925 the subsidy was reduced from £9 a year to £7 10s a year for houses completed after the end of September 1927, on account of the fall in building costs, with the result that local authorities hurried work along in order to complete as many houses as possible in time to qualify for the £9 a year subsidy. A further reduction in 1929 was decided on, from £7 10s to £6, with the 1923 Act subsidy (reduced to £4 a year or a £50 lump sum in 1927) abolished. The newly returned second Labour government in 1929 cancelled the reduction in the 1924 Act subsidy, but allowed the termination of the 1923 Act subsidy to go into effect (38). Otherwise the second Labour government administered the 1924 Act in the same way as the previous government had done. Termination of the 1923 Act subsidy, which was payable to private owners as well as to local authorities, was an action of the Conservative government; it was not a measure by the second Labour government to confine subsidy to local authorities.

In contrast to what happened in 1920-21, the Great Depression did not result in subsidized house building being stopped, though that was considered in the autumn of 1931 by the 'National' government but rejected (39), which goes to show how much more firmly established local authority housing had become. Local authorities' capital expenditure was however reduced by administrative means. The Ministry of Health urged local authorities to concentrate on providing smaller houses that could be let at rents that were within the means of people with lower incomes. Local authorities ".... should limit the provision of new houses to the number required to meet urgent need of applicants with children who are living under overcrowded conditions or insanitary houses and whose financial position is such that they cannot obtain accommodation in the absence of provision by the local authority". By 'smaller houses' the Ministry meant three bedroom houses with no parlour, and with a floor area of only 760 sq.ft., which was very small compared with the 950 sq.ft. maximum allowed by the Act. To ensure that local authorities took heed of what was asked of them, they were to submit their plans in preliminary form, with a statement of the facts on which their estimate of need was based (40). These more restrictive policies explain why completions were lower in 1932/33 and 1933/34. The fall in capital expenditure was greater: capital expenditure on state-aided housing schemes was £31.1 million in 1929/30, £28.6 million in 1930/31, £31.0 million in 1931/32, but only £20.4 million in 1932/33 and £20.2 million in 1933/34 (41). The subsidy under the 1924 Act remained in being until 1933, when it was terminated by the Housing (Financial Provisions) Act of that year. The circumstances of its termination were bound up with the beginning of the slum clearance drive, and so are best discussed after the slum clearance subsidy (introduced in 1930) has been described.

In terms of the number of houses built with its aid, the 1924 Act subsidy was the most important of all the subsidies in the inter-war years. Out of a total of 1,112,000 houses built for local authorities, 505,000 were built with the 1924 Act subsidy, compared with 74,000 with the 1923 Act. 363,000 houses were built for private owners with subsidy under the 1923 Act, most of them as a result of the subsidy being extended beyond the original termination date of 1925.

Apart from the subsidies provided under the 1923 and 1924 Acts, the other house building subsidy used on a large scale by local authorities in the inter-war years was that provided by the Housing Act 1930 for rehousing people displaced by slum clearance. The Housing Act 1930 was seen onto the Statute Book by the second Labour government, but was basically a departmental measure that had been at an advanced stage of preparation within the Ministry of Health under the previous government (43). The principal subsidy under this Act was an annual Exchequer contribution of £2 5s per person displaced and rehoused. For a 4-person household this was equivalent to the £9 a year originally provided under the 1924 Act; for a full account of the complicated detail of the subsidy reference should be made to Jarmain (44), but the most interesting innovation was the provision of a higher rate of subsidy, £3 10s a year per person rehoused instead of £2 5s where it was necessary to build blocks of flats more than three storeys high on sites costing more than £3,000 per acre. Enhanced subsidies for high rise building on expensive sites became much more important in the post-war years, and indeed the single enhanced rate provided in 1930 was developed into a sliding scale by legislation in 1935 and 1938; but the 1930 Act was the beginning.

The 1930 subsidy (sometimes known as the Greenwood subsidy from the name of the Minister of Health in the 1929 Labour government) was generally more advantageous to local authorities than was the 1924 subsidy: for the standard three-bedroomed house a subsidy of £11 5s a year was normally payable (i.e. for five people), and the rate fund contribution required was only £3 15s, the same as under the 1924 Act (as reduced). There were, indeed, extra costs incurred in slum clearance, notably the clearance work itself and compensation payable for business premises in the cleared areas. Even so, the subsidy was fairly generous. Nevertheless the number of houses built with its aid was small until the 1924 Act subsidy was repealed in 1933; up to and including 1933/34 only 17,400 houses had been completed with subsidy under the 1930 Act.

The repeal of the 1924 subsidy by the Housing (Financial Provisions) Act 1933 combined with an administrative drive undertaken by the Ministry of Health to secure more progress with slum clearance led to a complete change in the scale of house building with the 1930 Act subsidy. The original inspiration of the repeal of the 1924 Act was the fall in building costs and, from 1932, the much lower interest rates at which local authorities could raise long-term loans. If local authorities concentrated on building the cheaper houses they could build without subsidy, the argument ran, and with interest rates low, the rather better houses for letting could be provided by private enterprise. Only in the course of the passage of the Bill through Parliament did concentration on slum clearance come to prominence (45). The Ministry of Health in Circular 1331 called on local authorities to prepare and submit to the Ministry five year programmes for dealing with slums, and the programmes as submitted envisaged demolishing and replacing 267,000 houses (46). These programmes were added to from time to time, and by the end of the 1938/39 financial year 472,000 houses to be demolished or closed had been included in local authorities' programmes. In contrast to the 17,400 houses built under slum clearance powers up to 1933/34, 248,000 were built in 1934/35 to 1938/39 (inclusive), and 245,000 dwellings demolished or closed (47). This was a volume of slum clearance activity without precedent in Britain. An explanation may be found partly in terms of the administrative drive on slum clearance; but also in that the 1924 Act subsidy had resulted in local authorities building up an organization that could produce 50,000 to 60,000 houses a year, so that when that subsidy was terminated the organization had either to be switched to the only form of subsidized house building still open to local authrorities, or run down. That local authorities built an average of 50,000 houses a year in 1934/35 to 1938/39 under slum clearance powers and 53,000 a year in the previous five years with subsidy under the 1924 Act is unlikely to have been wholly coincidence.

The history of housing subsidies in the interwar years is completed by the legislation of 1935 and 1938. The Housing Act 1935 placed on local authorities a duty to take action, including the provision of houses, to abate overcrowding, and a subsidy was provided for building flats for this purpose. For houses (termed "cottages" at the time) as distinct from flats a subsidy of up to £5 a year for 20 years was payable, but only to authorities that could demonstrate that the cost would be an 'undue burden'. But for flats there was an entitlement to subsidy according to a sliding scale that depended on the cost of the site. The details do not matter greatly, as only 24,000 dwellings were built for relief of over-crowding. The interest of the 1935 subsidy lies in its being a stage in the development of the subsidy for high rise building on expensive sites that was to become much more important in the 1950s, 1960s and 1970s. In 1938 the subsidy for flats built for the relief of overcrowding and the subsidy for flats built for slum clearance were merged into a single subsidy, again according to a sliding scale: where the cost of land was between £1,500 and £4,000 per acre the subsidy was £11 a year per dwelling; between £4,000 and £5,000 - £12; between £5,000 and £6,000 - £13; and the £1 a year higher per £2,000 per acre up to a maximum of £21 per dwelling when land cost £18,000 to £20,000. These subsidies were not always sufficient to cover the extra cost of building high, so there were instances of rents of housing being set higher than they would otherwise have been in order to cross-subsidize flats (48). Here again what was done in the inter-war years in a fairly small way fore-shadowed what was to come on a far larger scale after 1945.

Until 1935, local authorities were required to keep separate accounts for houses provided under each of the Acts that made available Exchequer subsidy. The requirements about rate fund contri-butions and about rents were not the same in the different Acts; so there were many instances of very similar houses being let at different rents because they had been built under different Acts. The houses built under the 1919 Act stood out in this respect owing to their high rents, and the disparity with the rents of houses built under later Acts tended to widen as reductions in costs and interest rates, combined with continuation of subsidy, led in many instances to surpluses in the accounts for houses built under the later Acts. Subsidies would have been reduced by the amount of these surpluses unless rents were reduced suffi-ciently to absorb them. In such cases rent reduc-tions were generally made, so that rents of houses built under the 1924 and 1930 Acts were reduced while rents of houses built under the 1919 and 1923 Acts remained unchanged. The solution adopted in 1935 was to consolidate the accounts of all houses built by local authorities from 1919 onwards into a single Housing Revenue Account. Houses built under pre-1919 legislation (principally the Housing of the Working Classes Act of 1890) could be included at the local authorities' discretion.

The accounting system set up for local authority housing by the Housing Act 1935 remained in being throughout the period covered by this book. It worked in ways that its authors are unlikely to have foreseen, that made British local authority housing finance unique. The principles according to which the accounts were drawn up were referred to in Chapter I. There was to be a clear distinction drawn between expenditure chargeable to revenue, for which borrowing was not permissible, and capital expenditure, which could be financed by loans, provided that such loans were fully amortized over a period not exceeding the useful life of the asset being acquired. The loan charges (interest and amortization of principal) in such circumstances were chargeable to revenue. The rate fund was to be the residual source that ensured that all expenditure chargeable to revenue would be met from revenue. All loan charges on debt incurred in connection with providing the houses and all expenditure on management and upkeep of the houses were to be debited to the housing revenue account, and to it were to be credited all income from rents, Exchequer subsidies, and statutory rate fund contributions. If these sources of income were insufficient to balance the account, any shortfall that remained after drawing on balances (if such there were) was to be met by a contribution from the general rate fund. The provisions of the Housing Act 1935 about the rents to be charged gave authorities very wide discretion: they were to make "reasonable charges", and "take into consideration the rents ordinarily payable by persons of the working classes in locality", and "from time to time review rents and make such changes, either of rents generally or of particular rents ... as circumstances may require". The power to grant rent rebates, first provided specifically by the Housing Act 1930, but not made general, was likewise drawn in very broad terms: (the authority) "may grant to any tenant such rebates from rent subject to such terms and conditions as they think fit". That remained the law on rent rebates until 1972.

A summary of housing revenue accounts aggregated by class or authority is shown in Table VII.1.

313

Table VII.1 - Housing Revenue Account Summaries by Class of Authority 1935/36

(£ thousand)

	London (a)	County Boroughs	Municipal Boroughs	Urban Districts	Urban Districts	All Authorities
Expenditure						
Loan charges	3,254	10,086	4,288	5,834	3,502	26,964
Repairs, management, etc.	1,101	2,812	1,007	994	522	6,436
Transfers to capital accounts	18	23	20	9	4	75
Total	4,373	12,921	5,315	6,837	4,028	33,474
Income						
Rents, etc.	2,828	7,512	3,016	3,449	1,765	18,570
Exchequer grants	946	4,164	1,824	2,878	1,944	11,757
Rate fund contributions	609	1,407	523	565	358	3,461
Total	4,385	13,084	5,364	6,891	4,067	33,788
Increase in Balances	10	162	48	55	39	313
Per Dwelling **Expenditure**						
Loan charges	40.6	29.7	31.1	34.6	35.7	32.8
Repairs, management, etc.	13.7	8.3	7.4	6.0	5.3	7.8
Total (inc. transfers to capital)	54.5	38.1	39.1	40.6	41.1	40.7

Table VII.1 (continued)

(£ thousand)

	London (a)	County Boroughs	Municipal Boroughs	Urban Districts	Urban Districts	All Authorities
Income						
Rents, etc.	35.2	22.1	22.2	20.5	18.0	22.6
Exchequer subsidies	11.8	12.3	13.4	17.1	19.8	14.3
Rate fund contribution	7.6	4.1	3.8	3.4	3.7	4.2
Increase in balance	0.1	0.5	0.4	0.3	0.4	0.4
(Number of dwellings)	(80,230)	(339,500)	(136,000)	(168,600)	(98,000)	(822,300)
Percentage Proportions of Income						
Rents, etc.	65	58	57	50	44	56
Exchequer	22	32	34	42	48	35
Rate Fund	14	9	9	8	8	18

Notes: (a) Comprises London County Council, the Metropolitan Boroughs, and the City of London.

Detail does not always add to totals owing to rounding.

Source: Local Government Financial Statistics 1935/36, Summary and Parts II and III . Number of dwellings from Rents of Houses and Flats Owned by Local Authorities, Cmd. 5537)1937).

From the 1934/35 data on income and expenditure on houses built under the 1919 Act, it can be estimated that the proportions of income from rents, etc., Exchequer subsidy, and rate fund were 38:52:10 for houses built under the 1919 Act and 66:25:9 for houses and flats built under other Acts, when costs were lower.

The rents of council houses averaged about 11s a week in London (49), 7s 6d to 8s a week elsewhere except in rural districts, and 6s 4d a week in the rural districts, with a national average of 7s 4d a week, according to the 1936 returns. These rents averaged 20-25% (about 1s 3d outside London and 1s 9d in London) above controlled rents of privately owned houses, and were about 5% below non-controlled rents for pre-1914 "working class" houses outside London and 15-20% lower in London (see Chapter VIII). In view of the difference in standards the local authority tenant was getting at least as good value for money as the controlled tenant, and substantially better value for money than the tenant of non-controlled pre-1919 property. Only the very fragmentary information discussed in Chapter V is available about tenants' incomes, but if a comparison much used in the later years is taken, that with the earnings of men employed full-time in manual work, then the average rent of about 7s 4d a week excluding rates in 1936 was between 11% and 11½% of earnings. Rates paid can be estimated an average of 2s 6d a week (50), making rent and rates combined about 9s 10d a week, about 15% of the average earnings of men working full-time in manual occupations. This was definitely a lower proportion of average earnings than average rent (including rates) before 1914; average rents outside London were about 17% of average earnings of men in full-time manual work (51). Subsidies thus helped keep rents lower in relation to earnings than they had been before 1914. Average earnings in the mid-1930s were about 30% higher, in real terms, than they had been in 1914; the average rent, including or excluding rates, of a council house was about 10% higher, in real terms, than the average rent of a "working class" house before 1914, but for a much better house.

This picture drawn from the 1935/36 housing revenue account totals and the 1936 rent returns remained broadly valid for the remainder of the 1930s. Between 1935/36 and 1938/39 expenditure on repair, maintenance, and management per dwelling increased at about the same rate as the general price level, whereas the average capital cost of new houses built was sufficiently below the average outstanding debt per dwelling (£554 at the end of 1935/36) to bring the average debt per dwelling down to £518 at the end of 1938/39. About two-thirds of the reduction in average loan charges of almost £4 per dwelling was due to lower average debt per dwelling, and one-third to a lower average interest rate, mainly the result of the loans taken in the late 1930s being the rates of interest below the average for all housing debt (heavily influenced by the interest rates paid on loans taken in 1919-22 and still outstanding). The reduction in average rents between 1936/37 and 1938/39 appears to have been about 5%, bringing the average down from 7s 4d recorded by the 1936 survey to about 7s. Most of this was due to the rents of dwellings coming into the stock being lower than the average for the whole stock rather than to rents being actually reduced, though there were a few instances of actual reductions to avoid surpluses. Most of any surplus would have been repaid to the Exchequer.

The Finances of the Large Local Authority House Building Programmes in the Post-War Decade

The inflation associated with the Second World War had a dual effect on the finance of local authority housing. The value in real terms of loan charges in local authority housing revenue accounts, and hence the rents, likewise in real terms, that would be needed to balance the accounts after crediting Exchequer subsidies and the statutory rate fund contributions, were much reduced. But building costs rose extremely sharply. The severe housing shortage caused by the war (see Chapter IV) made necessary a large building programme. Before discussing this building programme and its financing, it is useful to show the financial starting point, the housing accounts as they emerged from the war. Exact figures for costs and receipts per dwelling cannot be calculated for 1945/46 owing to there being no firm figure for the number of dwellings in housing revenue accounts. Working forward from the 1936 base becomes increasingly dubious during the war years, when the number of council houses destroyed

317

Table VII.2 - Housing Revenue Accounts Before and After 1939-45

	Loan Charges	Other Costs	Total Costs	Rents etc.	Exchequer and Rate Fund	Increase in Balances
Totals (£ million)						
1938/39	30.34	8.62	38.96	21.93	17.35	+0.32
1945/46	31.09	11.37	42.46	25.56	17.14	+0.25
Per Dwelling (£ actual prices)						
1938/39	29.0	8.2	37.2	20.9	16.6	....
1945/46	26.8	9.8	36.6	22.0	14.8	....
Per Dwelling (£ 1938/39 prices)						
1938/39	29.0	8.2	37.2	20.9	16.6	....
1945/46	16.6	6.1	22.7	13.7	10.3	....

Notes: The number of dwellings in 1938/39 (mean of the totals at the beginning and end of the year) is taken as 1,047,000; and in 1945/46 1,160,000, obtained by working forward with the published number of completions, and allowing 20,000 for houses destroyed in the war. The price index used was the consumers' expenditure deflator.

is not known.   Nevertheless, estimates can be made
that are close enough to the mark to be useful.

Average loan charges per dwelling were reduced
by over 40% in real terms.   They were reduced even
in money terms as the result of lower interest
rates and re-financing at those rates of loans that
matured,   and debt repayment by means of the
principal   element in loan charges;   these routine
processes of local authority finance went on,
notwithstanding mobilization and total war.   The
reduction in other costs (nearly all of them upkeep
and   management)   of about 25% in real   terms was
likewise the result of the war.   Little maintenance
work could be carried out,   so there was little
point in raising the contribution to repairs
accounts (52).   For those authorities that did not
have a repairs account (mainly the smaller authorities) there was less expenditure on repairs to
debit directly to the housing revenue account.
Costs per dwelling in total fell nearly 40% in real
terms,   and rents by nearly 35%.   Whereas in 1936
average council house rents,   excluding rates, were
equal to between 11% and 11½% of average earnings
of adult men employed full-time in manual work,   at
the beginning of 1946 the proportion was only 6½%.
In   post-war controversies about council house
rents, much depended on whether the test of reason-
ableness was the percentage increase from the level
at the end of the war; or the amount in real terms,
or relative to incomes,   compared with before the
war.

Chapter IV outlined how the economy was
managed in the post-war years and how the size of
the house building programme was therefore determined in terms of the real resources that the
government considered could be made availabe,
mainly labour but also timber,   which was very
scarce owing to the limited volume of imports that
could be afforded.   Determining the total of house
building in this way did not necessarily mean that
the houses had to be built for local authorities.
The concentration on local authority house building
after 1945 was noteworthy in that the Labour election manifesto did not put any emphasis on subsidized house building;   in what it said about
housing,   drive and determination with if necessary
centralized purchasing of building materials,   were
the main themes.   The Conservative manifesto said
that   "subsidies will be necessary for local authorities and private enterprise alike" (53).   Nor was

319

the concentration on council housing as opposed to
building for owner-occupation part of the reform
(but not specifically socialist) programme of the
1930s and the war years from which came so many of
the 1945-50 Labour government's measures. The
explanation lay partly in the Second World War even
more than the First having led to great faith being
put in the efficiency of centralized direction,
that if something was needed badly enough administrative planning was the way to get it done quickly
and in very large quantities. There appears to
have been something of this train of thought
behind the concentration on council house building
as in the speech by the then Minister of Health,
Aneurin Bevan about "plannable instruments" having
to be used if house building was to be planned
effectively, and the private builder was not a
plannable instrument (54). As well as these
reasons for concentration on council house building, there was also the reason that allocation of
housing according to 'need' rather than ability to
pay went well with a public mood that esteemed
"fair shares", with council house waiting lists but
the longest and slowest moving of the queues that
had become part of everybody's life in wartime.

With decisions on the size of the local
authority house building programme taken and implemented in the way just described, finance for
capital expenditure was arranged so as to impose no
additional constraint, in contrast to 1920 when
difficulties about raising loans were a major
source of trouble. Local authorities were required
by the Local Loans Act 1945 to do all their
borrowing from the Public Works Loans Board (PWLB),
that is to say from central government: they were
not permitted to borrow directly from financial
markets at all. Central government thus provided
local authorities with whatever funds they required
to put into effect the building programmes determined by direct control. These funds were provided
at very favourable interest rates. Financially the
war had been a "3% war", and immediately afterwards
the Government pursued a policy of ultra-cheap
money, associated with the name of Dalton, the
Chancellor of the Exchequer, to bring interest
rates down still further. The government did not
succeed in holding the rate on long-term Gilt-edged
securities down to 2½ percent, and after the crisis
of the summer of 1947 it went back to 3% or just
over. At the end of the war the PWLB rate on long-

term loans was 3⅛%, it was reduced to 2½% in June 1946, and moved back to 3% in January 1948, where it remained until 1952. Although decisions about how many houses to build were not influenced by interest rates, the financial consequences of the building programme were greatly influenced by them. If post-war house building in 1945-50 had had to be financed at 6% as in 1919-21 instead of 3%, the subsidies needed would have been very different.

The main problems of financing local authority housing in the immediate post-war years consequently came not from interest rates but from capital costs. One important reason for high capital costs was the raising of standards, which can be attributed to the vision of a "better Britain" to be built (or re-built) after the war. The other was the increase in building costs that took place during the war. Both were discussed in some detail in Chapter IV (55).

The subsidies provided to local authorities after the war for permanent houses followed the classic pattern of £x a year for y years, but the financing of temporary houses (the "pre-fabs") was different, and was of all the post-World War II financial arrangements for housing the most similar to the subsidy provided in 1919. In both instances the reason was uncertainty about capital costs and what relationship they would bear to rents. We saw earlier in this chapter why the Exchequer had to carry the net cost in excess of the proceeds of 1d rate under the 1919 Act. The mass production of temporary houses planned in 1944 would use techniques never previously used for housing; indeed, one of the main reasons was to use the capacity of the munitions industries and their labour. What the cost would be was hard to foresee; so the Exchequer carried the capital cost. Local authorities were to provide the sites; central government would pay the capital costs; local authorities were to manage the houses, and charge rents at their discretion subject to the statutory powers (discussed in the previous section) which governed their ordinary housing and were to pay central government £23 10s a year (£21 10s in rural districts). This charge was based on a rate fund contribution of £4 a year and an average rent of 10s a week (56). The local authorities' liability was thus limited to £23 10s plus the cost of upkeep and management.

For permanent houses the subsidy provided by

the Housing (Financial Provisions) Act 1946 was of the classic £x a year for y years type, where y equalled 60 (instead of the pre-war 40) and x equalled £16 10s. The rate fund contribution required was £5 10s, one-third of the Exchequer subsidy instead of the pre-war half. In addition there were, as in the pre-war legislation, supplementary subsidies for flats and houses for agricultural workers; and a novel provision for a higher Exchequer subsidy and lower rate fund contribution for authorities that could show that the £5 10s rate fund contribution was unduly burdensome. The combined Exchequer subsidy and rate fund contributions were set with the intention of permitting local authorities to charge a rent of about 10s a week, though the Treasury preferred 12s a week and correspondingly smaller subsidies (57). With a rent of 10s a week total income from rent and subsidies would be £48 a year; average expenditure per dwelling on upkeep and management was about £10 a year (see Table VII.2), which left £38 for loan charges. That would cover a capital cost of £1,025 at 3⅜%, or £1,175 at 2½%. At the beginning of 1946 these would have been realistic estimates of capital cost had building productivity not been so low. The thinking behind such financing can, with hindsight, be seen to have been very much that of a world of low interest rates and stable prices, the pre-war world jacked up to a new and higher absolute price level. In case there should be a fall in costs and prices as in 1920 and after, the 1946 Act required an annual determination of subsidy amounts. The amounts could be set lower than in the Act itself, but not, of course, higher.

A rent of 10s a week for a new house built to the standards outlined above differed from the average of about 7s 6d a week for pre-1945 house by an amount that could be justified by reference to the extra cost of building to higher standards. Nothing had to be put onto the rent on account of the fall in the value of money since before the war, or higher earnings having increased the rents that tenants could have afforded to pay. If the post-1945 world had been one of stable prices (including building costs) at the new higher level, tenants would have kept the benefit of the historic costs of their houses having been sharply reduced in real terms by war-time inflation, and the tenants of post-war houses would have obtained the same benefit through high subsidy, intended (if

322

costs had come out as expected) to cover about 45%
of costs instead of the pre-war 34% for houses
other than those built under the 1919 Act.

The post-war years were far from being a
period of stable prices, of course. The information about rents in the late 1940s is much less
full than in later years, but a fair indication of
what happened in the immediate post-war years can
be obtained from the particulars of rents in
1949/50 collected from local authorities by the
Institute of Municipal Treasurers and Accountants
(IMTA, subsequently the Chartered Institute of
Public Finance and Accountancy, CIPFA) and published in the first of the Institute's Housing
Statistics series. From the incomplete figures
collected (the metropolitan boroughs were not
covered and the coverage of rural districts was
thin) the average rent of pre-war dwellings outside
London can be calculated at about 10 shillings a
week, which was about 3 shillings a week above what
it had been before the war. The average rent of
post-war dwellings was about 14 shillings a week.
The increase of three shillings a week in the rents
of pre-war houses was about equal to the increase
in expenditure per dwelling on maintenance and
management between 1938/39 and 1949/50. A rent of
14 shillings a week for post-war houses, plus a £16
10s a week Exchequer subsidy and £5 10s rate fund
contribution, would cover the costs of management
and maintenance plus the loan charges on about
£1,200 of the capital expenditure. The average
capital cost of dwellings built between the end of
the war and 1950 was £1,400 to £1,500, so the loan
charges on £200 to £300 had to be met from other
sources, either a rate fund contribution above the
statutory amount or by drawing on the balances that
had been built up during the war on the housing
revenue account or the repairs account. Most
authorities kept a housing repairs account; contributions to this account were debited to the housing
revenue account, and during the war when little
repair work was done, large balances were built up.
For a time these balances could be drawn on to keep
down rent increases. But unless there was going to
be a post-war slump and fall in costs and prices,
drawing on balances could only put off the day when
rents would have to be raised, without in any way
lowering the level to which rents would then have
to rise.

The much enlarged local authority house building programme of the 1951-55 Conservative government was among the more noteworthy episodes in recent British housing history. The government's general policies were opposed to greater public expenditure, and indeed looked for reductions; they were in favour of more reliance on private enterprise and less on state action; and in housing policy strongly favoured owner-occupation (58), as Conservatives had done in the 1920s and 1930s. The rearmament programme undertaken following the outbreak of the war in Korea was gathering pace and in 1953 expenditure on defence reached a proportion of gross domestic product previously seen only in the war years and not subsequently reached again during the period covered by this history, which makes the decision to increase capital expenditure on housing so drastically all the more surprising. But most notable of all, in view of the subsequent history, was the increase in subsidies to offset the increase in interest rates. As a means of restraining inflation restrictive monetary measures were brought back into use for the first time since the 'cheap money' policy was begun in 1932, and interest rates rose. The Public Works Loans Board rate on long-term loans, the key rate for local authorities' housing finance, was raised from 3% to $4\frac{1}{2}$% in March 1952. On a 60 year loan repayable by an annuity, the effect was to increase the annual payments by about £10 per £1,000 borrowed (i.e. by 28%), and hence added about £15 to £16 to the annual loan charges on the average cost of a new house in 1952. The Housing Act 1952 raised the standard subsidy from the £16 10s a year provided under the 1946 Act to £26 14s, with a pro-rata increase in the associated rate fund contribution from £5 10s to £8 18s. The increase in the Exchequer subsidy met two-thirds of the increase in interest costs, with the associated rate fund contribution the proportion of the increase to be met from subsidy, as distinct from recovered from tenants, was some 85-90%. On all future occasions when interest rates were raised for reasons of monetray policy, the reply of the government of the day to criticisms of the effect on housing costs was that housing, like other activities, could not be shielded from economic realities. But in 1952 it was shielded very substantially. As mentioned in Chapter IV, none of the published histories of the period have unfortunately given any attention to how this came to be.

The financing of the lare programmes of house building in the post-war decade may be illustrated by summary housing revenue accounts which show both totals and averages per dwelling. To maintain continuity with the comparison in Table VII.2, 1945/46 is included in Table VII.3 as well.

Table VII.3 - Housing Revenue Account Totals and Averages: England and Wales 1945/46 to 1955/56

Totals (£ million)

	1945/46	1951/52	1955/56
Expenditure			
Loan charges	31.10	68.41	122.82
Other expenditure	11.37	30.83	50.14
Total	42.46	99.23	172.96
Receipts			
Rents, etc.	25.56	64.13	110.25
Exchequer subsidy	12.31	24.93	45.42
Rate fund contribution	4.84	10.93	18.17
Per Dwelling (£)			
Loan charges	26.8	35.7	46.7
Other expenditure	9.8	16.1	19.9
Rents, etc.	22.0	32.5	41.9
Exchequer subsidy	10.6	13.0	17.3
Rate fund contribution	4.2	5.7	6.9
(Number of dwellings at mid-year in '000)	(1,160)	(1,915)	(2,630)
(Value of money - GDP deflator)	(100)	(75)	(63)

Source: HRA totals from Local Government Financial Statistics (annual)

Average rents in 1955/56 are estimated at about 14s 6d a week (59), which implies about 12s a week on average for pre-war dwellings and 16s a week for post-war dwellings; 12s a week in 1955/56 for pre-war dwellings exceeded the 7s 6d a week average in 1945/46 by little more than the increase

in costs of upkeep and management in the inter-
vening decade. Cross-subsidy in historic cost
terms between inter-war and post-war dwellings had
thus not become generally established by 1955, even
though there were individual instances of it. 'Two
tier historic cost' pricing was far more common as
a way of setting rents than full "pooling" even as
late as the mid-1950s.

Pooled Historic Costs and Cross-Subsidy as the Basis of Local Authority Housing Finance from the Mid-1950s to the Early 1970s

After the mid-1950s, pooling of historic costs
and cross-subsidy from older houses with low
historic costs to newer houses with much higher
costs became the basic principle of local authority
housing finance. Inflation reduced the real value
of the loan charges on older houses so far that
first the subsidy payable under pre-war Acts could
in effect be used to subsidize newer houses via
pooling of all costs and revenues within the
housing revenue account, and subsequently a surplus
of rents over historic costs of inter-war houses
could be earned and used to help cover the deficit
on newer houses with much higher costs, but not
correspondingly higher rents. This was what was
common to the financial arrangements for council
housing between the mid-1950s and the early 1970s,
notwithstanding several sharp changes of subsidy
policy.

The description of the system of local authority housing finance as it developed from 1924
onwards has emphasized the way in which it was a
system for a world of stable prices and stable
interest rates, in which the gap between the annual
costs chargeable to revenue and the rent that
tenants could be expected to pay would change
little, so that a subsidy of £x a year for y years
would be equally appropriate year after year for
bridging the gap. The post-war subsidy arrangements were in the same spirit; they were based, in
effect, on there having been a once and for all
increase in the price level after which the underlying assumptions of the 1930s of a stable price
level and low interest rates would continue to be
valid. Even the increase in subsidies in 1952 was
in the same vein; the increase in interest rates
made necessary a new value for x in £x a year for y
years, but nothing else was different.

But in the mid-1950s there was a radical change to a system that took the inflation since 1939 as a fact that would not be reversed, and relied on the widening gap between the rents that could reasonably be charged for older dwellings and the historically incurred costs (particularly loan charges) for those dwellings to provide the means of bridging the gap between the charge to revenue arising from building new houses and flats and the rent income that they would bring in. How such an arrangement would work would depend on the size of the surpluses (in historic cost terms) on the older dwellings, the size of the deficits on new dwellings and the balance between new houses built and the number of older dwellings in the accounts. The scope for stresses and strains was obviously great, and so it proved to be. But before recounting the history of the policies that sought to deal with these problems it is useful to describe what happened to average costs of new houses and to interest rates, which dominated the expenditure side of the housing revenue account in the 1950s and 1960s. Not until the 1970s did the growth of expenditure on repair and maintenance and super- vision and management become a major source of strain. Table VII.4 below shows year by year the average cost of new dwellings built for local authorities from the beginning of the 1950s to the beginning of the 1970s, and average rates of interest payable on debt on which the loan charges were debited to housing revenue accounts. From 1963 to 1970 the figures for costs are comparable; but before 1963 the only figures available are of the cost of two storey three-bedroom-houses. The changes in average cost include the effect of changes in quality, standards, and after 1963 in the mix of dwelling types built, as well as true price change. The change in average cost is com- pared with the change in the general price level.

Between 1951 and 1958 average costs of new local authority houses fell by about 25% in real terms, partly as a result of smaller sizes and lower standards. But between 1958 and 1968 the change was in the other direction, with average cost per dwelling rising by 60% in real terms. In view of the hybrid measure of changes in costs that is used in Table VII.4 these are not exact figures, but they are fully sufficient to show that not long after the move to reliance on cross-subsidy from older houses to new, the average cost of new houses

Table VII.4 - Average Costs of New Dwelling and Average Interest Rates:
Local Authorities in England and Wales

(£)

	Average Construction Cost (Two Storey Houses) Including Adjustments	Average Construction Cost (Tenders) (Two Storey Houses)	Average Construction Cost (Tenders) All Dwellings	Total Cost	Change Relative to Increase in General Price Level (%) (a)	Interest Rate (b)
1951	1,458		...	...	...	...
1952	1,415		...	...	-11.0	3.2
1953	1,403	1,384	...	...	-3.7	3.4
1954	...	1,383	...	...	-2.0	3.4
1955	...	1,418	...	...	-0.9	3.5
1956	...	1,472	...	...	-2.3	3.8
1957	...	1,486	...	...	-2.9	4.0
1958	...	1,485	...	...	-5.0	4.1
1959	...	1,515	...	...	+0.6	4.1
1960	...	1,611	...	...	+4.5	4.4
1961	...	1,786	...	...	+7.3	4.7
1962	...	1,967	...	...	+6.5	4.6
1963	...	2,129	2,229	2,910	+5.8	4.5
1964	...	2,303	2,434	3,140	+4.8	4.8
1965	...	2,579	2,655	3,540	+8.3	5.1
1966	...	2,782	2,929	3,790	+3.0	5.3
1967	...	2,951	2,989	4,150	+6.5	5.6
1968	...	3,046	3,046	4,340	+1.5	6.1
1969	...	3,159	3,090	4,190	-6.9	6.7
1970	...	3,383	3,194	4,560	+1.0	6.8

Table VII.4   (continued)

Notes: (a)   Change in the general price level measured by
the GDP deflator.
(b)   Average pool rates in financial years, e.g.
1952 refers to 1952/53.

Source: Ministry of Housing and Local Government,
Report for 1955, Cmd. 9876 (1956), Appendix I
Table M; Report for 1959, Cmd. 1027 (1960),
Appendix X, Table D; Report for 1961, Cmd. 1725
(1962), p.34; Handbook of Statistics 1965, p.5;
Handbook of Statistics 1967, Table 10; Handbook
of Statistics 1969, Table 13; Housing Statis-
tics Housing Policy Technical Volume, Table
VIII.13.   Interest rates calculated from Local
Government Financial Statistics.

turned sharply upwards at a rate well ahead of
inflation.   The reasons were various: rising
standards; changes of mix, in particular more high-
rise dwellings; and higher land prices. From 1959
onwards local authorities had to acquire land at
market values, and those values rose fast, as was
shown in Chapter IV.
    Increases in capital costs at such rates would
have strained the system of cross-subsidy even if
interest rates had remained stable, but they did
not.   The way in which the increase in interest
rates affected the finances of local authority
housing owed much to a major change of policy in
1955 about local authority borrowing.   Local
authorities had been free from 1953 onwards to
borrow directly from the capital market instead of
from the Public Works Loans Board, but were not
obliged to do so, and most of their borrowing was
in fact from the PWLB.   From October 1955, though,
local authorities were allowed to borrow from the
PWLB only if they could show that they were unable
to raise money from the capital markets.   The
purpose was to reduce the amount the Exchequer had
to borrow, and so allow a reduction in the Treasury
Bill issue, which in turn would lead to restriction
of the amount of bank lending (60).   The consequence of the local authorities having to turn to
the capital markets for their borrowing was that
they borrowed large sums at very short-term; in the
words of the Radcliffe Committee's report: "The
'unfunding' operation by the local authorities in

the last few years had to some extent been a consequence of their reluctance to borrow more long-term
money than they could help at what they regarded as
abnormally high rates of interest; but it has also
been forced on them by decisions of the central
authorities" (61). Loans taken at very short-term
could in practice always be renewed or replaced at
the going rate of interest, but when interest rates
rose the result was not only an increase in
interest payments generated by new capital expenditure but in interest on existing debt as well. The
vulnerability of local authority housing finance to
increases in interest rates was consequently
increased; loan charges per dwelling in housing
revenue accounts were increased not only by the
higher interest rates on debt that financed new
building but also by increases in the interest
payable on debt that had been generated by the
building of the present housing stock. By the
later 1950s most authorities operated a 'loans
pool' whereby money was borrowed for the purposes
of the authority generally, and notionally on-lend
to the various services (of which housing was one)
at an interest rate equal to the average rate on
the whole of the authority's debt (generally termed
the 'pool' rate). There was nothing anomalous,
therefore, in money borrowed at a week's notice
being used to finance capital expenditure on houses
amortized over 60 years. In the 1960s local
authorities were again allowed to borrow from the
Public Works Loans Board, subject to certain
limits, but large scale borrowing at short-term
continued, not least because rates of interest were
so high in relation to past experience as to be
considered 'abnormal'. In consequence the proportion of short-term debt rose sharply. In 1955,
5.8% of the outstanding loan debt of local authorities in Great Britain (62) had under one year to
maturity; five years later the proportion had risen
to 17.5%; in 1964 the proportion was 27.8%, and in
1968 28.5%. The "pool" interest rates that
resulted from these arrangements were shown in
Table VII.4 above.

That interest rates and capital costs would
rise in this way was probably not foreseen when a
complete change in subsidy policy was made in 1955
and 1956. In October 1955 the government announced
a complete change in policy, the intention to
terminate subsidies for houses built for general
needs. In view of how radical this change of

policy was, the stated rationale is worth quoting:

> ".... most, if not all authorities which
> have long waiting lists possess a big pool
> of existing houses upon which they receive
> large amounts of subsidy. These usually
> include pre-war houses built at much lower
> costs. Provided, therefore, that they
> subsidize only those tenants that require
> subsidizing, and only to the extent of their
> need, local authorities should well be able
> to continue building the houses they need
> with appreciably less Exchequer subsidy than
> hitherto" (64).

The government's intention was to terminate subsidies for new building for general needs, though as a transitional arrangement the immediate reduction (for houses in tenders approved after 3rd November 1955, the date of the introduction of the Housing Subsidies Bill) would be to £10 a year.

Local authorities were thus urged to charge "realistic" rents, and to charge differential rents according to income and household circumstances, and thereby confine the subsidy to those tenants that "needed" it. To give local authorities a greater financial inducement to do this, the 1956 Act repealed the statutory obligations on local authorities to make rate fund contributions in association with Exchequer subsidies. Such obligations were first introduced in 1924; in the inter-war years the ratio of the local authority's contribution to the Exchequer subsidy was generally 1:2, but in the post-war years it was 1:3. Local authorities could, of course, make higher rate fund contributions than these, so long as the rents met the statutory test of being reasonable charges; but once higher rents had eliminated any additional rate fund contributions, any further rent increases would benefit the Exchequer more than the rate fund, owing to the complex rules for distributing a housing revenue account surplus (broadly speaking pro-rata to past Exchequer subsidy and rate fund contributions). Abolishing the obligation to make associated rate fund contributions thus made it easier for local authorities to charge higher rents, and gave them a stronger inducement to do so.

The average rent of about 14s a week in 1955/56 was equal to about 6.3% of average weekly earnings of adult men employed full time in manual work. No information about the actual incomes of tenants was collected at this time, so any view about what level of rents was "realistic" in the sense of what tenants could afford to pay had to be based on opinion rather than fact. But just as important as any comparison with earnings, in all probability, was the comparison with rents paid to private landlords. Controlled rents in payment just before the 1957 Rent Act (and rents in 1955 could not have been much different) averaged some 10s 6d a week (see Chapter VIII). Since these were, with only limited exceptions, 1939 rents, decontrol would obviously lead to large increases of a size that would be difficult to defend or even sustain except as scarcity rents, if local authorities charged no more than an average of 14s a week for houses of which a majority had been built post-war. As was observed in Chapter IV, only when historians in the late 1980s have had an opportunity to study the papers of 1955 and 1956 as they become available under the '30 year rule' will it be known how far the Housing Subsidies Act 1956 and the Rent Act 1957 had a common origin in a consciously planned policy of putting provision of housing to rent for general needs into the sphere of private landlords and not local authorities, who would concentrate slum clearance and certain other needs. This would be the 1933 policy revived nearly a quarter of a century later. To stand any chance of success it would require rents to be much higher than they were in the mid-1950s. Abolishing compulsory rate fund contributions (other than for balancing the housing revenue account) could however not in itself make a great difference to rents straight away. Rate fund contributions were already heavily concentrated in London; the IMTA figures for 1957/58 (65) showed about one-third of all rate fund contributions to be made by the London County Council and the metropolitan boroughs, which owned under 10% of the total local authority housing stock. Over much of the country the rate fund contribution was too small in relation to total costs for abolishing it to make much difference to rents. Far more potent as an influence on rents would be the financial consequences of building new houses without Exchequer subsidy, which was terminated for building for general needs by the Housing Subsidies Order 1956 (SI No. 2015).

Before discussing the results of relying on

cross-subsidy (in historic cost terms) from older dwellings to meet the cost of new dwellings over and above what could be recovered from rents, it is convenient to look at the supplementary subsidies provided by the Housing Subsidies Act 1956 for high-rise building. Enhanced rates of subsidy for building on expensive sites had a history that went back to 1930, but subsidies increasing with storey height were an innovation in the 1956 Act. The subsidy scale provided for building for rehousing from slum clearance started at £22 10s for houses (or maisonettes in blocks of fewer than 4 storeys), for flats in a four-storey block £32 a year each; in a five-storey block £38 a year; in a six-storey block £50 a year, increased by £1 15s a year for each storey above six. These subsidies were in addition to the expensive site subsidy, £60 a year per acre if the site cost was between £4,000 and £5,000 plus £34 per acre for each £1,000 over £5,000. These supplementary subsidies for high-rise building and expensive sites taken together were considerably more advantageous for those authorities building high blocks of flats, particularly those building them on sites acquired by slum clearance, than the expensive site subsidies under the 1952 Act and earlier legislation. The sites on which the former slums stood were not necessarily all that valuable, given that they were valued in their existing use (housing), so that the amount of subsidy provided by the expensive site subsidy would not cover the extra cost of building high. Adequate financial support for high-rise building for slum clearance purposes was essential to the government's housing policy: great emphasis was being given to slum clearance as the primary purpose for which new dwellings were to be built by local authorities, and, as mentioned in Chapter IV, in 1955 'green belts' to restrain urban growth were made part of planning policy for cities and large towns generally, not just for London. The supplementary subsidies provided the finance for building high. With ten storey blocks the number of dwellings to the acre would be fifty or sixty (66). At these densities, subsidies on the 1956 scale would provide 6-7% more subsidy with land costs at £5,000 per acre; going to 20 storeys would increase the number of dwellings by only 13% or so, but would result in subsidy 37% higher under the 1956 Act than under the subsidy scale hitherto in effect (the 1952 Act as modified in October 1954).

333

Although high-rise building has subsequently been
strongly condemned, it was the outcome of policies
that were widely supported at the time, in their
land use aspects for reasons that had little to do
with council housing; and the subsidy system met
most of the extra costs of building high.

Under the financial regime provided by the
Housing Subsidies Act 1956, average rents rose from
about 14s a week in 1955/56 to 20s 9d a week in
1960/61. Considered as a rate of rise this was
rapid: 48% in money terms, 30% in real terms within
five years, that is to say an average of 5.4% a
year. But as so often in the period under review
here, what might be thought of the increases in
council house rents would depend greatly on whether
the focus was on levels or on rates of increase.
An increase of 5.4% a year in real terms was twice
as fast as the increase in earnings; but 20s 9d in
1960/61 was definitely below the average rent of
decontrolled unfurnished lettings in the private
sector, which was about 22s a week in 1959 (see
Chapter VIII).

In 1961 'general needs' building subsidies
were brought back. In place of nothing for general
needs and £22 1s for dwellings built for slum
clearance the new legislation (Housing Act 1961)
provided a subsidy of the standard form of £x a
year for y years, where y was equal to 60 as it had
been since 1946, but where x depended on the
balance between housing revenue account costs and a
notional rental income. If the account would
balance if credited with a notional rental income
equal to twice the rateable value of the dwellings
in the account (plus the subsidies payable under
earlier Acts) the basic subsidy would be £8 a year
per dwelling; if the account would be in deficit
the subsidy would be £24 per dwelling, except where
the authority's rate poundage was higher than the
England and Wales average. If it was higher, the
subsidy would be £28, £34, or £40 (the maximum)
according to the increase in the poundage that
would be required to meet the notional housing
revenue account deficit. The rationale of a
subsidy on such a pattern was purely cross-subsidy
via pooling: authorities with low housing revenue
account costs relative to income from rents that
could reasonably be charged could use the surplus
(in historic cost terms) on the older dwellings in
their stock to meet the deficits on new dwellings,
whereas those authorities that had little scope for

doing this needed more help through subsidies. At 1961 capital costs and interest rates though, £8 a year was only a token subsidy: at interest rates of just under 5%, £8 a year for sixty years was equivalent to about £160 capitalized, less than 7% of the average capital cost, compared with the 45% that the 1952 subsidy had provided. Even the £24 subsidy for authorities without much ability to cross-subsidize amounted to only about 20% of capital cost, too small to alleviate by much the burden that the costs of new building would impose on the rate fund or on other tenants. The high rise and expensive site subsidies were unaltered.

A novel feature of the subsidy provision of the 1961 Act was the power taken to reduce or terminate subsidies already in payment under the Act. This provision did not apply to subsidies under earlier Acts, where to go back on the commitment to subsidy for 40 years or 60 years would have been objectionable; it could not come into effect until 10 years after the Act became law, and was described by the Ministry of Housing and Local Government as "purely precautionary" (67). The need for it arose because experience had shown that far reaching changes could occur in the rent-paying capacity of tenants. In 1960/61, in fact, £10.3 million of subsidy was paid under pre-war Acts out of a total expenditure on housing subsidies of £57.0 million (68). The rents charged in 1960/61 would generally suffice to cover the full historic cost of pre-war dwellings (excepting only those built at the peak of building costs in 1920) without subsidy. Through pooling, the subsidy payable on dwellings built in the inter-war years could be used to subsidize more recently built houses. That this should be done was the rationale of the 1956 Act, modified only slightly in 1961.

Capital costs were rising too fast, though, for a subsidy in the form of £x a year for y years to be effective any longer. As Table VII.4 showed, average construction costs per dwelling rose by over 30% between 1960 and 1963, so the proportion of the cost offset by a subsidy of £x a year fell rapidly. The values of x and y were, of course, specified by the legislation itself, and could not be increased except by new primary legislation. Such a system was unsatisfactory, especially at a time when the government was encouraging local authorities to build more houses. By 1963 the Conservative government had come round to seeking a higher rate of house building by local authorities, and in the Housing White Paper in which it put forward this policy, it announced its intention of discussing with the local authority associations a reform of housing subsidies (69). The discussions were completed in September 1964, but there is no published record of what the government planned to do. Any plans it might have had were overtaken by the General Election in October 1964.

The incoming Labour government announced its intentions on housing subsidies in 1965 in the White Paper, The Housing Programme 1965 to 1970, and they were enacted into law by the Housing Subsidies Act 1967. The basic subsidy under this Act, which was payable for houses in tenders approved from November 1965 (but in certain priority areas houses completed from November 1965), was of a novel form and designed for conditions in which capital costs and interest rates would rise. Instead of the '£x a year for y years' formula, the annual payment was determined as the difference between the sixty year loan charge on approved capital cost at the average new borrowing rate for all local authorities and a loan charge on the same capital cost at 4% interest. The subsidy was an approximation to providing loans for housing at 4% interest; it was only an approximation, because not all authorities paid exactly the same interest rates and (more important) because the interest rate on new borrowing for purposes of calculating the subsidy was that in the previous year. For dwellings completed in 1966/67, for example, the average interest rate on new borrowing for calculating the subsidy was that for 1965/66. Working one year in arrears in this way was inevitable if the subsidy payable was to be determined immediately the dwelling was completed, because average new borrowing rates could only be calculated for complete years; but the lag worked to local authorities' disadvantage (compared with actual 4% loans) when interest rates were rising, as they were during the late 1960s. Once determined, however, the subsidy in respect of a particular dwelling remained fixed in money terms, regardless of what subsequently happened to interest rates, prices and incomes. In this the 1967 Act subsidy followed the practice of all previous subsidies back to 1923. Like the 1961 Act, the 1967 Act allowed for reduction, in 1977 and later, in subsidies already in payment under it.

The subsidy provided for by the 1967 Act was designed for inflationary times with unstable interest rates. Unlike its predecessors that provided amounts that were fixed in money terms and which could not be raised except by new primary legislation, it provided subsidies that were fully open-ended with respect to interest rates, and partly open-ended with respect to capital costs. To prevent it from being totally open-ended with respect to capital costs the number of new dwellings for which tenders were approved was controlled centrally, and cost per dwelling controlled by the 'Cost Yardstick', essentially a set of cost limits determined with respect to size of dwelling and density. Subsidy was payable only on capital expenditure up to the 'yardstick' limit; above that was a 10% tolerance which local authorities could use, but wholly at their own expense, and above that loan sanction would be withheld. Banning building at costs more than 10% above the yardstick was justified by the government of the day on grounds of the need for more houses being greater than the need for yet higher standards over and above the Parker Morris standard, itself a considerable step up from what had gone before (see Chapter IV). The 1967 Act brought about substantial increases in the subsidies paid on new houses; from an average of about £24 a year payable under the 1961 Act the average paid under the 1967 Act started at £67 per dwelling and by 1971 had increased to £187 (70).

Notwithstanding the much larger subsidies provided by the Housing Subsidies Act 1967, or possibly in part because of them, local authority housing finance and rents were the subject of increasingly acrimonious controversy in the later 1960s. To see why this should be so, we must look both at costs and subsidies and at rents. Total and average costs and subsidies are shown in Table VII.5. The increase in loan charges per dwelling was the dominant part of the increase between 1965/66 and 1970/71 in costs borne by housing revenue accounts. Average expenditure per dwelling on repair and maintenance and supervision and management rose by about 20% in real terms, but average loan charges by 30%. The main reason was the inter-action between a large building programme, high building costs, and rising interest

Table VII.5 - Housing Revenue Accounts 1955/56 to 1970/71

	1955/56	1960/61	1965/66	1970/71
Total Expenditure (£ million)				
Loan charges	122.8	195.3	310.9	580.5
Repair and maintenance	32.2	48.5	71.7	114.9
Supervision and management	12.8	19.3	33.8	67.0
Other expenditure	5.1	7.7	15.5	20.0
All expenditure	173.0	270.8	431.9	783.3
Total Revenue				
Rents of dwellings (a)	101.6	182.8	296.4	526.9
Rents of other properties and miscellaneous income (a)	8.7	11.0	20.4	48.9
Exchequer subsidy	45.4	59.7	76.5	159.0
Rate fund contribution	18.2	17.5	34.3	55.8
Per Dwelling (£)				
Loan charges	46.7	60.7	83.0	132.1
Supervision and management }	17.1	21.1	19.1	26.1
Repair and maintenance			9.0	15.4
Total expenditure	65.8	84.0	115.3	178.2
Rents of dwellings	37.4	56.8	79.1	119.9
Exchequer subsidy	17.3	18.5	20.4	36.2
Rate fund contribution	6.9	5.4	9.2	12.7
(number of dwellings in '000)	(2,630)	(3,220)	(3,745)	(4,395)
Rents of dwellings as % of net expenditure (b)	61.8	70.4	72.0	71.7
Value of money (GDP deflator)	100.0	83.6	71.3	58.1

Table VII.5 (continued)

Notes: (a) Division only approximate in 1955/56 and
            1960/61.
       (b) 'Net expenditure' is total HRA expenditure net
            of income from rents of non-domestic property
            and miscellaneous income.

            Some of the detail for 1955/56 and 1960/61 was
            estimated from IMTA data.

rates, though the increase in loan charges on 'old'
debt was also important. An approximate calculation shows that between 1965/66 and 1970/71 the
addition of about 650,000 houses to the stock
brought in about £165 million of additional loan
charges, of which about £85 million was offset by
higher subsidy, and about £50 million from rents,
net of expenditure (pro-rata) on repair and maintenance, and supervision and management. Some £30
million of the current costs of new houses had thus
to be recovered from tenants of houses built
earlier, or from rate fund contributions. The
cross-subsidy required was about £9 per dwelling
per year, as well as £105 million approximately
(£28 per dwelling per year) from increases in
interest charged on "old" debt. Subsidy to provide
the equivalent of loans at 4% net still required
considerable cross-subsidy from older dwellings to
new dwellings, and it is salutary to recall that in
1952 when the rate of interest on long-term loans
went up to 4½% the rates of subsidy were increased.
This requirement for cross-subsidy on new houses at
the time of a large building programme, on top of
the large increase in interest to be paid on 'old'
debt, was the main reason why the finance of local
authorities' housing was under such pressure in the
later 1960s notwithstanding the introduction of
larger Exchequer subsidies that rose with building
costs and interest rates.
    The pressure was increased by the subsidy
under the 1967 Act, like its predecessors, being a
building subsidy, and so not begun to be paid until
the house that qualified for subsidy was completed.
The entire cost of financing land bought for
housing purposes and work-in-progress on houses
under construction therefore fell on the rate fund
or rents. When rising interest rates coincided
with a much enlarged building programme in the mid-
1960s this burden became substantial, as did the

amount of complaint. Estimates of the loan charges on land awaiting development and work-in-progress for certain individual authorities were collected in 1968, and showed that in some instances the burden was considerable; for the Greater London Council in 1968/69 such charges were equivalent to £15.9 a year per dwelling, some 14% of all loan charges and 8.6% of total costs (71), and a massive (but exceptional) £59.3 per dwelling in the London Borough of Sutton. Costs of financing housing under construction were highest, of course, where a large building programme was being undertaken by an authority with only a small stock of houses already let.

The rent increases by which the local authorities sought to recover these increases in costs may be considered next. The importance of the distinction between percentage rates of increase and absolute levels cannot be over-emphasized when the course of rents from the mid-1950s to the end of the 1960s is examined. The percentage rate of increase in real terms was high; but the starting point was a level of rents that had been brought down a long way in real terms during the war. The average rent of a pre-war dwelling in 1955/56 was probably around 12s a week. This compared with about 7s a week at the outbreak of war; retail prices rose by about 135% between 1939 and 1955 (72), so if like is compared as near as possible with like, council rents in 1955 were between 25% and 30% lower in real terms than they had been in 1939, although real incomes were much higher. The relevance of pre-war rents would of course have been disputed, but the fact needs to be borne in mind here. Table VII.6 below shows the changes in average rents in money terms and in real terms between 1955 and 1970, broadly the period under discussion here. Rents are shown as a proportion of average earnings of adult men in manual work, not because that necessarily measures all that accurately the average earnings of local authority tenants, but because it is a reasonable measure of the proportionate change in incomes.

By 1970/71 average rents were between 85% and 90% higher in real terms than they had been in 1955/56. This increase in rents did not come about as a sequence of annual increases, for annual increases in council rents did not appear until the 1970s. Local authorities were required by law to review their rents from time to time, and in the

1950s and 1960s such reviews normally took place at two or three year intervals, with a tendency towards shorter intervals at the end of the period. In any one year in the late 1950s and 1960s only a minority of rents would actually increase: the sequence was normally of a steep increase, often as much as 25% or even 30%, followed by a period of stability.

Table VII.6 - Local Authority Rents 1955/56 to 1970/71

	Average Rents	Percent of Average Pre-Tax Earnings	Percent of Average Post-Tax Earnings (a)
1955/56	14s 6d	6.7	6.9
1960/61	20s 8d	7.3	7.8
1965/66	28s 7d	7.5	8.4
1970/71	£2.30	8.6	10.4

Annual Average Percentage Increases

	Money Terms	Real Terms (b)
1955/56 to 1960/61	8.1	5.3
1960/61 to 1965/66	6.6	3.0
1965/66 to 1970/71	10.0	5.3

Notes: (a) Tax payable by married man with two children.
(b) Index of retail prices used to convert from money terms to real terms.

In the 1960s rent rebates became an increasingly important and contentious aspect of rent policy. They had a history that went back to 1930, when they were authorized by the Housing Act of that year to assist households displaced by slum clearance and who could not afford the rents of replacement dwellings notwithstanding the subsidy provided to keep the rents down. The 1935 Housing Act extended the power to grant rent rebates to all dwellings in housing revenue accounts, at local authorities' discretion. Some authorities used the power extensively, Leeds being perhaps the best known instance in the inter-war years. Rent rebates were always controversial, and there were two sharply contrasting attitudes to them in the Labour party and among its supporters. One part of Labour opinion saw them as putting into practice the principle of "to each according to his needs", whereas others objected strongly to rent rebates as a form of "means testing", something that the administration of unemployment assistance in the 1930s had made a term of opprobrium. Conservatives, in contrast, generally had no such objections to means testing as a means of concentrating assistance where it was most needed or keeping down public expenditure, or (usually) a combination of the two. The principle at issue here went far wider, of course, than whether council house rents should be graduated according to tenants' incomes. Universalism versus selectivity in the social services, to use the rather grandiloquent terms current at the time, was much debated in the 1960s, with 'universalism' (services available on the same terms to all who needed them irrespective of income) championed very forcefully by Professor R.M. Titmuss and those who had studied under him. Pressures on public expenditure, however, pushed policy in the direction of selectivity, and council house rents and subsidies were an early example of this trend.

The (Conservative) government of the day in 1955 had exhorted local authorities to use rent rebate systems, or differential rents of like effect, to concentrate subsidies on tenants who most needed them, and not to subsidize tenants who could afford unsubsidized rents. That continued to be the policy of the Conservative governments in the later 1950s and the early 1960s. When the Labour government took office in 1964, the pressures on housing costs and subsidies led it to the same general conclusion about the need to make extensive use of rent rebates. In June 1967 the Ministry of Housing and Local Government (in Circular 46/47) said that in the words of the 1965 White Paper on the Housing Programme (paragraph 44) "subsidies should not be used wholly or even mainly to keep general rent levels low. Help for those who most need it can be given only if the subsidies are in large part used to provide rebates for tenants whose means are small", and provided a model rent rebate scheme for guidance. Advocates of rent rebate schemes recognized the great range of circumstances of tenants and hence the wide variations in the rent that they could reasonably afford to pay. Building for slum clearance and for old people, the two categories of building singled out for encouragement by the subsidies being retained in 1956, brought into local authority tenancies large numbers of people who could not afford the kind of rents that would be manageable for tenants in averagely paid employment. If rents for all tenants were to be kept to the level that the poorest tenants could afford, the cost of the subsidies would be very high indeed. Not all Labour local authorities accepted the arguments for rent rebates and correspondingly higher standard rents, notably the Greater London Council (GLC) which had no rebate scheme until the Conservatives won control there in 1967. The GLC acquired the housing responsibilities of the former London County Council (LCC) where Labour had been in control continuously since 1934, and firmly opposed to rent rebates.

The proportion of tenant households receiving rebates, however, was not high in the mid-1960s, and the increase in the next few years that resulted from the efforts to secure greater use of rent rebates was not very great. In the financial year 1965/66 the number of households receiving a rent rebate was estimated at 355,000 out of a total of 3,850,000, and the total amount of rebates £9.6 million (73), equal to 8.6% of the total of Exchequer subsidies and rate fund contributions. In 1970/71 the total amount of rebates was put at £15.6 million, according to returns collected by IMTA and the proportion of tenants receiving rebates at 9.3% (74). These were not complete returns, but clearly the growth of coverage was slow. Since the various local authorities' rent rebate schemes were so diverse, the number of households eligible for rebates cannot be estimated, so a 'take up rate' cannot be calculated for comparison with the national standard scheme introduced in 1972. Nearly all schemes in the 1960s excluded households receiving Supplementary Benefit, on the ground that rebates would be offset by a corresponding reduction in the amount of benefit paid, since the benefit scales were in the form of £x a week plus rent. Exclusion of households receiving Supplementary Benefit from rent rebate schemes was a contentious matter, and there were allegations that some authorities were putting tenants in receipt of Supplementary Benefits into the highest rented modern dwellings, in the knowledge that the Ministry of Social Security would in effect be paying. The 'inter-face' between rent rebates and Supplementary Benefits was a continuing source of difficulty even after the 1972 reform, owing to the complicated calculation required to work out which would give the better result for a householder entitled to both and hence could choose which one to claim.

The rent rebates were prominent in the controversies over rent policies in the later 1960s. The pressures on rents from the causes already described were the basic reason; but the controversies were exacerbated by the prominence accorded to prices and incomes policy in managing the national economy; and by the party political conflict that arose from there being a Labour government nationally but with political control of very many local authorities, including the Greater London Council, the largest local housing authority of all, passing from Labour to Conservative in 1967 and 1968. By the late 1960s well over one-quarter of all households were local authority tenants, so in the context of prices and incomes policy council rents were an important and highly visible price. On grounds of general economic management, therefore, the central government sought to restrain the rise in council rents at the same time as its housing policy, specifically the large building programme and the subsidy system which were leading to large increases in the amount of expenditure to be met from rent or rates. At the same time many of the Conservative local authorities were trying to reduce or eliminate rate fund contributions. The method usually preferred was to combine substantial increases in standard rents with the introduction or improvement of rent rebate schemes. The Greater London Council was a prominent instance. It did not previously have a rent rebate scheme, and the stated intention of the Conservative majority that took control there in 1967 was to raise rents as to meet the costs of a rent rebate scheme and reduce the rate fund contribution from £15 14s a year in 1966/67 to zero in 1970/71 (75). The effect of this on un-rebated rents would, of course, come on top of the effects of increases in costs. A clash with central government was inevitable, which central government sought to resolve by taking powers to control local authority rents.

The legislation about rents need be sketched only briefly. As part of the prices and incomes "standstill" announced in July 1966 local authorities were asked not to increase rents during the six months standstill period (76), a request that was the more readily complied with as most local authorities' rent increases took effect in April at the beginning of the new financial year. But when it became clear that many local authorities planned to raise their rents by substantial amounts, not least to catch up with the increase in costs that had occurred during the period of the standstill, the government in December 1967 referred council rent increases to the National Board for Prices and Incomes, which under the Prices and Incomes Act 1966 had the effect of postponing the increase for the three months (subsequently extended to four) during which the Board had to report. The Board found, as it was bound to do, that the rent increases arose from increases in costs, with reduction in rate fund contributions important only for a few authorities (77). It recommended as maximum increases in any one year 7s 6d in average rents and 10s for any individual dwelling. The Prices and Incomes Act 1968 made rent increases illegal unless the Minister of Housing's agreement had been given, and the Minister announced (Circular 37/68) that agreement would not be given for increases in excess of 7s 6d (average) or 10s a week (maximum). Approval of lesser increases was not automatic; they had to be justified by inescapable cost increases. The 1968 Act expired at the end of 1969, and was replaced by the Rent (Control of Increases) Act 1969, under which increases of more than 7s 6d average of 10s maximum required the Minister's agreement. Alongside these statutory restrictions went an informal agreement that local authorities would raise rents only to cover inescapable increases in costs or the introduction or improvement of rent rebate schemes. They could not raise rents in order to make lower rate fund contributions than they were accustomed to make (78). As well the House of Commons Select Committee on Estimates reviewed housing subsidies extensively but inconclusively in 1969 (79); they found that the high expenditure on subsidy was the consequence of the rise in capital costs and interest rates, just as the Prices and Incomes Board had found in the previous year about rents. The terms of reference of the Estimates Committee precluded it from considering policy, so it was not able to consider reform of the subsidy system, and had to confine itself to fairly minor (though in their own way radical) changes, such as that loan charges on land before development should be met from a rate fund contribution, and that housing revenue accounts might be balanced over a three year period instead of annually. For a more comprehensive study the Committee looked to the Ministry of Housing and Local Government. In 1968-70 the Ministry undertook a study and review of housing finance (80), but the findings were never published, as they were overtaken by the change of government after the general election of 1970. The incoming Conservative government had well defined views about the direction in which it wanted to move on council house rents and subsidies, and its statements of policy made no mention of having drawn on the work done by the Ministry under the previous administration.

The pressures on rents and rate fund contributions that were generated by new house building were one reason why in 1969 building by local authorities fell short of what central government was prepared to allow, even though the programme had been reduced (by 10,000 in both 1968 and 1969) in the post-devaluation cuts. But there were other reasons as well: the Ministry of Housing and Local Government observed in its report for 1969 and 1970: ".... in some areas local authorities had reappraised their own house building programmes because, they said, they were finding a diminishing demand for their houses and (in some cases) they were able to meet demand to a greater extent from their existing stock. There was also apparent a feeling among some local authorities that on social grounds more emphasis on owner-occupation was desirable" (81). The effect of the reduction in the demand for tenancies, rising re-lets, and policy decision to build fewer council houses was that: ".... the overall level of activity came to be dictated not by any limitation on the number of houses the Ministry was prepared to authorize, but by the proposals of the local housing authorities themselves as to what new building they should undertake" (82). These were novel developments, at any rate in the post-war years, but they foreshadowed what was to happen on a much larger scale in the later 1970s. With hindsight, 1969 can be seen to mark the stage when in England (though not yet Scotland) the growth in the demand for council houses began to slacken and hence the number of new houses and flats built began to tend downwards. The increase in new building in 1973-75 was only a temporary interruption to this change of trend,

caused by the surge in house prices in the early
1970s and then the change of government in 1974.
But before that the policies that went with the
change of government in 1970 must be considered.

The Reform of Local Authority Housing Finance in 1972

The Conservative government that took office
in 1970 came in with firm views about the direction
in which it wanted council rents and subsidies to
move. The policies that it had developed while in
opposition owed much to the experience and practice
of Conservative local authorities in the later
1960s, particularly the GLC whose housing policies
from 1967 onwards in many ways foreshadowed what
the 1970 Conservative government would try to do
nationally. It wanted to reduce total expenditure
on housing subsidies, and to concentrate the expenditure on those most in need of assistance (83),
and the instruments by which it planned to put this
policy into effect were "fair rents" and a national
system of rent rebates. "Fair rents" in this
context meant rents aligned with those registered
under the Rent Act 1965 (subsequently the Rent Act
1968) for accommodation rented unfurnished from
private landlords. This legislation, its antece-
dents, and results are discussed in some detail in
the next chapter. Here the important point is that
the rents that resulted from it were much higher
than the general run of local authority rents. In
1969 fair rents as registered averaged £270 a year
for houses in London and £311 for flats, and
outside London £135 for houses; whereas average
local authority rents in London were equivalent to
£143, and outside London £99, a year (84). The
flats and houses for which rents were registered
might well have been not exactly comparable with
council houses and flats, but the differences in
average rents were so great, over 90% in London and
35% elsewhere, that if council rents were to be set
by analogy with fair rents as registered for houses
and flats rented from private landlords, they would
be very substantially above the rents actually
charged by councils at the end of the 1960s.

Experience in the 1960s could be (and was)
held to support a move away from dependence on the
state of the housing revenue account as it then
stood. That setting rents according to the state
of the housing revenue account, as modified by rate

fund contributions that reflected widely differing
policies, gave rise to anomalies was not, indeed,
open to doubt. As the government's White Paper,
Fair Deal for Housing (85) pointed out, "....
variations .... also arise from historic accidents
which have determined the composition of each local
authority's housing stock. An authority which
built most of its houses when costs were lower can
balance its housing revenue account by charging
rents far below the present value of its houses.
But an authority which has had to build most of its
houses recently may be obliged to charge much
higher rents for houses of similar quality. The
difference in historic costs works out to the
disadvantage of the authority with unsolved housing
problems, and of its tenants". The reason why
housing revenue accounts worked that way lay, of
course, in subsidies being so set as to leave a
substantial gap between the costs of new houses
falling on HRAs, net of subsidy, and the rents that
tenants could be expected to pay, with the gap left
to be covered from increases in rents for the
existing dwellings, or a rate fund contribution.
That increases in rents paid by tenants of houses
that had been built earlier should be used to
bridge much of the gap between the costs generated
by new houses and their rents had been the basis of
council house finance since 1955, but by 1970 high
interest rates, high building costs, and large
building programmes meant that it produced hard-to-
justify variations in rent levels and rent
increases between one authority and another. One
logical way out was to have rents set by criteria
other than the costs, net of subsidies, falling on
the housing revenue account; the other was an
equalization levy on authorities that had a proportionately large stock of older houses built at low
costs and a corresponding grant to authorities in
the opposite situation. Such a proposition, particularly under the name of national pooling of loan
charges, was widely discussed in the mid-1970s, but
attracted little interest at the beginning of the
decade. The course chosen by the government of the
day in 1970 and 1971 was to have rents set by
reference to criteria other than the state of the
housing revenue account. The state of the account
would be unlikely to bear much relationship to what
the houses were worth, so relating rents to an
objective measure of what the houses were worth had
much to be said for it (86).

The decision to set rents independently of the housing revenue account was logically separable, of course, from the decision that they should be set at levels aligned to "fair rents" as they emerged from registration of rents of accommodation let by private landlords. The height at which rents should be set, when separated from costs falling on housing revenue accounts, was a distinct policy decision. As far as can be gathered, the decision to go for the same level as registered rents was inspired mainly by the aim of sharply reducing expenditure on subsidies (87). A case could also be made on housing market grounds for rents being set on the same basis in both the public and private rented sectors. Aligning council rents with registered rents in the private sector meant an increase in council rents of 40-50 percent, more in London and rather less in the rest of England. Whether such an increase could be fairly or reasonably sought after the increase of 85 to 90 percent in real terms between 1955 and 1970 was of course strongly contested. Arguments one way tended to be in terms of rates of increase, arguments the other way in terms of levels. An average rent of £3.50 a week (compared with £2.45 a week before rebates), it could be argued, was not high in relation to what could be afforded by the better paid tenants, notably households where there was more than one earner. In 1969 approximately 56% of local authority tenant households had incomes (before tax) of over £30 a week, and 25% had incomes of £40 a week or more (88). Some advocates of higher rents and lower subsidies were given to citing expenditure on cars and overseas holidays as evidence that council tenants could afford to pay more rent, a line of argument that could readily degenerate into class-based antagonism and malice in direct descent from the nineteenth century assertion that 'the working classes' could afford decent housing if only they did not waste their money on alcoholic drink. An important part of the case for much higher standard rents being equitable and reasonable was that they would be accompanied by a mandatory rent rebate scheme that would provide effective help to tenants with low incomes.

The method by which rents were proposed to be set may be commented on briefly. The principle of setting rents for council houses by comparison with rents charged for houses and flats rented from

private landlords was not novel: controlled rents
plus a margin for higher quality had been the basis
according to which local authorities were supposed
to set rents under the 1919 Act, and the
"appropriate normal rent" under the 1924 Act was
similarly linked to rents in the private sector.
In 1935, though, the link was reduced to the
obligation on local authorities to "take into
consideration" rents of working class houses in the
district. But as a source of precedents and
experience, this was more than thirty years old by
the 1970s, during which time the local authority
housing stock had quadrupled in size and the
private rented sector had halved. The rationale of
aligning local authority rents with private sector
rents was quite different when renting from private
landlords was the majority tenure from what it
would be when local authority dwellings were
substantially more numerous than dwellings rented
from private landlords and the private rented
sector was diminishing fast. This was the reason
cited by the National Board for Prices and Incomes
in 1968 for rejecting private sector registered
rents as a basis for setting local authority rents
(89). How great the difficulties would be in
practice was in the event never tested. Local
authorities were responsible in the first instance
for assessing fair rents of their dwellings, with
their assessments to be reviewed by specially
appointed commitees (termed Rent Scrutiny Boards)
from the Rent Assessment Panels, which would revise
them as appropriate. Before the work of the Rent
Scrutiny Boards had got very far, however, they
were stopped following the change of government in
March 1974. So during the period when the reformed
system was in operation, rents were governed by the
transition rules laid down by the Housing Finance
Act 1972, not by the level at which 'fair rents'
would have actually been set for council houses and
flats.
    The basic principle of the transition provi-
sions was that average rents should be increased by
50p a year until 'fair rents' were reached, subject
to the proviso (Housing Finance Act 1972, Secion
62(4)) that the Secretary of State for the Environment could authorize a smaller increase if he was
satisfied that the full 50p increase would result
in the rents of more than 2 percent of a local
authority's stock being raised to more than the
'fair rent' level. These "Section 62(4) dispensa-

tions" were extensively used. The detail of the
transition was made much more complicated by the
provisions needed to ensure that local authorities
raised rents sufficiently to bring in an average of
50p a week more per dwelling in 1972/73 considered
as a whole than in the previous year, even though
the Housing Finance Bill could not become law until
part way through the 1972/73 financial year. Until
it became law, local authorities were under no
obligation, of course, to put up their rents.

Requiring rents to be set by criteria other
than the state of the housing revenue account would
make necessary a radical re-casting of subsidies.
If rents determined the state of the account
instead of the state of the account determining the
rents, then subsidies (and rate fund contributions)
had to be certain to be sufficient to balance the
account by meeting all the difference between
expenditure chargeable to revenue and rent income.
Where loan charges per dwelling were low as a
result of many of the houses having been built
before the war or in the post-war decade, rents at
levels comparable to private sector registered
rents would produce surpluses. New financial
arrangements would be needed.

The structure of the 1972 system of subsidies
was complicated. An observation at the time was
that subsidies of the £x a year for y years type
could be understood by someone with the 'O' level
of the General Certificate of Education, but the
1967 system required 'A' level ability to understand it, and the 1972 system a university degree.
The function of the detail of the subsidies was to
determine the way in which any shortfall of income
relative to outgoings was to be shared between the
Exchequer and rate fund. Central government could
control capital expenditure (by loan sanctions and
by the cost yardstick, which remained in force) and
hence the loan charges generated, but it could not
control expenditure on repair and maintenance and
supervision and management, which remained under
the local authority's own hand. An Exchequer
subsidy equal to 100% of the deficit was therefore
unacceptable: there had to be a sharing of any
deficit with the local authority. This was done by
means of four subsidies:

(a) 'Residual subsidy', in effect the subsidies
    payable under previous Acts consolidated and
    tapered out.

(b) 'Transition subsidy', to make up any differ-
     ence between the increase in rent income and
     the reduction in residual subsidy.
(c) 'Operational deficit subsidy', a subsidy equal
     to one-half of the rate fund contribution in
     1970/71 or 1971/72, whichever was the smaller,
     plus one-half of the increases in HRA
     expenditure between 1970/71 and 1971/72 in
     excess of £15 per dwelling.
(d) 'Rising cost subsidy', a subsidy equal to the
     increase in the sum of all reckonable costs
     per dwelling over the year before.

Of these, transition subsidy and rising cost
subsidy were to be divided between the Exchequer
and the rate fund in proportions beginning at 90:10
in 1972/73 with the Exchequer's share reduced by 5
percentage points each year to 75% in 1975/76. The
sum of the subsidies (including the associated rate
fund contributions) was to be limited to the amount
to balance the housing revenue account, by notionally crediting the subsidies in a prescribed order
and stopping when enough had been credited to
produce the balance. When the rent income exceeded
costs falling on the housing revenue account (which
was expected to happen fairly quickly in authorities where a higher than average proportion of the
stock had been built when costs in money terms were
low), a balance of up to £30 per dwelling might be
built up, but any excess over £30 per dwelling was
to be paid to the central government. Against the
amount so paid was to be set the cost of rent
allowances (i.e. allowances to tenants of private
landlords) for that particular local authority; and
of any remainder one-half was to be repaid to the
local authority. The rent allowances were to be
administered by the local authority, but with the
full amount of the allowances payable funded by
central government subsidy. The first charge on
any surplus on the housing revenue account would
therefore be the rent allowances paid to tenants of
private landlords.
     The remaining part of the 1972 arrangements to
be described, and in the event the longest lasting,
was the national rent rebate scheme. Local authorities were obliged to set up rent rebate schemes at
least as favourable to tenants (in the sense of the
entitlement produced by any specified combination
of income, household circumstances, and rent) as
the national scheme, with a limited discretion to

make their schemes somewhat more favourable to
tenants. The cost of the national model scheme was
divided between the Exchequer and rate fund in
proportions that began at 90:10 but changed in
steps to 75:25 in 1975/76; the extra cost of a
scheme more favourable to tenants was to be borne
entirely by the local authority. The scales specified for the national model scheme when announced
in the Fair Deal for Housing White Paper were more
advantageous to tenants than the Ministry of
Housing's model scheme set out in Circular 46/67;
the 'needs allowance', i.e. the income at which
only the minimum rent would be payable, was set at
£13.50 a week for a married couple plus £2.50 for
each dependent child as against £8 and £1 in 1967;
and the 'taper', i.e. the reduceion in rebate in
proportion to the amount of income in excess of the
needs allowance, was set at 17% whereas the 1967
provided a taper of one-sixth of the first £5 above
the allowance and one-quarter of the rest. With a
rent of £3 a week a married man who had two
dependent children and who earned £22 a week
(three-quarters of average earnings in 1971 for men
employed full time in manual work) would receive a
rebate of £1.20. Under the Circular 46/67 scheme
he would have received 37p, assuming that the
allowances had been up-rated since 1967 in line
with prices. Tenants receiving Supplementary
Benefit were included in the rent rebate scheme.
To start with, administrative arrangements were
made for local authorities to be notified about
which tenants were receiving Supplementary Benefit,
so that tenants would not have to claim twice; but
from 1974/75 onwards the Supplementary Benefit
scales in effect included the rebate, with local
authorities reimbursing the Department of Health
and Social Security for the cost of these so-called
'indirect' rebates.

The Housing Finance Act 1972 was a highly
controversial piece of legislation, fiercely
attacked as being hostile and unfair to tenants.
It was also objected to as taking away from elected
local authorities the power to determine their own
rent policy, something they had had since 1923; and
for planning to "make profits out of tenants". The
last allegation depended on a housing revenue
account surplus being equated with "profit", but
the concepts of inflation accounting that were
highly relevant here had not in 1971/72 achieved
the currency that they were later to do. The

passage of the 1972 reform into law and the early
stages of implementing it were made more stormy by
being embroiled in a wider conflict over whether
the legislation of the government of the day could
be resisted by extra-legal means. The Industrial
Relations Act 1971 was the prime example, but the
threatened refusal of some Labour local authorities
to implement the 1972 Act was in the same spirit.
In the end only one (Clay Cross UDC) persisted in
its refusal and had its housing affairs transferred
to a commissioner appointed by the government.
Ill-will was further exacerbated when the government of the day had recourse in 1972 and 1973 to a
statutory incomes and prices policy, with which a
policy of requiring large rent increases could be
alleged to be incompatible.

There was no doubt that by the standards of
past experience the rent increases required by the
1972 Act looked large at the time when they were
decided on. 50p was an increase of almost 20% over
the average rent in payment in 1971, and more than
twice as large, in real terms, as the average over
the past 5 years. An increase in rent every year
was, moreover, a novelty; as mentioned above, in
the 1960s most local authorities reviewed their
rents every two years or three, with two year
intervals becoming more common as the rate of rise
of costs accelerated in the second half of the
decade. In the first year of the new financial
regime the Act had the effects intended of it.
Average un-rebated rents in May 1973 at £3.44 were
25% higher than a year earlier, 15% higher in real
terms. In real terms this was the sharpest
increase in a single year on record, and brought
rents to a higher proportion of average earnings
than in any post-war year. Exchequer subsidy and
rate fund contributions to housing revenue accounts
(excluding rebates) were lower in money terms in
1972/73 than in 1971/72, and in total between 13%
and 14% lower in real terms. All this was as
expected.

What was not expected, as far as is known,
were the large increases in expenditure on subsidy
that the 1972 Act generated when interest rates
rose sharply in 1973 and the boom in land prices
and construction costs further increased the loan
charges falling on housing revenue accounts. With
rents no longer influenced by the state of the
housing revenue account, they were not affected by
even a large increase in the costs falling on the

account. More rapid inflation could affect rents only as it affected 'fair rents' as determined; and so long as rents actually paid were governed by the transition rules, in particular the 50p a year, they were not affected at all by an acceleration of inflation. The transition rules and the 50p a year progression were part of the Housing Finance Act itself (Part VI) so a greater increase than this would require new primary legislation. Nothing at all was said in the White Paper Fair Deal for Housing about how the system would work with different rates of inflation and interest rates. To show what happened the course of interest rates must be outlined, and then the housing revenue accounts summarized.

Table VII.7 - Average Rates of Interest Charged to Housing Revenue Accounts 1970/71 to 1978/79

(percent)

1970/71	6.8	1975/76	9.8
1971/72	6.6	1976/77	10.4
1972/73	6.7	1977/78	9.6
1973/74	8.1	1978/79	10.2
1974/75	9.5		

Source: Housing Policy Technical Volume, Chapter 4, Table IV.6; and Department of the Environment.

In the two years 1973/74 and 1974/75, average pool rates rose by 2.8 percentage points, an increase wholly without precedent. What happened to costs falling on housing revenue accounts during the period of the Housing Finance Act 1972 is shown in Table VII.8. 1970/71 is taken as the year for comparisons and not 1971/72 because in the latter year the figures were distorted by transfers to general rate funds out of balances on housing revenue accounts and repair accounts.

In terms of constant (1970/71) prices, total costs per dwelling rose by about £49 (27%) between 1970/71 and 1974/75. Just under one-half of this was the result of higher loan charges, for which the reasons have already been discussed. Expenditure on repair and maintenance and supervision and management rose by £22 per dwelling (just over 50%) at 1970/71 prices. Increases at this pace in expenditure on upkeep and management were something entirely novel. Why expenditure on repair and

Table VII.8 - Housing Revenue Accounts: England and Wales 1970/71 to 1974/75

	1970/71	1972/73	1973/74	1974/75
Expenditure (£ million)				
Repair and maintenance	115	183	203	264
Supervision and management - general	39	62	72	107
Supervision and management - special	29	44	54	81
Loan charges	581	649	827	1,104
Other expenditure	20	40	51	65
Total	784	978	1,207	1,621
Income				
Rents of dwellings (*)	527	703	823	919
Rents of other properties and miscellaneous income	49	63	80	81
Exchequer subsidy (**)	159	184	237	485
Rate fund contribution (***)	56	26	65	136
Total subsidy including rent rebates	215	278	457	814
Per Dwelling (£)				
Repair and maintenance	26.2	40.1	44.1	56.3
Supervision and management - general	8.9	13.6	15.7	22.8
Supervision and management - special	6.6	9.6	11.7	17.3
Loan charges	132.3	142.1	179.8	235.5
Total expenditure	178.5	214.3	262.4	345.9
Rents (un-rebated)	120.0	154.0	178.9	196.1
Exchequer subsidy (excluding rebates)	36.2	40.3	51.5	103.5
Rate fund (excluding rebates)	12.8	5.7	14.1	29.0
All subsidies including rebates	49.0	60.9	99.3	173.7
Rebated rents	120.0	139.1	145.2	154.9
Number of dwellings ('000) at mid-year	4,392	4,564	4,600	4,687

Table VII.8   (continued)

Notes: (*)   Un-rebated rents in 1972/73 and subsequently.
        (**)   Excluding rent rebates in 1972/73 and subse-
               quently.
Source: Housing and Construction Statistics, Depart-
               ment of the Environment, Housing Policy
               Technical Volume, Chapter 4, Table IV.9.

maintenance and supervision and management should
have risen so much at this time, in a way that it
had never done before, has never been explained.
The exceptional increases in the price of oil and
other fuels can be dismissed as a major part of the
explanation: costs of heating and hot water, where
these are supplied by the authority, come under
'special' supervision and management, but of the
£22 increase in average expenditure per dwelling,
less than a quarter consisted of 'special' supervision and mangement.   Increases in pay more rapid
than elsewhere could not explain the increase
either (90), so we are left with increases in the
amount of service per dwelling (or at any rate
increases in the resources employed in providing
it) or accounting changes by which larger amounts
of expenditure were charged to the housing revenue
account.   Where work is done in connection with
housing revenue account dwellings by local
authority departments that do other work as well
(for instance the Treasurer's department collecting
the rents, or the works department doing repairs)
an apportioned part of the cost is charged to the
housing revenue account.   Rising cost subsidy made
expenditure on supervision and management and
repair and maintenance subsidizable, which it had
not been at any time since the 1919 Act.   That the
biggest increase came in 1972/73, the year in which
the expenditure became subsidizable, seems too much
of a conincidence for there to have been no connection between the increase in expenditure and the
subsidy, but there is nothing (apart from the
expenditure itself) to suggest that the standard of
upkeep of management of local authority housing
improved much in the early 1970s.
     The progression of rents provided for by the
1972 Act, in practice the transition rules, could
not keep up with these increases in costs. Between
1972/73 and 1973/74 un-rebated rents rose in real
terms by about 8½% (91), whereas costs per dwelling
rose by 14%.   In 1974/75 the rise in un-rebated

357

rents, if the increases due in 1974 had gone into
effect as scheduled, would have barely kept pace
with the general price level whereas costs per
dwelling rose by another 10% in real terms. Even
if the 1974 increases had gone into effect instead
of being 'frozen', average un-rebated rents in
1974/75 would have been only about 15% higher in
real terms than they had been in 1970/71. Such a
rate of increase, 3½% a year in real terms, was
well below what occurred in the late 1960s, which
is an ironic comment on how far off course the
policy was driven by unforeseen inflation.

The consequence of un-rebated rents rising
much more slowly than costs was that Exchequer and
rate fund subsidies had to rise very fast. If
rebates were excluded in 1970/71 the average
subsidy would have been £45.3 per dwelling; in
1974/75 it would have been £115.4 per dwelling,
excluding the effect of the rent freeze. In real
terms there was thus in the four years an increase
of almost 70% in real terms in subsidies per
dwelling.

The cost of rent rebates came on top of the
general subsidies just described. If the cost of
rent rebates is added in, the expectation of a
reduced total subsidy bill can be seen to have gone
even further astray. The total cost of subsidies
including rebates in 1974/75 is shown in Table
VII.8 as £814 million, of which £193 million was
for rebates. If the net cost of the rent freeze,
including consequential savings or rent rebates, is
taken off, the figure would have been about £750
million (92). To make the figure comparable with
1970/71, adjustment is needed for Supplementary
Benefit. Before 1972 hardly any rent rebate
schemes included households receiving Supplementary
Benefit, but from 1972 the rules of the model
scheme required that they should be included. In
1972/73 and 1973/74 for the first eight weeks after
claiming benefit, the benefit was assessed on the
scale plus un-rebated rent, but after that on the
scale plus rebated rent, with the tenant receiving
a rebate. From 1974/75 onwards Supplementary
Benefit was assessed throughout on the un-rebated
rent, in order to avoid the administrative burden
of changing the amount of benefit and transferring
the tenant to rebate, but local authorities made
block payments to the Department of Health and
Social Security broadly equal to the rebates to
which households on Supplementary Benefit would

have been entitled if they had received them individually. The amount was £95 million in 1974/75 (93), and would probably have been about £100 million in 1974/75 if the increases in rents scheduled for 1974 had taken their course. The figure for subsidies including rent rebates in 1974/75 that is comparable with the total of £215 million in 1970/71 was thus about £650 million, excluding the effect of the rent freeze. In money terms the cost trebled; in real terms it doubled. That the cost of rent rebates rose so much, even excluding the Suplementary Benefit tenants, was due partly to take-up and partly to the rebate scale being more advantageous to tenants than most of the schemes which it superseded. The IMTA figures showed 308,000 tenants in 1970/71 receiving rebates averaging £1.04 a week (94), whereas in 1974/75 nearly 850,000 rebates were in payment, excluding households receiving Supplementary Benefit, averaging £2.39 a week (95). The number of rebates paid had nearly tripled and the average rebate had risen from just over 40% of the average rent to just over 60%. In 1974/75 an estimated 70-75% of households eligible for rebates claimed them. Most of the increase in expenditure on rent rebates was the result of the national scheme, not the increase in rents. The Fair Deal for Housing White Paper made no estimate of the number of households eligible for rent rebates, or the amount of rebates, hence it is not possible to say whether the increase in expenditure was foreseen or not. But the success of the rebate scheme was a major reason why public expenditure on housing subsidies rose so much.

In view of all the controversies attending the Housing Finance Act, a question of some interest is what would have happened had the previous system remained in force. A definitive answer cannot be given because how the difference in the subsidy system would have affected behaviour is unknown; but there is no doubt that the financial pressures on local authority housing would have been very severe indeed. An attempt may be made to calculate the subsidy that would have been payable under the 1967 Act, and hence what the aggregate of housing revenue accounts would look like. Exactly how much subsidy the 1967 Act would have provided is impossible to say, owing both to the calculation of the new borrowing rate for subsidy being so complex, and also the timing of payment of the subsi-

359

dies that became due on completion. But a reasonable estimate is that the total subsidy would have
risen from £187 million in 1971/72 to £310 million
(approximately) in 1974/75 (96). But for the rent
freeze Exchequer subsidy would have been about £420
million (£485 million less four-fifths of the £81
million effect on un-rebated rents). The difference of £110 million is not all of the extra
revenue that would have had to have been found from
rent and rates if the 1967 Act had continued in
force: under that Act there was no rent rebate
subsidy, and at the very least the cost of rebate
would probably have risen pro-rata with un-rebated
rents if the 1967 system had remained in force.
The pressures that would have fallen on the financing of local authority housing in those hypothetical circumstances are outlined in Table VII.9,
which shows how much more would have had to be
raised from rent and rates over and above the rents
and rate fund contribution that the 1972 Act would
have produced. A major unknown in such a calculation is what would have happened to expenditure on
supervision and management and repair and maintenance. Reasons were adduced above for thinking that
the 1972 Act led to increases in expenditure under
these heads being charged for housing revenue
accounts; so one of the hypothetical calculations
has expenditure per dwelling risen in real terms at
the same average rate as between 1965/66 and
1970/71, about 4% a year plus 10% for the larger
public service pay increase and, in 1974/75, the
rise in fuel costs. The actual figures for 1974/75
are compared with three hypothetical sets of
housing revenue account totals: 'Hypothesis A', the
1972 Act with no rent freeze; 'Hypothesis B', the
1967 subsidy system but actual increases in costs,
and 'Hypothesis C', the 1967 subsidy system with
costs per dwelling for supervision and management
rising with the general price level plus 10%.

Had the 1967 Act subsidies remained in force
it is highly likely that local authority housing
would have been in a state of financial crisis by
1974/75. For the 1967 system gave no protection at
all against increases in interest rates on existing
debt or on debt that financed land holdings and
houses not yet completed; and the representative
interest rate for calculating the subsidy on new
houses being one year in arrears would have worked
very harshly when interest rates rose so fast. If
the expenditure side of housing revenue accounts

Table VII.9 - Hypothetical Housing Revenue Account Totals in 1974/75 if the 1967 Act had continued in Force

(£ million)

	Actual Out-turn	Hypothesis A	Hypothesis B	Hypothesis C
Expenditure				
Loan charges	1,104	1,104	1,104	1,104
Repair, maintenance, supervision, management	452	452	452	379
Other expenditure	65	65	65	65
Total	1,621	1,621	1,621	1,548
Income				
Un-rebated rents at 1972 Act levels	919 (a)	1,000	1,000	1,000
less Rebates under 1967 system			29	29
Rent income under 1967 system			971	971
Exchequer subsidy (excluding rebates)	485	420	310	310
Rate fund contribution (as under 1972 Act)	136	120	120	120
Rents of non-domestic property and miscellaneous income	81	81	81	81
Total income	1,621	1,621	1,482	1,482
Gap between expenditure and income from 1972 Act rents	nil	nil	139	66
Average extra weekly rent if gap closed entirely by rents	nil	nil	58p	28p
Implied average weekly rent (un-rebated)	£3.85	£4.20	£4.78	£4.58

Note: (a) Actual, as affected by the rent freeze.

had changed as it did even if the 1967 subsidy system had remained in force an extra £140 million would have been required from rents and rates, over and above what the 1972 Act would have produced. If it all came from rents (very likely, owing to the way in which other increases in local authorities' expenditure had already led to very large rate increases) an average rent of about £4.80 would have been required. That would have been double the 1970/71 average in money terms and 30-35% higher in real terms. Even if some of the rise in expenditure on supervision and management and repair and maintenance is taken to have been the consequence of the 1972 Act and so taken out of a calculation of what would have happened if the 1967 Act had remained in force, a rent 90% higher in money terms would still have been needed. Such increases would have been unprecedentedly large, and there must be great doubt about whether they could have been secured. If they could not, capital expenditure on housing would have had to have been very sharply cut.

With hindsight, therefore, the Housing Finance Act 1972 can be seen to have effectively shielded investment in local authority housing against what would otherwise have been severe cuts, and tenants against what would otherwise have been even larger rent increases. It did so by providing for an open-ended subsidy, as was inherent in making rents no longer dependent on the state of the housing revenue account. In the circumstances of accelerating inflation and wholly exceptional increases in interest rates, open-ended subsidy was very expensive indeed.

Subsidies and Rents from 1974 to 1979

The rent increases scheduled for April 1974 (for some authorities October) were cancelled under Prices and Incomes Act powers which were used to "freeze" all rents for the rest of 1974, including rents in the private sector. The rents freeze was part of a policy of trying to secure wage restraint by means of price restraint. What the policy, embodied in what was termed the "social contract" between government and trade unions, achieved in slowing down the rate of inflation is debatable but not for discussion here. In local authority housing finance, though, it widened still further the already rapidly growing gap between costs and rents.

When the Bill that became the Housing Finance Act was passing through Parliament the opposition pledged to repeal it, and after the 1974 general elections the pledge was carried into effect by the Housing Rents and Subsidies Act of 1975. It was avowedly a temporary measure to keep local authority housing finance going until longer lasting and thorough-going reforms could be made in the light of the fundamental review of housing finance that the government announced that it was setting in hand. In comparison with the Housing Finance Act 1972 it was a much more conservative measure (small c of course). Exchequer subsidies in payment under the previous Act were consolidated into the "basic element" of subsidy, which was in substance the time-honoured practice under all Acts before the Housing Finance Act of leaving unaltered the subsidies payable under earlier Acts while the new Act provided a fresh layer of subsidies. Also in line with past practice was leaving the fixing of rents to local authorities, subject to the legal duty (in words unchanged since 1935) to make "reasonable charges". The only novelties here were a power for the central government to set a maximum limit to increases and the prohibition of transfers from the housing revenue account to the general rate fund, though a balance could be carried forward provided it was "no larger than is reasonable having regard to all the circumstances". This was more restrictive than the pre-1972 legislation (in substance unchanged since 1935, though consolidated in 1936 and 1958) which allowed repayment to the rate fund of contributions made during the previous five years. Also in line with pre-1972 practice, increases in expenditure on repair and maintenance and supervision and management would no longer attract subsidy (some special transition provisions and high cost areas apart); subsidies became capital expenditure subsidies once more, apart from the "supplementary financing element" of subsidy, which met 33% of any increases above 1974/75 levels in loan charges on pre-1975/76 debt.

The main subsidy was the 'new capital cost element', a 66% subsidy on the loan charges on debt incurred as a result of 'reckonable' capital expenditure in 1975/76 and after. Such a subsidy provided support for new investment that was proportional to capital costs and to pool rates in the same way as rising cost subsidy under the 1972 Act; like the 1972 subsidy, and in contrast to that

363

under the 1967 Act, it provided subsidy on the loan charges on land and on dwellings under construction. 66% of all loan charges was, in general, more advantageous to local authorities than the rising costs subsidy of 75% less (effectively) the excess of rent income over the cost of repair and maintenance and supervision and management generated by new houses built or houses acquired. The government of the day favoured a large programme of house building by local authorities, together with improvement of their existing stock and (where appropriate) purchase of houses from private owners. The 'new capital cost element' was intended to fund this capital expenditure programme in conditions of rapid inflation and high though variable interest rates. On debt incurred in 1975/76 and later, 66% of the cost of any increase in loan charges due to higher 'pool' rates would be met by the Exchequer, and on pre-1975/76 debt 33%. The total proportion met by the Exchequer would thus be a weighted average of 66% and 33%, and would move towards 66% as debt generated by capital expenditure raised the amount of post 1975/76 debt, and debt repayment slowly diminished the amount of 'old' debt. The protection would gradually come to exceed that given by the rising cost subsidy under the 1972 Act. Earlier subsidies had given no cover at all against increases in loan charges caused by increases in pool rates being applied to existing housing revenue account debt.

The outline of the 1975 Act subsidies may be completed by describing briefly the 'high cost' and 'special' elements. The 'high cost element' was payable, as its name suggests, to authorities with high average costs per dwelling. It had some affinities with the operational deficit subsidy under the 1972 Act, not least in being primarily a London subsidy. The 'special element' was intended to assist authorities to manage in 1975/76 with only moderate rent increases, and provided a 50% subsidy on the deficit on a notional housing revenue account (notional because the entries for supervision and management and repair and maintenance were to be the previous year's expenditure plus a prescribed percentage increase) that would remain after all other subsidies had been credited and rents credited at the previous year's level plus £23 per dwelling. This subsidy would be consolidated into the basic element in subsequent years, and would be payable whether or not the £23

(45p a week) rent increase was actually charged. A
somewhat different 'special element' was provided
for 1976/77 under the Remuneraton, Charges, and
Grants Act 1975 (the 1975 prices and incomes policy
legislation), which was only paid to authoities
that raised their rents by at least the £31 a year
(60p a week) stipulated, and was not consolidated.
The 'special element' subsidies were basically
ad hoc subsidies to hold down rent increases for
reasons of prices and incomes policy. The same
motive probably lay behind the powers taken by
central government (s.11) to restrict increases in
local authority rents. In the event this power,
which would set the same maximum increase for all
authorities, was never used. Comment is called for
on how small was 45p a week as a 'standard'
increase in 1975. It was about 12% of average un-
rebated rents in payment; and (owing to the 1974
rent freeze) would be the first increase since
April or October 1973. During the two or one-and-
a-half years between then and April 1975, the
general price level had risen by 44 or 37% and
average earnings by 47 or 38%. The government's
policy at this time clearly gave much more weight
to holding down rents as a contribution to attempt-
ing to secure wage restraint than it did to
restraining the growth of expenditue on subsidies.
The average increase in rents in 1975, counting in
October increases, was 59p a week (15%), but there
were very wide variations. At one extreme were
four London boroughs (Islington, Lambeth, Lewisham
and Tower Hamlets) and Manchester, which did not
put up their rents at all during 1975, even though
rents had last been increased in October 1973. In
contrast 107 authorities put on two increases,
including Leeds which increased rents by 90p a week
in two stages and Newcastle by 95p a week in two
stages. Liverpool and Coventry each raised rent by
£1 a week in one stage. The variation between rent
increases was not due just to party politics, but
there is little doubt that the zero and very low
increases were the result of the political conflicts over the 1972 Act being followed through
when councils again were responsible for setting
rents.

After 1975, moreover, un-rebated rents rose
more slowly than the general price level, taking
one year with another. Such a fall in rents in
real terms contrasted sharply with the rapid
increase in the 1950s and 1960s, to say nothing of

those intended under the Housing Finance Act, and so is worth looking at in a little more detail. Table VII.10 shows average rents in comparison with average prices and earnings.

Table VII.10 - Average Local Authority Rents (Un-rebated) Compared with the General Price Level and with Earnings

(April of each year)

	1975	1976	1977	1978	1979	1975-79 Total
Average rent (actual)(£)	4.16	4.77	5.52	5.85	6.40	+2.24
Average rent in real terms (a)	4.16	4.12	4.06	3.99	3.95	-0.21
Change in rents in real terms (%)	....	-1.0	-1.5	-1.7	-1.0	-5.0
Increase in rents in money terms	....	+14.7	+15.7	+6.0	+9.4	+53.8

Note: (a) Re-valued by the index of retail prices.

Such a fall in rents in real terms could be the consequence of any or all of: a fall in real terms in costs per dwelling falling on housing revenue accounts; higher subsidies under the 1975 Act; or local authorities' own decisions, put into effect through higher rate fund contributions. What happened is shown in Table VII.11

Although in money terms costs per dwelling continued to rise very fast, in real terms the rise slowed down, and between 1974/75 and 1977/78 costs actually fell in real terms. Loan charges were the main reason: interest rates fluctuated, but until 1978 and 1979 there was nothing resembling the steep increases in 1973; and in 1977 interest rates fell fast. Real loan charges per dwelling fell by 15% between 1974/75 and 1977/78, and the increase in 1978/79 reversed only one-fifth of this fall. Expenditure per dwelling on supervision and management and repair and maintenance continued to rise in real terms after 1975/76 even though such expenditure no longer attracted subsidy, but the rate of increase (which averaged just over 3% a

Table VII.11 - Summary of Housing Revenue Accounts 1974/75 to 1978/79: England and Wales

	1974/75	1975/76	1976/77	1977/78	1978/79
Expenditure (£ million)					
Supervision and management - general	107	144	168	186	213
Supervision and management - special	81	110	135	161	191
Repair and maintenance	264	340	395	479	590
Loan charges	1,104	1,317	1,580	1,664	1,942
Other expenditure	65	66	83	97	105
Total	1,621	1,977	2,361	2,587	3,041
Income					
Rents of dwellings (un-rebated)	919	1,079	1,267	1,467	1,600
Interest on houses sold	30	35	38	42	50
Rents of non-domestic property and miscellaneous income	51	65	88	104	129
Exchequer subsidy (excluding rebates)	485	633	838	894	1,054
Rate fund contributions (excluding rebates)	136	175	154	154	219
Total subsidies including rebates	814·	1,031	1,277	1,384	1,628
Per Dwelling (£)					
Supervision and management - general	22.8	29.9	34.0	36.8	41.2
Supervision and management - special	17.3	22.9	27.3	31.9	36.9
Repair and maintenance	56.3	70.7	80.0	94.8	114.1
Loan charges	235.5	273.9	319.9	329.3	375.6
Total	345.9	411.1	478.0	512.0	588.1
Rents of dwellings (un-rebated)	196.1	224.4	256.5	289.7	309.4
Exchequer subsidy (excluding rebates)	103.5	131.6	169.7	176.9	203.8
Rate fund contribution (excluding rebates)	29.0	36.4	31.2	30.5	42.4
All subsidies including rebates	173.7	214.4	258.6	273.9	314.8
Total of dwellings at mid-year ('000)	4,687	4,809	4,939	5,053	5,171
Price level (GDP deflator)	100.0	79.8	70.6	62.1	56.2
Rents (un-rebated) as percent of net HRA costs	59.7	57.5	56.7	60.0	55.9

year between 1975/76 and 1978/79) was no more in percentage terms than it had been in the later 1960s, if anything less. But the steep increases in 1972/73, 1973/74 and 1974/75 proved permanent, whether they had been 'real' or only accounting charges, so that the more modest rates of increase in percentage terms after 1975/76 were therefore compounded onto a higher base. Average costs per dwelling in total fell by 5% in real terms between 1974/75 and 1975/76, and rose by under 1% between 1975/76 and 1978/79. The fall in rents in real terms after 1975 was therefore not the consequence of an outright fall in costs in real terms, though of course costs rose much less than they had previously done.

Exchequer subsidies, however, rose substantially more in real terms than did costs. At 1975/76 prices the increase between 1975/76 and 1978/79 was about £12 per dwelling (just under 10%) in real terms, compared with an increase of about £3 in costs per dwelling. Generally speaking, therefore, the explanation of why un-rebated rents fell in real terms between 1975/76 and 1978/79 lay in the subsidies provided by the 1975 Act. Rate fund contributions fell even in money terms between 1975/76 and 1977/78; the increase in 1978/79 can be explained mainly by the rise in interest rates during the year, after decision on rents had been taken. Rate fund contributions (other than for rent rebates) were heavily concentrated in London; many authorities in the provinces found that the combination of falling costs in real terms per dwelling and the subsidies provided under the 1975 Act enabled them both to reduce rate fund contributions and to raise rents by less than the increase in the general price level.

One reason why average costs per dwelling rose so little in real terms after 1975/76 was the fall in capital expenditure which held down the increase in loan charges. Although the 1975 subsidy system had been designed to support large programmes of capital expenditure, not long afterwards local authorities' capital expenditure on housing began to fall as Table VII.12 shows.

Central government controls over the number of dwellings approved for tenders were reintroduced in 1976 in the course of the cuts in public expenditure introduced when drawings were made from the International Monetary Fund in response to the foreign exchange crisis. The controls checked the

Table VII.12 - Capital Expenditure on Housing by Local
                Authorities in England

(£ million at constant (1980 Survey) prices)

	1975/76	1976/77	1977/78	1978/79
Land	264	194	108	75
New dwellings	1,850	1,944	1,734	1,359
Acquisition of dwellings	291	180	103	90
Improvement investment (*)	509	497	504	600
Other	148	126	102	81
Total	3,062	2,941	2,551	2,205

Note: (*) Improvement of dwelling owned by local
         authorities.

Source: Cmnd. 8175 (1981) Table 2.7.

rise in expenditure and probably contributed to the
fall in expenditure on new building in 1977/78, but
they can hardly have explained the continuing fall.
What, then, did cause the fall in new building by
local authorities, which was steeper than the fall
from 1968 to 1972, and still more so than the fall
from 1955 to 1960? Financial pressure was
suggested, in particular the size of burden falling
on the rate fund even after bringing new capital
costs element to account. Certainly 66% of loan
charges at the pool rate did not finance all of the
cost not recovered from rents, but a fair estimate
of the proportion of loan charges on new building
not recovered from subsidies and rents is about 10-
15%, which was not large, especially in view of the
fact that rate fund contributions were relevant for
rate support grant. Expenditure on improving local
authorities' own dwellings, which attracted subsidy
in the same way as new building, rose sharply in
1978/79, even though it usually produced much less
extra rent income (in proportion to expenditure)
than did new house building. The increase in
expenditure on improvement tells with considerable
weight against the reduction in house building
being due to any significant extent to local
authorities being unable to carry the residual cost
on their rate funds or pass it on in increased
rents paid by other tenants.

Probably more important than any financial
pressure after 1976 to restrain capital expenditure
on local authority housing was the emergence on a
large scale of 'difficult to let' housing as a
problem for local authorities' housing management.
This problem was both novel and disturbing. From
the end of the war to the late 1960s most local
authorities had experienced excess demand for
virtually all their housing everywhere. At the end
of the 1960s, as noted earlier in this chapter, the
situation began to change and the pressure began to
fall. The reversion to increasing demand for
tenancies that followed the surge in house prices
and the leap of interest rates proved to be only
temporary and although the new government attempted
in 1974 and 1975 to boost local authority house
building the problem of hard to let houses and
flats re-appeared, and on a much larger scale than
at the beginning of the 1970s. Dwellings on the
least popular estates became hard to let to tenants
who were in a position to wait. That some estates
were less popular than others was nothing new, but
real difficulty in letting houses and flats was
much more novel. The difficulties were much
increased by complex allocation procedures that had
their origin in equity in managing the queue: when
an applicant had been selected for an offer of a
dwelling and he refused, selecting a new applicant
to whom to offer if had to start again. At the
very end of the period some authorities had
introduced 'first come first served' arrangements
for letting the least popular dwellings, though not
without some misgivings, for the notion that local
authority tenancies were for those who 'need' them
was deep rooted. One conclusion that could be
drawn from this state of affairs was that the stock
of dwellings was large enough to meet needs. Here
almost certainly was one of the main reasons for
the fall in the number of new dwellings built.
Another without doubt was the way in which the
unsatisfactory aspects of some of the houses and
flats built in the 1950s, 1960s, and early 1970s
diminished the public reputation of local authority
housing. In consequence there was a fall in the
demand to rent from households with any scope for
choice in the matter; and a diminished disposition
on the part of many local authorities to spend as
much as before in adding still further to the
stock, particularly to replace older privately
owned housing. As noted in Chapter IV slum

clearance activity was falling fast. "Pensioning off the bulldozer" meant much less new building to rehouse the people whose former houses and flats had been bulldozed.

British Council Housing and its Financing:
An Overview

If one looks at the history of local authority housing subsidies as recounted in this chapter it is possible to discern a linking thread in adaption to live with higher and higher interest rates and then successively higher rates of inflation. The financial framework was laid down in conditions of fairly stable prices and interest rates of 3% to 4%, and depended on fixed-interest loans in contrast with equity financing. With this framework went rents based on costs as abated by subsidies (the Housing Finance Act 1972 alone excepted). 'Costs' meant historically incurred costs, notably loan charges on debt actually incurred in providing the houses. Because houses have such long useful lives, the scope of divergence between historic costs and current values is greater than for any other asset, and this difference was from the mid-1950s onwards the other key feature of British council house finance.

How so much of the British housing stock came to be governed by such a financial system is itself a question of interest, where 'revisionist' arguments about the origins of council housing show that the answer should not be taken for granted. On the evidence, one can dismiss fairly summarily the contention that repeal of rent restriction in the early 1920s would have led private landlords to do unsubsidized what the boroughs, urban districts and rural districts did with subsidy. The history of rent restriction in the inter-war years and the consequences of the policy pursued are discussed in some detail in the next chapter, and there is nothing there to suggest a return to the pre-1914 regime would have led to better results than it had produced before 1914. If treating the private landlord as expendable does explain why council housing came to bulk so large, it must do so either through the reasons why subsidized building for letting was in the form of publicly owned houses for rent, and not subsidized private ownership; or why subsidizing building was preferred to subsidies to households.

The second aspect has been alluded to several times already, with mention of attitudes to supplementation of wages, means-testing, and the mechanism for 'negative income taxes' and the like not existing until after World War II. Here it is important to note that in times of shortage when the policy is to encourage house building, as was so in the 1920s, the 1940s, and much of the 1950s and 1960s, building subsidies tend to appear more attractive and effective than do income supplements, whether housing-related or not. Building subsidies have the advantage of 'not much building, not much subsidy', so if the money has been spent the houses have been built. Payments to households to increase their ability to afford housing are more problematical in their effect on the number of houses built, and never more so than in circumstances of post-war shortages. It is highly unlikely that mere chance explains why income-related payments to households in preference to building subsidies became more prominent in many countries in Europe in the 1970s when shortages were considered to be a much smaller part of the problem than they had been previously.

There is therefore nothing surprising about the subsidies for rented housing being building subsidies. But building subsidies in no way imply that a public authority has to own the subsidized houses: many countries make extensive use of subsidies to private and semi-private landlords, often with restrictive conditions about the rents that may be charged and sometimes about the incomes of tenants. Britain, indeed, provided subsidies to private landlords in the inter-war years: the Housing (Additional Powers) Act of 1919 provided a capital grant, and the Housing Act 1923 an annual payment or an equivalent capital payment. Neither were confined to houses for letting, and could be taken for building for sale for owner-occupation. The 1923 Act subsidy was terminated by the Conservative government in 1928 (to take effect in 1929), but the Conservatives in 1945 envisaged subsidy for private owners as well as for local authorities. Given the result of the 1945 general election, of course, subsidized privately owned rented housing in Britain is only a historical 'might-have-been'.

In financial terms, subsidized building for letting by private owners would have worked very differently from subsidized local authority housing after the mid-1950s. Pooling of costs of houses built at different dates and at different price levels can only work where the houses belong to an agency that has built up a sizeable housing stock over the years. This cannot be counted on for private landlords, and hence cost-based but subsidized rents have to be determined separately for individual schemes, which in inflationary times leads very quickly to very different rents for substantially similar properties. This has been a source of very considerable difficulty for the European countries that have subsidized private owners, and the different rates of interest at which loans were taken aggravated the problem. To discuss policy in other countries would be out of place in a history of policy in Britain; but it is worth noting that pooling of costs and rents is unique to Britain (and extremely difficult to explain to someone accustomed to scheme-by-scheme financing as in the European countries). That it exists in Britain, and from the mid-1950s onwards was the basis of the financial systems for subsidized rented housing, was the consequence of the subsidized rented housing being owned by a sufficiently small number of authorities.

The way in which pooling worked depended on the rate of inflation, and on interest rates. High nominal interest rates in a regime of fixed interest financing, with interest paid as it fell due and not capitalized, produced a "front-loading" or "front-end loading" of interest charges in real terms. How this worked is illustrated in Table VII.13, which shows the proportion of loan charges in real terms paid off in the early years of a 60 year term when the real interest rate is (approximately) 3% but with different rates of inflation and nominal interest rates.

Even if the rate of inflation is fairly slow the "front-loading" effect is by no means insignificant; and with a 7% nominal interest rate and 4% inflation (broadly speaking the average for the 1960s) the proportion of real loan charges that fall to be met in the first five years is nearly $2\frac{1}{2}$ times as great as it would be if the real interest rate and the nominal rate were the same and the price level stable. But the double figure nominal interest rates experienced from 1973 onwards produced a truly massive heaping up of the real cost of loan charges in the early years. The "front-loading" of loan charges produced a gap between costs and rents that was very large in the

Table VII.13 - Proportion of Total Loan Charges Real Terms
                in Early Years when Real Interst Rates is 3%

(percent)

Infla- tion Rate	Nominal Interest Rate	First 5 years	First 10 years	First 15 years	Whole 60 Year Life
0	3	8.3	16.7	25.0	100.0
2	5	13.5	25.8	36.9	100.0
4	7	19.7	35.8	49.1	100.0
6	9	26.1	45.6	60.1	100.0
8	11	32.1	54.1	69.1	100.0
10	13	38.1	61.6	76.3	100.0

early years, but diminishing rapidly as loan
charges fell in real terms as inflation eroded them
or (according to the way one looks at it)
increasing income in money terms raised the rents
that tenants could reasonably be expected to pay.
Instead of a gap between costs and rents that was
broadly constant from year to year, the gap was
wedge-shaped. How to close this gap was in reality
the central problem to which the successive subsidy
regimes were addressed.

The policy of the mid-1960s was to rely on
cross-subsidy from older dwellings built when costs
were lower. This was in effect a policy of using
the capital appreciation on the older stock to
offset the front-loading of costs in more recently
built houses. In the first decade after the war
the benefit from the capital appreciation (or
alternatively of the fall in the real value of the
money originally borrowed to finance the building
of the houses) had gone for the most part to the
tenants. The mid-1950's policy was to withdraw it
from them and use it to finance new building. The
amount of financing that could be mobilized from
cross-subsidy, of course, depended on the size of
the rent increases that were tolerable and the size
of the older stock, whereas the amount of financing
needed depended on the level of interest rates (and
hence the amount of front-loading generated by any
given volume of capital expenditure) and the amount
of new building. That the relationship between the
size of the older stock and the amount of new
building would vary between different authorities
was recognized, but whether it could be lived with

was a matter of quantities. With the more modest capital programmes of the later 1950s and interest rates that were still fairly moderate by later standards the stresses and strains were not too severe. But that changed in the 1960s when building programmes, building costs, and interest rates all increased. Unaided cross-subsidy could no longer cope, and subsidies on new building had to be brought back. The 1967 subsidy system was designed for a world of rising capital costs and interest rates, with the value of x in £x a year for y years being altered yearly by formula instead of requiring new primary legislation to amend it. The 1967 subsidies, although large by previous standards, did not remove the need for cross-subsidy. Notwithstanding the heavy expenditure on subsidies there were strong pressures on rents and rate fund contributions in authorities that were building on a large scale.

This, in the present author's view, was the underlying reason why local authority housing finance became the centre of increasing acrimony in the later 1960s. Cross-subsidy from older dwellings as the way to cope with front-loading was ceasing to work adequately, because with much heavier front-loading and a large building programme the costs falling on existing tenants gave rise to increasing complaint and the anomalies between authorities were increasingly serious.

What then was to be done? One route was that of the Housing Finance Act 1972, which severed the connection between rents and costs falling on housing revenue accounts. That the distribution between authorities of the stock of older housing and hence the scope for cross-subsidy should match the distribution of need for new building and hence capital expenditure could come about only by chance, and there were plenty of instances where they did not match at all well. In such situations separating rents from the state of the housing revenue account would remove troublesome anomalies and inequities. But there was a major disadvantage: separating rents from the state of the housing revenue account meant that rents were no longer set as a cost-determined charge for a service, but appeared as a charge determined on policy grounds. In a time of inflation that was serious: that increases in any price do no more than cover increases in costs is a powerful reason for accepting the price increase, however grudg-

ingly. That indeed has always been the basic
principle of price control. When the link with
costs had gone, rent levels became the more readily
the subject of party political conflict, with
consequences that would be hard to present as
desirable. Costs falling on an account that was in
terms of historic costs could be criticized as an
unsatisfactory basis for setting rents, but in the
early 1970s inflation accounting was not sufficiently well developed to have anything practical
to contribute to housing finance.

A method of resolving the "front-loading"
problem that had its advocates in the 1970s was to
charge interest at an appropriate 'real' rate, 3%
say, and capitalize or 'roll up' the rest. The
result would be to spread the cost of loan charges
evenly (or nearly so) in real terms over the life
of the house. If that could be done the advantages
would be great: rents could be linked to costs
without cross-subsidy, and without the need for
tapering down the subsidy as tenants' incomes rose;
capitalizing excess interest would not only 'taper
out' the subsidy automatically, but would later on
retrieve the subsidy when tenants' ability to pay
allowed this to be done. But there were disadvantages that at the time appeared insuperable. One
was that the pervasive instability in the relationships between rates of interest and inflation could
cause trouble and might in some circumstances leave
part of the debt not amortized at the end of the
useful life over which amortization was originally
calculated. Another was that no way could be found
of applying the arrangement to debt already in
existence. A third was that the effect on the
public sector borrowing requirement, which by the
mid-1970s had become the centre-piece of public
finance, of capitalizing interest was just the same
as outright subsidy up to the point when some of
the capitalized interest began to be repaid. So in
the short-term there was no fiscal advantage
compared with subsidy. The Housing Policy Review
of 1975-77 concluded against capitalizing interest
(97), and instead recommended a deficit subsidy
which would require an annual determination of the
increase in the sum to be found locally from rent
and rates. High but stable interest rates and
rates of inflation could be coped with by subsidy
paid according to a formula, or even variable rates
of inflation and rates of interest so long as the
difference between the rate of interest and the

inflation rate was constant or nearly so. But high
and variable rates of inflation in conjunction with
high but unstable interest rates could not be coped
with by any formula. The recommendation of an
annual determination was embodied in the Housing
Bill introduced just before the dissolution of
Parliament in 1979, and was included in the Housing
Act 1980.

Towards the end of the 1970s, and too late to
have any real impact on the Housing Policy Review,
a very different line of thought about housing
finance began to gain ground, an application to
rented housing of ideas that were gaining ground in
the world of commercial accounting about valuing
assets in balance sheets at replacement cost. The
subject is far too complex, and appeared on the
scene too close to the end of the period studied,
to warrant extended dicussion here, but was implied
as setting un-rebated rents by reference to a
target rate of return on the current value of an
authority's stock of dwellings plus costs of supervision and management and repair and maintenance.
Like the 1972 system, it would remove the anomalies
arising from differences in historic costs caused
by differences in the age structure of the stock of
dwellings. Housing is indeed the extreme example of
what inflation can do to conventional historic cost
accounting. But even at the end of the period
studied, setting rents by reference to a rate of
return on the market value of the stock was still
an idea for discussion (98), not a worked-out
scheme, and so not appropriate for further discussion here.

If costs as calculated according to standard
accounting principles (historic costs) could not
give an appropriate guide to what level of rents
would be reasonable, there was no obvious alternative that took proper account of tenants' ability
to pay and of the policy aim of 'a decent home for
every family at a price within their means' (99).
The latter would frequently imply a better house
for poorer households than they would get if they
had to pay a fully 'economic' price or rent. The
contrast between "subsidizing buildings" and
"subsidizing people" was a facile contrast, for the
purpose of subsidizing houses was to subsidize
people in the sense of providing them with better
houses than they would otherwise get. As termino-
logy, the distinction between income-related and
non-income-related subsidies is much more helpful.

purpose of subsidizing houses was to subsidize
people in the sense of providing them with better
houses than they would otherwise get. As termino-
logy, the distinction between income-related and
non-income-related subsidies is much more helpful.
The 1970s saw a substantial development of income-
related subsidy, the part of the 1972 Act that the
Labour government retained without substantial
change. This development, though, coincided with
non-income-related subsidies that responded to an
open-ended way by happenstance (1972) or by design
(1975) to a cost explosion. There is here the main
explanation of why a total expenditure on subsidies
was nearly eight times as great in 1978/79 as in
1970/71 (three times higher in real terms, notwithstanding the very rapid inflation). A subsidiary
explanation was the holding down of rents from 1974
onwards for reasons of prices and incomes policy.

Notes and References

(1) B.R. Mitchell and Phyllis Deane, Abstract of British Historical Statistics, Cambridge University Press, Cambridge, 1962, Chapter XIV, Tables 4 and 4a.

(2) M. Swenarton, Homes for Heroes, Heinemann, London, 1981, pp.46-47.

(3) The Standing Orders of the House of Commons have since the 18th century provided that the House will entertain a motion to impose a charge (i.e. levy taxation or incur expenditure) only with the commendation of the monarch, i.e. with the support of the government. As a consequence taxation cannot be increased or expenditure voted without the government's approval.

(4) Swenarton, Homes for Heroes, pp.51-62.

(5) Report, Cd. 8663, 1917.

(6) Quoted by P.B. Johnson, Land Fit for Heroes, University of Chicago Press, Chicago, 1968, pp.62-64.

(7) Housing in England and Wales, Memorandum by the Housing Advisory Panel of the Ministry of Reconstruction. PP 1918, p.4.

(8) K. and J. Morgan, Portrait of a Progressive, The Political Career of Christopher, Viscount Addison, Oxford University Press, Oxford, 1980.

(9) Building Construction: Report of a Committee appointed to consider questions of building construction in connection with the provision of dwellings for the working classes, Cd. 9191 (1918); XIV.

(10) Swenarton, Homes for Heroes, pp.92-108.

(11) See Swenarton, Homes for Heroes, Chapter 7 for full discussion.

(12) P. Wilding, Government and Housing (unpublished Manchester University D.Phil thesis, 1970), citing Cabinet minutes and the papers of the Ministry of Health and its predecessors.

(13) S.K. Merrett, State Housing in Britain, Routledge and Kegan Paul, London, 1979.

(14) Housing, Town Planning, etc. Bill: Estimate of Probable Expenditure, Cmd. 125 (1919).

(15) First Interim Report, VII, Cd. 9182, (1918).

(16) Merrett, State Housing, Chapter 2.

(17) Swenarton, Homes for Heroes, pp.130-135.

(18)   Quoted by Johnson, Land Fit for Heroes,
        pp.345-346.
(19)   M. Bowley, Housing and the State, Allen and
        Unwin, London, 1945, p.271, tabulated from
        the Ministry of Health's annual reports.
(20)   The Local Taxation Returns for 1924/25 (the
        first to distinguish expenditure on housing
        provided under the 1919 Act from other local
        authority expenditure on housing) showed
        total outstanding debt incurred on housing
        under the 1919 Act as £180.8 million, i.e.
        £1,060 per dwelling averaged over 170,000
        dwellings.
(21)   Morgan and Morgan, Portrait of a Progres-
        sive, p.98.
(22)   Departmental Committee on the High Cost of
        Building Working Class Dwellings, Report,
        Cmd. 1447 (1921), p.55.
(23)   See J.R. Jarmain, Housing Subsidies and
        Rents, Stevens, London, 1948, pp.38-39 for
        full details.
(24)   Jarmain, Housing Subsidies and Rents,
        pp.54-62.
(25)   Jarmain, Housing Subsidies and Rents, p.68.
        The total reductions allowed were equivalent
        to £461,000 a year.
(26)   Quoted by Swenarton, Homes for Heroes, p.133;
        see also Morgan and Morgan, Portrait of a
        Progressive, p.129.
(27)   House of Commons Debates 4th series,
        Vol. 143, col. 400.
(28)   Cabinet on 22 June 1921, cited in Wilding,
        Government and Housing at pp.187-188.
(29)   In Daily News 28 March 1923, Citation from
        M. Kinear, The Fall of Lloyd George,
        Macmillan, London, 1973, p.11.
(30)   Morgan and Morgan, Portrait of a Progres-
        sive, p.141.
(31)   Merrett, State of Housing, p.41.
(32)   Morgan and Morgan, Portrait of a Progres-
        sive, p.140.
(33)   M.J. Daunton, Councillors and Tenants, Local
        Authority Housing in English Cities, 1919-39,
        Leicester University Press, Leicester, 1984,
        pp.6-15.
(34)   Jarmain, Housing Subsidies and Rents,
        pp.80-86.
(35)   Bowley, Housing and the State,
        Appendix Table 6.

(36) Report on the Present Position in the Building Industry ... Prepared by the National Building Committee Cmd. 2104 (1924)

(37) K. Middlemass and J. Barnes, Baldwin, Weidenfeld and Nicholson, London, 1969, p.287.

(38) Housing Acts (Revision of Contributions) Order, 1928; Housing (Revision of Contributions) Act, 1929.

(39) Wilding, Government and Housing, p.317.

(40) Ministry of Health Circular 1238 (1932); see also Ministry of Health, Annual Report 1931/32, Cmd. 4113 (1932) p.98.

(41) Ministry of Health, Local Taxation Returns (annual).

(42) Ministry of Health, Annual Report 1938/39, Cmd. 6089 (1934) Appendix XVIII.

(43) Wilding, Government and Housing, p.277.

(44) Jarmain, Housing Subsidies and Rents, pp.122-23.

(45) Wilding, Government and Housing, Chapter XII.

(46) Particulars of Slum Clearance Programmes Furnished by Local Authorities, Cmd. 4555 (1933).

(47) Bowley, Housing and the State, Table XII, p.152, and Appendix 2.

(48) Jarmain, Housing Subsidies and Rents, p.192.

(49) Figures from the returns of rents collected by the Ministry of Health and published in Rents of Houses and Flats Owned by Local Authorities, Cmd. 5537 (1937). Most of the difference from the £35.2 a year (13s 6d a week) shown for London in Table VII.1 is due to the number of dwellings there being too low.

(50) Local Government Financial Statistics for 1934/35 shows rates paid on dwellings in "State assisted housing schemes" in 1934/35 at £4,757,000. The number of dwellings at mid-year in 1934/35 is estimated (by working backwards from the June 1936 total) at 780,000, which gives an average of £6.1 a year. The rise in rate poundages between 1934/35 and 1936/37 would raise the figure to £6.5 a week.

(51) See page 33 above.

(52) Under the Housing Act 1935 authorities were permitted but not obliged to have housing repairs accounts. The principle was that regular contributions to such accounts would

even out the effects on the housing revenue account, and hence on rents and the rate fund, of 'lumpy' repair work. During the war substantial balances were built up in housing repairs accounts as so little repair work would be done.

(53) The manifesto texts can be conveniently consulted in F.W.S. Craig, British General Election Manifestos 1918-1966, Political Reference Publications, Chichester, 1970.

(54) M. Foot, Aneurin Bevan 1945-60, (Paladin Edn.), 1965, p.71.

(55) See pages 119 and 141 above.

(56) Ministry of Health, Temporary Housing, 1944.

(57) K.O. Morgan, Labour in Power, Clarendon Press, Oxford, 1984, p.164.

(58) In the White Policy Housing: The Next Step (Cmd. 8996) (1953) owner-occupation was referred to as: ".... of all forms of ownership .... one of the most satisfying in the individual and the most beneficial to the nation".

(59) The starting point was the published figures of 18s 9d in April 1958 and 19s 0d in October 1958, giving an average for 1958/59 of 18s 10d. This was projected back pro-rata to "rents, etc." in housing revenue accounts as shown in Local Government Financial Statistics divided by the estimated number of dwellings.

(60) See Committee on the Working of the Monetary System, Report Cmd. 827 (1959) Chapters V and VI for the way in which the process was considered to work.

(61) Cmnd. 827, (1959) paragraphs 597 and 598.

(62) Annual Abstract of Statistics 1963, Table 327. Separate figures for England and Wales were not published.

(63) Annual Abstract of Statistics 1969, Table 350. This figure refers to the United Kingdom, but Northern Irish local authority debt was too small in relation to the UK total to make the 1964 and 1968 UK figures materially non-comparable with the GB figures.

(64) Statement by the Minister of Housing and Local Government (Sandys) in House of Commons 27 October 1955. Quoted by Ministry of Housing and Local Government Report for 1955, Cmd. 9876 (1956) pp.4-5.

(65) Institute of Municipal Treasurers and Accoun-

tants, Housing Statistics 1957/58.

(66) P.A. Stone, Urban Development in Britain, Standards Costs and Resources 1964-2004, Cambridge University Press, Cambridge, 1970.

(67) Report of the Ministry of Housing and Local Government, 1961, Cmnd. 1725 (1962) pp.11-12.

(68) House of Commons, Fourth report from the estimates Commitee Session 1968/69 Volume II, Memorandum by Ministry of Housing and Local Government, Annex B.

(69) Housing, Cmnd. 2050 (1963) paragraph 76.

(70) Housing Policy Technical Volume, Chapter VIII, Appendix A, paragraph 9.

(71) National Board for Prices and Incomes, Report No. 62 Increases in Rents of Local Authority Housing, Cmnd. 3604 (1968), pp.47 and 53.

(72) C.H. Feinstein, National Income Expenditure and Output of the United Kingdom 1855-1965, Cambridge University Press, Cambridge, 1972, Table 65. (The index calculated by the London and Cambridge Economic Service was used by Feinstein to span the war years when the official cost of living index was stabilized by subsidies.

(73) Natiional Board for Prices and Incomes, Report No. 62 (1968) (Cmnd. 3604), Appendix C, Table 4.

(74) Housing Statistics 1970/71, Part 2, p.2.

(75) National Board for Prices and Incomes, Report No. 62, Increases in Rent of Local Authority Housing, Cmnd. 3604 (1968) para. 33.

(76) Prices and Incomes Standstill, Cmnd. 3073, 1966.

(77) Report No. 62, Increases in Rents of Local Authority Housing, Cmnd. 3604, (1968).

(78) Ministry of Housing and Local Government Circular 1/70.

(79) Fourth Report from the Estimates Committee Session 1968-69, HC 473, October 1969.

(80) Report of the Ministry of Housing and Local Government 1969 and 1970, p.10.

(81) Report of the Ministry of Housing and Local Government 1969 and 1970, Cmnd. 4753, (1971) p.4.

(82) Report of the Ministry of Housing and Local Government 1969 and 1970, Cmnd. 4753 (1971), p.4.

(83) R. Harris and B. Sewill, British Economic Policy 1970-74, Institute of Economic Affairs, London, 1975, p.30.

(84) See page 425 below.
(85) Cmnd. 4728 (1971), paragraph 6 (iv).
(86) For an economist's favourable comment on this aspect of the 1972 Act, see D. Maclennan, Housing Economics, Longmans, London, 1982, pp.250-251.
(87) Harris and Sewill, British Economic Policy.
(88) Housing Statistics No. 22, Table XII.
(89) National Board for Prices and Incomes Report No. 62, Cmnd 3604 (1968), paragraph 64.
(90) Housing Policy Technical Volume, Chapter 4, paragraph 27.
(91) The difference from the 15% increase in real terms in the year to May 1973 (page 354 above) is explained by the rent increases in the summer and autumn of 1972, which made the average rent in 1972/73 higher than the average in April and May 1972.
(92) See reference (90).
(93) Housing and Construction 1971-1981 Table 126.
(94) IMTA, Housing Statistics 1970/71 Part 2, p.2.
(95) Housing and Construction Statistics 1971-1981 Table 125.
(96) The representative new borrowing rates for 1972/73, 1973/74 and 1974/75 were taken to be 8%, 10% and 13%, which were the average rates paid (approximately) on new borrowing one year previously. The average costs of dwellings completed were taken as £4,500, £5,140, and £6,130, the average cost of dwellings for which tenders were accepted in 1970, 1971 and 1972, with allowance for a six-month lag between approval and start and eighteen months between start and completion. Since the subsidy was equal to loan charges on these costs at the new borrowing rates less 4%, the subsidies are put at £202 per dwelling completed in 1972/73, £318 in 1973/74, and £555 in 1974/75. The number of new dwellings completed for local authorities in England and Wales were 76,000, 76,000 and 94,000 respectively. The three annual layers of subsidy would have totalled £92 million on this reckoning. Exchequer contributions for improvement of local authority dwellings under the Housing Acts 1969 and 1971 increased by £25 million between 1971/72 and 1974/75, £5 million might be added, notionally, for increases in the supplementary subsidy for flats, making £122 million to be added to the

1971/72 total of £187 million, to make £309 million (hypothetically) in 1974/75.

(97)   Housing Policy Technical Volume, Chapter 8, Appendix B; and Housing Policy Green Paper (Cmnd. 6851, 1977, paragraphs 9.44 and 9.46).

(98)   See, for example, A. Grey, N.P. Hepworth, and J. Odling-Smee, Housing Rents, Costs, and Subsidies: A Discussion Document, Chartered Institute of Public Finance and Accountancy, London, 1981.

(99)   Fair Deal for Housing, Cmnd. 4728 (1971) paragraph repeated almost word for word in Housing Policy (Cmnd. 6851, 1977) paragraph

CHAPTER VIII

PRIVATELY OWNED RENTED HOUSING

The history of public policy towards housing rented from the private sector is primarily the history of rent restriction and its consequences. The term 'rent restriction' may strike the reader in the 1980s as old fashioned; but it is used here in preference to 'rent control' (the generally used word in international comparisons) because in the 1960s and 1970s 'rent control' had a technical meaning in Britain, contrasted with 'rent regulation' (1). An important point to be made at the outset is that rent restriction was not only about limiting rents but about security of tenure as well. Without security of tenure legislation to limit rents would be ineffective, because fear of dispossession would in practice nullify any legal rights. The converse is also true: for if the rent could be raised to any level without limit, the tenant could always be dispossessed for non-payment of rent. Few landlords, it might be argued, would demand a rent higher than the market rent in order to get rid of a tenant; but exceptional behaviour is what most legislation is about. Not until 1965 was security of tenure separated from fixed rents; that an innovation that with hindsight seems so obvious took fifty years to come is one of the more surprising features of the history of the private rented sector in Britain.

Policy on Rent Restriction to 1939

The history of rent restriction began with the 1915 Act, of which the full title was the Increase of Rent and Mortgage Interest (War Restrictions) Act. The origins of this Act have of late been the subject of controversy. Englander has sought to

386

dismiss as a "legend" the view that the Act was
passed in response to the rent "strikes" in Glasgow
in 1915 (2), and contended that "The Rent Act 1915
represented, to a degree which hitherto has not
been appreciated, the culmination of the pre-war
struggle between landlord and tenant ...." (3).
Evidence for there having been such a struggle in a
sense more specific and direct than the clash of
interests on opposite sides of the market, is
however sparse thus far. Englander produced
evidence about rent "strikes" in 1913 and 1914 in
parts of Wolverhampton, Birmingham, Bradford and
Leeds, but not (very important) in London.
Lansbury (who was of couse a London man) talked of
a rent "strike", but there is no record of any
action. Englander himself terms the Victorian and
Edwardian tenant agitations "evanescent" (4), and
until evidence is produced of much more widespread
collective action by tenants and by landlords, it
seems reasonable to regard the 1915 Act as a
response to wartime conditions rather than as the
outcome of pre-1914 struggles between landlord and
tenant. That there was so little of such struggles
is perhaps surprising. There might have been an
example in the Irish land legislation, which since
the 1880s had provided for security of tenure and
limitation of rents.

Besides Englander's interpretation of rent
restriction in terms of class struggle between
landlords and tenants, and Daunton's interpretation
of private landlords being regarded as expendable
in the interest of defending large property ownership (5), there is a third which in the present
author's view goes further to explain the policy
that the 1915 Act embodied. That is to see rent
restriction as part of the development of direct
controls for running the war economy. Direct
controls over prices, materials, and manpower came
step by step as the government, the business world,
and the public came to realize that the war would
last a long time and required manpower, munitions,
and supplies on a scale hitherto unthought of. To
meet these requirements shifts were required in the
allocation of resources far larger than market
mechanisms could cope with. Housing was a case in
point. With very large numbers of men already in
the forces, and many more in the armaments industries, the capacity of the building industry was
for the time being greatly reduced and new house
building at a virtual halt (the only important

exception was building for munitions workers).
Higher rents and larger returns to landlords could
not, therefore, lead to an increase in the number
of houses built for letting and hence an increase
in the supply of rented accommodation. One half of
the mechanism of supply and demand could thus not
function; if the price mechanism was to balance
demand and supply, it would have to do so by
choking off demand. The rent increases needed to
do this would have been large, and the redistribution of income from tenants to landlords substantial. A large increase in the cost of so prominent
an item in the household budget as rent would be
sure to lead to pressure for substantial pay
increases, which would cause industrial unrest and
interruption of production of munitions of war if
resisted, and financial problems if conceded. The
increase in landlords' incomes would also have been
objected to as a form of 'profiteering', always
highly unpopular in wartime and already the subject
of complaint in 1915. There remains the question
of why rent restriction as a form of price control
was applied earlier in the war than many other
price controls. The answer here is likely to
include the Clydeside 'rent strike' (6).

There is no convincing reason for regarding
the inclusion of rents in wartime price control as
a sign of landlords being treated as expendable.
The 1915 Act was indeed not wholly to landlords'
disadvantage, as Professor Nevitt pointed out in
1970 (7). The Act restricted interest rates on
mortgages to what they were at the outbreak of war
and prohibited the calling-in of mortgages. A
substantial proportion of landlords financed their
investment with money borrowed on mortgage, so
restriction of rents was workable only if the
mortgage interest paid by landlords was correspondingly restricted. But at the end of the war, rent
restriction took a different course from the other
wartime controls. Controls over production and
materials were quickly brought to an end, and
consumer rationing and price controls soon
followed. Rent restriction in contrast, was extended. The procedure followed at the end of the war
set a precedent that was followed through the
inter-war years: legislation was preceded by a
review of the subject by an independent committee
that took evidence from interested parties and the
public, and the extension of rent control was for a
specified term of years, not indefinitely. The

Rent Restrictions Acts were reviewed five times, by
committees usually known by the names of their
chairmen: 'Hunter', 1918 (8), 'Salisbury', 1920
(9), 'Onslow', 1923 (10), 'Marley', 1931 (11) and
'First Ridley', 1937 (12) (Viscount Ridley chaired
another committee on the Rent Restrictions Acts
which reported in 1945) (13). These committees
ascertained and drew together majority informed
opinion, and their recommendations were for the
most part followed by successive governments. That
may, perhaps, have been the line of least resistance; but it probably helped to keep down the
temperature of an inherently 'hot' subject.

The development of policy in this period may
be considered in four stages: the immediate post-
war changes (Hunter and Salisbury and the 1919 and
1920 Acts); relaxation of control with a view to
its early ending (Onslow and the 1923 Act);
retention of control until the shortage was at an
end (the continuation of control in 1925, Marley,
and the 1933 Act); and proposals for selective
decontrol in the later 1930s. The fourth stage
merges readily with the third, for the basis for
partial decontrol was to be the passing of
shortages in particular parts of the market or
areas of the country.

The 1919 and 1920 Acts, and the reports of the
Hunter and Salisbury Committees, that preceded
them, can be taken together. The restrictions on
rents imposed by the 1915 Act were due to expire
six months after the end of the war, so consideration of whether legislation would be needed to
prolong them had obviously to be part of preliminary planning for post-war 'reconstruction'. The
review of the matter by the Committee chaired by
Lord Hunter was but one of a large number of
reviews of various aspects of reconstruction policy
that were set in hand in 1917 and 1918. That the
war had resulted in a worsening housing shortage
was evident, and in the light of that shortage the
Committee recommended that rent restriction should
be continued in force, and its coverage extended to
more highly rated houses not subject to control
under the 1915 Act. The 1919 Act extended the
controls until March 1921, with the important
exclusion of dwellings completed, or provided by
conversion, from April 1919 onwards; and raised the
rateable value limits below which the Rent Restriction Act applied to double those set by the 1915
Act (i.e. from £35 in London and £26 elsewhere in

England and Wales to £70 and £52), which added an
estimated three-quarters of a million houses to the
number subject to the Acts (14). The reason
adduced was that the shortage of houses had become
more widespread during the four years since the
original Act, hence occupiers of higher rented
houses needed protection against being dispossessed
by people buying houses for their own occupation.
The 1919 Act was no more than an interim
measure, and the question of the Rent Restrictions
Acts was reviewed again by Lord Salisbury's Committee in 1920, in time for the legislation that would
be needed if rent restriction was not to come to an
end in early 1921. The Committee concluded that if
rent restriction was brought to an end then, the
severe shortage of housing would result in an
increase in rents "beyond the point that public
opinion would .... regard as equitable" (15). Not
all of the increase would be the result of
scarcity: some would be due to the fall in the
value of money and the rise in building costs. Not
to give the owners of houses some relief from the
effects of rising costs and prices would be unjust,
but any relief must exclude the effects of
scarcity. In assessing the increase in rent that
should be allowed for the purpose of giving this
relief to owners of house property, costs of repair
were considered first. The Committee estimated
that they were some 2½ times what they had been in
1914, i.e. an increase of 150%. They estimated
further that in 1914 repair costs had averaged one-
sixth of the rent (exclusive of rates), hence to
offset the increase in repair costs an increase of
25% in the rent would be required. The Committee
then recommended that provision should be made for
an increase of one percentage point in the interest
on mortgages financing rented housing: with the
mortgage assumed to equal two-thirds of the cost, a
10% increase in rent would be required (which
implies a ratio of rent to capital cost of six and
two-thirds percent, and with costs of upkeep equal
to one-sixth of the rent, a ratio of rent net of
costs of upkeep to cost of 5.6%). To give the
owner a similar increase in his return, and to
provide for instances where the mortgage was a
different proportion from the assumed two-thirds, a
further 5% was allowed, making 40% in all (16).
The increase of 1% in the interest on mortgages was
considered equitable in relation to the yield on
other securities. Since the mortgagee was not

390

permitted to call in the mortgage, to give him a return more in line with other securities was required on grounds of fairness. So too was a similar increase in the return the investor received on his own capital that was tied up in the house.

The recommendations of the Salisbury Committee about rents were enacted into law in the Increase of Rent and Mortgage Interest (Restrictions) Act 1920, and the 1914 rent plus 40% (in the normal case where the landlord was responsible for external repairs) remained the controlled rent throughout the inter-war years for houses and flats to which the Rent Restrictions Acts applied. The rationale of 1914 rents plus 40% is therefore important. As was emphasized in the previous paragraph, Lord Salisbury's Committee reasoned in terms of equity; and their conclusion about equity in the circumstances of 1920 was that landlords should get their 1914 net rent in money terms (hence the increase to offset the rise in the cost of repairs), enhanced in line with the rise in interest rates in the economy generally. Such a concept treated rented houses as an investment fixed in money terms (like Gilt Edged securities) as distinct from an equity investment, but where the interest rate could be re-negotiated to keep it in line, perhaps with some lag, with interest rates generally. This would in fact, be a fair description of the private mortgage on house property that was the principal source of finance for rented housing before 1914. The Salisbury Committee did not seek to provide landlords with a return based on the current (i.e. 1920) value of their property, even with scarcity value excluded. Encouraging landlords to re-let rather than sell was mentioned nowhere in the Committee's report. The inducement to invest in new houses to let was not affected, since the 1919 Act had excluded new houses from the Rent Restrictions Acts. To treat landlords as if they owned investment fixed in money terms made sense if the 1920 price level was not expected to last. If prices fell (and a return to 'normal' was very widely expected), then the real value of their income would recover in the same way as the incomes of holders of other investments fixed in money terms. The Committee recommended that the Rent Restrictions Act, together with the rent increase that they proposed, should be extended for a further three years. That would give what they termed 'the emergency' time to pass; and the subject could then be considered again.

The Committee's recommendation for a three year extension of the Act and the 40% increase in rent was enacted into law by the Rent Restrictions Act 1920, which remained the principal Act throughout the inter-war years. At the time the 1920 Act took effect, the general price level was almost 160% higher than in 1914 and had reached its peak; towards the end of the year the post-war slump began, and by 1923 prices had fallen back to 90% above the 1914 level. When the approaching expiry of the three years' prolongation of rent control provided by the 1920 Act made a further review of rent control necessary, the return of prices and costs to where they had been in 1914 seemed well under way.

The Onslow Committee in its report in 1923 considered that any further fall in costs and prices would be slower than in the immediate past. But nonetheless it recommended in emphatic terms that rent control should be extended for a further two years only: and then brought to an end. Houses made subject to the Rent Restrictions Acts for the first time by the 1920 Act should be decontrolled straight away; those brought in by the 1919 Act should be decontrolled a year later; and the rest at the end of two years. In the meantime, the Acts should cease to apply to any house that was re-let to a fresh tenant (subsequently termed "decontrol by movement" or "creeping decontrol"). The Committee reached these conclusions primarily on the ground that the controls were a deterrent to investment in new houses to let. Their report reads:

> ".... the demand for houses at a rent .... is so great that this [i.e. the gap between the commercial rent of new house and controlled rents for similar houses] would probably not deter investors .... were it not for the psychological factor. The factor is .... the aversion to statutory control of any kind .... the property owner dislikes the prospect of increasing interference by the state in relations between himself and his tenant; and both he and .... the mortgagee desire securities which can be realized at short notice ...."

> ".... houses erected since April 1919 and
> money invested in such houses do not suffer
> disabilities of this character, [but] inves-
> tors feel that they have no security that
> future legislation will not bring those new
> houses under restrictions" (17).

The Committee concluded:

> "They [i.e. the Rent Restrictions Acts] have
> helped to prolong the shortage of accommoda-
> tion that rendered them necessary, so that
> if the country is ever to get back to the
> position whereby the bulk of its houses is
> to be provided by private enterprise, the
> sooner all restrictions can be removed the
> better" (18).

Because in the circumstances of shortage an immediate ending of the controls would lead to hardship
on a scale "sufficient to cause great agitation and
unrest", the controls should continue but terminate
at the latest in 1925. "During this period it is
hoped that a sufficient number of working class
houses will have been provided .... to have reduced
the shortage to a point at which the house owners
would no longer be in a position to demand and
obtain excessive rents" (19).

The Onslow Committee's arguments were far from
cogent: there were strong reasons other than the
"psychological effects" of controls on pre-1914
houses why there had been so little building to let
by private enterprise; and the expression of hope
that two years hence the shortage would be at an
end was no more than wishful thinking unsupported
by analysis or calculation of any kind. As was
emphasized in the previous chapter, building costs
had been expected to fall after the war, and as a
consequence of the slump had fallen sharply in
1921. So long as there were expectations of a
further fall, few would invest in new houses to let
for fear of competition from houses built subsequently at lower costs and hence able to show an
acceptable return on the capital invested with
lower rents. The size of the gap between households and dwellings compared with 1911 and the rate
at which the number of household was increasing
rendered altogether vain any hope that housing
shortages would be at an end by 1925. The full

results of the 1921 Census were not yet ready when the Onslow Committee was sitting, but there is no mention in their report of their having made any enquiries about figures for houses and households, or even having regarded them as relevant.

The legislation that followed the Onslow Committee's report extended the Rent Restrictions Acts for two years, with provision for decontrol on re-letting ("decontrol by movement" or "creeping decontrol"), but not the Committee's recommendation for earlier termination of control over houses first brought in by the 1919 and 1920 Acts. In 1925 the Rent Restrictions Acts were extended for a further two years (Rent Restriction (Continuance of Restrictions) Act, 1925), and after that they were extended for a year at a time by the annual Expiring Laws Continuance Act. From 1925 onwards rent restriction, like subsidized house building to let, had ceased to be a post-war emergency measure that would lapse as soon as peace-time normality had returned, but had become something much more long lasting. The fall in the general price level and in building costs provided landlords with a gradual increase in rents in real terms, and there were no real pressures to extend the Rent Restriction Acts to newly built houses. None of the Minority Reports of the various committees on the Rent Restrictions Acts recommended it; and, perhaps more significantly, neither the 1924 nor the 1929-31 Labour governments made any move in that direction. The 1924 government's legislation in this area, although termed the Prevention of Eviction Act, made only a limited change to the grounds for possession of houses to which the Rent Restrictions Acts applied1; and the 1929-31 Labour government did not legislate on the subject at all, apart from prolonging the Rent Restrictions Acts a year at a time as the previous Government had done. In 1930 it set up another committee to review the Rent Restrictions Acts, under the chairmanship of Lord Marley.

The change in the status of the Rent Restrictions Acts was made plain by the recommendations of the Marley Committee, which reported in 1931. The Committee made a far more considered assessment of the housing situation than the Onslow Committee had done eight years earlier: they noted that because the number of separate families was believed to be rising faster than the total population (20), the increase in the housing stock relative to popula-

tion since the end of the war had probably not
reduced the shortage of housing by as much as might
at first sight have appeared (21). Careful
estimates were made of the number of dwellings
subject to the Acts, the number decontrolled under
the 1923 Act, and the rents of controlled and
decontrolled houses. The source of the Committee's
information about decontrol and rents was enquiries
made by the Ministry of Labour, which collected
information about rents for calculating the cost of
living index number, and had the national organization (the Labour Exchanges) that could be used to
make more extended enquiries. The sample survey
carried out by interviews lay in the future, of
course: not until 1941 did the government have the
organization to conduct such enquiries. Nevertheless, the evidence collected was sufficient to show
that shortages remained, particularly of the
cheaper houses to rent. The extent of shortages
determined the Committee's recommendations about
the different classes:

> ".... the question of continuing control of
> any particular class of house must be regar-
> ded as dependent on whether the shortage of
> that class is at an end or likely to end
> within a reasonable period. The shortage is
> both a measure of the need for control and
> the main barrier to its removal.
>   While it is not desirable to retain con-
> trol longer than is necessary, we cannot
> accept the suggestion that, regardless of
> the shortage, a date must be fixed for final
> decontrol" (22).

The contrast with the Onslow Committee's approach
could not be more pointed.
    The Committee recommended a three-fold divi-
sion of the pre-1919 housing stock by reference to
rateable values: the highest group (termed Class A)
should be decontrolled altogether; in the middle
group (termed Class B) controls should remain, but
with 'decontrol by movement' as provided by the
1923 Act; but for what the Committee regarded as
"real working class houses", termed Class C, not
only should controls be retained but the decontrol
by movement permitted by the 1923 Act should be
brought to an end. The Class A group comprised
houses with current rateable value of £35 and over
(£45 and over in London). A high proportion were

considered to be owner-occupied and so outside the
purview of the Rent Restrictions Acts; in the
absence of survey evidence there must be some
uncertainty about whether this was really so, but
the information collected for the Fitzgerald
Committee in 1938 indicated that about two-thirds
of dwellings in the Marley Committee's Class A were
owner-occupied. Equally important was the substantial number of new houses built, which made it
unlikely that scarcity rents could be exacted. If
accepted, the recommendation about Class A houses
would withdraw the Rent Restrictions Acts from the
houses first controlled by the 1920 Act and most of
those first controlled by the 1919 Act.

By Class B houses the Committee said (23) that
they meant "the small house that is sometimes
rented and sometimes owned, and occupied at one end
of the scale by the artisan and at the other end by
the less well paid members of the middle classes".
Two main reasons were given by the Committee for
recommending that 'decontrol by movement' should
continue for these houses: large numbers had been
built, and more were being built, which would
alleviate the shortage; and that decontrol on re-
letting had "checked the widespread practice of
holding this class of house empty for sale when it
became empty" (24). These considerations did not
apply, though, to the "real working class house":
"We do not think that this class of house has ever
been held for sale in large numbers when empty or
is likely to be and in this we are supported by the
testimony of a most experienced witness - the
Valuer to the London County Council" (25). On the
strength of this judgement, the Committee recommended that decontrol by movement should be
stopped, owing to the harm it did to mobility by
working class tenants. With decontrol by movement
a tenant who moved would have to move to a decontrolled house at a substantially higher rent;
the ".... immobilizing effect .... is a point to
which we attach the greatest importance, not merely
because of its effect in impeding post-war housing
policy but also .... on account of its effect on
the national industrial economy" (26). Where to
draw the line between Class B and Class C was not
an easy matter, but the Committee decided on the
"compounding limit", that is to say the rateable
value below which the local authority could require
the landlord to pay the rates (to be recouped from
the tenants) instead of the occupier. The boundary

396

between Classes B and C was therefore set at £20 rateable value in London and £13 elsewhere in England and Wales.

The Marley Committee's recommendations were enacted into law by the Rent and Mortgage Interest Restrictions (Amendment) Act 1933, apart from the recommendation that no expiry date should be provided: rent restriction was continued, on the terms enacted, for five years. Rent restriction was due to expire in June 1938; so another committee to review the Rent Restrictions Acts was appointed, this time under the chairmanship of Lord Ridley. When it reported in December 1937, its approach was explicitly that of the Marley Committee applied to the facts of the housing situation six years later. During that time the house building boom of the 1930s had greatly increased the stock of dwellings relative to households, which implied that shortages had diminished. The 1936 Overcrowding Survey (27) provided numerical evidence of geographical differences in the severity of shortages. Although those differences could have other explanations (in particular the proportion of large families) there is no reason to doubt the validity of the Committee's view that the degree of shortage varied greatly from district to district, and that consequently the length of time before controls could be ended (according to the Marley Committee's doctrine which the Ridley Committee explicitly endorsed) varied just as greatly. This was the origin of the Committee's recommendations for the longer term, for a stage by stage decontrol, with the staging determined by the percentage of working class households that were statutorily overcrowded. For districts where the proportion overcrowded exceeded 4%, an eight year period of decontrol (by lowering the rateable value limit in £5 stages) starting in 1942 was recommended. Setting an ultimate date for total decontrol in this way, even though it was up to 13 years distant, was at variance with the professed adherence to the Marley Committee's doctrine, and appears to have owed something to the view that 'control must end some day' (28), though there was no doubt force in the argument that uncertainty about the future of control was disturbing. Not all of those who signed the Committee's report agreed; two members added a note of reservation dissenting from the recommendation of automatic decontrol and proposing a simple five year extension, followed by a further review.

The Ridley Committee's Minority Report is of
interest in that it attempted to argue a case for
permanent control. The Minority wrote:

> "We cannot agree that housing is a fit sub-
> ject of commodity economics, but rather ....
> that, so long as it is left to private
> enterprise, its management should be subject
> to public utility principles .... a social
> service of such extreme importance ought to
> be controlled ...." (29).

By 'public utility principles' was meant the body
of principles governing the regulation of charges
by such industries as the railways and electricity
supply, when these were privately owned but their
charges subject to public regulation to prevent
misuse of monopoly power. By 'commodity economics'
was presumably meant freedom to charge what the
market would stand. The historian must beware of
reading the views of the future into the words of
the past; but nevertheless there can be seen here
the beginnings of a line of argument that in the
1960s would carry the day.

The government of the day did not take up the
Ridley Committee's proposals for staged decontrol
and different staging area by area. The 1938
legislation (the Increase of Rent and Morgage
Interest (Restrictions) Act) did no more than
extend the Rent Restrictions Acts for a further
four years to 1942, and implement the Committee's
recommendation that Class B under the 1933 Act, the
£20-£45 rateable value range in London and £13-£35
elsewhere in England and Wales, should be split.
The upper part would be decontrolled, and the lower
part would remain subject to control, with decontrol by movement brought to an end. The Committee
had criticized decontrol by movement on the ground
that "sporadic decontrol is likely to mean attempts
to increase rents in the case of individual houses
which would not be possible if a substantial number
of houses of the same type were simultaneously
decontrolled" (30). Looking back on the inter-war
years from 1944-45, the second Ridley Committee
recommended against decontrol by movement after
World War II in emphatic terms:

> ".... we are emphatically of the opinion
> that .... that principle of decontrol on
> vacant possession should not be revived,

since the evidence shows that in the past this principle has been responsible for many of the hardships and anomalies that have arisen" (31).

Little more than a year later in August 1939 a new Rent Restrictions Act was one of a group of Acts hurried through Parliament in preparation for war which by then could be seen to be imminent. By the Rent and Mortgage Interest (Restrictions) Act of 1939, rents of dwellings (and parts of dwellings) let unfurnished were restricted to the rent charged on 1 September 1939; those rents would be August 1914 plus 40% for accommodation that had remained subject to control through the inter-war years, or market rents for accommodation that had been decontrolled or had been built after 1919. Such a way of setting controlled rents had obvious disadvantages in that very different rents could be charged for identical houses, but in the circumstances there was insufficient time to devise anything better, and anomalies in rents came very low among the horrors of war that were expected in 1939.

Rent Restriction and the Private Rented Sector in the Inter-War Years

Rent restriction could affect the size and composition of the stock of rented houses in three sets of ways:

  i) new building;
 ii) sales for owner-occupation of formerly rented houses; and
iii) improvement and upkeep of the rented houses.

In the absence of any inter-war house condition surveys there is no evidence about (iii); but some comments may be made about (i) and (ii). Table V.1 put the number of dwellings in the private rented sector in 1939 at 6,530,000, 6.5 million in round terms. There are no firm figures for earlier years, but if the conventional figure of 10% of dwellings owner-occupied before 1914 is anything near correct, the stock of rented dwellings then would have numbered about 7.1 million (32), only 600,000 less than in 1939. If the conventional 10% is an understatement, then the decrease was even less; but if for present purposes the conventional proportion is retained, then the components of change, rounded to the nearest 100,000 were: new building, +0.9 million; conversions, +0.1 million; slum clearance, -0.3 million; sales for owner-occupation, -1.2 million; miscellaneous demolitions and changes of use, -0.1 million.

The number of new houses and flats built for letting by private owners is fairly securely estimated from the returns collected for the Fitzgerald Committee (see Chapter V), and is much larger than is sometimes assumed. The only currently collected figures are those shown in Table VIII.1 The Ministry of Health's half-yearly figures of houses completed distinguished houses and flats built for letting by private owners only between October 1933 and March 1939, but the figures of dwellings built for letting are probably incomplete even for the period they cover.

Table VIII.1 - Dwellings Built for Letting by Private Owners England and Wales 1933/34 to 1938/39

	Rateable Value £13 or Under (a)	Rateable Value Over £13 but not over £26 (b)	Total
1933/34 (c)	22,000	17,000	39,000
1934/35	33,200	22,500	55,700
1935/36	35,400	25,100	60,500
1936/37	39,900	31,300	71,100
1937/38	42,400	31,900	74,400
1938/39	38,100	30,100	68,200

Notes: (a) £20 or under in London.
(b) Over £20 but not over £35 in London.
(c) Figures available only for second half of the financial year; first half estimated on the assumption that the proportion of all houses completed for private owners that were for letting was the same as in the second half of the year.

Source: Ministry of Health, twice yearly Housing return.

Some useful evidence about building for letting by private owners in the inter-war years was provided nearly forty years on by the National Dwelling and Housing Survey (NDHS) from which an estimate could be made of 113,000 households renting from private landlords who were living in dwellings recorded (in Valuation Office rating records) as having been built in 1919-1920, and 202,000 in dwellings built in 1930-39, of whom 19,000 and 59,000 respectively lived in flats (33). The absolute figures signify little owing to the large number of sales for owner-occupation, not all the dwellings in NDHS have a known date of construction, and some of the tenants being occupiers of parts of houses and not the whole house. But as indicators of the proportions of inter-war privately rented houses built in the 1920s and the 1930s they should be more reliable, as there are no obvious reasons why sales should have been proportionately more numerous among houses built in the 1930s than in the 1920s or vice versa. The NDHS figures suggest proportions of about one-third built in the 1920s and two-thirds in the 1930s, in round terms about 300,000 dwellings built in the 1920s for renting by private owners, and 600,000 in the 1930s. The estimate of about 300,000 houses and flats built for letting by private owners in the 1920s is noteworthy in that it is equal to just over a third of all building for private owners, in a period when there was generally supposed to have been very little building for letting by private enterprise. The Marley Committee's discussion of the housing situation (34) was in terms of building by private enterprise being virtually all for sale. There must be a measure of uncertainty here; but there is no doubt about the reality of a large number of houses being built for letting by private landlords in the 1930s, or about such building having already started in the 1920s.

The substantial number of houses and flats built for letting by private enterprise can be more readily explained when we look at returns on investments. Information collected by the Ministry of Labour for the Ridley Committee indicated that a representative rent in 1936 for houses built after 1919 for letting to 'working class' households was about 10s a week. Against this must be set expenditure on upkeep and management; no figures are available about the amounts that landlords actually spent, but local authorities spent a weekly average of 2s 1d (35). Private landlords are unlikely to have spent more than local authorities, and so would have a net income of 8s to 8s 6d a week. £20 16s to £22 2s a year. Such a net income amounted to a return of 5-5½% if the capital cost was £400 or 4½-5% if it was £450. Houses could be built for £450, and in many instances for £400: the average tender cost for a three bedroomed council house in 1932/33 was £300, and in 1936/37 £323 (36), so with the cost of land and site works about £70 (37), total cost would be about £370 and £390. This was the cost of a council house without a parlour (the commonest type), so the cost of a house with two reception rooms and kitchen (the type most frequently built by private owners) would have been somewhat higher. Figures for the cost of council houses with parlours, collected down to 1930/31, suggested that a parlour added 15% to the tender cost. Even so, a 5% return seems to have been obtainable from the rents that could be charged. 5% was quite an attractive yield on what was generally regarded as a safe investment. Consols yielded about 3½% in 1932/33, and in 1935/36 just under 3%. Money invested with building societies yielded 4½% to 5%, and as mentioned in Chapter IV, there were extended periods when building societies limited the amounts of new money they would accept from investors, and times when they would not accept any. Moreover, with rents yielding a net return of 5% on the capital cost, housing to rent could be financed by loans from building societies for those investors who could not finance it wholly from their own funds. In the 1930s building societies advanced considerable sums to finance houses for letting, as was shown in Chapter VI. Clearly the market for houses to let by private landlords produced returns that were sufficiently competitive to attract substantial amounts of investment.

New houses and flats were of course a part of the market to which the Rent Restrictions Acts did not apply after 1919. A controlled and a non-controlled sector existed side by side, with large amounts of new building in the non-controlled sector. This showed that in the circumstances of the 1920s and 1930s the existence of a controlled sector need not have a depressing effect on building to rent not subject to the controls, contrary to the views of the Onslow Committee in 1923. The effects of the Rent Restrictions Acts on the pre-1919 rented housing stock are a separate question. Economic theory predicts that holding down the rate of return will lead to disinvestment; there were two ways in which disinvestment in privately owned rented housing could take place, namely sale for owner-occupation when the dwelling became vacant, and not carrying out repairs. How much disinvestment took place through not doing repairs is impossible to estimate in the absence of house condition surveys. Before discussing disinvestment by sale for owner-occupation, though, a brief mention is called for of the effect that rent control had on the rate of return that landlords received from their properties. Any such discussion can only be tentative, seeing how sparse the information is. The estimate of a 5% return from a rent of 10s a week for post-war houses provides a starting point from which to deduce rates of return from the average rents about 7s 6d for pre-1918 "working class" houses not subject to control and 6s a week for controlled lettings (38). If, as is reasonable first approximation, vacant possession capital values were proportional to rents where rents were not controlled, a range of £400 to £450 for post-1919 houses would imply a capital value of £300-£340 for pre-1918 houses. To estimate the return on investment the amount to be set against the rent on account of repairs and management must be estimated: the Marley Committree reckoned one-quarter of the rent of small houses was absorbed by repairs in 1914 (39), which implies about a shilling, equivalent to about 1s 9d at the prices of the 1930s, rounded to 2s to include something for management. The net income to the landlord of 5s 6d a week amounted to $4\frac{1}{4}$ to $4\frac{7}{8}$% of the estimated capital value in the absence of control; a similar calculation for the average controlled rent of about 6 shillings (giving a net income of 4 shillings a week) would show a net return of 3 to $3\frac{1}{2}$% on the capital value. Such a return was about in line with what could be obtained on Consols or from building societies; with prices fairly stable, these were real yields as well as nominal interest rates. Seeing how illiquid an investment house property was, the return on houses let at controlled rents was not particularly attractive; but neither was it so low as to be patently unattractive. The fall in the general price level down to 1933 meant that the controlled rents that had been fixed by the 1920 Act in money terms gradually increased in real terms and so gave landlords a slowly improving return.

The only firm evidence about sales for owner-occupation is what can be inferred from the estimates of the number of pre-1914 dwellings let on controlled tenancies, non-controlled tenancies, and owner-occupied in 1938. These estimates are based on information collected by the Ministry of Health for the Fitzgerald Committee and published in the Committee's report (see Chapter V). The estimates are summarized in Table VIII.2

Table VIII.2 - Analysis of Pre-1914 Housing Stock by Tenure and Gross Value for Rating 1938

(thousands)

	.... Pre-1914 Dwellings		
	Rented Controlled	Rented Not Controlled	Owner-Occupied
Houses with gross value less than £20 10s	2,165	1,235	730
Houses with gross value £20 10s to £40	430	500	595
Houses with gross value £40 to £60	20	125	235
Houses with gross value £60 to £100	-	40	105
Houses with gross value over £100	-	15	55
Flats		470	-
Shops, etc. with living accommodation		430	50
Rented farmhouses		200	-
Total	2,800	2,830	1,770

Note: Gross value of £20 10s was equivalent to £13 rateable value; gross value of £40 was equivalent to a rateable value of £28 in London and £30 elsewhere; gross value of £60 was equivalent to a rateable value of £44 in London and £48 elsewhere; and gross value of £100 was equivalent to rateable values of £76 in London ands £80 elsewhere.

404

There were some 730,000 owner-occupied pre-1914 houses that had rateable values below £13 and so were in the Marley Committee's Class C, a figure high enough to suggest that that Committee were in error in their judgement that few rented houses in this category had been or would be sold for owner-occupation. The conventional assumption about the number of houses owner-occupied in 1914 would suggest about 800,000 in total: if this is anywhere near right, it is improbable in the extreme that all but 100,000 or so were of the type rated at £13 or under in 1938, as there were over one million pre-1918 dwellings that in 1938 were owner-occupied and rated at over £13 in 1938. The error may be one of the many instances of 'what everybody knows' about rented housing proving to be incorrect when tested against evidence; another possibility is that sales of small houses for owner-occupation were more numerous outside London, so that the experience of the London County Council's Valuer was not a reliable guide to the national picture. Perhaps half a million, or possibly rather less, of these dwellings had been sold for owner-occupation. Nearly three times as many had been re-let on non-controlled tenancies, which could only have occurred legally between 1923 and 1933. How many were re-let on controlled tenancies before 1923 or after 1933 is not known and there is thus far no evidence on which to base an estimate.

The difference between controlled rents and the rents of comparable non-controlled lettings is shown in Table VIII.3.

Table VIII.3 - Average Weekly Net Rents of "Working Class" Houses in 1937

	Controlled	Pre-1914 Decontrolled
Greater London	8s 6d to 9s 0d	12s 6d to 13s 0d
County Boroughs (excl Greater London)	5s10d to 6s 2d	7s 6d to 7s 9d
Other Boroughs and Urban Districts (excl Greater London)	5s 6d to 5s10d	7s 0d to 7s 4d
Rural Districts	4s 6d to 4s10d	5s 9d to 6s 0d

Source: Inter-Departmental Committee on the Rent Restrictions Acts, Report., Cmd. 5621, 1937 paragraph 41.

405

Controlled rents averaged about 9% of average
earnings of adult men working full time in manual
occupations, and non-controlled rents about 11-11½%
of average earnings. In the absence of a survey,
what differences there were (if any) between the
incomes of households with controlled tenancies and
the incomes of households in decontrolled lettings
is unknown. Rent control thus made a difference of
about 2% of earnings to rents paid. Put another
way, in 1924 1914 rents plus 40% amounted to a
reduction of just over 25% in real terms compared
with 1914; in 1937 the reduction in real terms was
about 17%. Decontrolled rents of pre-1914 dwellings, on the other hand, were about 5% higher in
real terms in 1937 than they had been in 1914. The
impact of controlled rents on housing costs went
beyond the 3 million households that paid them at
the end of the 1930s; through the "appropriate
normal rent" that local authorities were to charge
for houses built under the Housing (Financial
Provisions) Act 1924 and the obligation under the
Housing Act 1935 to have regard to the rents of
working class dwellings in the locality, controlled
rents had an effect on council house rents as well.
They were a very important part of the process by
which the supply price of housing to the householder was forced downwards relative to incomes and
prices generally from what it had been before 1914,
with a consequent increase in the quantity and
quality of housing demanded.

Rent control was not only about rents: it was
about security of tenure as well. Including
lettings of parts of house (which could constitute
controlled tenancies if let unfurnished with
exclusive use of at least one room) the number of
controlled tenancies in the late 1930s was probably
about 3 million, and for the tenants security of
tenure was a great advantage. The Marley Committee's report in 1931 expressed the view that "....
before the Rent Restrictions Acts were passed, the
working class tenant could be turned out of his
home at a week's notice. For sixteen years this
fear has been removed from his mind. The ....
tenant who pays his rent has been given almost
complete security of tenure during all these years,
and now attaches as much importance to this as to
the restricted rent" (40).

The total size of the private rented sector
was less than 10% smaller in 1939 than it probably
was in 1914, and new building for letting by

private owners was as high in the 1930s as it had been in the two decades before 1914 excepting only the peak of the boom at the turn of the century. In the world of stable or falling prices and low interest rates building for letting by private owners flourished to a greater extent than is sometimes acknowledged. This activity was outside the scope of the Rent Restrictions Acts; in the economic circumstances of the time the existence of the Acts was fully compatible with there being an active non-controlled sector, as there was no pressure to extend the controls. The history of rent restriction in the 1920s and 1930s is not one of landlords being treated as 'expendable'. The policy that could be criticized as treating them in this way was slum clearance with its compensation rule of site value only. This could be regarded as harsh, and occasioned a substantial amount of complaint.

The Private Rented Sector from 1939 to the Early 1960s

The new Rent Restrictions Act that was hurriedly enacted in August 1939 restricted rents to their September 1939 levels, and applied to all unfurnished lettings with a rateable value of £75 or under (£100 or under in London). Table VIII.2 shows that there were only about 20,000 to 25,000 rented houses above these limits; there could well have been some flats with high rateable values, but all told the number of rented dwellings excluded by the rateable value limits could not have exceeded 50,000 out of 6½ million lettings (some would have been excluded because they were let furnished, or were service tenancies). To restrict rents to September 1939 levels was to perpetuate an amalgam of market rents and 'old control' rents, and was defensible only on the ground that in the press of war there was no opportunity for anything better. Direct controls were introduced straight away; that such controls were essential for running a war economy was a non-controversial conclusion drawn from experience in 1914-18.

What to do after the war was considered by yet another committee on the Rent Restrictions Acts that was set up late in 1943, again under Lord Ridley. Experience in the inter-war years warned them against thinking that early decontrol would be feasible, and they advised that post-war legisla-

tion should be framed in the expectation that
control would last ten years after the war was
over. Their recommendations about what to do about
rents during that period flowed from their view
that "The incidence of the Rent Restrictions Acts
is so uneven that no single and simple formula can
be devised which can be universally applied to
produce fair rents" (41). In other words, the
amalgam of different kinds of rents that had been
in force in 1939 meant that a 40 percent (or any
other percentage) increase over pre-war rents could
be much more inequitable as between different
tenants and between different landlords than it had
been in 1920. The committee were emphatic in
rejecting rateable values as a basis for post-war
rents, as rating assessments varied so widely (42),
and in this their judgement was fully supported by
the available evidence (43). In the absence of a
formula, the committee recommended an administrative process, Rent Tribunals that would determine
fair rents. Local authorities would be required to
register all rents actually in payment, and these
(almost always the controlled rents under the 1939
Act) would be the rents legally recoverable unless
the Tribunal determined a different rent. The
committee's view about how the Tribunals should
determine fair rents should be quoted, not least
because the concepts enacted 20 years later were so
similar. The Tribunals should ".... determine what
is a fair rent for the tenancy or sub-tenancy
having regard to all the circumstances of the case,
including the situation of the premises, the
accommodation, furniture or services to which the
tenant is entitled, the expenditure necessarily
entailed .... [in] .... fulfilling .... obligations
as regards repairs .... and the general level of
rents of comparable houses in the distrit which are
in good repair" (44). As we shall see, the 1965
legislation defined a 'fair rent' in a very similar
way.

To deal with nearly six million rents in this
way would have been a daunting administrative task,
and was not in the event attempted. Whether the
administrative burden was the main reason or
whether others (such as holding down those prices
that were within the reach of government in seeking
wage restraint from the trade unions from 1948
onwards) is not known. The housing policy,
including rents, of the Labour governments of 1945-
51 still awaits a historical study that draws on

the official papers now open to the public under
the '30 year rule'. The principal study of the
1945-51 governments that is based on official
papers, that by Morgan (45) does not mention rent
control. The Labour governments' legislation on
rents was concerned with furnished lettings. The
main body of rent control legislation from the 1915
Act to the 1939 Act had applied only to accommodation let unfurnished, the form of letting that was
customary for permanent residences. Legislation in
1946 and 1949 (the Furnished Houses (Rent Control)
Act 1946 and the Landlord and Tenant (Rent Control)
Act 1949) extended regulation of rents and security
of tenure to furnished lettings, and provided that
Rent Tribunals could, at the instance of either
tenant or landlord (but in practice almost invariably the former), determine a 'reasonable' rent for
accommodation let furnished, which became the maximum legally recoverable; and grant limited security
of tenure. This difference between the statutory
regimes for unfurnished and furnished lettings was
to be an important question for policy for many
years, and was a distinctively post-1939 issue in
rent policy.

Leaving controlled rents where they were in
money terms meant a sharp fall in rents in real
terms, and a sharper fall still in landlords' real
income because costs of house maintenance rose
substantially faster than the general level. The
price of consumers' goods and services in 1945 was
just over 50% higher than in 1939, but between 1945
and 1951 it rose by a further 35% (46), making 105%
in total. The price of building maintenance work
nearly trebled in the same period (47). With the
income from rented house property so sharply
reduced there is nothing surprising about the
volume of sales for owner-occupation of hitherto
rented property. Reasons were advanced in Chapters
V and VI for thinking that is was in the later
1940s that such sales began to be numerous, and
that their volume was very large in the 1950s.

The first measure to permit an increase in
rents is unlikely to have made any significant
difference to the inducement to sell. The Housing
Repairs and Rents Act 1954 permitted increases in
controlled rents where the house was in good repair
and the landlord had spent specified sums on repair
in the recent past. The starting point was the
estimated trebling of the cost of house repairs and
maintenance since before the war. To offset that

increase in costs of upkeep, landlords were allowed (on conditions) to raise the rent by twice the 'statutory deduction' for rating purposes. The 'statutory deduction' was the deduction from gross rateable value (in principle the market rent as assessed) allowed for costs of upkeep in arriving at net rateable value, the net income yielded after setting against the rent the cost of keeping the property in the condition that would continue to command the rent. The 'statutory deduction' in 1954 was in fact that applying to gross and net rateable values as assessed in 1935 and varied from two-fifths of the gross value for the lowest rated houses to one-fifth for houses of £100 gross value (48). There was an element of arbitrariness about using the 'statutory deduction' as a bench-mark for spending on repair for individual houses, but it was the only one available. Since repair costs had trebled, the current cost of upkeep was taken to have been three times the statutory deduction. The 'statutory deduction' itself should be covered by the 1939 rent, so a rent increase equal to twice the statutory deduction should leave the landlord's net income (after deducting costs of upkeep) equal in money terms to what it had been in 1939, provided the statutory deduction measured what it was supposed to measure and the landlord did in fact do the repairs needed to keep the house in good order.

The rationale of the increases in controlled rents permitted by the 1954 Act was closely similar to the Salisbury Committee's reasoning in 1920. In 1945 however, two sets of conditions were imposed: the landlord must have spent on repairs sums equal to three times the statutory deduction in one year, or six times it in three years; and the house must be in good repair. Only then could the increase be recovered. The increase in controlled rents was much more tightly tied to repairs in 1954 than it had been in 1920, and indeed formed part of a package of measures directed at the conditions of the housing stock (49). As such it was purely a measure to allow increases in controlled rents in the circumstances defined: it was not in any way a decontrol measure, and the only provision that pointed in the direction of a non-controlled private rented sector was the exclusion from control of newly built or converted houses and flats. This provision of the 1954 legislation corresponded to that of 1919; but the fact that

410

such an exclusion was not made until nine years after the end of World War II was of little practical importance since house building work was strictly limited by licensing until 1953, and building licensing was not finallly ended until November 1954. How many increases in controlled rents took place under the provisions of the 1954 Act was never ascertained; there was no administrative process that would record them, and no survey was conducted to collect the information. The rent increases that did take place were reckoned to be in the region of 5 shillings a week (corresponding to a rateable value of about £20), which if accurate imples that the houses affected were generally of the larger and better kind.

In complete contrast with the very limited and highly conditional rent increases permitted by the 1954 Act were the very sweeping proposals for reform announced by the government in the autumn of 1956 and enacted into law by the Rent Act 1957. It had four main parts:

  i)   decontrol of lettings above £30 rateable value (£40 in London);
 ii)   decontrol on vacant possession of lettings below these limits;
iii)   for lettings remaining subject to control, the controlled rent to be twice the gross value for rating purposes (where the landlord was responsible for structural repairs; there were special provisions for other cases); and
 iv)   power to extend decontrol by lowering the rateable value limits by Statutory Instrument as distinct from new primary legislation.

Of these, (i) and (ii) had inter-war precedents, and so, in a way, had (iii), but (iv) was new: on both occasions pre-war when dwellings were decontrolled by a lowering of rateable value limits (in 1933 and 1938) this was done by primary legislation. The 1957 Act, in contrast, made provision for the ending of rent control without any further primary legislation being needed. A general increase in controlled rents was at last made possible by the new rating valuations, which provided the "simple formula" that was lacking when the Ridley Committee considered the level of controlled rents. To secure uniformity and consistency in valuations, responsibility for valuations for rating was transferred in 1948 from local authorities to the Board of Inland Revenue, and in 1956 new valuations made by the Inland Revenue's District Valuers came into force. Houses and flats were assessed at 1939 market rents, on the ground that 1939 was the last occasion on which there were enough market rentals to assess all houses in a consistent way. For the purpose of rent control, of course, what was important about the new rating assessments was not their absolute level but their consistency: that the absolute values were at 1939 levels could be offset by making controlled rents as a multiple of the gross values. This was the course adopted, in setting the new rents at twice the gross values (i.e. twice 1939 market rents). Controlled rents in 1937 had been on average about 75% of market rents (see Table VIII.3; the 1937 rents shown there are unlikely to have changed much by 1939), so rents set at twice 1939 gross values would be likely to exceed actual average controlled rents (i.e. 1939 rents) by an amount similar to the increase in the general price level since 1939, about 150%.

The Rent Act 1957 was highly controversial not only because it was drastic in itself but because it gave the government the power to end rent control altogether without any further primary legislation. It was an act of government policy, not the outcome of a review by an independent committee as were the inter-war Rent Restrictions Acts. Its basis and origins await study when the '30 year rule' makes the papers available to historians in the late 1980s. The one full length scholarly monograph, M.J. Barnett's The Politics of Legislation (50) was written from the standpoint of a student of polictical science and not of a historian of housing, which shows clearly in his account of the development of the policy, what the consequences were expected to be, and the Ministry of Housing's assessment of the housing situation. One possible interpretation, already referred to in Chapter VII in connection with the 1956 legislation on subsidies, is that the Rent Act 1957 and the Housing Subsidies Act 1956 were separate parts of a combined policy of making the further provision of housing a matter for private enterprise, other than slum clearance and associated rehousing, and certain special kinds of housing (of which housing for old people was the most important). A revival

412

of building for letting by private enterprise was essential if such a strategy could succeed, and a large measure of decontrol was considered necessary to that end. In favour of such an interpretation are the powers of further decontrol by statutory instrument and the complete absence of any such powers to raise controlled rents. By 1956 there had been more than a decade of peace-time inflation and no good reason to think that it was at an end. To set new levels for controlled rents in money terms that were unalterable except by new primary legislation made no sense in a policy directed at reviving letting by private enterprise, unless rent control would be quickly at an end. It is not possible, though, to exclude the alternative inter-pretation, that after seventeen years an increase in rents to offset the effect of the fall in the value of money on landlords' incomes was long overdue and that the 1956 revaluation at long last provided the opportunity to raise controlled rents by a simple formula.

Decontrol, including ending of security of tenure, of lettings above the rateable value limit aroused strong opposition from among the govern-ment's own supporters as well as the the official opposition. An early result was legislation (Land-lord and Tenant (Temporary Provisions) Act, 1958) to postpone for three years the full effect of decontrol of lettings above the rateable value limits. During that time eviction was permitted only after a Court Order, with fairly wide powers for the Court to suspend a possession order. Unless the tenant had unreasonably refused the offer of a three year tenancy at a rent of not more than twice the gross value (the formula for controlled rents) any order for possession was required to be suspended. Further decontrol by use of the power to lower the rateable value limits ("block decontrol") was in effect suspended indefi-nitely by the inclusion in the Conservative 1959 general election manifesto of a pledge that if the Conservatives were returned, the power to decontrol by lowering the rateable value limits would not be used during the lifetime of the next Parliament. Decontrol would therefore be restricted to decontrol by movement, and the expiry of the temporary provisions enacted in 1958.

The effects of the Rent Act 1957 may be considered under the headings of decontrol; rents, the size of the private rented sector; and

413

insecurity and abuses. The number of lettings decontrolled through being above the rateable value limits specified in the Act was about 400,000 or perhaps slightly less (51), which was little more than half the number (750,000) estimated at the time the Bill that became the Rent Act was introduced (52). At the end of 1964 the number of controlled tenancies was estimated at 1,755,000 and the number of non-controlled unfurnished lettings at 1,550,000 (53). Not all of the non-controlled lettings had been subject to control, of course: some were fresh lettings; some of the others are likely to have been 'tied' accommodation not subject to control. But plainly 'decontrol by movement' was the principal source of non-controlled unfurnished lettings, probably in the region of 800,000 between the time when the Act came into force (July 1957) and the date of the 1964 survey (November 1964). The number of controlled lettings was about 4.3 million immediately before the Rent Act took effect (54), and 1.75 million at the end of 1964. Sales for owner-occupation and slum clearance contributed to the reduction as well as decontrol of course, but the rapid reduction merits note. What effect the 1957 Act had on the rate of reduction in the private rented sector in total is however best reserved for discussion later, against the background of what came after as well as what went before.

Increases in rent under the 1957 Act may next be considered. For controlled tenancies the new controlled rent was twice the gross value where the landlord was responsible for all repairs other than internal decorations, one and one-third times gross value when the tenant was responsibile for all repairs, and two and one-third times gross value where the landlord was responsible for internal decoration as well as repairs. The controlled rent of a letting could increase further only as a result of an addition of 8% of the landlord's expenditure on improvement (excluding grant, if any); since improvements were generally considered to have been fairly rare, increases through time in average controlled rents would pick up lags in the raising of rents to the levels permitted by law, and changes in the mix of dwellings as a result of sales and demolitions. Table VIII.4 shows rents and ratio to gross value (arithmetic means in 1957 and 1959; and in 1963 and 1964 medians).

Table VIII.4 - Median Rents and Gross Value:
            Lettings Below the Controlled Limit

| | ..... London ..... | | Rest of England ... and Wales .... | |
	Net Rent	Ratio of Net Rent to G.V.	Net Rent	Ratio of Net Rent to G.V.
1957 (before Act took effect)	14s	1.1	9s 4d	1.2
1959 (March-May)	22s 4d	1.8	13s 1d	1.7
1963 (Nov.)	25s 9d	1.99	......	...
1964 (Nov.)	......	...	14s 7d	1.99

Source: Rent Act Inquiry (Cmnd. 1246)(1960); Tables 5 and 6
         (figures for lettings where occupier is unchaged);
         1957 ratio to G.V. calculated; Report of the Com-
         mittee on Housing in Greater London (Cmnd. 2605)
         (1965) Tables 31 and 33, and The Housing Survey in
         England and Wales 1967, Tables 2.21 and 2.22.

        The Rent Act Inquiry in 1957 and 1959 produced
figures that were not in all ways exactly
comparable with those produced by the 1963 and 1964
surveys (the former in Greater London, the latter
in the rest of England and Wales). Nevertheless,
it is clear that putting the permitted increases
into effect took several years, especially outside
London. The 1959 interview found that in England
and Wales outside London, 37% of the occupiers of
premises below the control limit and who had been
there in 1957 were paying rents of less than 1.5
times gross value; in 1964 the proportion was 16%,
in London the proportions were 22% in 1959 and 12%
in 1963 (55). At the other end of the range, there
were rents being paid for controlled tenancies that
were higher than were legally recoverable (56).
        The increases in controlled rents between 1957
and 1959 of about 8s a week in London and 4s a week
elsewhere were equivalent to 3.3% and 1.7% of
average earnings of adult men in manual work.
These were not necessarily the average earnings of
tenants, of course. Not until the 1964 survey did
information become available about the income of
tenants of controlled tenancies, and even then the

distinction was not drawn between earning and non-earning householders. The median head of household income of tenants of controlled tenancies was just under £10, and their average rent about 17s a week (57), so in very round terms controlled rents averaged 8-9% of head of household income in 1964. Incomes rose by about 50% between 1957 and 1964 (58), so the permitted increase in controlled rents in 1957, if implemented in full, would have taken rents up from 7% to 12-13% of head of household incomes; or from 4% to 7% of average earnings of adult men in manual work, if that is used as a yardstick. Controlled rents were not high relative to incomes, it could be argued, even after the increase, but the increase was nevertheless sharp: it was equal to all of the increase in average earnings net of tax (on the income of a couple with two children) between October 1957 and April 1959 and nearly half of the increase in the National Insurance retirement pensions for a married couple that took place in 1958 (the first such increase for nearly three years). At this time tenants not receiving National Assistance paid the increase in rent entirely from their own incomes. Rent allowances did not appear until 1972.

The comparison between rents of controlled and uncontrolled tenancies is made more difficult by differences in the type of dwelling. The best that can be done with the information available to take account of differences in type and quality of accommodation is to use gross value as an indicator of the volume of housing service supplied. The figures about this are shown in Table VIII.5.

To look at averages, though, is to overlook a very important part of the benefit of rent control to the tenant, namely protection against "non-average" behaviour. There was a far wider dispersion around the average both of rents and ratios of rents to gross values for non-controlled than for controlled accommodation. Table VIII.6 shows this for England outside London and Wales; in London the contrast was even sharper (59).

Table VIII.5 - Controlled and Non-Controlled Rents Compared with Gross Value

| | ... Net Rent as Percent of Gross Value ... | | | Average Non-Controlled Rent |
	Controlled	Non-Controlled	Difference %	
1959 (Below control limit)				
London	1.8	2.6	+44	29s 7d
Rest of England and Wales	1.7	2.4	+41	20s 2d
1963 London				
Singly occupied house	1.94	2.65	+37	50s 4d
Purpose built flat	2.01	3.46	+72	64s 10d
Part of house or flat	2.02	4.18	+107	47s 0d
1964 Rest of England and Wales				
All dwellings (median)	1.99	2.42	+22	20s 7d

Source: 1959: Cmd. 1246, Tables 5 and 6.
         1963: Cmd. 2605, Tables 31 and 32.
         1964: The Housing Survey in England and Wales, Table 2.21 and 2.22.

Table VIII.6 - Ratios of Rent to Gross Value:
England (outside London) and Wales 1964

(percent)

Ratio of Rent to Gross Value	Controlled	Not Controlled
0.01 to 0.50	1	3
0.51 to 1.00	5	7
1.01 to 1.50	11	6
1.51 to 2.00	33	19
2.01 to 2.50	36	17
2.51 to 3.00	6	13
3.01 to 3.50	3	11
3.51 to 4.00	1	8
4.01 or more	3	15
Total	100	100

Source: The Housing Survey in England and Wales, 1964,
Table 2.22. Gross Values are pre-1963 gross
values.

Decontrol affected not only rents but security
of tenure, and the ending of security of tenure
through decontrol aroused as much hostility as the
rent increases, if not more. This was not, indeed,
something novel in the late 1950s. As mentioned
above, the report of the Marley Committee in its
report in 1931 had laid emphasis on the value that
tenants set on security of tenure. From 1939 to
1957 all tenants of private landlords renting their
accommodation unfurnished ('tied' accommodation
alone excepted) had had security of tenure provided
that they paid the rent and did not maltreat the
property. The Rent Act 1957 replaced the former
one week's notice by four weeks for non-controlled
lettings, as a consequence of an amendment moved by
back-bench MPs on the government side. But otherwise the law remained that the landlord could give
the tenant of non-controlled accommodation notice
to quit for any reason or none; and at the end of
the period of notice the former tenant became a
trespasser who could be evicted by the landlord
himself or bailiffs employed by him without
recourse to the courts. The prospect of loss of
security appears to have aroused more apprehension

than did possible rent increases among tenants
whose accommodation might be decontrolled by the
powers in the Act to lower the control limit by
Order; and for that reason the Conservative
manifesto for the 1959 general election pledged
that a future Conservative government would not use
these powers of decontrol during the lifetime of
the next Parliament.

Insecurity and abuses to do with possession
did far more to discredit the policy that the Rent
Act embodied than did rent increases. The kind of
abuses that took place were discussed in detail in
the Report of the Committee on Housing in Greater
London (60), and so need be referred to only
briefly. Some of the abuses consisted of harass-
ment, threats, or trickery to get rid of tenants
with controlled tenancies; others took such forms
as vindictive notices to quite to tenants who went
to the local authority to get action taken under
the Public Health or Housing Acts about disrepair.
That such actions were far from rare in the early
1960s was not in doubt, and they added a new word
to the language, "Rachmanism", to connote oppres-
sive conduct by landlords (61). The incentive for
such conduct did not arise entirely from the Rent
Act, of course. For houses that were saleable for
owner-occupation the value if offered for sale with
vacant possession had for years been greater than
the prices they would fetch if sold subject to a
controlled tenancy. The Rent Act made no difference here (except through block decontrol) and gave
no new inducement to get rid of the tenant and sell
with vacant possession. Where the Rent Act did
make a major difference was to property that would
not be saleable for owner-occupation. Before 1957
such property had to be let furnished if it was to
be outside rent control, but after the Rent Act
became law it could be let unfurnished without
attracting security of tenure or limits to rents.
The Rent Act widened substantially the range of
property where there was a financial advantage to
the landlord in getting a controlled tenant to go.
And in the non-controlled sector the threat of
notice to quit could render ineffective and
unenforceable the considerable body of legislation
imposing obligations on landlords to keep their
property in proper repair, provide rent books, and
so forth. The market's safeguard against oppres-
sive conduct by suppliers is that the buyer can
take his custom elsewhere and not have to rely on

anyone's sense of propriety, fairness, restraint or humanity (62); but at the end of the 1950s the demand for rented housing was much too far in excess of the supply for competition to provide such protection, particularly in London.

Rent Regulation: Adjustable Rents with Security of Tenure

In the early 1960s the climate of opinion moved away from reliance on market mechanisms in favour of more state action and regulation. That shift of opinion generally, together with growing concern about the abuses referred to in the previous sector, led to a major shift of policy on security of tenure and rents. Security of tenure was brought back in 1964 by the Prevention of Eviction Act, a stop-gap measure intended to prevent landlords from dispossessing tenants in anticipation of reintroduction of security of tenure and rent restriction. The following year a new system of rent regulation was introduced by the Rent Act 1965, which remained in being for the rest of the period covered by this history. The principle introduced in 1965 was that for accommodation let unfurnished that was not subject to control under the 1957 Act there should be security of tenure but the rent was to be a "fair rent" determined by a new administrative process created for the purpose, comprising in the first instance the Rent Officers and on appeal the Rent Assessment Committees. What was novel was first the separation of security of tenure from completely fixed rents; and second the rents being determined by reference to the facts of the individual case and not by reference to the rent at a previous base date (e.g. 40% above the August 1914 rent under the 1920 Act) or valuation for rating (e.g. twice gross value as under the 1957 Act). Rents as registered could be re-registered not less than three years later, which provided a mechanism that could allow for general inflation of costs and prices. To combine security of tenure with a mechanism that could be used to review (and in practice raise) rents periodically may appear to be the obvious way of running rent restriction in an era of inflation; but not until 20 years after the end of the war did it appear in Britain.

The provisions about security of tenure followed patterns that had been well established

since the 1920s, apart from the introduction of a
"second succession", i.e. the protected tenancy
could pass not just from the original tenant to
another member of his family living with him
(allowed since 1920), but then to a member of the
successor's family. The protected tenant had
security of tenure provided he paid the rent and
did not maltreat the property. As under all
previous legislation, furnished lettings were
subject to arrangements different from those for
unfurnished lettings.

The provisions on the 1965 Act about rents
merit a more detailed description both because they
were novel and because they remained in effect and
were the centre-piece of rent policy generally in
1970-74. In determining a fair rent, regard was to
be had to ".... all the circumstances (other than
the personal circumstances) and in particular to
the age, character, and locality of the dwelling
house and its state of repair". And then: "For the
purposes of the determination it shall be assumed
that the number of persons seeking to become
tenants of similar dwelling houses in the locality
on the terms (other than those relating to rent) of
the regulated tenancy is not substantially greater
than the number of dwelling houses in the locality
that are available for letting on such terms",
(originally Rent Act 1965, s.27; then Rent Act
1968, s.46; at the time of writing Rent Act 1977,
s.70). An attempt was made to exclude any scarcity
element from fair rents as measured. Although the
concept of a hypothetical balanced market attracted
criticism on the ground that both the demand and
the supply would be influenced by price, the idea
that excluding the effects of scarcity is part of
fairness between landlord and tenant went back as
far as Lord Salisbury's Committee, at least (63).
The idea of setting restricted rents individually
by reference to the characteristics of the accommodation was likewise not completely novel. The
similarity between the words of the 1965 Act and
the Ridley Commiteee's recommendations twenty years
before has already been mentioned. In their
pamphlet Housing to Let that was published by the
Conservative Political Centre in 1956, G. (later
Sir Geoffrey) Howe and C. Jones advocated replacing
controlled rents by "reasonable rents" that took
account of the state of repair, costs of upkeep,
and comparable rents in the locality, but with the
personal circumstances excluded. Setting rents

would be the job of 'Rent Officers' or 'Rent
Controllers' attached to the County Courts, an
arrangement explicitly modelled on practice in
Australia and New Zealand; an appeal from the
officers' decisions would lie to the County Court
itself. The similarity to the administrative
machinery actually set up by the 1965 Act is
evident, though under the 1965 Act appeals from
decisions of Rent Officers lay to Rent Assessment
Committees, not to the Courts (but with a right of
appeal to the Courts from the Rent Assessment
Committees on points of law). Who first thought
of an idea is usually difficult to ascertain, and
who influenced whom is seldom clear; but there is
no doubt that both the concept of the "fair rent"
determined on the facts of the individual case and
the administrative arrangements had a varied
ancestry of considerable length before 1965.

To describe the concepts is one thing; to
explain the level of rents that they generated is
quite another. The statutory provisions governing
the determination of fair rents had nothing to say
about the level at which the rents would come out;
that could only emerge when Rent Officers had
Registered rents and Rent Assessment Committees had
given decisions. To compare the average rents
registered as fair rents with the average
controlled and non-controlled rents reported by the
1963 and 1964 surveys is not wholly straightforward, both owing to the difficulty of ensuring
that like is compared with like, and the time
interval between those surveys and the detailed
analyses of registered rents prepared for the
Francis Committee (64). The best that can be done
is to use gross rateable values to allow for
differences in the quality of dwellings. They are
not ideal for the purpose, but are better than
nothing. As for the time interval, comparisons can
be made with the rise in the general price level.

Registered rents in 1969 were some 90% higher
in relation to gross values than were, on the
average, non-controlled rents in 1963 and 1964.
During that period the general price level, as
measured by the index of retail prices, rose by 23-
27%. The fair rents that emerged from the arrangements set up by the 1965 Act were thus on the
average substantially higher than non-controlled
had been before that Act was passed, when like is
compared as far as possible with like. The survey
carried out in 1970 for the Francis Committee found

Table VIII.7 - Registered Fair Rents in 1979 as Proportion
of Gross Value: Comparisons with
Non-Controlled Rents in 1963 and 1964

(Rent as proportion of 1963 Gross Values)

		1963	1964	1969
England and Wales				
Houses:	Mean	....	....	1.73
	Median	....	....	1.68
Flats:	Mean	....	....	1.89
	Median	....	....	1.79
Rooms:	Mean	....	....	2.24
	Median	....	....	2.06
London				
Singly Occupied House: Mean		0.83	....	....
Purpose Built Flat: Mean		1.00	....	....
Part of House or Flat		1.36	....	....
Rest of England and Wales				
All lettings: Median		....	0.87	....

Sources: 1963 from Report of the Committee on Housing in
Greater London, Cmd.2605, (1965) p.356; 1964 from
The Housing Survey in England and Wales 1964,
Table 2.22; 1969 from Report of the Committee on
the Rent Acts, Cmd. 4609, (1971) Table 20.

that the same was true if registered rents were
compared with the rents charged for lettings not
subject to rent control but not the subject of
recourse to rent registration (65). But, to take
up a point referred to several times already,
averages were not all that mattered about rent
restriction; dispersions around averages were also
very important and here the effect of the registration system can be seen in the much smaller proportion of rents that were very far above average.
Table VIII.8 shows the medians, upper quartiles,
and highest deciles of rents in relation to gross
value as recorded in the 1963 and 1964 surveys and
the rent registration statistics published by the
Francis Committee.
    Registered rents had a much narrower spread
than did non-controlled rents earlier in the

423

Table VIII.8 - Measures of the Dispersion of Rents 1963-69

(ratios to Gross Value)

| | Non-Controlled Rents .... | | | Registered Rents | |
	Houses in 1963 (London)	Flats in 1963 (London)	All Lettings 1964 (Excluding London)	Houses in 1969	Flats in 1969
Median	0.85	0.95	0.76	1.68	1.79
Upper Quartile	1.28	1.28	1.15	1.95	2.09
Ninth Decile	1.70	1.75	1.30	2.29	2.53
Upper Quartile as percent of Median	150	135	150	116	117
Ninth Decile as percent of Median	200	185	170	136	141

Notes on Sources: 1963 from Cmnd. 2605, (1965) Table 35 p.356. Median, upper quartile, and ninth decile all derived by interpolation from published percentage distribution by rent/gross value range 1964 from The Housing Survey in England and Wales, (HMSO 1962) Table 2.23. Median as published, quartile and decile interpolated.

1969 from Cmnd. 4609, (1971) Table 20. Median and upper quartile published, decile interpolated.

decade, which suggest that rent regulation afforded to tenants protection against exceptionally high rents. In this context, it is significant that where the tenant applied for registration of rent, the rent previously in payment averaged 2.27 times gross value in 1966, 2.32 in 1967, 2.37 in 1968 and 2.50 in 1969 (66); where tenants invoked the 'fair rent' machinery they were usually paying rents that were untypically high. But although it protected tenants against extremes of rent, it cannot be said to have brought about levels of rent that were low in general. In 1969 the average rents registered were £270 a year for houses and £311 for flats in London, and £135 and £150 in the rest of England and Wales (67); average un-rebated local authority rents at 31 March 1970 (which would have been close to rents in payment in most of 1969 by tenants not receiving rebates) averaged £143 in London and £99 elsewhere in England and Wales. That registered rents came out as high as they did was a disappointment to many of those who had pressed for renewed restriction of rents, and the difference of almost 2:1 between average rents in London compared with the rest of England and Wales aroused particular complaint. A 2:1 difference was greater than the difference in house prices, and as great as the difference in non-controlled rents under the 1957 Act. It was therefore argued that registered rents in London did not really exclude the effect of scarcity as the 1965 Act intended that they should. The Francis Committee did not accept this argument (68), but their attempt to distinguish between that part of excess demand for rented housing in London that was relevant to exclusion of the effect of 'scarcity' and that which was not does not read convincingly and demonstrates the ambiguities in the concept that Rent Officers and Rent Assessment Committees had to apply. Before very long, though, the determination of fair rents became increasingly influenced by 'comparables', that is to say that the best evidence of what rent should be registered for a particular property was a rent recently registered for a fairly similar property not too far away. Presenting 'comparables' was the normal way of proceeding in appeals against rating valuations or in cases of dispute about market rents for business premises, and so came naturally to the surveyors who sat as members of Rent Assessment Committees or appeared before them on behalf of landlords or tenants objecting to

Rent Officers' determinations.

Evidence presented to the Francis Committee indicated that 'fair rents' as registered averaged about 20% below market rents (69), but this must be taken with some reserve owing to how sparse was evidence about market rents. Perhaps more enlightening is the estimate by the Valuation Office that in 1970 the average ratio of registered rents to hypothetical vacant possession sale values of the properties was about 7% (70). Costs of management and upkeep must be deducted to estimate the net yield, but although there is no information about them specifically for the private rented sector, the local authorities' average expenditure of £42 per dwelling in 1970/71 is unlikely to be too low if used to represent private landlords outgoings. Rents registered in 1970 averaged £216, so taking off £42 for upkeep and management would make the net yield about four-fifths of the ratio of rent to market value, i.e. about $5\frac{1}{2}$%, which compares reasonably well with yields in the 1930s (71). In 1970, however, money invested in building societies earned the equivalent of 8.5%; the yield on Consols was just over 9%, and the dividend yield on ordinary shares averaged 4.5%. Since re-registration would enable rents to keep up with inflation, it is with the yield on ordinary shares rather than Consols and building societies that the yield provided by registered rents should be compared. A net rent equal to $5\frac{1}{2}$% of the capital value was equivalent to a rate of return of $4\frac{1}{2}$% if the asset had a life of 40 years. Such a return was no greater than that on ordinary shares, and so not very attractive in comparison because as investments rented houses were much more difficult to turn into cash quickly, should that be required, than shares. The level of rents that rent registration produced in the later 1960s was thus not far out of line with other investments, even though it was not high enough to encourage investors to buy houses with vacant posession with a view to letting them.

Registered rents were much more advantageous to landlords, obviously, than were controlled rents under the 1957 Act. These were fixed in money terms (apart from the addition of $12\frac{1}{2}$% of landlords' expenditure on improvements) and so were falling further and further out of line with current values. Even in 1965, rents that were the same in money terms as in 1957 were already 20%

lower in real terms, and with decontrol (in the 1957 sense) not envisaged, keeping 1957 rents could not be justified as an interim arrangement until decontrol. The Rent Act 1965 did not touch controlled rents; the first move to transfer lettings from control to regulation (i.e. the registered rent regime) was made by the Housing Act 1969, which provided for such a transfer of dwellings for which the local authority issued a "qualification certificate" of good repair and presence of all the standard amenities. 76,000 dwellings were the subject of rents registered through this procedure by the end of 1972 (71). The Conservative government's policy was to transfer to the registered rent system all tenancies subject to rent control under the 1957 Act except where the dwelling had been formally represented as unfit. Transfer from control to regulation would bring about a steep increase in rents: in 1971 rents registered under the "qualification certificate" procedure for former controlled tenancies averaged £221 a year compared with controlled rents of £74 (72). Tenants were to be protected against financial hardship by the introduction of a mandatory scheme of "rent allowances", the equivalent for tenants of private landlords of rent rebates for tenants of local authorities. Statements that the inability of some tenants with controlled tenancies to pay market rents should be a matter for "the welfare state" or "social services" had indeed been for many years a commonplace of discussion of controlled rents, particular in advocacy of market rents. Tenants receiving National Assistance, of course, would have been protected, for the scale of £x a week plus rent ensured that any increase above the controlled rent would be matched by an increase in the assistance payments they received; but that was of no help to the householder in low paid work or with a large family, since National Assistance (Supplementary Benefit from 1967) was not payable to people in work. Rent allowances filled the gap, and provided the mechanism by which rent increases could be partially offset if the means of the tenant were insufficient. This was the private sector counterpart of the policy of combining a mandatory rent rebate scheme for local authority tenants with rents at the same level (after a transition period) as rents registered for similar properties in the private sector. The Housing Finance Act 1972

427

provided for transfer from control to regulation in six batches, defined by rateable value, at half yearly intervals beginning in January 1973. Transfer in batches was simply to spread out the workload on Rent Officers and Rent Assessment Committees; it was not that the severity of the shortage or tenants' incomes were thought to be related to rateable values.

In 1974 when the Labour government took office, the first three batches of controlled tenancies had been transferred to regulation, but transfer of the other three batches was stopped. Also in 1974 a new Rent Act extended full security of tenure to tenants renting their accommodation furnished from a landlord who did not live in the same building. Security of tenure for tenants of furnished lettings was a highly controversial question that had been much debated over the years. Tenants of furnished accommodation had only very limited security of tenure, which led to allegations of "a few sticks of furniture" being provided to keep lettings clear of full security, and a substantial amount of litigation about what kind and quality of furnishings made a letting 'furnished' for the purpose of the Rent Acts. The majority of the Francis Committee recommended against extending security of tenure to furnished lettings on the ground that such action could reasonably be expected to reduce the supply of accommodation to let (73); the Minority Report recommended extension of security of tenure to furnished lettings, except for householders letting off parts of their homes while remaining in occupation; most of the accommodation let furnished would continue to be let even if security of tenure applied, because so little of it was saleable for owner-occupation (74). The 1974 Act drew much the same distinction: tenants of accommodation rented furnished from a non-resident landlord were accorded the same security of tenure as tenants renting unfurnished; tenants renting furnished from a resident landlord had only restricted security as before, as did tenants renting unfurnished from a resident landlord where the letting began after the Act came into force. In 1976 greater security (though not full Rent Act protection) was extended to tenants of agricultural tied cottages by the Rent (Agriculture) Act. This was as far as the Labour governments of 1974-79 went in legislation on privately owned rented accommodation. In 1976

the Department of the Environment set in hand a
review of the Rent Acts with a consultation paper
issued to invite evidence from interested organizations, and the general public; but no conclusions
had been published before the 1979 general election.

During the 1970s the much higher rates of
inflation had the effect of cutting sharply the
rate of return yielded by registered rents. At the
rates of inflation experienced in the early 1960s
(which were the relevant part of the background
against which the 1965 legislation was framed)
triennial increases provided by the Rent Act 1965
would work reasonably well in the sense that the
landlord's real income would not fall very far in
the interval between revisions of the rent, nor
would revision face the tenant with an increase in
his rent that would be large enough to be burdensome. But at the much higher rates of inflation
experienced in the 1970s, that ceased to be true.
The sheer size of the increase in the rent if
revised at three year intervals would create
difficulties for tenants. The 1975 legislation
(Housing Rents and Subsidies Act) accordingly
provided for "phasing" of rent increases, by which
they took effect in three annual steps. The
registered rent did not become payable in full
until the second anniversary of its being
registered. There were precedents for such an
arrangement in temporary legislation of 1968 and
1969 (75) that was part of the prices and incomes
policy of the government of the day, but the
phasing provisions of the 1975 Act, were intended
to be permanent. Even had rents as registered kept
up with inflation, rents actually paid would have
lagged behind as a result of phasing. But when
inflation was at its height, rents as registered
did not keep pace, as Table VIII.9 shows. The
average interval between re-registration of
registered rents is not known exactly; but since
the minimum interval was three years the average
must be greater than this, so the increases in the
general price level over a three year and a four
year period are both shown.

Whether a tendency to lag behind inflation was
inherent in the mechanism for determining fair
rents is open to argument, but obviously a system
that in practice depended heavily on 'comparables'
would have difficulty in keeping up with accelerating inflation. The combined effect of registered

429

Table VIII.9 - Increases in Registered Rents Compared with the Rise in the General Price Level

(percent)

| | Increase in Rents on Re-Registration | | Increase in Index of Retail Prices | |
	Greater London	Rest of England and Wales	3 years	4 years
1969	+10	+11	+13	...
1970	+11	+11	+17	+20
1971	+17	+20	+23	+28
1972	+21	+29	+25	+31
1973	+25	+36	+28	+36
1974	+23	+35	+36	+49
1975	+30	+44	+57	+69
1976	+38	+52	+68	+83
1977	+43	+57	+68	+95
1978	+44	+61	+46	+82

Source: Housing and Construction Statistics No. 11, Table 43; No. 22, Table 44; No. 30, Table 43.

rents not keeping up with inflation and phasing of rent increases keeping rents actually paid and received below the rents registered led to a sharp fall in rents in real terms during the 1970s. While rents fell back relative to the general price level, house values with vacant possession surged ahead of it in the boom of the early 1970s. The balance of financial advantage shifted heavily in favour of selling with vacant possion and against re-letting, when the opportunity offered and the dwelling was saleable. During the period building societies were being pressed to be more willing to lend 'down-market' which increased the range of properties saleable for owner-occupation.

The Changing Size, Composition, and Functions of the Private Rented Sector in the Post-War Years

Before the effects of the policies just described can be discussed, the changing size, composition, and functions of the private rented sector must be outlined, for the timing of changes in the rate of reduction in the size of the privately rented housing stock are vital to any conslusions about the effects of the various policy measures. Estimates of the total of dwellings in the private rented sector (in the statistical sense, including public as well as private employers) were shown in Table V.1. Here estimates are given of the components of change. They are necessarily approximate only. In 1971-81 housing associations are excluded, but up to 1971 they have to be included for lack of data with which to separate them.

Table VIII.10 - Estimated Components of Change of the Private Rented Sector in England and Wales 1939-81

(thousands)

	1939-53	1953-61	1961-71	1971-81
Stock at Start of Period	6,530	5,945	4,557	3,195
New building for HAs	+13	+31	+46	...
New building (other)(a)	+76	+126	+124	+50
Converted Flats (gross)	+125	+125	+85	+60
Slum Clearance	-120	-290	-470	-335
Other losses, including dwellings converted (b)	-160	-108	-104	-67
Transfers to owner-occupation	-505	-1,245	-850	-825
Transfers to local authorities	-14	-27	-33	-40
Total net change	-585	-1,388	-1,202	-1,157
Stock at end of period (c)	5,945	4,557	3,355	2,038

Notes: (a) Includes building for public sector employers, e.g. armed forces married quarters.
(b) Includes 120,000 losses by enemy action in 1940-45.
(c) Difference between 3,355,000 at end of 1961-71 and 3,195,000 at the beginning of 1971-81 is due to the former including and the latter excluding Housing Associations.

Source: See Tables V.1 and V.2.

None of the figures in Table VIII.10 is at all precise, but together they give a reasonable picture of the components of change in the private rented sector over the years. Attention is usually focused on the transfers to owner-occupation, but it is important not to overlook the effect of slum

clearance. Between the announcement in 1953 of the
government's intention to re-start slum clearance
and the "pensioning off of the bulldozer" at the
end of the 1970s, well over a million dwellings had
been removed from the private rented sector by slum
clearance. Given the history, the private rented
sector was bound to bear the brunt of slum
clearance. It also appears to have been most
affected by other demolitions, notably for urban
roads which were generally routed through areas of
older and poorer housing as far as possible.
Between 1953 and 1981 over one-fifth of the private
rented housing stock was simply demolished.

Transfers to owner-occupation were, however,
even more numerous. The chronology was discussed
in Chapter V (76). There is no doubt about the
peak rate of sales having been in the 1950s, and
the evidence from building society lending, plus
the figures for the 1950s, suggested strongly that
most the the half million sales between 1939 and
1953 took place at the very end of the 1940s and
the early 1950s. The annual rate of sales in 1957-
59 appears to have been if anything a little lower
than in the mid-1950s, and in the early 1960s the
rate of sales was very distinctly lower. That can
hardly be taken as evidence of the 1957 Rent Act
having led to a slowing of the contraction of the
private rented sector, however, since the annual
rate of sales in the second half of the 1960s,
after security of tenure and rent restriction had
been brought back, was lower still. There is thus
no firm evidence of the individual changes in the
regime of rent restriction having affected
materially the number of sales year by year for
owner-occupation. That is not to say that there
was certainly no effect, but only that such effects
as there were were not large enough to be measured
with the information available.

The private rented sector is extremely hetero-
geneous, and the rates of reduction were far from
being the same in all sectors. Table VIII.11 shows
estimates for the main sub-sectors. Households
rather then dwellings have to be used because so
much of the furnished sub-sector consisted of
lettings of parts of dwellings. Housing associations are shown because until the later 1970s most
surveys included them in the private rented sector,
and the census did not distinguish them until 1981.
A certain amount of estimation was required in
constructing the table and is described in the

432

notes and references (77).

Table VIII.11 - Households in Sub-Sectors of the Private
Rented Sector: England and Wales

(thousands)

	1961	1966	1971	1981
Housing Associations	110	125	160	361
Occupied by virtue of employment	665	672	575	305
Rented with farm and business premises	198	174	150	69
Other unfurnished	3,654	2,786	2,065	1,077
Other furnished	491	526	165	510
Total	5,108	4,283	3,565	2,322
Total excluding Housing Associations	4,998	4,158	3,495	1,961

Notwithstanding uncertainties arising from how
comparably defined were 'separate households' in
practice in the four censuses, there is no doubt
that furnished lettings changed differently from
the rest of the private sector. The comparison
between 1971 and 1981 argues against the extension
of security of tenure in 1974 to tenants renting
furnished accommodation from non-resident landlords
having led to a fall in the amount of accommodation
let furnished in the same way as the Rent Acts were
alleged to have led to a fall in the amount of
unfurnished accommodation for letting. The amount
of "tied" accommodation, and accommodation rented
with business premises, fell more sharply in the
1970s than in the 1960s, but was not in either
decade subject to the Rent Acts.
Comparison of the fall of some 3.0 million
households in the private rented sector (excluding
housing associations) with the reduction of about
2.4 million in the number of dwellings according to
Table VIII.10 (with an estimate for housing
associations in 1961) shows that there was a steep
reduction in the number of lettings of parts of

433

dwellings. The information about lettings of parts
of dwellings in the censuses is not very detailed,
so recourse must be had to surveys. The first
survey providing information about lettings of
parts of dwellings was in 1964; the most recent
survey was in 1978, the Private Rented Sector
Survey and the Sharers Survey that were based on
the National Dwelling and Housing Survey (NDHS).
Notwithstanding the difficulties with the figures,
including scaling the 1964 survey figures to agree
with the census-based totals in Table VIII.11 and
adjustment to exclude Wales for comparability with
the 1978 surveys for England only, the reduction in
the number of lettings of parts of houses is worth
some attention as it is an important aspect of both
the causes and the consequences of the diminution
of the private rented sector.

Table VIII.12 - Types of Letting by Private Landlords:
England 1964 and 1978

	1964 ('000)	1978 ('000)	Change ('000)	Change (%)
Lettings of parts of dwellings by resident owner-occupiers	280	90	-190	-68
Lettings of parts of dwellings to sub-tenants by resident tenants	100	40	-60	-60
Lettings of parts of houses by non-resident landlords	555	300	-255	-46
Lettings of whole houses or flats	3,255	1,995	-1,280	-39
Total	4,190	2,405	-1,785	-43

Source: See text for methods of estimation.

Lettings of parts of their houses by owner-
occupiers, and by tenants of public and private
landlords, declined most rapidly of all in proportionate terms, and lettings of parts of houses by
non-resident landlords declined by more than did
lettings of whole houses or flats. Clearly the

434

causes were different, as parts of houses could not be sold for owner-occupation. In view of the persisting signs that the demand for rented accommodation exceeded the supply, the fall in the number of householders letting off parts of their houses must be explained mainly in terms of a reduction in the number wishing to do so, perhaps as rising incomes led fewer people to be willing to forego privacy in the interest of the income from letting. Letting of houses in rooms is different again. Letting in rooms of what was previously a singly occupied dwelling house constitutes a 'change of use' that requires consent under the Town and Planning Acts, and many authorities followed a policy of refusing such consents. Where that happened, there was no new supply of such lettings, and as existing lettings went out of use (e.g. through clearance, conversion to self-contained flats, or sale) the total diminished. Here, it may be argued, was one of the causes of the rise in homelessness during the 1970s. Accommodation in lettings of parts of houses was generally very expensive for what it offered, and often poor in quality; but it was usually available quickly, with none of the formalities that went with buying a house or flat or being allocated one by a local authority. The reduction in the supply of such lettings was leading increasingly to an all-or-nothing contrast between sole use of a self-contained house or flat and homelessness.

There were also changes in the circumstances of the households living in the private rented sector. Here again surveys must be used, rather than the census; the comparison is therefore between 1964 and 1978, for England (see Table VIII.13).

The general pattern of changes between the early 1960s and the late 1970s is clear: a large reduction in the number of family households in the private rented sector, a somewhat smaller fall in the number of childless couples, a substantial increase in the number of young and middle-aged people living alone, and a fall in the number of older households that was smaller, proportionately, than among families. The reduction in the number of families would be shown as even greater, in proportional terms, if accommodation rented from employers were excluded from the comparison.

Table VIII.13 - Types of Households in the Private Rented
                Sector England 1964-78

(thousands)

	1964	1978	Change 1964-78 ('000)	(%)
Individuals under 60 living as separate households	315	390	+75	+24
Small adult households (a)	650	430	-220	-34
Small families (b)	780	340	-440	-56
Large families (c)	365	125	-240	-66
Large adult households (d)	815	300	-515	-63
Older small households (e)	1,265	770	-495	-39
Total	4,190	2,360	-1,830	-44

Notes: (a) Two adults (both under 60), no children.
       (b) One adult or two, one child or two.
       (c) One adult or two, three children or more.
       (d) Three adults or more, not more than one child
           (all persons above the minimum school leaving
           age count as "adults").
       (e) Individuals aged 60 or over living alone, and
           two-person households where at least one member
           is aged 60 or over.

Sources: The Housing Survey in England and Wales
           Table 2.31; Private Rented Sector Survey,
           Table 3.3 (rounded).

    The analysis of the way in which the composi-
tion and functions of the private rented sector
changed in the 1960s and 1970s as its size
diminished may be taken a stage further by looking
at length of residence by tenants renting from
private landlords. There is information to be
found about length of residence in the private
rented sector in the late 1950s and early 1960s in
three different surveys (78) and the 1961 Census.

Privately Owned Rented Housing

This information was fitted together to provide an estimate for the "early 1960s". This is compared in Table VIII.14 with the distribution of tenants according to length of residence in 1977. The report on the 1978 Private Rented Sector Survey did not analyse length of residence in a way that can be directly compared with the earlier information, so the 1977 data from the National Dwelling and Housing Survey (NDHS) is used instead.

Table VIII.14 - Length of Residence of Tenants of Private Landlords

| | Proportions (%) | | .. Absolute Totals ('000) .. | | | |
	"Early 1960s"	1977	"Early 1960s	1977	Change	Change (%)
Less than one year	12	20.7	500	500	Nil	Nil
1 year but less than 2	8	10.1	340	240	-100	-29
2 years but less than 3	6	8.8	250	190	-60	-24
3 years but less than 5	11	8.2	460	200	-250	-54
5 years or more	63	52.2	2,640	1,270	-1,370	-52
Total	100	100.0	4,190	2,420	-1,770	-42

Sources: Estimate for "early 1960s" from 1964 survey by Government Social Survey and the 1958 and 1962 surveys sponsored by the Rowntree Trust 1977 from National Dwelling and Housing Survey.

That the "short-stay" part of the private rented sector declined much less than did the rest of the sector is the exact opposite of what would have been expected if the reduction had occurred primarily through decisions by landlords not to re-let. If decisions not to re-let had been the principal part of the process of decline, the proportion of households that had been resident for only a short period would have fallen, with households that had been resident at their addresses a

long time being an increasing proportion of all
households renting from private landlords. This is
the exact opposite of what happened, which tells
heavily in favour of an interpretation in terms of
a fall in the demand for accommodation there by
families, and couples intending to have families,
at the same time as the demand from non-family
households rose. There was during the later 1950s,
the 1960s and the early 1970s a very marked
shortening in the average length of time that
married couples who set up home in accommodation
rented from private landlords stayed there before
moving to owner-occupation or local authority
tenancies (79). That was the main cause of the
rapid fall in the number of family households in
the private rented sector that was shown in Table
VIII.14. The corollary of the increased demand for
owner-occupation was a reduced demand to rent, and
in consequence increasing numbers of formerly
rented houses and flats were sold for owner-occupation.

The fact that the short-stay part of the
private rented sector declined least in the 1960s
and 1970s demonstrates that very considerable
amounts of accommodation were re-let when vacated,
contrary to the very frequent assertions that owing
to the Rent Acts any accommodation vacated would be
sold with vacant possession or (if not saleable)
left empty. These assertions were an instance of
'what everybody knows' being in error, as reference
to readily accessible survey information would have
shown. The first survey to collect such information was the survey of landlords in London carried
out in 1963 by the Government Social Survey for the
Milner Holland Committee. Their findings are
summarized in Table VIII.15; landlords were asked
what they would do if the sample lettings "became
vacant tomorrow".

The next survey to enquire of landlords about
whether they would re-let or sell if their tenanted
properties became vacant was the survey carried out
in 1970 for the Francis Committee. The survey
proved to be predominantly a London survey, so
comparisons may be made with the 1963 survey. The
sample was of properties for which rents had been
registered (or set by Rent Tribunals), hence the
classifications in Table VIII.16.

Table VIII.15 - Landlords' Intentions on Securing Vacant Possession: London 1963

(percentages)

	Re-let	Sell	Live in All of it	Other	Total	(Sample Number)
A. By Type of Letting						
Controlled						
Singly occupied house	51	42	–	7	100	(141)
Purpose built flat	83	14	–	3	100	(65)
Part of house or flat	60	21	8	11	100	(172)
Non-Controlled Unfurnished						
Singly occupied house	77	14	2	7	100	(45)
Purpose built flat	98	–	–	2	100	(90)
Part of house or flat	70	12	11	7	100	(161)
Furnished						
(Mainly parts of houses)	76	11	12	1	100	(108)
B. By Type of Landlord						
Resident landlord	62	6	27	5	100	:
Non-resident individual	55	37	4	4	100	:
Company	86	8	–	6	100	:
Other bodies	84	9	–	7	100	:

Source: Cmnd. 2605, Appendix V, Tables 26 and 28 (1965).

Table VIII.16 – Landlords (including Landlords' Agents) Intentions on Tenancy Falling Vacant, 1970

(percent)

	Re-let Unfurnished	Re-let Furnished	Sell or Occupy	Don't Know	Total	(Sample Number)
Registered Unfurnished Tenant Applications						
Landlords	17	23	33	28	100	(18)
Agents	43	12	33	11	100	(105)
Landlord Applications						
Landlords	64	5	18	14	100	(22)
Agents	48	9	33	9	100	(133)
Joint Applications						
Landlords	50	-	50	-	100	(8)
Agents	49	8	33	9	100	(76)
Furnished (Rent Tribunal Cases)						
Landlords	8	75	16	-	100	(12)
Agents	6	70	11	13	100	(46)

Source: Committee on the Rent Acts, Report, (Cmnd. 4609) (1971), p.336.

If the 'don't knows' are excluded, the landlord or agents said that more than one-half of the
sample of unfurnished lettings would be re-let
unfurnished if they became vacant, not re-let
furnished or sold. The detail provided by the 1970
survey was not the same as that in the 1963 survey,
so close comparisons are not possible; but clearly
the proportion of instances where the dwellings
would be re-let was lower in 1970 than in 1963.

Information about what landlords would do with
lettings if they became vacant was next collected
in 1976 by the "Attitudes to Letting" survey. This
was a more specialized survey than those of 1963
and 1970, with a sharper focus on attitudes and
intensions, and drew the destinction (not drawn in
either of the previous surveys) between what the
landlord would do if the individual letting became
vacant and what he would do if the whole building
was vacated. Table VIII.17 summarizes the replies.

The proportion of lettings which, landlords
said, they would sell if vacated individually was
about the same in the 1976 survey as in 1970 (when
resident landlords were not included); but if the
whole building were vacated the proportion of sales
would be greater. The distinction was most pro-
nounced for corporate landlords, who were more
likely to own blocks of flats than individual landlords; flats were much easier to sell for owner-
occupation if all in the block could be sold than
if some would remain rented, and blocks that were
partly rented and partly owner-occupied could have
management problems not present where all the flats
were rented or all owner-occupied.

Sales of flats for owner-occupation were a
distinctive aspect of the reduction in renting from
private landlords in the 1960s and 1970s. Flats
built in the 1930s and earlier had been built for
renting; problems about responsibility for the
maintenance of the structure and upkeep of common
parts militated against owner-occupation of flats,
and the 1960 survey found that only one-fifth (or
perhaps slightly less) of privately owned flats
were owner-occupied (80); but by 1977 the proportion had risen to over one-half (81). Long lease-
hold tenure in which the terms of the lease obliged
the ground landlord to maintain the structure and
see to the common parts, and obliged the lessees to
pay service charges that covered the costs, was
accepted as providing adequate protection for the
owner-occupier's investment, and during the 1960s

441

Table VIII.17 - Landlords' Intentions if a Vacancy Occurred at Sampled Addresses: England 1976

(percentages)

	Resident Individual (excluding Sub-letting)	Non-Resident Individual	Company
A. Individual Vacancy			
Re-let (or improve for re-letting)	51	50	56
Sell (or improve for sale)	10	39	35
Occupy it himself (or let relations occupy)	34	5	1
Leave vacant	13	5	8
Other	-	2	-
Total	100 (*)	100	100
B. Whole Building Vacant			
Re-let (or improve for re-letting)	40	40	36
Sell (or improve for sale)	34	52	60
Occupy it himself (or let relations occupy)	43	4	1
Leave vacant	1	2	3
Other	-	2	2
Total	100 (*)	100	100
(Sample Number)	(93)	(342)	(244)

Note: (*) Individual percentages sum to more than 100 because some landlords said that they would use part of the letting/building in one way and part in another.

Source: Office of Population Censuses and Surveys: Attitudes to Letting 1976 (HMSO 1978) Tables 4.5 and 4.6.

came to be recognized as providing a sufficient security for a mortgage loan. Acceptability to building societies made flats saleable in the 1960s and the 1970s in a way that they had not been in the 1950s and the inter-war years. During the boom of the early 1970s there were many reports of sales or flats, and in some instances criticisms of pressure being put on tenants to buy.

The dominant importance of building societies as house purchase lenders made their criteria for lending a considerable influence on the number of sales for owner-occupation of formerly rented dwellings. Sales of flats have already been mentioned; and it is highly likely that the public pressure put on building societies from the mid-1970s onwards to be more ready to lend 'down market' lowered the threshold of what property was saleable. This is the most likely reason for the large increase between 1971-72 and 1977-78 in the number of pre-1914 dwellings sold with building society and local authority mortgages. The number is estimated at 145,000 in 1971 and 155,000 in 1972, but 190,000 in 1977 and 210,000 in 1978; in contrast the number of inter-war dwellings sold is estimated at 145,000 and 135,000 in 1971 and 1972, and 145,000 in both 1977 and 1978 (82); since there was no increase in the number of inter-war dwellings sold, the increase in the number of pre-1914 dwellings sold is evidence of an increase in the supply of them coming onto the market rather than a faster turnover. The slow growth of real incomes after 1973, and high mortgage interest rates are likely to have increased the demand for comparatively cheap houses relative to new and modern houses; given the building societies' greater readiness to lend on older houses made this demand effective, its consequence appears to have been a faster reduction in the private rented sector.

Rent Restriction and the Reduction in Renting from Private Landlords

Rent restriction has in general attracted little but criticism. Comment from the world of property including the property professions has been adverse; and most economists who have written about rent restriction have been very critical. The essays re-published by the Institute of Economic Affairs in 1972 (83) are a fair sample, and the

443

author of the introduction contended that the
record showed that rent restriction ".... has done
much more harm than good in rental housing markets
- let alone the economy at large - by perpetuating
shortages, encouraging immobility, swamping
consumer preferences, fostering dilapidation of
housing stocks and eroding production incentives,
distorting land use patterns and the allocation of
scarce resources" (84). He might have added that
in Britain wartime rent restriction, by holding
rents constant in money terms while the general
price level rose fast, was instrumental in forcing
housing outgoings sharply downwards in real terms,
with long lasting effects on public perceptions
about what level of outgoings in relation to income
was reasonable, that carried over into the setting
of council rents. The demand for housing,
including separate accommodation in place of part
of a house, was sufficiently price-sensitive for
such a forcing down of the price of accommodation
to produce a substantial increase in the quantity
of housing demand, which successive governments
considered had to be met. Critics of rent restriction both in the world of property and among
economists have seen it as the main reason why the
number of households renting from private landlords
declined as it did.

This conclusion requires, however, to be
heavily qualified, and distinctions drawn between
rent restriction as such and holding rents constant
in cash terms at a time when the price level is
rising. But before developing those lines of
argument, it is important to reiterate that rent
restriction was not just about holding rents below
market levels but about security of tenure. Most
of the comment on rent restriction has been in
terms of the advantage to tenants being rents that
were below market levels with security of tenure
virtually ignored. The only important exception
known to the present author is in the works of
Professor Nevitt (85). But it could be fairly
argued that security was just as important as lower
rents. Reducing insecurity was an important aspect
of the social policies that developed during World
War II and were enacted into law between 1945 and
1950. The revised and expanded National Insurance
scheme was intended to reduce the financial
insecurity arising from the risk of interruption of
earnings through sickness, injury, or unemployment,
and the National Health Service removed the risk to

444

household finances that the cost of lengthy or complex medical and hospital treatment might bring. Reduction or elimination of insecurity of families' housing could be seen alongside the reduction in insecurity in other aspects of life. Most people regard secure housing as desirable, and it had always been obtainable, by purchase or by leasing for a term of years, by those who could afford it. So what in Chapter I was termed the "specific egalitarian" aim of raising the standard of housing that people could have, if they wanted it, irrespective of their income, could as well include security of tenure against arbitrary dispossession as it could include a bathroom and inside WC. Dispossession at a week's notice for any reason or none had become an anachronism in the post-1945 climate of opinion in Britain, and substitution of one month for one week in the Rent Act 1957 made no material difference in this respect. In retrospect it is surprising that in 1956/57 a return to no more security than a month's notice was thought to be "on" for family housing. As was observed earlier in this chapter, abuses to do with insecurity did far more harm to the reputation of the policy of decontrol than did excessive rents. But for security of tenure to be effective it had to be combined with restriction of rents, otherwise a tenant could be dispossessed by charging a rent known to be beyond his means.

For security of tenure to be workable in conditions of inflation it had to be separated from fixity of rents in money terms. In post-1945 conditions such fixity of rents was unworkable, and in this respect as well the setting of a fresh money value for rents without provision for change (except after improvement) other than by new primary legislation by the Rent Act 1957 was an anachronism. Not until 1965 was security of tenure separated from fixity of rents, and with hindsight this could be said to have been twenty years too late. There was nothing anomalous about security of tenure combined with market rents: this was broadly what the 1954 legislation on landlord and tenant provided for business tenancies, whereby the tenant who had observed the conditions of tenancy is normally entitled to a new lease but at a market rent. Much the same applied to agricultural tenancies. And the German legislation on rent restriction in the 1970s was directed primarily at security of tenure with rents so set as to be close

445

to market rents (though with the landlord prevented from charging rents higher than market levels). It is worth noting here that the provisions in the Housing Act 1980 about security for tenants of houses and flats let as "assured tenancies" was modelled on the law related to business tenancies. Why the government of the day did not make any provision for security of tenure in the Bill that became the Rent Act 1957 will repay study when the official papers for 1956 and 1957 become available in the Public Record Office. The 1954 legislation on business tenancies would have provided a precedent, should one have been needed.

Whether a combination of market rents with security of tenure would have resulted in the housing history of post-1945 England being very different, though, is very arguable. The principal reason is that the conventional view that regards rent restriction as the predominant cause of the diminution of the private rented sector gives insufficient weight, in the present author's view, to the strength of the demand for owner-occupation. We saw in Chapter V how the proportion of households expressing a preference for owner-occupation grew; and in Chapter VI how owner-occupiers came to have the advantage of very favourable rates of interest, and a tax relief that provided the equivalent of a substantial subsidy. It is easy to overlook the fact that the preference for owner-occupation was just as much a preference against renting from private landlords as against renting from local authorities. The favourable rate of interest on house purchase loans plus tax relief meant that most households that could afford a market rent would get better value from buying than from renting, particularly in view of the way in which house values rose. Put another way, the owner-occupier who had the advantage of tax relief could normally out-bid the tenant who had to pay rent out of taxed income.

The near-continuous inflation after 1945 combined with high nominal interest rates means that new building for letting by private enterprise would have had to have been financed very differently from in the inter-war years or before 1914. The basis then was finance by fixed interest borrowing on mortgage, with the mortgagee having the right to call in the loan on notice, in practice to allow him to raise the interest rate when the general level of interest rates rose.

446

This way of financing new building depended on the interest rate at which the money could be borrowed being slightly less than the rent (net of costs of upkeep and mangement) as a proportion of the capital cost. That was feasible enough when the rate of interest was 5% or 4½%, but in the late 1950s and early 1960s when mortgage money cost from 6% to 7% it would hardly have been so, and when in the 1970s interest rates were in double figures, net rents that at the outset were high enough to cover the interest on a fixed interest loan were wholly impossible. Virtually anyone who could have afforded such rents could afford to buy, and with tax relief the net outgoings would have been lower for purchase than for renting right from the start. In inflationary times market rents could be expected to keep up with the general price level and perhaps exceed it, but if fixed interest financing were used there would be a very large cash shortfall in the early years when rents were insufficient to cover interest, even if on a long enough view the yield on the investment compared favourably with shares. Local authorities covered the gap between rent and loan charges on new houses by pooling and subsidies, but private owners received no subsidies and only large and long established landlords could use pooling of costs of old and new houses in the way councils did. With rents rising but at an unforecastable rate (in money terms), houses to rent were an equity investment analogous to shares, not something analogous to government securities but at a higher yield, as they had been in the inter-war years or before 1914; so they would have had to be financed by money raised on the same kind of terms. A public company could issue shares, but the individual landlord obviously could not; and since he could not, it is hard to see how he could have invested in new houses to let to an extent greater than he could finance from his own accumulated savings. In the conditions of the late 1950s, the 1960s and the 1970s, the hope that the individual private landlord could again finance houses to let was thus a vain hope, irrespective of whether market rents could have been secured. Letting newly built houses would have been confined to companies financially strong enough to issue shares, or able to make the financing arrangements with insurance companies and pension funds of the kind used to finance investments in commercial property.

447

That the financing of new houses and flats to let by private owners would have had to have been analogous to the financing of shop and office property is vital to any judgement about whether private investment in new houses and flats would have been forthcoming if the same legal regime had applied to them as to commercial property. For most of the period, yields of 5% to 6% were obtainable on commercial property, let on leases that made the tenant responsible for repair, so rents that gave at least as good a yield as this would be needed to make house property an attractive investment. But a rent high enough to provide such a yield would generally be unattractive to anyone who could afford to buy, unless frequent moves made the costs, in trouble as well as cash, of buying and selling houses onerous. Likewise, such "economic" rents would frequently be beyond the reach of those who could not afford to buy. One can only conclude that in the conditions of the late 1950s, the 1960s and the 1970s, large scale new building for letting by private enterprise was never at all likely without substantial subsidy, given the strength of demand for owner-occupation and the powerful inducement to buy rather than rent that the tax relief gave. To make extensive new building for letting by private owners financially feasible, either overt subsidy (as in 1923-29) or tax reliefs equivalent to a subsidy would be needed. Other countries have the one or the other, and sometimes both; in the period studied here Britain had neither.

The strength of the preference for owner-occupation, the favourable terms on which money could be borrowed for house purchase, and the tax relief on house purchase help explain not only why there was so little new building for letting by private enterprise but also how so much of the existing stock of privately owned rented housing was sold for owner-occupation. Even with market rents there would still have been a gap between the price which houses would fetch if sold with vacant possession and their value as investments producing an income. That gap was the most important element in the economics of rented housing in post-war Britain, and more than anything else was what set housing apart from other kinds of rented property. Commercial property was an investment held to produce an income. The owner of rented business premises at no time during the period studied had anything to gain from getting the tenant out; on the contrary, tenants whose financial strength was good enough to obviate any doubts about their ability to pay the rent were an asset to a commercial landlord. But the owner of rented houses frequently stood to gain if the tenant left; this gain from being able to sell with vacant possession rather than subject to a protected tenancy put much increased pressure on security of tenure, both through litigation at the edges of it and through extra-legal and (at times) plainly illegal action. Rent restriction increased the gain from selling with vacant possession, but was rarely the origin of it. In the house price boom of the early 1970s the gains from selling with vacant possession would have been very large even in the absence of rent restrictions.

Not to be overlooked as a reason why sales for owner-occupation of formerly rented accommodation were far more numerous (as far as can be seen) in England than in the USA or in the European countries, was that far more of the rented housing stock in England consisted of individual houses as opposed to flats. Owner-occupation of flats is much more complicated under any legal system than is owner-occupation of individual houses. 'Condominium' ownership of flats in the USA, for instance, came on the scene only in the 1970s as a way of selling flats for what was effectively (seen through English eyes) owner-occupation. Nor should the importance of slum clearance be under-rated. As Table VIII.10 shows, about a million dwellings rented from private landlords were demolished between 1953 and 1981.

The reduction in the number of lettings of parts of houses deserves separate comment. The reduction was not a simple process in which houses and flats that once had been let were sold and fewer and fewer householders let off parts of their houses to sub-tenants. On the contrary, there were flows in both directions, with dwellings let which had hitherto been owner-occupied, and lettings of parts of houses which hitherto had been wholly occupied by the owner or main tenant. As late as the 1970s the number of fresh lettings of parts of houses was far from negligible: of the dwellings in the Attitudes to Letting sample that in 1976 were owner-occupied with lettings, 17% had in 1971 been owner-occupied with no lettings. From the nature of the sample there is no way in which an estimate for the whole country can be derived, and the sample number of addresses which in 1971 were owner-occupied with lettings but in 1976 were owner-occupied with no lettings was twice as great. Similar information was not collected on earlier occasions, so nothing definite can be said about changes through time; but it is far from unlikely that the fall in the number of lettings of parts of houses came from a diminished number of new lettings rather than an increase in the number of lettings taken off the market.

A particular reason for there being fewer new lettings of parts of houses was the use by local authorities, as mentioned earlier, of their planning powers to prevent houses hitherto used as single family residences from being let in rooms to tenants. Letting such a house in rooms was held to constitute a change of use under the Town and Country Planning Acts, and hence to be unlawful unless planning permission had first been obtained from the local authority. This requirement did not extend to the owner-occupier letting off part of his house, or the tenant sub-letting, but it definitely did apply to letting a large house in rooms to several tenants, whether the owner lived in part of it or not. Although there was some variation in local authorities' attitudes, the general disposition was not to allow more houses to become multi-occupied. Occupiers of such houses could readily become in need of local authority tenancies, as a supply of multi-occupied accommodation could attract people in from elsewhere, to be housed later, particularly if they had children, by the authority within whose area the accommodation in question was to be found. This was primarily a London issue, and attempts to prevent the letting in rooms of houses in London has a history that reaches back to the 1590s.

The reduction of the stock of lettings by private landlords in England was thus a complex process, with powerful causes other than the holding down of rents through rent restriction. The suggestion is not made that rent restriction was of no importance, of course; only that rent restriction by itself was only a limited part of the explanation. In the inter-war years, in the 1930s in particular, a non-controlled sector not only existed side by side with a controlled sector but was the setting for investment on a large scale in new house building for rent. The existence of

controls applying to part of the rented stock <u>may</u>
generate expectations that controls would in time
be extended to the currently non-controlled sector
and thereby dissuade investment there; but there is
nothing automatic about it, and it did not happen
that way in Britain in the 1930s. One reason why
not, in all probability, was the stability of the
general price level: it is rent increases that put
the steam behind pressures for rent control, and
with a stable price level and low interest rates
enabling landlords to obtain satisfactory returns
from stable rents, extension of rent control to
post-1919 dwellings did not come onto the agenda of
British politics in the 1930s. Falling prices and
costs down to 1933 likewise took some of the
aggravation out of rent restriction in the
controlled sector: with falling costs landlords'
returns in money terms slowly increased, a falling
general price level increased them in real terms,
and falling interest rates in the economy as a
whole reduced the attraction of selling out from
rented housing in order to re-invest elsewhere.

After 1945 the economic context was completely
different. Continuing inflation meant that for
private enterprise renting to be workable, security
of tenure had to be separated from fixed rents. As
was suggested earlier in this chapter, they were
separated twenty years too late. What would have
happened if security of tenure had been separated
from fixed rents in the late 1940s or early 1950s
can only be a matter for conjecture. There would
have been major problems of financing to be solved
if building for letting by private owners were to
return to the scale on which it took place in the
1930s, and whereas in the 1930s building societies
were eager for opportunities to lend money, from
the mid-1950s they experienced (as described in
Chapter VI) a chronic inability to raise enough
money to meet the demand for loans for house
purchase for owner-occupation, let alone to finance
building and purchase for letting. Absence of
finance could well have been an important reason
why the provision in the Housing Repairs and Rents
Act 1954 of an exclusion for new dwellings (as in
1919) did not lead to much new building for
letting, as well as the political risk that the
opposition of the day, were they to be returned to
office at a subsequent general election, would
extend rent control to such dwellings. Given the
strength of the demand for owner-occupation, it is

451

all too easy to over-state the extent to which an absence of rent restriction and security of tenure would have diminished the inducement to sell into owner-occupation, let alone lead to new building on a large scale for letting. With the other sectors subsidized, it is not easy to see how the non-subsidized sector could be expected to keep up with them. It seems reasonable in the light of the historical record to put more emphasis on subsidy (including tax relief); the growing preference for owner-occupation; efficient financial arrangements for making that demand effective; and the financial problems for renting that high nominal interest rates would have generated, than on rent restriction as reasons for the shift in the tenure pattern of English housing. The present author would therefore reject as exaggerated Paish's use of the term "the disastrous incubus of the Rent Restriction Acts" (86) as applied to the period about which he was writing (down to 1952) or subsequently. Treating landlords as politically expendable likewise would not appear as an apt description of policy on rent restriction in the inter-war years. In the post-war years unsubsidized renting by private enterprise was not an alternative to subsidized renting by public authorities: it was an alternative to owner-occupation; and the growing preference for owner-occupation, reinforced by the tax relief, ensured that owner-opccupation would expand and private enterprise renting would contract. With a combination of security of tenure and restriction of rents better adapted to continuing inflation the contraction would have been slower. But a radically different outcome would have been likely only if building to let had received fiscal support on the same scale as owner-occupation, or building by private owners subsidized as "social housing" in the same way as in some of the European countries.

Notes and References

(1) "Controlled tenancies" were abolished by the Housing Act 1980.

(2) D. Englander, Landlord and Tenant in Urban Britain, Clarendon Press, Oxford, 1983, p.205.

(3) Englander, Landlord and Tenant, p.208.

(4) Englander, op. cit p.184.

(5) M.J. Daunton, House and Home in the Victorian City, Arnold, London, 1983, p.295.

(6) For accounts of the Clydeside "rent strike" from a standpoint of sympathy with the tenants that were involved as taking part in the class struggle, see S. Damer, 'State, Class, and Housing: Glasgow 1885-1915' and J. Melling, 'Clydeside Housing and the Evolution of State Rent Control' in J. Melling (Ed.) Housing, Social Policy and the State, Croom Helm, London, 1980.

(7) A.A. Nevitt, The Nature of Rent Controlling Legislation in the United Kingdom, Centre for Environmental Studies, London, 1970.

(8) Report of the Committee of the Ministry of Reconstruction on the Increase of Rent and Mortgage Interest (War Restrictions) Act 1915, Cmnd. 9235 (1918).

(9) Report of the Committee on the Increase of Rent and Mortgage Interest (War Restrictions) Acts, Cmd. 658 (1920).

(10) Final Report of the Inter-Departmental Committee on the Rent Restrictions Acts, Cmd. 3911 (1931).

(11) Final Report of the Inter-Departmental Committee on the Rent Restrictions Acts, Cmd. 5621 (1937).

(12) Report of the Inter-Departmental Committee on the Rent Restrictions Acts, Cmd. 5621 (1937).

(13) Report of the Inter-Departmental Committee on Rent Control, Cmd. 6621 (1945).

(14) Estimate made for the Marley Committee, Report, Cmd. 3911 (1931) para.27.

(15) Report (Cmd.658) (1920), para.4.

(16) Ibid, paras.7-9.

(17) Report, (Cmd) 1803, (1923) pp. 7 and 8.

(18) Cmd. 1803 (1923), p.8.

(19) Cmd. 1803, (1923) p.9.

(20) The 1931 Census confirmed that this was so. See Chapter III above.

(21) Inter-Departmental Committee on the Rent Restrictions Acts, _Report_ Cmd. 3911 (1931), para.32.
(22) Cmd. 3911 (1931), para.38.
(23) Cmd. 3911, para.42.
(24) Cmd. 3911 (1931), para.46.
(25) Cmd. 3911 (1931), para.47.
(26) _Ibid_, para.48.
(27) See page 76 above.
(28) See the observations on this point in the _Minority Report_. Cmd. 5621 (1937) p.55, para.7.
(29) Cmd. 5621 (1937), p.55, para.7.
(30) Cmd. 5621 (1937), para.64.
(31) Report of the Inter-Departmental Committee on Rent Control, _Report_, Cmd. 6621 (1945), para.17.
(32) The 1911 Census total of dwellings was 7,691,000, and the House Duty figures suggest a net increase of 200,000 in the stock of dwellings between 1911 and 1914. 90% of the combined total is 7.1 million.
(33) Department of the Environment, unpublished tabulations.
(34) Cmd. 3911 (1931), pp.18-24.
(35) Committee on Local Expenditure, _Report_, Cmd. 4300 (1932). para.78 and footnote.
(36) J.R. Jarmain, _Housing Subsidies and Rents_, Stevens, London, 1948, Appendix 1, taken from Ministry of Health Annual Reports.
(37) Committee on Local Expenditure, _Report_, Cmd. 4300 (1932) footnote to table on p.54.
(38) The Ridley Committee's estimates, from information collected by the Ministry of Labour, Cmd. 5621 (1937) para.42.
(39) Cmd. 3911 (1931), para.63.
(40) Inter-Departmental Committee on the Rent Restrictions Act, _Report_, Cmd. 3911 (1931), para.113.
(41) Inter-Departmental Committee on Rent Control, _Report_, Cmd. 6621 (1945) para.43.
(42) Cmd. 6621, para.35.
(43) See J.R. Hicks, U.K. Hicks, and C.E.V. Leser, _The Problem of Valuation for Rating_, Cambridge University Press, Cambridge, 1944, Chapters III and IV.
(44) Cmd. 6621, para.55.
(45) K.O. Morgan, _Labour in Power_, Clarendon Press, Oxford, 1984.

(46) C.H. Feinstein, National Income, Expenditure, and Output of the United Kingdom 1855-1965, Cambridge University Press, Cambridge, 1972.

(47) Ministry of Housing and Local Government, Committee of Enquiry into the Cost of House Building, The Cost of House Maintenance, 1953.

(48) Slightly different figures applied in London.

(49) The others were the resumption of slum clearance, with a tightening up of the definition of "unfit", and larger improvement grants.

(50) Weidenfeld and Nicolson, London, 1969.

(51) The Government Social Surveys estimate was 367,000 to 391,000 (subject of course to sampling variation): Rent Act 1957 Report of Enquiry, Cmnd. 1246 (1960), p.21. The estimate provided by the 1958 survey sponsored by the Rowntree Trust was 400,000.
D.V. Donnison in Manchester Guardian, 9 and 10 July 1959 (subsequently republished in D.V. Donnison and others, Essays on Housing, Codicote Press, Welwyn, 1964.

(52) Rent Control Statistical Information, Cmnd.17 (1956).

(53) Government Social Survey, The Housing Survey in England and Wales 1964, (HMSO 1967), Table 2.31.

(54) Cmnd. 1246 (1960) estimates 3,890,000 lettings subject to control immediately after the Act took effect, to which must be added the lettings decontrolled by the rateable value limit.

(55) Cmnd. 1246 (1960) Table 6; Cmd. 2605 (1965) Table 33; The Housing Survey in England and Wales 1964 Table 2.22.

(56) See J.B. Cullingworth, Housing in Transition, Heinemann, London, 1963, for discussion of this phenomenon.

(57) Head of household income from The Housing Survey in England and Wales 1964, Table 2.31, rents from Table IX.4 above, with rents in London and the rest of England and Wales combined in proportions taken from Table 2.3 of The Housing Survey in England and Wales.

(58) Average earnings of adult men employed full-time in manual work in manufacturing and certain other industries. The National Insurance pension for a married couple was 68% higher in 1964 than in 1957.

(59) Committee on Housing in Greater London, Report, Cmnd. 2605 (1965) Table 31 (p.351). The Committee and its report are commonly known by the name of the chairman, Milner Holland.

(60) See previous reference. Abuses are discussed in Chapter VII and Appendix III.

(61) See Milner Holland Committee Report, Appendix II, for a short account of Rachman and his activities.

(62) Qualities considered by the Milner Holland Committee to be shown by the great majority of London landlords, Cmnd. 2605, (1965) p.176.

(63) See page 390 above.

(64) Committee on the Rent Acts, Report, Cmnd. 4609 (1971).

(65) Cmnd. 4609 (1971) Chapter II, and Table 20 and Supplementary Table VI (pp.200-302).

(66) Cmnd. 4609, (1971) Table 16.

(67) Housing Statistics, No.22, Table VIII.

(68) Cmnd. 4609, (1971) pp.87-88.

(69) Ibid, p.62.

(70) The results of the Valuation Offices's analysis were circulated to Rent Officers and Rent Assessment Committees in a note that was cited in J. Doling and M. Davies, 'Fair Rents and Capital Values', Estates Gazette, Vol. 260, pp-677-678.

(71) Housing and Construction Statistics No. 4, Table 44.

(72) Ibid.

(73) Report, Cmnd. 4609, (1971) Chapter 32.

(74) Cmnd. 4609, (1971) pp.233-235.

(75) Prices and Incomes Act 1968, which applied to rents registered before the end of 1969, and Rent (Control of Increases) Act 1969, which applied to rents registered in 1970 and 1971.

(76) Pages 173-5 above.

(77) Housing association figure for 1971 is from National Dwelling and Housing Survey, Table 2.5; earlier years were estimated by working back from 1971 by subtraction of dwellings completed, with a small allowance for acquisition. The other 1961 figures are as enumerated in the census, adjusted on the basis of the post-enumeration check (General Report pp.166-168). The 1966 figures are from the Quality Check apart from household renting furnished, where

the number is as enumerated. The difference
between the enumerated and Quality Check
figures for furnished lettings was due to
separate households found by the Quality
Check but not identified as such in the
census were taken to have been renting
furnished, and such housholds were not
checked in 1971.

For 1971 the proportion of households
occupying their dwellings through their job
or business was taken from the General
Household Survey for 1971 and 1972 (pooled),
and the estimate split between rented with
business premises and occupied by virtue of
employment pro-rata to 1966. 150,000 of the
households renting with job or business were
assumed to rent furnished (see Housing Policy
Technical Volume Chapter IX, Note to Table
IV.13. The rest were unfurnished.

The 1981 figures are as enumerated (Housing
and Households), Table 2.

(78)   The 1958 and 1962 surveys sponsored by the
       Rowntree Trust, with results published in
       D.V. Donnison (and others), Essays on
       Housing, Codicote Press, Welwyn, 1964; and
       J.B. Cullingworth, English Housing Trends,
       Bell, London, 1965; and The Housing Survey in
       England and Wales 1964, by Government Social
       Survey.

(79)   A.E. Holmans, 'Housing Careers of Recently
       Married Couples' Population Trends No. 24,
       1981.

(80)   The Housing Situation in England and Wales,
       Table 17, P.G. Gray and R. Russell
       (cf. Government Social Survey).

(81)   National Dwelling and Housing Survey.

(82)   For building societies' loans the building
       society mortgage survey provided information
       on the age of dwellings purchased in all
       years from 1968, and the local authority
       mortgage survey did so from 1974; for 1971
       and 1972 an estimate was made by assuming
       that the age distribuition of second-hand
       dwellings sold with local authority mortgages
       (for which there are published figures) was
       the same as in 1974. This is not necessarily
       correct, but the margin of error introduced
       is small.

(83)   F.G. Pennance (Ed.) Verdict on Rent Control,
       Institute of Economic Affairs, London, 1972.

(84)   Pennance, <u>Rent Control</u>, p.xi.
(85)   See, for instance, A.A. Nevitt, <u>The Nature of
       Rent Controlling Legislation in the United
       Kingdom</u>, Centre for Environmental Studies,
       London, 1970.
(86)   F.W. Paish, 'The Economics of Rent
       Restriction', <u>Lloyds Bank Review</u>, 1952.

CHAPTER IX

OVERVIEW AND CONCLUDING OBSERVATIONS

The theme of this book has been how, why, and with what results government became so deeply involved with housing, and particularly why the degree of involvement increased so much after 1945 even though households' real incomes rose at an unprecedented rapid rate (for Britain) and owner-occupation took the place of renting as the majority tenure. This chapter attempts to draw together the threads of the argument, and from the review of results of policies to highlight some of the reasons why by the mid- to later 1970s the support for housing policies of the kind in effect for the previous thirty years (or even fifty years) was beginning to decline.

Why government came to be deeply involved with housing is a comparatively straightforward question to answer; why its involvement increased so much is less readily answered; and what the involvement achieved most difficult of all. Chapter II attributed the beginning of government involvement with urban living conditiions (including housing) to the combined effect of a massive change of scale in urban living and a change in attitudes towards conditions that had existed for centuries. The industrial revolution did not cause bad housing in the sense of causing housing conditions to be worse than they would otherwise have been. The basic cause was poverty, and that was not a consequence of the industrial revolution. The growth of industry at a time when the population was growing fast (for basically non-industrial reasons) led to an enormous increase in the urban population and so made the consequences of the insanitary conditions in towns far more important in quantitative terms. With the change in the numerical scale of the

"health of towns" problem went a change of
attitudes. That the health of towns became the
subject of a great deal of concern in the nineteenth century whereas similar conditions (or
worse) in London had excited no such interest even
though they were on the doorstep of the Court,
government, and legislature must be attributed to
the same movement of opinion that brought about the
abolition of slavery, the reform of the criminal
law, the great increase of missionary activity at
home and abroad, and a general flourishing of
charitable activity. Just as concern for the souls
of their fellow men led some well-to-do nineteenth
century men and women to support education for the
poor lest they should be prevented by illiteracy
from reading the Bible, so it led others to
interest themselves in the housing of the poor lest
crowding and squalor should make moral living
impossible. The body of opinion that had come to
regard public executions and bare-knuckle prize-
fighting as offensive to decency tended to the same
view about squalid housing when attention was
focused on it.

Squalor and crowding might appear as public
scandals, but effective action could only be taken
through state policy. The advantages of an uncon-
taminated water supply, a sewerage system, and
collection and disposal of waste were well understood. But water supply and sewerage and drainage
systems are inherently local monopolies and so must
be provided by public bodies (or private organizations with statutory powers). The development of
these services was therefore closely bound up with
the growth of nineteenth century local government,
and hence proceeded at a pace that varied greatly
from place to place, sometimes for largely
fortuitous reasons and sometimes owing to ratepayers' resistance to the expense. The powers of
central government to hurry things along were
limited; but by the 1870s public health engineering
had become well established as part of the responsibilities of urban local authorities. The 'health
of towns' question had passed from reforming
philanthropists to Borough Engineers and Medical
Officers of Health.

Important as was public health engineering as
a function of government, however, its effect on
housing conditions could not go beyond drainage, a
cold water tap, and (often later on in the day) a
water closet. That was as far as public health

engineering would reach; if 'the health of towns' was coterminous with control of communicable disease, that was the point at which public health and housing reform separated. But protection of health of the occupiers of houses could reach further; and protection of morals further still. Protection of occupiers' health called for minimum standards of space, ventilation, and light. Public concern for morals called for separate sleeping quarters instead of young and old of both sexes being crowded together. The minimum standards for protection of health were the basis of powers to close or demolish as "unfit for human habitation" houses that fell far short of those standards. Separation of the sexes in sleeping quarters was the basis of powers to control overcrowding. Concern for physical health and morals made the worst housing conditions appear as a public scandal, even if they no longer posed a threat to those who lived elsewhere by facilitating the spread of communicable disease.

What should be done about those conditions that constituted the "housing question", as it came to be termed in the later nineteenth century, when the earlier all-embracing "condition of England question" began to sub-divide into a number of more specific "questions"? The earliest answer was in the form of 'a law against it'. Until well into the nineteenth century, English civil government was much more about prohibitions of various kinds than about providing services, poor relief alone excepted. Social reform increased the array of prohibitions in such ways as forbidding women to work underground in coal mines and forbidding children to work longer than specified hours in mills and factories. There was thus nothing particularly revolutionary or even startling about powers to forbid the building of houses that did not comply with statutory standards, to close or demolish houses that fell short of a different (and much lower) set of standards, or to forbid landlords to have more than a maximum number of people in the accommodation they let. The limitations to this answer to the "housing question" did not take long to discover. The building bye-laws under the Public Health Acts, the powers under the Torrens and Cross Acts to demolish insanitary dwellings and clear insanitary areas and bye-laws to abate nuisances provided the means with which to try to drive the worst housing off the market. But

461

reformers very quickly found that demolishing insanitary dwellings without building better houses to replace them merely drove the displaced occupiers into crowded accommodation elsewhere, and that to cover its costs replacement housing had to be let at rents that were beyond what the displaced households could afford. Against the facts of the distribution of income and sheer poverty, a policy that relied solely on driving the worst accommodation off the market was bound to fail.

The consequence was an impasse. The various ways out of this impasse that had their supporters in the decade before 1914 were discussed in Chapter II, where it was argued that given the powers of the state and subsequent experience with land taxation, only building for letting at subsidized rents was reasonably likely to work as a way of reconciling the housing standards that would protect health and morals with the amount of rent that large numbers of households could afford to pay. Subsidized housing did not ineluctably mean council housing, of course. It is this distinction, a much narrower distinction than that between subsidized renting and land reform or redistribution of incomes, that provides such justification as there is for the criticisms lately directed at the argument that the minimum standards of housing canvassed before 1914 could lead only to council housing. That there were few if any parallels in other countries with the British council housing stock in 1939, let alone in later years, is certainly true. That other countries relied far more heavily on subsidized building by private onwers and non-profit-making bodies is likewise very clear. Why Britain relied so heavily on stocks of houses owned directly by local authorities and not on subsidies and tax reliefs for private owners deserves asking more frequently.

There is in the present author's view no conclusive answer, but private landlords being especially vulnerable in political terms and treated as expendable is not part of such answers as there are. One may first note the very special circumstances of the immediate post-war years when building costs were very high but expected to fall. For reasons discussed in Chapter III, these were not conditions in which private enterprise could be expected to build. It is important to note, though, that the Housing (Additional Powers) Act 1919 did make subsidy available to private owners, and so, much more important, did the Housing Act 1923. It was the 1924 Labour government that made the 1923 Act subsidy permanent; and a Conservative government that discontinued it in 1929. Chamberlain was the responsible Minister at the time, and the rather brief reference to it by his most recent biographer (1) conveys the impression that the subsidy was discontinued on grounds of economy, because building costs had fallen, and not from any strategic decision about the comparative merits of subsidized local authority housing and subsidies to private owners. The only subsequent occasion on which subsidized private housing to rent might have come to the fore, on present evidence, would have been if the Conservatives had won the general election in 1945. Whether the 1951-55 Conservative government considered subsidizing private landlords has yet to emerge from the official papers of the period.

Unsubsidized building for letting by private landlords in place of subsidized building by local authorities was never really 'on'. The Tudor Walters' recommendations on standards for new houses and the Ministry of Health's 'manual' that gave effect to them were a very large step up from pre-1914 standards for 'working class' housing. If housing of Tudor Walters' standards, even as eroded in the interest of economy in 1923 and after, was to be built for 'working class' households, it would have to be subsidized, and subsidized heavily. If private enterprise was to build for them with no aid, tenants would have to be content with pre-1914 standards, and that likewise was something that would not come under starter's orders. When building for letting by private enterprise did revive, it catered for a different section of the market. For decades hopes were expressed that private enterprise would again build for letting and thereby obviate the need for more council house building. These hopes always contained a heavy admixture of wishful thinking, and in the early 1960s were effectively abandoned. From then on the alternative to an ever-increasing stock of council housing was perceived to lie in the encouragement of owner-occupation.

Owner-Occupation

From the standpoint of the government's involvement with housing from the 1920s to the

1950s, a growth of owner-occupation meant an increase in the number of households whose housing caused government neither expense nor trouble. Subsidies, with the exception of those under the Housing (Additional Powers) Act 1919 and the Housing Act 1923, were confined to rented housing. The other great branch of housing policy, the Rent Restrictions Acts, was necessarily concerned with renting and not owning. Encouraging owner-occupation was thus a way of limiting the state's involvement with housing. Support for owner-occupation on these grounds went with support for it as contributing to political stability or (put another way from a more critical standpoint) strengthening the security of large property interests by linking with them the interests of a large number of small property holders (2). Some of what was said and written in the 1920s about owner-occupation as a defence against "Bolshevism" now reads oddly, but that is no reason for not believing that the sentiments in question were genuinely held. They were, indeed, the direct ancestors of the belief in the 1960s and later that owner-occupiers were natural Conservative voters (3). Government encouragement of owner-occupation, though, did not extend to spending money. The arrangements that the Inland Revenue made with the building societies about administering tax relief on mortgage interest, for example, and a composition settlement of tax on investors' interest facilitated building societies' operations and hence house ownership, but they did not provide a subsidy. The starting point of liability to income tax was high enough, and the reduced rates charged on the bottom band of taxable income low enough for tax treatment of owner-occupied housing to have little or no effect on the cost of house purchase for all but quite well-off households. Not until the 1960s did tax relief become really important in reducing the cost of house purchase for very large numbers of households.

The mechanics of tax relief on mortgage interest have a long history (4), but how recently they came to be important for large numbers of house buyers with mortgages is very easily over-looked. The continuing reduction in the starting point of income tax in real terms and the rise in real incomes greatly increased the number of people who would benefit from the tax relief were they buying on mortgage; the ending of the reduced rates

464

of income tax during the 1960s much increased the
value of the relief to owner-occupiers with mortgages with modest incomes. In 1967 the option
mortgage subsidy was introduced to give the equivalent of tax relief to those owner-occupiers with
incomes too low to benefit from tax relief proper,
by then a small minority. The abolition of the
Schedule A charge on owner-occupiers in 1963 added
to the financial attractions of owner-occupation;
and the exclusion of sole or main residences
ensured that the introduction of capital gains tax
did not impair those attractions. That tax relief
developed in this way just in time to mitigate the
accelerating rise in interest rates in the later
1960s may however be attributed to coincidence.
The fiscal support for owner-occupation came into
being as the by-product of a series of changes to
the starting point and rates of income tax interacting with tax principles (in particular relief
for interest) which in their origin had nothing to
do with support for owner-occupation. The structure of tax relief and exemptions "just grew"
without being planned. If fiscal support for
owner-occupation had been deliberately planned, a
flat percentage subsidy (5) on interest that was
completely open-ended (except for the £25,000 limit
introduced in 1974) would not necessarily have been
everyone's first choice, least of all at a percentage that rose and fell with tax rates. But be
that as it may, the emergence of what was effectively a flat rate 30% (or thereabouts) interest
rate subsidy to owner-occupation meant that the
earlier contrast between subsidized council housing
and non-subsidized private housing, whether owner-
occupied or rented, no longer existed. A faster or
slower growth of local authority housing compared
with owner-occupation might affect the rate of
growth of total subsidy (broadly defined) in total,
but not how much of the housing stock was subsidized, and how much not. A flat percentage subsidy
was bound to prove very expensive if interest rates
increased or house prices rose fast. When in the
1970s much higher interest rates followed hard on
an exceptional rise in house prices, the tax relief
on mortgage interest became very costly indeed.
Here was a very large part of the explanation of
why public expenditure on housing (broadly defined
to include so-called 'tax expenditures') rose so
fast.

The Increase in Public Expenditure on Housing and the Sense of Crisis in Housing Finance and Policy

The steep rise in the cost of tax relief on mortgage interest was a large part of the increase in the total cost of housing to the public purse. The details were discussed in Chapter IV (see especially Table IV.19). During the 1960s, especially the later 1960s, it was local authority housing finance that was the centre of concern, with subsidies growing rapidly despite increases in rents well in excess of the rate of inflation. When in the 1970s a large growth in the cost of tax relief was added to the increase in public sector subsidies, the view that housing finance and particularly the contribution to it from public funds was going astray attracted increasing support. By the later 1970s sweeping condemnations of the housing subsidy system (in the broadest sense, including tax relief) had become commonplace. "Haphazard", "ineffective", "patent inequities", and "bizarre" were how two leading economists specializing in public finance described it (6). Just as dismissive was the view of a most distinguished specialist in housing administration, Professor J.B. Cullingworth: ".... so complex and haphazard is the system that it bears some of the characteristics of a lottery" (7). On the assumption that no one would design a housing subsidy system that way from choice, how the British system came to take on these attributes, at least in the eyes of critics, deserves consideration. As well as being criticized for inequity as between people, the system was criticized for spending too much on subsidy and too little on investment; and for the manifestations of unsatisfactory housing (like homelessness and the unpopular blocks and estates) that existed in spite of all the expenditure. Probably the majority view by the later 1970s was that the results were disproportionately small in relation to the amounts spent, and that much of what was spent on subsidizing housing or on council house building could have been spent to better effect elsewhere. This was not, indeed, the conclusion of the Housing Policy Green Paper in 1977 (8), but was the main thrust of most of the comments on it.

The main explanation is to be found, in the present author's view, in the effects of high nominal interest rates and inflation on a system

466

that grew up in days of stable prices and 3 to 5% interest. Prolonged inflation introduces anomalies when accounts are in historic cost terms, and the very long life of houses and the long terms of housing loans made the scope for inflation-induced anomalies in housing finance particularly great. There is here to be found the explanation for the strictures just quoted. The way in which rising interest rates resulted in much increased costs of tax relief on mortgage interest was discussed in Chapter VI and the effects of local authority housing costs and subsidies were discussed in still more detail in Chapter VII. A distinction must be drawn between 'front-loading' generated by the interaction of high nominal interest rates and inflation, and higher real interest rates. From the mid-1950s to the late 1960s, rising real interest rates were present as well. The historical record of interest rates and prices was summarized in Table IV.3; the average real interest rate (measured from the rate on Consols) was minus 1.7% in 1948-52, plus 1.2% in 1953-57, 3.1% in 1958-62, and 2.9% in 1963-67 (falling to 2.4% in 1968-72 and minus 2.6% in 1973-77). Different views were held about the reasons for the rise in real interest rates in the 1950s and 1960s. One line of argument would emphasize the strong demand for capital, translated into a strong demand for investible funds, generated by the long economic expansion. An alternative line of argument would stress the reductions in the barriers to international movements of capital and the very large and rapidly increasing amounts of money that could be moved across the exchanges. Interest rates became important for influencing the expectations of those with the power to move these funds into and out of sterling, and in the 1950s and 1960s the exigencies of "confidence" clearly had a ratchet effect on short-term interest rates in Britain. The 7% bank rate in 1957 was seen as a very startling move but further use diminished its impact, so that in 1968 8% was necessary and in 1973 13%. Likewise when the pressure was off, interest rates did not go back to where they had been before; the low point for bank rate had been 3% in 1953, but only 4% in 1958 and 1963, and 6% in 1967.

In the 1970s real interest rates were low or even negative, but nominal interest rates were at hitherto unheard of heights. Such interest rates in a system that depended on fixed interest (as

contrasted with equity or indexed) financing
generated a heavy burden of front-loading of
interest costs, in the way described in Chapter VII
(see in particular Table VII.13). This front-
loading effect of inflation and high interest rates
generated problems around the world for tenants and
house purchasers, and was the main cause of what in
the USA was termed the problem of the "affordability" of housing, that is to say very high
outgoings in relation to income until rising
incomes and static outgoings in money terms relieve
the burden. The "affordability" problem was thus
of limited duration, unlike the gap between the
cost of adequate housing and ability to pay that
was the core of the pre-1914 and inter-war housing
problem. But the "affordability" problem was
serious at an important stage in a household's
career, and generated needs for assistance much
further up the income scale than would be required
to make accessible to households with the lowest
incomes housing that approaches in quality that
enjoyed by households with average income or a
little higher. The emphasis on "affordability" has
been criticized: the contrary view holds that
against the high outgoings must be set the increase
in the value of the dwelling acquired, and that
when this is done the net cost of house purchase
was low or even negative. There is, though, a
great difference between outgoings that must be
paid in cash and increases in the value of houses
that can neither be encashed nor used to provide
the security for "rolling up" (i.e. capitalizing)
part of the interest due. A house buyer with a
mortgage knows only too well the difference between
the effect on his finances of payments on a
mortgage at 11% interest when the price level is
rising at 14% a year (say) and a mortgage in a time
of stable prices that melts away at 3% a year
without his having to pay anything, even though the
real interest rate would be negative by approximately 3% (2.7% exactly in the former case) in both
instances. A by-product of house purchase on
mortgage in times of inflation and high nominal
interest rates was a more rapid acquisition by the
purchaser of the equity in the house compared with
what would happen with lower interest rates and
more stable prices. The combination of increased
outgoings and a faster acquisition of the equity
might reasonably be termed "forced saving".
Indexed mortgages where the nominal and real

468

interest rates were the same provided in theory a
way round this problem and a way of avoiding
subsidizing the acquisition of the equity in
houses; but such mortgages were not on offer during
the period studied. Financial institutions (and
for that matter borrowers as well) adjusted only
gradually to inflation; and indexed mortgages have
problems of their own, because everybody's income
does not rise at the average rate nor do all house
prices rise at the same rate (9).

The much higher current expenditure on housing
from the public purse and householders' own funds
in the 1970s is thus readily explicable. Because
interest was so uniquely high a proportion of
current expenditure on housing, the costs of high
and volatile interest rates would have fallen
disproportionately on local authority housing and
on owner-occupiers with mortgages. The provisions
for subsidy and tax relief redistributed part, but
hardly all, of the discriminatory effects of high
interest rates away from tenants and mortgagors and
back to taxpayers at large, including those immune
to the effect of those interest rates on housing
costs (because they owned outright or had only the
tail ends of mortgages taken out long ago) but
benefiting from much higher returns on their
investments.

The other reason besides interest rates for
the increase in private and public outlays
concurrently was the rise, relative to prices
generally, of building costs and land and house
prices. As was shown in Chapter IV the trend of
building costs from the 1940s to the 1970s was
upwards in real terms and so was the trend of land
prices. On a very long view, these increases in
the price of housing relative to the general price
level were a continuation of a trend that had
persisted from as far back in the nineteenth
century as evidence exists. The inter-war years
were the great exception, extremely important but
an exception nevertheless. Only on an inadequate
time perspective could the course of housing costs
and prices in the inter-war years be taken as the
norm with which performance in the 1940s and later
should be contrasted unfavourably. A faster rise
in pay in the building industry and the building
materials industries can be excluded from an
explanation of rising building costs in real terms.
There remains a slow rise in productivity in house
building. Building itself is impossible to

469

mechanize, and the attempt to raise productivity
and cut costs by off-site prefabrication (the basis
of "industrialized" building) proved unsuccessful.
Land prices and site values are a separate
question. The rise in rents (in real terms)
relative to prices generally in the years before
1914 was explained in Chapter II in terms of travel
costs in time and money limiting the amount of
useable building land. A fast growing demand
pressed against a slower growing supply, with the
result that the price rose in real terms over the
longer term. In the inter-war years the motor bus
and the electric train greatly increased the area
of land accessible to places of employment and
hence useable for house building, and this great
increase in the supply of building land was
considered in Chapter III to be the main reason why
land and house prices did not rise in real terms in
the inter-war years as they had done before 1914,
and in particular why the housing boom of the
1930s did not run into rising house prices and
land shortages. The reductions in travel costs and
travelling times in the inter-war years were due to
the development of public transport; private cars
were still far from common even at the end of the
1930s. The great expansion of car owning came from
the mid-1950s onwards. From the experience of the
1920s and the 1930s when there was a large increase
in the supply of useable building land as a result
of the growth and improvement of public transport,
the growth of private transport in the 1950s and
1960s and the reduction in its costs might have
been expected to lead to a further large increase
in the supply of useable house building land in the
same way as in the inter-war years, and to hold
down land prices in the same way.
That it did not may be attributed to there
having been put in place in 1947 a land use
planning system inspired by the belief that the
virtually unrestricted spread of house building in
the 1920s and 1930s on land that the improvement in
transport had made useable for the purpose had had
undesirable results and should not be repeated.
What is here described neutrally or benignly as
increasing the amount of useable building land was
described in discussion of land use policy as
'urban sprawl'. The post-war system of land use
controls was strict enough to prevent it, and the
system was administered in a way that ensured that
there could be no repetition of the 1930s. The

results ranged from rising house prices and land
prices in the market for owner-occupied houses to
pressure on urban local authorities to adopt
expensive high density forms of building to meet
their housing needs within their own areas. The
increase in land prices generated in the private
housing market put further pressure on local
authorities' housing costs, because from 1959
onwards local authorities had to acquire land at
the market price, and the evidence of what were
market prices to be paid by an authority acquiring
land compulsorily could only come from the private
market. By this mechanism private housing booms
like that of the early 1970s pulled up the costs of
local authority housing and hence the amount of
subsidy needed, at the same time as raising
directly the cost of tax relief on mortgage
interest. As was emphasized in Chapter IV, the
advantages and disadvantages of the land use policy
pursued fairly steadily and consistently under
governments of both parties go far wider than the
effects of housing costs borne by households and by
the public purse. This is not the place to attempt
a judgement about the balance between all the
advantages and disadvantages. The point is simply
that the very different policy in control of land
development probably goes some way towards
explaining why the unsubsidized private housing
boom of the 1930s could not be repeated after the
war.

The Results of Public Policies Towards Housing

The criticisms of British housing policies
stemmed not just from the mounting cost but also
from the results being perceived as disproportionate to those costs. What exactly the policies
and expenditure achieved is an extremely complicated question, to which definitive answers cannot
be given for want of ability to provide proof of
what would otherwise have happened. Nevertheless
the attempt must be made, if only to comment on how
far the history bears out the verdict on housing
policy as "The Great British Failure" (10). That
housing conditions improved enormously in the
inter-war years and between the 1940s and the later
1970s is not open to dispute. Nor is there any
room for disagreement about expenditure on new
house building being far higher in relation to the
total national product in the years from 1919

471

onwards when the state invested heavily in house
building than before 1914 when it did not. Where
there is a great deal of debate, of course, is over
what public policies contributed to the rise in
housing standards, over and above what would have
happened any way as a result of the rise in real
income. The improvement in housing conditions was
both in quantity and in quality. The detail is in
Chapters III and IV, but some of it warrants high-
lighting here. In the 1920s a separate house for
every family was a reformer's aspiration; in 1945
it became a commitment of government policy but
achievable only in the distant future; but by the
1970s it was well on the way to achievement. A
housing stock large anough for nearly all households to have a house or flat to themselves had
become not only a reality but taken for granted,
with living in only part of a house or as part of
someone else's household a criticized exception
instead of being the commonplace consequence of
poverty (before 1914) or shortage (in much of the
inter-war years and the two decades after 1945). A
'separate house for every family' went far beyond
the natural family of two or more people related by
birth or marriage: by the 1970s most widows and
widowers kept their own households, and a fast
rising number of single people lived on their own.
Between 1945 and the end of the 1970s the number of
households rose by more than a million as a result
of these changes in household headship, over and
above the increase due to the growth of the population, earlier marriage, and most couples being able
to set up on their own soon after marriage instead
of after a long spell with in-laws. This was the
new regime of household formation, which began
(apparently) in the inter-war years, but did not
develop fully until the 1950s, 1960s and 1970s.
There was a marked contrast with the half century
before 1914, when the number of households at most
kept pace with what would be expected just from the
population of household-forming age, and sometimes
did not do even that.

With the increase in the quantity of housing
went a very substantial rise in quality. The way
in which some of the houses and flats built for
local authorities in the 1950s, the 1960s and the
early 1970s have turned out badly has tended to
divert attention from the extent of the improvement
in the quality of housing that went alongside the
improvement in the quantity. From being a majority

in 1947, houses and flats without one or more of a hot water system, bathroom, and inside WC had by the end of the 1970s become a comparative rarity. Bathing in a portable galvanized iron bath with water heated in kettles or pans, still very common at the end of the war, was nearly a thing of the past; so too was the fixed bath in the scullery and not in a bathroom (a design used in some inter-war council houses to cut costs). Central heating was by the end of the 1970s more common than a fixed bath had been at the end of the 1940s. That these changes had come to be taken for granted by the later 1970s does not on a longer view make them less noteworthy. Apart from the growth of the housing stock, with the additions built with bathroom, inside WC, and hot water system, and increasingly with central heating, the rise in standards came about through the modernizing of large numbers of houses built before 1914 and in the inter-war years; and through the demolition and replacement of most of the very poorest of the old houses, those that were unfit for habitation, by post-1945 or even post-1919 standards, from the day they were built.

Increasing the number of houses and flats in the stock at a faster rate than the increase in households until dwellings exceeded households by a margin sufficient to ensure that the family without a separate house was a comparative rarity was inherently a finite task. So too was replacing the pre-1880 houses that were 'unfit' from the day they were built. So also was putting the basic amenities of a fixed bath, inside WC, and hot water system into houses that lacked them. The first had been done by the mid-1970s; the second was also substantially finished by then; and the last at the end of the decade. These three achievements were not all that needed to be done, by the standards of the time to secure "a decent home for every family at a price within their means" (11), but together they amounted to a transformation of English housing compared with 1910 or even 1950. In explaining why this transformation took so long, sight must not be lost of how important were the two world wars. Out of the half century between 1911 and 1961, a full decade was spent in war. That meant the equivalent of ten years' housing output lost, plus the equivalent of another year's output destroyed by air attack.

The extent of the improvement in housing

conditions may be acknowledged, of course, while doubting whether public policy achieved anything over and above what would have happened in any event as a consequence of rising income. Criticisms could also be made on grounds of the improvement in housing conditions having been achieved at undue cost to the performance of the economy, or (not quite the same thing) undue cost to public funds. Criticisms under the last two heads increased greatly during the 1970s as noted above. The three lines of criticism or scepticism are not wholly consistent with each other; if public policy did not really bring extra resources into housing, and particularly if public expenditure merely displaced private expenditure, then resources could hardly have been diverted away from the rest of the economy. But that all the criticisms could not have been wholly valid simultaneously does not, of course, mean that none of them could be valid individually or even up to a point in combination.

That rising real incomes had much to do with improved standards of housing is hardly open to dispute. Rising real incomes could lead to higher housing standards both through market processes and through raising the standard of public services that could be afforded from given tax rates. To measure the amount of displacement of private expenditure on housing by public expenditure would require a far more comprehensive theory than we have about what determines the amount of private expenditure. But the beginning of a way into the question can perhaps be found from comparisons over time of the number of houses and flats built for private and public owners, with the increase in the adult population shown to standardize (crudely) for the growing needs for housing, and slum clearance demolitions shown to identify a category of public authorities' building that demonstratively did not displace building for private owners.

There is no reason for thinking that house building would have run exactly level in relation to the growth of population if local authority house building had not come upon the scene, but that there would have been building for private owners in the inter-war years equal to the sum of actual building for private owners plus local authority building defies belief. The one international study of the relationship of house building to stages of national economic development, that by Burns and Grebler (12), gives no

474

Table IX.1 - Comparisons of House Building Over Time

(annual averages in thousands)

| | .... Houses Completed .... | | | Slum Clearance | Increase in Adult Population |
	Private Owners	Public Authorities	Total		
1870-89	..	..	100	..	180
1890-1914	..	..	115	..	290
1920-29	95	53	148	2	311
1930-39	229	51	280	40	267
1946-55	47	163	210	15	157 (*)
1956-70	169	132	301	60	139
1971-78	151	122	273	53	79

Note: (*) 1939-55.

Source: See Chapters II, III and IV.

reason at all for expecting so great an increase in house building in the inter-war years compared with the two decades before 1914. That the advent of large scale building by local authorities merely, or even mainly, displaced building for private owners, can be rejected as highly improbable, even though logically possible. A more interesting question on the figures is whether the much higher level of building for public authorities in the 1950s and 1960s than in the inter-war years helps much to explain why even in the boom of the 1960s building for private owners was still some way short of the levels reached in the 1930s. The answer that the present author would give is 'no' on the ground that the unsubsidized private enterprise housing boom of the 1930s owed much to uniquely favourable conditions (plentiful mortgage credit at 5% or less, and a much enlarged and rapidly expanding supply of cheap building land) that were never to return in the three post-war decades. If iprovement in housing conditions at the inter-war rate was required for those who could not afford the full cost in post-war conditions, a much larger recourse to subsidy was inevitable.

International comparisons also suggest that public policies made a substantial contribution to improving housing conditions in Britain. Such comparisons are inevitably restricted in their scope in being limited to aspects of housing conditions that are easily measured. Table IX.2 shows such comparisons for around 1970. A comparison at this date is of more interest than earlier in the post-war years, in that it is less affected by war damage, and also because by the beginning of the 1970s the lower level of real income in Britain than in many of the European countries was attracting critical comment. At the time of writing, data from the censuses in 1980 and 1981 for a comparable range of countries had not yet become available.

Of the thirteen countries included in Table IX.2, only the USA and Canada had better housing (in terms of the aspects compared) than Britain. The comparison is consistent with public expenditure on housing and a financial system that was held to favour house purchase having made Britain well housed, by international standards, given its income. On this reckoning there was something to show in Britain for all the money and resources that went into housing.

Table IX.2 - International Comparisons of Housing Conditions

			.... Proportion of Dwelling with:		
Country and Year		Persons per Room	Hot Water Supply within Dwelling	Flush Toilet within Dwelling	Fixed Bath or or Shower
Austria	(1971)	1.1	62.7	69.8	52.9
Belgium	(1970)	0.6	....	55.3	47.8
Canada	(1970)	0.8 (b)	92.6	94.2 (a)	90.7
Denmark	(1970)	0.8 (b)	....	.... (d)	76.5
France	(1968)	0.9 (c)	50.1	54.8	47.5
Germany (Federal Republic)	(1972)	0.7	83.8	86.1	81.8
Italy	(1971)	1.0	....	82.8	64.5
Luxembourg	(1970)	0.6	....	77.7	68.9
Netherlands	(1971)	0.7	....	94.5	81.4
Norway	(1970)	0.7	....	70.0	66.1
Sweden	(1970)	0.7	....	90.1	78.3
Switzerland	(1970)	0.6	88.8	90.1	80.9
USA	(1970)	0.6	95.2 (e)	93.3	95.1
England and Wales	(1971)	0.6	86.1	89.5	90.5

Notes: (a) Include dwellings where the toilet is in the same building but not necessarily within the dwelling.
(b) Kitchens not counted as rooms.
(c) Kitchens with floor area greater than 12 sq. metres counted as rooms.
(d) Location of toilet not reported.
(e) Hot water supply to sink, wash hand basin, and bath.

Source: UN Economic Commission for Europe, A Statistical Survey of Housing Conditions in the ECE Countries Around 1970 (United Nations, New York, 1978) Tables III.3 and III.5.

The Costs

The counterpart to these probable results of public policies was the cost. That can be measured in several ways, but it is convenient to look first at investment. Did the resources put into house building so depress investment in industry and trade as to retard Britain's economic growth? As has been reiterated at several places earlier in this book, the rate of growth of the British economy from the later 1940s to the early 1970s was exceptionally rapid by past British standards, however much criticized it was in comparison with the European countries. This was the time when gross fixed investment in dwellings was at its highest in relation to gross domestic product. The estimates of investment in dwellings before 1914 (discussed in Chapter II) and in the inter-war years (Chapter III) are subject to margins of error, especially the former, but there is no room at all for doubting that investment in dwellings was much lower in relation to gross domestic product than it subsequently became. But so too, as Table IX.3 shows, was investment other than in dwellings. The half century before 1914 was not an era of high investment in commerce and industry (even including investment overseas) even though investment in dwellings and public social services was much lower than it subsequently became.

The historical record summarized in Table IX.3 is sufficient to reject any simple version of the contention that the improvement of housing conditions was bought at the expense of a retardation of economic growth. There are many controversies in economics and economic history about how important is investment in fixed capital for economic growth and about the advantages and disadvantages of investment abroad (particularly important in 1880-1913) compared with investment at home. Those controversies cannot be gone into here; the reason for mentioning them is that the only route by which increased outlays on housing could have retarded economic growth in Britain was through reducing the amount of investment in other kinds of asset. The large volume of non-housing investment in 1948 and later is evidence against this having happened systematically, as distinct from at the peaks of booms when the building industry had more demand than it could meet (e.g. 1955-56, 1964-65 and 1973). In the 1930s there was

Table IX.3 - Gross Fixed Capital Formation and Gross
Domestic Product in the United Kingdom
1870-1979

... Investment as Percent of GDP ...

	Dwellings	Other Domestic Fixed Investment	Other Domestic Plus Overseas (a)	Rate of Growth of GDP (b)
1870-1883	1.6	6.7	11.2	2.0
1883-1899	1.4	6.0	10.8	2.2
1899-1913	1.5	6.9	12.8	1.4
1924-1937	2.9	6.0	6.0	2.2
1948-1957	3.5	12.5	13.0	2.6
1957-1965	3.5	15.5	15.8	3.2
1965-1973	4.1	17.3	17.6	2.6
1973-1978	4.0	17.1	16.2	1.6

Notes: (a) Net overseas investment as defined in the
national income, equal by definition to the
balance of payments surplus or deficit. on
current account.

(b) The rate of increase (annual average rate)
between the three years centred on the first
and last years of the periods distinguished
before 1914, e.g. 1869-71 to 1879-81.

Source: 1924-37 and earlier from C.H. Feinstein,
National Income, Expenditure and Output,
Tables 3 and 39; 1949 and later from Economic
Trends Annual Supplement 1984.

a superfluity of funds seeking investment
opportunities, with the demand to invest depressed
by the slump. In such circumstances, the housing
boom could hardly have displaced other investment.

In a somewhat similar way, a 'not proven'
verdict on the responsibility of investment in
housing for slow economic growth in Britain is
reached from comparisons with housing investment
and other gross fixed investment in relation to
gross domestic product in other countries. Table
IX.4 shows such a comparison for the 1960s and
1970s, using the Organization for Economic Co-
Operation and Development's (OECD) standardized
national income accounts statistics. Gross fixed
capital formation is divided into "residential

Table IX.4 - Categories of Gross Fixed Investment as Percent of Gross Domestic Product in the Main OECD Countries

	1963-1970			1971-1979		
	Residential Buildings	Government Services	Industry Services, etc.	Residential Buildings	Government Services	Industry Services, etc.
Australia	4.9	4.2	17.2	4.7	3.4	14.9
Canada	4.9	4.6	15.3	5.8	3.3	13.7
New Zealand (a)	...	...	...	5.0	2.9	14.2
USA	4.1	2.8	11.2	4.7	2.1	11.7
Belgium	5.9	2.6	13.3	6.3	2.9	12.1
France (a) (b)	...	...	...	6.8	2.9	13.4
Germany	7.1	3.6	14.0	6.4	3.8	12.3
Italy	...	...	...	5.2	1.8	12.7
Netherlands (c)	5.3	4.9	15.5	5.7	3.7	12.1
Norway	4.6	4.3	18.6	5.4	4.8	21.8
Sweden	6.4	4.6	13.0	4.5	3.5	12.9
United Kingdom (d)	3.6	2.5	12.2	3.4	2.3	12.9

Notes:
(a) Figures not available for 1963-1970.
(b) Division between "government services" and "industry services, etc." available for 1973-1979 only.
(c) 1964-1970.
(d) Percentages are lower than in Table IX.3 because denominator in gross domestic product at market prices, not factor cost.

Source: OECD National Accounts 1963-1980 Vol. II, Tables 1a and 4a (for each country).

buildings"; "government services"; and "industry, services, etc."

Investment in "industry, services, etc." in the United Kingdom was not notably lower relative to gross domestic product than in many other countries, particularly in the 1970s, but investment in housing was definitely lower. Exact comparability cannot be taken for granted, but it would be surprising if differences of definition could explain why, contrary to widespread belief, the OECD national income accounts statistics do not show Britain in the 1960s and 1970s as investing much more in housing and much less in industry and services compared with other countries.

How, then can one explain why there was so much support for the view that too much was being spent on housing in Britain, and that public policies were the main reason why this was so? The answers given are a matter for judgement rather than proof, but a few observations would seem to be called for here. In the present author's view, the explanations are to be found partly in the very rapid rise in public expenditure and tax relief in the later 1960s and still more so in the 1970s which has already been discussed, partly in the persistence and indeed increase in overt homelessness; and partly in the diminishing esteem in which much local authority housing was held. The juxtaposition of the first and the second encouraged the view that the expenditure was mis-directed if not wasted; and the third cast doubt on what for fifty years had been a major instrument of housing policy.

The reasons for the steep increase in public expenditure have been discussed at some length above, notably the way in which high and unstable nominal interest rates raised the current cost of housing so sharply owing to the 'front-loading effect'. But for the higher expenditure, improvement in housing conditions would have been much slower and may well have halted. That conditions did improve considerably in the 1970s was argued in Chapter IV, and the prominence of homelessness does not demonstrate the contrary. The explanation of the paradox, in the present author's view, lies in the sharp reduction in the supply of lettings of parts of houses, commented on in Chapter VIII. Such lettings were frequently inferior accommodation, and expensive for what it offered, but it was available quickly; and quickly available accommodation was what was needed to prevent homelessness. With progress towards the 'separate house for every family' and the decline in sharing, there came increasingly to be an all-or-nothing contrast between a separate house and nothing at all.

The other reason (in the present author's view) for growth of dissatisfaction with the results of housing policy was the way in which substantial amounts of local authority housing built in the later 1950s, the 1960s and the early 1970s turned out unsatisfactorily in practice. This is far too complex a subject to discuss at length here, and one where the numerical dimensions, as distinct from the seriousness of individual instances, were far from clear at the time of writing. There was a degree of modishness about the design fashions of the late 1950s and the 1960s, and likewise probably about the aversion to some of them that grew in the 1970s. There were at the end of the 1970s still unresolved disagreements about the relative importance of the designs and concepts and of the way the finished product was managed; and about what methods of management would work better and what they would cost. Difficult-to-let housing did not consist solely of the 'mistakes' of the industrialized building era, but they were a considerable part of it. For many years council tenancies were regarded almost as if they were prizes that had to be fairly allocated and if there were more of them, so much the better. The emergence of difficut-to-let housing was a very marked change, and future observers will probably consider it important in explaining why the demand to build by local authorities was falling away fast in the later 1970s.

That the housing problem was not eliminated by the prolonged rise in real income in the three post-war decades is not altogether surprising. Its physical aspects were transformed with sheer shortage and crowding much reduced and older deficiencies well on the way to being eliminated, notwithstanding a rise in the proportion of adults living as separate households with a place of their own far beyond anything that might have been foreseen by those who thought of a better Britain after the war. Home ownership became the tenure of a substantial majority; and for most others security was ensured by public provision or by legislation. The interacting effects of inflation, high nominal interest rates, and financial

482

mechanisms that had evolved in times of more stable prices and lower interest rates ensured that housing financed in all its forms was a continuing source of trouble and difficulty. The general improvement in housing made the condition of those who did not share in it the more keenly felt; the types of disadvantage less easy to deal with than shortage, crowding, or lack of a fixed bath, hot water supply and inside WC were coming to constitute an inceasing part of the housing problem, in the sense of what gave rise to dissatisfaction. How far this was due to mistakes in the post-war years, and whose mistakes they were, are matters which must be remitted to subsequent students of the history of English housing.

Notes and References

(1) D. Dilks, Neville Chamberlain, Vol. 1, Cambridge University Press, Cambridge, 1984, p.561.

(2) See A. Offer, Property and Policies 1870-1914, Cambridge University Press, Cambridge, 1981, for the argument that this was the basic strategy of nineteenth century Conservatives to defend property interests against feared attacks from radical reformers (or worse).

(3) Curiously, the argument commonly advanced after the 1959 general election that the "affluent society" had diminished the appeal of the Labour party made very little mention of owner-occupied housing. The "affluence" in question was seen as being manifested in ownership of cars and household durable goods, not home-ownership.

(4) For a summary, see Housing Policy Technical Volume, Chapter VI (HMSO 1977).

(5) Relief on mortgage interest at the higher rates of tax (surtax before 1973) was an anomaly in terms of housing finance.

(6) A.B. Atkinson and M.A. King, 'Housing Policy, Taxation, and Reform', Midland Bank Review, March 1980.

(7) J.B. Cullingworth, Essays on Housing Policy, Allen and Unwin, London, 1979.

(8) Cmnd. 6851 (1977).

(9) For a discussion of dispersions in rates of rise of house prices and rates of rise of earnings and the problems they would cause, see Housing Policy Technical Volume, Chapter VI (HMSO 1977).

(10) F. Berry, The Great British Failure, Knight, London, 1974.

(11) Fair Deal for Housing, White Paper, Cmnd. 4728 (1971), para.5.

(12) L.S. Burns and L. Grebler, The Housing of Nations, Macmillan, London, 1977.